MANUFACTURE AND REPAIR
OF TABLA

THE COMPLETE REFERENCE FOR TABLA
VOLUME 3

MANUFACTURE AND REPAIR OF TABLA

First Edition

by
David R. Courtney, Ph.D.

Sur Sangeet Services
Houston
2001

First Edition
$35.95

Distributed by Sur Sangeet Services
Box 270685
Houston TX 77277

Spiralbound
ISBN   1-893644-02-2

The author can be reached at:
(713) 665 4665 (tel)
(713) 665 0186 (fax)
david@chandrakantha.com (E-Mail)
http://chandrakantha.com (Personal web page)

TABLE OF CONTENTS

PREFACE

Here we go again. I presume that you have been with me through the first two volumes, so by now you know what I have going for you. You are in for several hundred pages of obscure and tedious discussions of the extreme minutia of *tabla*. Let us face it, the average person does not even know what *tabla* is, but you have made it through two volumes, and are working your way through the third. By reading this book, you are proving yourself to be almost as crazy as I am.

So now that we both know where we stand, we can proceed with our insanity.

I think that a few words concerning the overall style are in order. This will help us put things into some type of perspective.

I am trying to strike a balance in this book. It should be neither too academic nor to informal.

We are all familiar with the informal style. On its positive side, it is very accessible. Over the years a number of non-academic books have been written on the subject of *tabla*. Although these books may have their strong points, their lack of rigour has made them harmful. They are harmful because they mix up misinformation with facts in such a way that few are able to keep a clear perspective on the subject. This is a common problem with the informal style.

However, academic writings are not without their faults. The biggest fault is that the form is so inaccessible. Marxist economists may speak of "objectified labour" when what they are trying to say is "wealth". Musicians inexplicably become "practitioners" and music teachers suddenly become "informants". I do not wish to point my fingers at any of my colleagues, but I feel that such obscurantism is not necessary for a work to be intellectually rigourous. Therefore, I have endeavoured.... (sorry) I have TRIED to write a book which is intellectually rigourous, yet at the same time is easy to read.

Learning the Craft in India

I would just like to say one more thing about the style of writing. This style is a mixture of British and American. The mixture is not arbitrary; it has been carefully thought out. There are two overall areas; spelling and style.

I preferred to use British-English spellings for words. Today, the English speaking world is a single market. This book is just as likely to be read in Birmingham, Alabama as it is to be read in Birmingham, England. In this broad English speaking world, Americanisms may be regarded as quaint, parochial and extremely provincial. This can be a big distraction, and it does not reflect the serious nature of this work.

The style of writing is not British. The British academic style tends toward circumlocution. Indeed it is this circumlocution, that has become characteristic of the "English" style, that I am trying to avoid. By avoiding these awkward, and at time unreadable, and long sentences, that really do not convey any real content, that I am attempting, for the sake of clarity, to write this book (which you are now reading). Then, we can more easily understand this work, without the unnecessary verbiage that we have sometimes, though not always, come to expect from the British academic style.

I am shooting for brevity, even to the point of single sentence paragraphs!

A few words are in order concerning the research behind this work. Generally the information is derived in three different ways: personal experience, training under the guidance of experienced craftsmen, and pre-existing published sources.

Much of the information was derived from personal experience. I have been repairing *tablas*, *dholaks*, *pakhawajs* and other Indian instruments since 1972. Some of the techniques that I have developed are being revealed here for the first time. I have placed these techniques in separate chapters and appendices so that the information should not be confused with traditional techniques.

My own experience has also had an advantage in that I have been able to acquire firsthand experience with instruments from all over south Asia. Most *tabla* repairmen will only have access to the materials and techniques which are locally accessible. India is a vast subcontinent, and the techniques will vary from one region to another. I feel fortunate to have been able to get a sampling of instruments from all over the subcontinent and get a glimpse of the various techniques and approaches.

I have also obtained a lot of my information from my personal apprenticeship. Between the years of 1976-1980, I learned the craft of *tabla*-making from the craftsmen of Hyderabad. This was considered to be a great novelty because working with skins is considered the lowest form of work, one which few Indians are willing to do. However, this apprenticeship has given me a knowledge of the details of construction that I could not have obtained in any other fashion.

I have also obtained information from pre-existing works. This material is almost entirely peripheral to the topic of *tabla*-making. This includes such material as general principles of metallurgy, woodcrafting, and the sciences associated with skins and leather.

I have done everything that I could to make this work as complete as possible, however I am not claiming that this book is the *Principia* of *tabla*-making. As such, it must be considered merely a first work on the subject.

Further work is necessary because there are areas of this book that are incomplete or just simply wrong. Although I have tried to make this work as accurate as possible, there is a lot of material which is based upon hearsay. At times I am forced to include such hearsay because it is impossible for me to go all over India and study under every craftsman. Therefore, when I hear of a technique, and it seems consistent with my experience, then I am willing to include it. However, the danger is that a certain percentage must turn out to be wrong.

Let me also say a few words about the overall structure. This book, like its predecessors, is not really intended to be read from cover to cover. It is written to make the maximum information available in the minimum amount of pages. Therefore, it is written so that one may skim through areas that are of only slight interest, but provide great detail in the areas that are of special interest.

The body of the book concentrates on material that is directly relevant to the construction of *tabla,* while the appendices concentrate on areas that are either background or tangential. Appendix 2 and Appendix 3 contain material that is very important background for the *tabla*-maker. These are such things as a wood, cloth, rope, and other materials that the *tabla*-maker uses. Although it is important, it is tangential to the topic of *tabla*; therefore, it is placed in the appendices. There is also a brief discussion of other Indian drums as well. This clearly is not directly related to *tabla.* However any craftsman who makes *tabla* will definitely be making some of these other drums. By the same token, any repairman dealing with *tabla* will also have to repair these other drums. Therefore, this material is too valuable to be ignored.

The appendix also contains a glossary. There are so many foreign terms that it is easy to lose track of things. Check the glossary whenever there is some doubt about the meaning of a word.

I would like to thank the many people who have made this book possible. I would especially like to thank Orlando Fiol. I very much enjoyed our endless e-mails where we discussed the minutia of *tabla*-making. I would also like to thank my friends, students, and colleagues who assisted with the proof-reading of the early drafts. I would especially like to thank Mohammad Siraj Haque, Gary Salamone, Akhtar Siraj, Partha Mukherji, Kalyani Giri, and Siraj Parmer. Two people who were especially helpful were Jay Kruse and Shawn Mativetsky.

I would especially like to thank my wife Chandrakantha, for her patience.

There is another thing that I must thank. I must thank the very thing that has made this possible. It is the modern world. Much of the research was done 30 years ago, yet it has only been possible to publish this detailed information now. So, why has it not been possible with pre-existing systems? The answers are simple.

Mainstream academia has been powerless to do something like this. The machinery of grants, tenure tracks, and other academic processes, lead researchers around like bullocks with rings in their noses. Independently directed research is very rare today, and *tabla*-making has never been a popular area. Furthermore, most research is such that it has to be completed in one academic year. In real terms this is usually only about nine months. *Tabla*-making and repair is so complicated, that it requires many years just to get a handle on it.

The corporate world has been equally impotent when it comes to independently directed research. The direction within the corporate world has been in areas that are likely to produce immediate profits. This clearly is not the case with *tabla* (at least not with traditional manufacturing techniques).

All this work is possible now only due to strides in technology. The internet allows me, the author, to have a nearly direct relationship with you, the reader. There is no big academic or corporate machine to nix the project because it is not mainstream enough. The widespread use of the DocuTech and similar printing machines have also made it possible to produce small runs of high quality printed books without the expense of the older offset machines. The result is simple: working in a tightly focused niche market is practical today in ways that were never possible.

So I really must thank all of you who are working in companies like Cisco Systems, AOL, IBM, Apple, Xerox, Adobe, and other high-tech companies for making this book possible (not Microsoft - sorry, but you guys don't make the grade).

With these things in mind we can begin.

CHAPTER 1

INTRODUCTION

INTRODUCTION
This book deals with a large amount of obscure material. Although this material is obscure, it need not be esoteric. If we have a clear understanding of a few basics, then this book will easily be understood by anyone. Therefore, it is appropriate that we review our subject. We will look at Indian drums in general and the *tabla* in specific. This will allow us to place things in some type of perspective.

OVERVIEW OF INDIAN DRUMS
There is a traditional taxonomy of Indian instruments. The group of instruments that we are interested in are the membranous percussive; these are the drums. In traditional Indian works, this is referred to as *avanaddh* (अवनद्ध). Here is a brief overview of Indian drums.

<u>Tabla</u> (तबला)(figure 1.1)- *Tabla* is a pair of hand drums. They consist of a small right hand drum called *dayan* (दांया) and a larger metal one called *bayan* (बांया).

The *tabla* has an interesting construction. The *dayan* (right hand drum) is almost always made of wood. The diameter at the playing surface may run from just under five inches to nearly seven inches. The *bayan* (left hand drum) may be made of iron, aluminium, copper, steel, or clay; yet brass with a nickel or chrome plate is the most common material. Undoubtedly the most striking characteristic of the *tabla* are the large black spots on each of the playing surfaces. These black spots are a mixture of gum, soot, white flour, and iron filings. Their function is to create the characteristic timbre of the instrument.

There is a very formalised system of training for the *tabla*. It is an apprenticeship that takes many years. In this period the compositions are taught by a series of mnemonic syllables known as *bol* (बोल).

Although the origin of *tabla* is somewhat obscure, it is generally believed that it evolved from the barrel shaped drum called *pakhawaj* (पखावाज). This was about 250 years ago.

Figure 1.1. Tabla

Figure 1.2. Daf

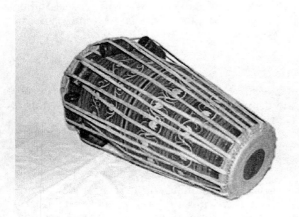

Figure 1.3. Pakhawaj

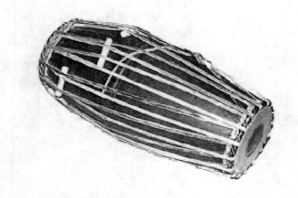

Figure 1.4. Mridangam

<u>Daf</u> (डफ़)(figure 1.2) - *Daf* is similar to a tambourine. It is quite large, about two feet across, with a conspicuous absence of jingles. It is commonly used in folk music, but is rarely heard in other styles. It is also called *dapphu, daffali,* or a number of other names. It is related to the *kanjira* of South Indian music.

<u>Pakhawaj</u> (पखावज) (figure 1.3)- *Pakhawaj* is essentially a north Indian version of the *mridangam.* It is the most common north Indian representative of the class of barrel shaped drums known as *mridang.* It was once common throughout north India, but in the last few generations, *tabla* has usurped its position of importance. It has a right head which is identical to the *tabla dayan* except somewhat larger. The left head is similar to the *tabla bayan* except that there is a temporary application of flour and water instead of the black permanent spot. It is laced with rawhide and has tuning blocks placed between the straps and shell.

There are several styles of *pakhawaj* playing. The most well known and important is for the accompaniment of *dhrupad* and *dhammar* singers; this however, is falling out of fashion. *Pakhawaj* is also very much used for Odissi dancers and occasionally for *kathak.* It is also found in a classical form from Rajasthan known as *Haveli Sangeet.*

<u>Mridangam</u> (मृदंगम)(figure 1.4) - *Mridangam* is a South Indian version of the *pakhawaj.* It bears a strong superficial resemblance to *pakhawaj,* but there are major differences in construction and technique. The tone of the instrument is also quite different. This is due to differences in construction.

The sitting and playing technique is well formalised. One sits cross legged with the left foot below and the right foot over and slightly extended. The *mridangam* rests upon the right foot and ankle. Since the instrument is very heavy it is also cushioned by some rolled up cloth placed at the right foot. The right hand plays the smaller head, while the left hand plays the head with the temporary application of flour.

The *mridangam* is an indispensable component of the south Indian classical performance. In these performances, the artist plays very intricate patterns to accompany south Indian vocalists, *vina*, violin, or *gottuvadyam* players. It is a very demanding art and requires many years to master.

Tabla Tarang (तबला तरंग) - *Tabla tarang* consists of a number of *tabla dayans* tuned to different notes of the scale. Complete melodies are played by striking the appropriate *dayans*.

Dholak (ढोलक)(figure 1.5) - *Dholak* is a very popular folk drum of northern India. It is barrel shaped with a simple membrane on the right hand side. The left hand side is also a single membrane with a special application on the inner surface. There are two ways of tightening the *dholak*. Sometimes they are laced with rope, in which case, a series of metal rings are pulled to tighten the instrument. Sometimes metal turnbuckles are employed. It is said that this instrument used to occupy a position of considerable prestige. Today it is merely relegated to *filmi* and folk music.

Nagada (नगाड़ा)(figure 1.6)- *Nagada* are the kettle drums of the old *naubat* (traditional ensemble of nine instruments). These drums are about one to two feet in diameter, and are played with sticks. Today this instrument is usually used to accompany *shehnai*.

Dholki (ढोल्कि)(figure 1.7) - *Dholki*, also called *nal*, is a drum with a barrel shaped shell. The left side resembles the *bayan* (large metal drum of the *tabla*) except that it uses *dholak massala* (oil based application) on the inner surface instead of a *syahi* (permanent black spot). The right head is unique in its construction. Goatskin is stitched onto an iron ring. In the centre of this skin is a *syahi*, similar to *tabla* except much thinner. The traditional *nals* were laced with rope and had sticks to function as turnbuckles. Today, metal turnbuckles have replaced the rope lacing in most models. The *nal* is very popular in the *tamasha* (street performance) of Maharashtra. It has been absorbed into the Hindi film industry and today the *nal* is very popular for *filmi* music.

Figure 1.5. Dholak

Figure 1.6. Nagada

Figure 1.7. Dholki

Figure 1.8. Kanjira

Figure 1.9. Tavil

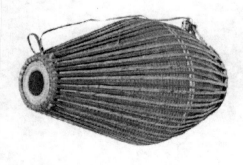

Figure 1.10. Khol

Kanjira (कंजीरा)(figure 1.8) - The *kanjira* is a small tambourine. It is made by stretching lizard skin over a wooden frame. The frame is about seven inches in diameter with one metal jingle. The *kanjira* is very popular in South Indian classical performances. It is related to the *daf* of folk music.

Tavil (ताविल)(figure 1.9) - *Tavil* is an instrument found only in the southernmost part of India. It has a shell of nearly spherical proportions which is open on both sides. There are two skins wrapped around two large hemp hoops. The left side is played with a stick. The right side is played with the hands, with metal thimbles placed over the fingers to give a sharp sound. This instrument is commonly played in South Indian temples and weddings. It is the most common accompaniment to the large oboe-like instrument known as *nadaswaram*.

Khol (खोल)(figure 1.10) - *Khol*, also called *mridang*, is a folk drum of northeast India. It has a body made of clay, a very small head on the right side (approximately 4 inches), and a larger head on the left side (approximately 10 inches). A fibreglass version of the *khol* has become popular in the West among the members of ISKCON (International Society for Krsna Conciousness). It is very popular in the *kirtans* of Bengal.

Pung (पुंग)(figure 1.11) - *Pung* is a drum from the north-east Indian state of *Manipur*. This association is so strong that it has come to be known as the *Manipuri mridang*. It is held in very high esteem and is very much used in the *Manipuri* style of dance. There is even a whole dance form based upon it known as *Pung Chalom*.

The *pung* is very similar to the *khol* in its construction and technique. There are really only a few differences. The *pung* has a body made of wood while the *khol* has a body of clay. Another difference is that both left and right sides of the *pung* are similar in size while the *khol* has sides that are very different. Another difference is that the *khol* has a greater girth while the *pung* is more cylindrical.

No one knows how long this drum has been in existence. It is said that it was introduced into the area by king Khuyoi Tompok in the year 154 AD.

Thanthi Panai (figure 1.12) - *Thanthi Panai (tantipanai* or *tanti panai)* is a pot drum used by tribals of southern India. It consists of a clay pot with a skin stretched over it. There is a metal string which attaches to the centre of this skin, then passes through the pot and through a small hole drilled in the bottom. From here, the string passes through a series of beads or wooden blocks, then ties to a tuning peg. This tuning peg is used to tune to the tonic. When the instrument is played, some small metallic rings which surround the string inside the resonator begin to vibrate.

The name *Thanthi Panai* is a reflection of the metal string used in its construction. It is based upon an older instrument that used gut strings. This was known as *Narakunda Panai.*

Figure 1.11. Pung

Damaru (डमरु)(figure 1.13) - *Damaru* is the most common hourglass drum in India. It has a shell which is anywhere from four-to-ten inches in length and three-to-eight inches in diameter. The shell is usually either metal or wood. There are two drumheads on each side of the shell which are laced together with cord. Near the centre of the lacing are two loose, knotted cords. The knots on each end strike both heads to produce a rattling sound. This is affected by rotating the drum rapidly in alternating directions. The pitch is bent by squeezing the lacing.

The *damaru* has very strong religious associations. It is strongly associated with the God Shiva and the *sadhus* (wandering Hindu religious men).

The *damaru* appears to be the last common representative of a family of hourglass drums. Although other representatives (e.g., *udaku, hurduk, idakka,* etc.) may be found, they are very rare. This is in stark contrast to the abundance of forms that are depicted on the walls of ancient temples.

Figure 1.12. Thanthi Panai

Figure 1.13. Damaru

Figure 1.14. Chenda

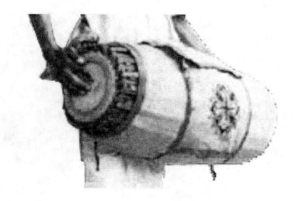

Figure 1.15. Shuddha Madalam

Chenda (figure 1.14) - *Chenda* is a drum from the South Indian state of Kerala. It is played upright with a pair of drumsticks. It is an indispensable accompaniment for the *Kathakali* and *Mohini Attam* dance forms.

Shuddha Madalam (figure 1.15) - *Shuddha madalam* is a drum from the South Indian state of Kerala. It is a two faced drum, similar to the mridangam, that is played with the hands. Like the *chenda*, it is an indispensable accompaniment for the *Kathakali* and *Mohini Attam* dance forms. It is very similar to the *mridangam*.

Idakka and Udaku - *Idakka* and *udaku* (*udakai*) are hourglass drums from south India. They are very similar to the *damaru* which is found throughout India. However, where the *damaru* is played by rattling knotted cords against the resonators, the *idakka* is played with a stick and the *udaku* is played with the hand. The *udaku* is structurally different in that it has a small snare made of hair, fishing line, or similar material stretched over one side. Like the *damaru,* both the *udaku* and the *idakka's* pitch may be bent by squeezing the lacing in the middle.

This previous section was a brief overview of the drums of India. Future discussions of the *tabla* and related drums will make much more sense when it is understood within the larger context of Indian drums.

THE TABLA

The *tabla* is composed of two drums. Strictly speaking, only the smaller wooden drum is the *tabla*. Still, it has become a common practice to refer to them collectively as the *tabla*. Therefore, we may bow to common usage. If we wish to indicate one drum over the other, we can call the wooden drum the *dayan* (दायां) and the metal drum the *bayan* (बायां). *Dayan* and *bayan* mean right and left respectively.

The parts of the *tabla* are shown in figure 1.16. There is the lacing known as *tasma* (तस्मा), also called *dori* (डोरी), *vadi* (वादि), or *baddhi* (बद्धी). There is also the wooden shell called *lakadi* (लकड़ी), also called *kath* (काठ). There is the drumhead which is known as *pudi* (पुड़ि), also called the *chamada* (चमड़ा). There is also the metallic shell called *pital* (पीतल), also called *kudi* (कुडी). There are wooden dowels used to tighten the drums, called *gatta* (गट्टा). There is a ring at the bottom which may be made of either rawhide, iron, or tightly woven metal wires, called *kundal* (कुण्डल).

Now that we have a rough idea as to the parts of the *tabla,* we should take a closer look at them.

Lakadi - *Lakadi* is the wooden shell upon which the right hand drum *(dayan)* is made (figure 1.16). This is called *lakadi* (लकड़ी) or *kath* (काठ). Good woods are teak and *shisham* (rosewood). *Bija* is another wood that is found in the North and is quite good. In the deep South, one tends to find jackwood. Although jackwood is a fine wood, south Indian *tablas* tend to be of poor quality for other reasons. Woods to be avoided are mango and *deel.*

Pital - The *pital* (पीतल), also called *kudi* (कुडी), is the brass shell upon which the left hand drum *(bayan)* is made (figure 1.16). Although brass is the most common metal, one sometimes finds iron, copper, and aluminium. It is best to get the heaviest shell possible. Aluminium shells tend to have a poor sound because of the low weight. Iron shells give an acceptable sound but rust easily. A heavy copper or brass is preferred.

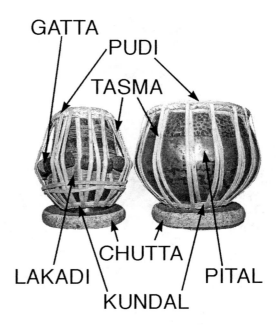

Figure 1.16. Parts of Tabla

Tasma - The rawhide lacing is known as *tasma* (तस्मा). It is also called *dori* (डोरी), *vadi* (वादि), or *baddhi* (बद्धी) (figure 1.16). The finest lacing is made of buffalo hide, although one often finds cowhide, leather, or even goat skin. One should definitely avoid leather or thin rawhide. These do not have an acceptable strength and will give problems.

Kundal - This is the counter-ring used for lacing the *tabla* (figure 1.16). These are commonly made of metal wire or rawhide.

Gatta - The *gatta* (गट्टा) are the wooden dowels used to control the tension (figure 1.16).

Pudi - The *pudi* is the drumhead, and is the most critical, complex component of the *tabla.* It is also known as *chamada* (चमड़ा). The parts of the *pudi* are shown in figure 1.17. There is the outer weaving which is called *gajara* (गजरा). There is a skin with a hole cut in it; this is called the *chat* (चाट), *kinar* (किनारा), *chati* (चाटी), *chanti* (चांटी), or *got* (गोट). There is the main membrane that covers the entire opening, called the *maidan* (मैदान), the *lab* (लब), sur (सुर) or *lav* (लव). The most distinctive portion of the *pudi* is called the *syahi* (स्याही), or *gab* (गाब). There is also an inner lining; this is known as *bharti* (भरती). The above nomenclature is but a small sampling of the variations in terms. India is a land with extreme linguistic diversity and it is beyond the scope of this book to attempt to give every possible variation.

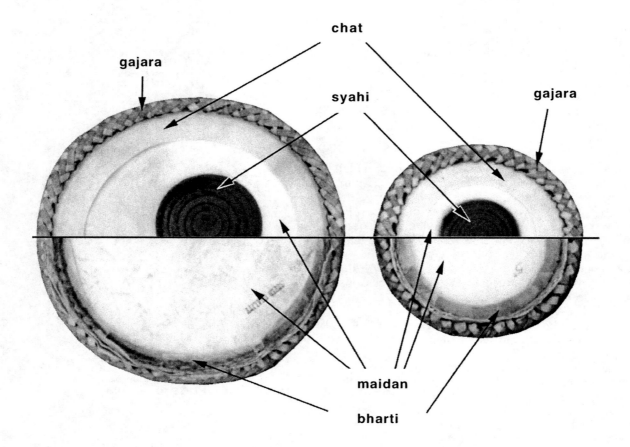

Figure 1.17. Parts of Pudi (outer and inner surfaces)

HISTORY OF TABLA-MAKING

We really know almost nothing about the history of *tabla*-making. It is unfortunate that the history of the world tends to be preoccupied with battles and kings. The affairs of craftsmen and artisans tend to be overlooked. This is especially problematic in India where any craft that uses rawhide, leather, or animal products of any kind, is looked upon as being the lowest form of work, a work which has traditionally been deemed not worthy of any serious attention.

What little we can say about the history of *tabla*-making has to be derived in two ways. On one hand, we can look at the present situation of *tablawalas* (*tabla*-makers) and see if it is reasonable to think that the same conditions, or at least similar conditions, existed several hundred years ago. In most cases there does not seem to be many major changes. Another way that we can get information is by examining instruments from that period. This too is extremely difficult because the rawhide of *tablas* is only good for a maximum of about 20-30 years. At some point it simply rots away. Therefore, we must look to pictures and written accounts from that period.

The bottom line is clear; our knowledge about the history of *tabla*-making is less than adequate. All we have are a collection of inferences, assumptions, deductions, and presumptions.

It appears that hundreds of years ago the manufacture of *tabla* was already spread among several different professions. The presence of dissimilar materials such as metal, rawhide, and wood suggest that these materials were in someway processed and/or formed before the *tablawala* purchased them. The similarities between the *tabla, pakhawaj, dholak,* and *nagada* suggest that the same craftsmen were involved in making all of them.

The metallurgical techniques used to fabricate the shells do not seem to have changed much in many centuries (see Chapter 3 for more information). The 19th century ethnomusicologist C.R. Day refers to copper being used for the *tabla.* We may also be sure that aluminium was not originally found in the *bayan* shells. The fabrication of aluminium parts requires a much more sophisticated technological infrastructure than was found in the early history of *tabla.*

The dimensions of the *tabla* were substantially different from what they are today. This is clear from the numerous photographs that come down to us from the 19th century. Figure 1.18 and 1.19 are two examples.

CONCLUSION

This chapter was a basic overview of the things that we need to know to make sense of this book. We looked at the drums of India. From here we may move into the next chapters and look at everything in greater detail.

Figure 1.18. Early tabla from miniature (circa 1750)

Figure 1.19. Tabla from Day's Treatise (19th Century)

WORKS CITED

Bhattacharya, Dilip
1999   *Musical Instruments of Tribal India*. New Delhi, Manas Publications

Courtney, David
1980   *Introduction to Tabla*. Hyderabad, India, Anand Power Press
1998   *Elementary North Indian Vocal*. Houston, TX, Sur Sangeet Services
1998   *Introduction to Tabla*. Houston, TX, Sur Sangeet Services
2000   *Advanced Theory of Tabla*. Houston, TX, Sur Sangeet Services

Day, C.R.
1990   *The Music and Musical Instruments of Southern India and the Deccan*. Delhi, Low Price Publications

Nevile, Pran
1996   *Nautch Girls of India: Dancers, Singers, Playmates*. Delhi: Ravi Kumar Publishers.

Stewart, Rebecca Marie
1974   *The Tabla in Perspective*. (Unpublished Doctoral Dissertation) Dept of Ethnomusicology, UCLA

CHAPTER 2

THE CRAFTSMEN

INTRODUCTION

There are a number of craftsmen involved in the manufacture of *tabla*. These craftsmen are connected to the larger tradition of the crafts in India. For the manufacture of *tabla*, there is the central occupation, which is known as the *tablawala* (तबलावाला), plus a number of peripheral occupations. It is appropriate that we take a quick overview of the complex relationship between the crafts, craftsmen, and Indian society.

CRAFTS, CRAFTSMEN, AND INDIAN SOCIETY

India has a long history of crafts. Metallic goods, textiles, wooden articles, etc., have been highly sought after in world markets for generations. However, there are some curious contradictions that are seen in the relationship between the skilled crafts and the larger society. In some ways Indian society bestows respect, but in other ways, craftsmen are looked down upon. In a similar way, the Indian economy is dependent on their production, yet there is a long history of economic neglect.

Viswakarma (विश्वकर्मा) - The respect and importance given to skilled craftsmen is reflected in traditional Hindu views. This is best summed up in the various myths concerning the god Viswakarma (fig. 2.1)(Saletore 1985).

Indian gods are known by a plethora of names; Viswakarma is no exception. He is variously called Tvasta (त्वष्ट), Prajapati (प्रजापति), Karu (कारु), Takshaka (तक्षका), and Sudhanvan (सुधान्वन).

The religious significance of Viswakarma is profound. He is considered the creator of the material world. One of the oldest Hindu texts, the *Rigveda,* describes him as being beyond mortal comprehension. As the creator of the material world and celestial artificer, he is often elevated to the highest position.

Hindu mythology is mixed as to the origins of Viswakarma. The *Nirukta* (निरुक्त), which is the traditional authority of etymology, states that he is the son of Bhuvana (भुवन). However, he has also been said to be the son of Prabhasa, who was the God of dawn, and one of the eight *Vasus.*

There is an interesting reference to him in the *Ramayan*. In this epic, Ram (राम) is planning to move his army onto the island of

Figure 2.1. Viswakarma

Lanka by shooting a magic arrow into the ocean, thus drying it up. Varuna (वरुण), the God of the waters, becomes apprised of the situation, and persuades Ram that such drastic action is not necessary. Varuna then convinces Ram to take the help of Nala (नल), who is the son of Viswakarma, to build a bridge across the ocean to allow his troops to pass. Nala was an able artificer in his own right, having learned the craft from his father. Nala complies and Ram is able to move his army and defeat his foe Ravana (रावण).

The *Ramayan* is not the only epic to make references to Viswakarma; the *Mahabharat* too makes several references. For instance, it is said that he sacrificed the entire earth when he gave it to Kashyapa (कारयप)(one of the seven cosmic rishis). He also designed the celestial vehicle for Kubera (कुबेर) (the cosmic treasurer and God of wealth). Furthermore, he constructed a magical bow named Vijaya (विजय). One other item of note is that he is the one who fashioned the emblem of an ape that was on Arjun's standard.

Viswakarma is credited with many other things as well. He is said to have presented the goddess Chandika a number of gifts, including jewellery, armour and weapons. He is also said to have fashioned palaces for Yama (God of death) and Indra (King of the gods).

These remarkable creations make Viswakarma very important to Hindu craftsmen. Not only is he a source of spiritual inspiration, but he is believed to be the divine protector of all artisans and craftsmen. He is commonly worshipped in a ceremony known as *Viswakarma Puja* (विश्वकर्मा पूजा). In this ceremony the tools of the craftsmen are the centre point for reverence. Not only is he considered the protector of craftsmen, but he is also believed to be the actual progenitor of all craftsmen.

Muslim Craftsmen - A large number of India's craftsmen, especially those who make *tablas*, are Muslim. It is obvious that the myths of Viswakarma do not have much meaning for them. Nevertheless, these craftsmen also have their traditional sources of respect.

Much of the respect that Muslim craftsmen derive is from a fundamental dignity of labour. Work itself is considered noble and a form of worship. It is for this reason that devout Muslims may commence their workday by saying *"Al Hamdu Lillahi Rabbil 'Alamin"*, which means "Praise be to Allah, the lord of the Worlds".

The Prophet Mohammed (p.b.u.h.) said, "Whoever finds himself at nightfall tired of his work, God will forgive his sins." The prophet himself did not shirk his duties when it came to physical labour. For instance, it is said that he injured his shoulder due to carrying large stones, in the reconstruction of the *Ka'bah* (the sacred edifice at Mecca) (fig. 2.2).

With so many traditional sources of respect and fundamental declarations about the dignity of labour, it is surprising that there are also deeply rooted stigmas.

Stigma of Manual Labour - Today there is a stigma attached to any manual labour. Traditional Hindu attachments or Islamic declarations are no match to present prejudices. It is very difficult to say exactly what the reasons for these prejudices are.

The social stigma that is attached to manual labour has adversely affected the crafts. Today

Figure 2.2. Ka'bah at Mecca

there is a tendency for families to discourage their children from going into the crafts. It is extremely common for the children of craftsmen to get a basic degree (e.g., B.Com) and seek government jobs. Often these jobs have extremely poor pay and are sometimes comparable to what a skilled craftsman can make. Still these government positions are considered to be much more prestigious.

Economic Importance of Crafts - Crafts are important to the economic well being of India. Silk, cotton cloth, clothing, brassware, goods made from sandalwood, and a variety of goods have become synonymous with India. Although manufactured goods, software, and other commodities are starting to eat into the traditional stronghold of handicrafts, the market is still very significant.

Indian crafts have been important world-wide for as long as anyone knows. Indian silk was popular in ancient Rome and China. Cotton material from India has been found in Egyptian tombs at *Fostat*. By the 3rd century BC, India was a major exporter of gems. Indian crafts were ubiquitous throughout the classical world.

The Middle Ages also saw tremendous interest in Indian crafts. It was not just tea and spice that spurred the sea trade with India in the late Middle Ages, but silks, gems and other items played their part. The creation of the East India company was, in part, a desire to exploit trade in these commodities.

The importance of Indian crafts continues even today. Although the advent of modern manufacturing techniques have cut into these traditionally strong areas, it is still a major part of the Indian economy. The 1999 exports of handicrafts are listed at over 26 billion (26 thousand-million) rupees. Remember these are the export figures; they do not include the production of handicrafts for internal consumption. Any way that you look at it, the crafts in India are a major portion of the Indian economy.

However, the economic importance of crafts do not necessarily translate to a secure financial position for the craftsmen. There is a long history of economic neglect.

Economic Disadvantage - Today the craftsmen tend to be economically disadvantaged. The reasons for this economic disadvantage are complex and long standing. They involve very complex mixtures of economics, politics, and other social pressures.

The downward spiral for the crafts began at the end of the Mogul empire. During this period the British began to have more of an influence over South Asia. It was during this period that European goods started to show up in the Indian markets. Indian craftsmen began to feel the competition with imported British goods.

The height of British rule in India was the depth of the economic situation for Indian craftsmen. There were high tariffs placed upon Indian goods while British manufactured goods had a minimal tariff. This made British goods inexpensive in the world markets, while Indian goods were expensive. This decimated the market for finished Indian products. Furthermore, the introduction of large factories and modern mass production allowed the British to produce quantities and qualities that the individual handmade goods from India could never match.

The result was that the economy of India shifted to a system whereby raw materials, such as cotton, were exported to Great Britain while finished goods, such as cloth, were imported back into India. In this system economic resources were lost.

The *swadeshi* (स्वादेशी) movement during the early part of the 20th century offered a ray of promise. This movement was pivotal to the Independence movement. According to the concept of *swadeshi*, Indians would boycott British manufactured goods in preference to indigenously manufactured ones. This was a brilliant example of economics as a political tool. By making their own goods and selling them in the local markets, it denied the British raw materials at the same time that it denied the British a market for their manufactured goods. *Swadeshi* is considered to be an import factor in India's independence.

Unfortunately, *swadeshi* was completely mismanaged after independence. This thrust the craftsmen back into economic hardship. After independence, India was pursuing the path of a centralised economy. Nothing could be imported or exported without government permission. The complex situation regarding licenses, paperwork and bribes meant that it became very difficult to find avenues into the world market for many Indian goods. Furthermore, since Indian craftsmen did not have to compete in the international markets, there was never the pressure to come up to international standards of quality.

There were numerous efforts on the part of government institutions to create outlets into the world markets. Government shops, co-ops, and a host of other schemes were set up with the express purpose of helping the craftsmen. However, deep rooted corruption and mismanagement coupled with an impenetrable wall of red tape doomed these efforts to failure.

Today the centralised economy has largely been dismantled. There are more avenues into world markets and most craftsmen are able to work to full capacity. Furthermore, there seems to be an improvement in the overall quality of goods produced.

LABOUR, RAW MATERIALS, AND THE CRAFTSMEN
It is interesting to look at the situation concerning labour and raw materials. We will see throughout this book that fundamental economic conditions have a profound effect upon the design and manufacture of *tabla*.

India is a land where labour is plentiful. Laws of supply and demand alone dictate that the value of manual labour is going to be very cheap in such conditions. This situation is further exacerbated by a constantly depressed rupee. The combination of these factors makes Indian labour especially cheap by international standards. Unskilled labour is valued at only pennies a day while highly skilled labour is measurable in only a few dollars.

This abundance of cheap labour stands in sharp contrast to the scarcity of raw materials. Many of the conditions that have caused there to be a abundance of cheap labour have also caused the cost of raw materials to be high.

India's large population is one reason for the scarcity of raw materials. It stands to reason that a larger population is going to demand more manufactured goods, more wood, more leather, more food, etc. If these demands are to be met locally then there are problems. One problem is that the density of population is very high. Therefore a smaller land mass must service the needs of a larger population. This will certainly cause the cost of raw materials to be high.

The economics behind the entire situation is extremely complex. It is not possible to even begin to discuss this in any detail. It must suffice for us to simply remember that labour is very cheap and raw materials are very dear. We will see throughout the rest of this book that this economic fact has profound implications for the design, manufacture and repair of *tabla*.

OVERVIEW OF INDIAN CRAFTSMEN
Indian craftsmen fulfill a number of duties. Some are involved with the production of utilitarian items while others are involved in the production of works of art. There is no clear distinction between utility and art. Even the most humble of utilitarian devices have artistic elements that must be appreciated.

It is very helpful to have a clear idea as to how Indian craftsmen relate to other forms of manual labour. There are two overall classes of labour. The lowest class of labourer is unskilled. Some common examples are agricultural labourers *(kisan)*, domestic labour *(naukar)*, and peons *(chaprasi)*. People who perform these occupations are at a tremendous social and economic disadvantage. A higher level of labourer is the skilled craftsman, known as the *karigar*. Common examples are the mason *(maistri or thawai)*, carpenter *(badhai)*, goldsmith, blacksmith *(luhaar)* etc. People who occupy this section of society may or may not have a better social and economic status. Many of these common occupations are shown in table 2.1.

Table 2.1 - Common Craftsmen and Labourers

English	Sanskrit	Hindi	Urdu
farmer	karshaka (कार्षक)	kisan (किसान)	kisan (کسان)
Ironsmith	lohakaarah (लोहकारः)	luhaar (लुहार)	luhaar (لوہار)
carpenter	takshakah (तक्षकः)	badhai (बढई)	badhai (بڑھاُئی)
goldsmith	swarnakaarah (स्वर्णकारः)	sunar (सुनार)	sunar (سونار)
tailor	sauchikah (सौचिकः)	darji (दर्जी)	darzi (درزُئ)
washerman	rajakah (रजकः)	dhobi (धोबी)	dhobi (دہوُی)
barber	naapitah (नापितः)	nai (नाई)	hajaam (حجام)
servant	sevakah (सेवकः)	das (दास)	naukar (نوکر)
tablamaker	-na-	tablawala (तबलावाला)	tablawala (طبلاوالا)
peon	dvahastha (द्वाःस्थ)	chaprasi (चपरासी)	chaprasi (چپراسُی)

TRAINING

Craftsmen learn their craft by apprenticeship. In this system a child learns from an older established professional. It is interesting to note that the system of apprenticeships is not confined to the crafts, but is also a common means of pedagogy for music, business, religious education, and a host of other activities in India.

The apprenticeship starts young. Generally it starts when a child reaches 7-9 years of age (fig. 2.3). The apprenticeship usually is for a period of several years, normally until the apprentice is 16-17 years of age.

The financial relationship between the apprentice and the master varies widely. If it is a field which is financially lucrative and apprenticeships are hard to come by, then it is common for the apprentice to pay the master for the privilege. Money or gifts that are given to the master may be referred to as *gurudakshana* (गुरु दक्षिणा). At the opposite end of the spectrum are low wage, low skill jobs. In such cases it is common for employers to pay a lump sum of money to the parents and take the child. This is really bonded labour. There are legal restrictions on this type of relationship because of frequent abuse, but the laws are seldom enforced. The most common relationship is where there is little or no financial imbalance. In such relationships, the apprentice works for free in exchange for training.

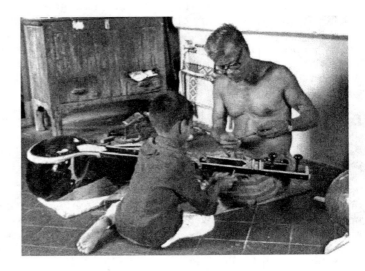

Figure 2.3. Sitar Maker and Young Apprentice.

page 15

It is normal for craftsmen in a particular industry to have their sons and daughters marry the children of fellow members of the craft. This traditionally has been done by arranged marriages. This is done primarily for financial and social reasons. A consanguineous relationship between the craftsmen has the effect of creating a social entity that functions very much like a guild or a union. It provides a basic support structure and allows for price fixing, control of raw materials and other related functions. This consanguineous relationship also extends into the apprenticeship. When it comes time for a child to become an apprentice, there is a good likelihood that it will be to a relative.

There are a number of things that are learned during the apprenticeship. The obvious things are the actual techniques of the craftsmanship. The less obvious, yet possibly more important, are the procurement of raw materials, knowledge of distribution channels, the grading of raw materials, tricks to reducing the workload, and other "tricks of the trade".

THE DUKAN

The shop that the craftsmen work in is known as a *dukan* (दुकान). The word *dukan* literally means a shop, workshop, or small store. They are invariably small affairs, usually no larger than a walk-in closet. Within this small space, one will find anywhere from two to eight people working. The exact characteristics of the *dukan* may vary from one craft to another; still there are many common factors.

Storage is very important in the *dukan*. When one enters the *dukan* the first thing that one notices is that most objects are stored at head level or above. This is a practical arrangement. There is also at least one cupboard used for a sundry of things. One thing that seems conspicuously absent is any type of display case.

Work space is another concern of the *dukan*. Generally all work must be done on the ground. The floors are usually either cement or rough-cut stone slabs. Either case is uncomfortable. Therefore, *ad hoc* mats made from old burlap bags (*gunny* sacks) or grass mats are common. There are other special purpose working surfaces which may vary from craft to craft.

The *dukans* have a minimum of amenities. Generally they are wired for electricity, but not for water. Even the electricity is not supplied constantly, for it is usually turned off for several hours a day; this is common throughout India. There are almost never any toilets in a *dukan*. Since they are open, mosquitoes are always a problem. One keeps the mosquitoes away by taking oil-soaked rags, and setting them on fire. They are then extinguished but allowed to smoulder and create a lot of smoke. This smoke is very effective at repelling mosquitoes. Obviously there is no air conditioning.

Working in cramped quarters without any amenities may seem terrible, but it is not really. The relaxed pace of Indian life coupled with a strong sense of camaraderie makes for a tolerable work environment. If one compares this with the fast-paced, high pressure life in the "corporate cubicle", then the craftsman's life is really not bad.

Economics of the Dukan - The *dukan* is pivotal to the economic well being of the craftsman. You may be thinking that this is so obvious that it does not deserve to be discussed here. However, the relationship between the *dukan* and the craftsman is extremely complex and is not obvious. It is especially not obvious to one who has never lived in India.

We may briefly say that the economic advantage that a craftsman receives is variable. It is proportional to his degree of control of the *dukan*. If you control the *dukan*, then you are in the position to control the distribution of money to the workers. As a general rule, the apprentices do not have to be paid. If the other workers are immediate members of your family, then distribution is dictated by a myriad of personal matters. If the worker is outside of the family, then distribution is according to prearranged agreement.

I must stress that "control" is not the same as "ownership". Ownership of the *dukans* is very vague in India. This may require some explanation.

India has a complex economic system that is based upon two types of money: there is black money and there is white money. White money is legal money; it is taxed and accounted for. Black money, on the other hand, is illegal, untaxed, and unaccounted for. Within the Indian economy the balance and relationship between the black and white economy is both important and extremely complex. Any major purchases, such as property, will invariably be based upon the transfer of both black and white assets.

When a craftsman acquires a *dukan,* the transaction will typically be made as follows. On the white side, there will be a rent which is often fixed. This is known as *kiraiya* (किराया) and is normally paid monthly. On the black side there is a lump sum which is very substantial; this is known as *pagadi* (पगड़ी). The rent (*kiraiya*) usually tends to be much less significant than the lump sum payment (*pagadi*). Although this is the normal arrangement, one may easily visualise all of the disputes that may arise between the building owner and the craftsman. This is an interesting topic, but one that we need not expand upon here.

OVERVIEW OF CRAFTS RELATED TO THE MANUFACTURE OF TABLA

The manufacture of the *tabla* is not done by any one craft or craftsman. There are a number of different crafts involved. It is appropriate for us to review these various crafts and see how they contribute to the overall endeavour.

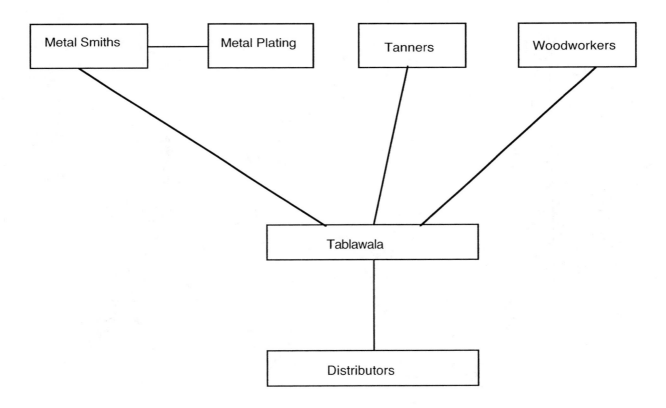

Figure 2.4. Crafts Related to Tabla-Making

The professions that are involved are shown in figure 2.4. This diagram shows woodworkers, metal smiths, metal platers, tanners, *tablawalas*, and distributors. It is surprising how specialised each part of the system has become. There is a remarkable lack of overlap in these various enterprises.

Woodworkers - Woodworking is a very ancient craft in India. There are particular castes whose hereditary function is to craft a variety of items in wood. Many of these communities ascribe their origins to Viswakarma, the celestial artificer.

Woodworking has very different characteristics in different areas of India. This is due in part because different woods have very different qualities. Over the years, the craftsmen have developed industries which are suitable for the characteristics of the local woods. It is impossible to cover all of the different woods and specialities because it is simply too diverse. However, a few famous ones come to mind. Karnataka for instance, specialises in decorative crafts based upon sandalwood; Kashmir is famous for walnut. Uttar Pradesh is known for crafts, usually utilitarian, based upon *sisam, sal*, and *dudhi*. Madura is famous for finely carved rosewood tables and household furniture.

Woodworking is not just for decorative crafts or utilitarian household goods; it is one of the basic enterprises in the manufacture of the *tabla*. The woodworkers, known as *badhai*, deal with the loggers, or their representatives, sort through and grade logs for their suitability, purchase and take them back for work. They take the wood, season it, cut it, then turn it on a lathe. The rough shells will then be sold to the *tablawalas*.

Metal Workers - Indian metal workers engage themselves in producing a variety of utilitarian as well as decorative items. Silver, gold, iron, brass, copper, bronze, steel, and zinc are the metals that they most commonly use. The metal workers are known by many names. The goldsmith may be known as *sunar*, and a blacksmith is known as *luhaar*, etc.

Figure 2.5. Brassworkers in Bombay

The fortunes and social position of the metalsmiths vary tremendously according to their products and their metals. It is no surprise that the goldsmiths and the silversmiths are in economically strong positions while blacksmiths tend to be at the bottom level.

Tanners and Cobblers - The rawhides are handled by a community of tanners. These are known as *chamar* (चमार) and are a class of untouchables. The *chamars* have also come to be known as *mochis* (मोची). This reflects the fact that their major activities revolve around the manufacture of shoes, handbags, belts, and a variety of handicrafts.

Indian tanners and cobblers deal in a variety of skins. Buffalo and cattle are the most common for utilitarian items. However, goats and sheep also provide skins for a variety of purposes. Supplying rawhide for the manufacture of *tablas* is but a very small part of their business.

Platers - The platers are the ones who plate the metal shells that are used for the *bayan*. Their main occupation is for plating automotive parts, cooking utensils and other similar things. Again, plating the shells for *tablas* is but a small part of their business.

Tailors - The tailor is known as a *darji* or *darzi* (दर्ज़ी). There is no cloth used for the *tabla,* however it is used for the cushioned rings and the covers. The sewing of cushions and covers is a totally insignificant part of their business. Their normal business revolves around shirts, blouses, pants, and other ordinary clothing.

Cloth is called *kapada* (कपडा) in Hindi and in Urdu. One generally finds ordinary machine woven cloth used; these are typically leftovers from the clothing trade. There is a handspun fabric known as *khadi* (खाड़ी), but it is quickly falling out of fashion.

Distributors - The distributors have become an important part of the entire system. Since very few people outside of India will be able to get their *tablas* directly from the *tablawala*, the distributors are an important consideration.

The distributors are not craftsmen, but businessmen. However, they have become so important to the system that it is necessary to undertake some discussion.

The distributors have only recently entered the equation as a significant social and economic force in the system. When I first started my association with the *tablawalas,* the majority of musicians dealt with the *tablawalas* directly. One seldom would go to a store to purchase a pair, especially if one wanted a good pair. Therefore, there really was no distribution system. More importantly, there was no major system for the export of *tablas*.

The reasons for a lack of a distribution system were varied. One of the biggest impediments was the Indian government and its maze of red tape. It was only with the reduction of red tape that things got easier. Slowly the large music stores such as Bina, Bharghava, and others began to venture into the export business. Today, there are numerous distribution channels that carry *tablas* out of India and into the world market.

The opening of new distribution channels has not been without its teething pains. One perennial problem has been quality control. Cultural factors have made it difficult to create a system that consistently assures high quality *tablas*.

The quality control issue is further complicated by the fact that vigilance must be maintained at every step. Even a superb, professional quality *tabla* can go bad by exposure to high humidity somewhere in transit. The distribution network is one area where we expect to see great expansion in coming decades.

TABLAWALA

The *tablawala* (तबलावाला) is the key position in the manufacture of *tablas*. The term "*tablawala*" may literally be translated to mean "*tabla*-man". It is their job to take the metal shells, the wooden shells, rawhide, and various materials and bring them all together to make *tabla, dholak, daf,* and a variety of Indian drums.

The social position of the *tablawala* is very low. Any occupation that deals in hides is considered one of the lowest occupations in India, and is usually performed by untouchable classes. This is perhaps one reason why a large number of the craftsmen are Muslim. There is not the same level of ostracism that one would find within the Hindu communities.

The craftsmanship of the *tablawala* is very high. It is one of the most difficult crafts and requires a very high level of skill and many years of training.

Figure 2.6. The Tabla-Dukan

Curiously enough, the combination of high level of skill coupled with the social ostracism has had desirable economic consequences. Both have combined to restrict the supply of *tablawalas*, while the opening up of world markets has created greater demand for their products. *Tablawalas* are therefore in a better position to demand a decent return for their services.

TOOLS OF THE TABLAWALA

There are a number of tools that the *tablawala* have at their disposal. These are shown in figure 2.7. It is very important to have a good understanding of these tools because there will be frequent allusions to them throughout this work.

a) *Chini* (चिनी) - *Chini* also called *chheni* (छेनी) is a carpenter's chisel. It is used to make slits in the skin. Occasionally it is used to make slits in the *tasma* (thong for the lacing).

b) *Patti* (पट्टी) - This is a section of metallic ribbon, usually about 3/8th of an inch wide. It is used to scrape off extra *syahi massala* during the process of applying the *syahi*. This process will be described in greater detail in Chapter 6.

c) *Palir* (पलिर) - *Palir* is merely a corruption of the English word pliers. These are ordinary pliers as may be found in any hardware store.

d & e) *Suva* (सुवा)- This is a kind of awl with a broad flat point. The flat point has a slit through which rope or string is passed.

f) Razor - This is used to shave hair from goatskin.

g) *Churi* (छुरी)- Churi is a large knife, similar to a kitchen knife.

h) *Jal* (जाल)- The *jal* is the template used to lay out and mark the hide. These are really nothing more than large, round steel gaskets as one might find in the piping industry. The sizes run anywhere from under one foot to nearly two feet.

i) *Hathodi* (हथौड़ी) - Hathodi is a hammer used for a variety of purposes, including tuning the *tabla*.

j & k) *Rampi* (रम्पि) - Rampi is a blade that is beaten out of a single piece of iron. The blade is perpendicular to the handle.

l) *Ghorta* (घोटा) - The *ghorta* is a rounded, highly polished stone used to apply the *syahi*.

m) *Badda* (बद्दा) - The *badda* is a flat section of bamboo. It is very reminiscent of a doctor's tongue depressor. It has one side sharpened to resemble a chisel. However, the sharp edge is not for cutting, but simply to facilitate its insertion into tight places.

n) Rasp - The rasp is used to remove and shape wood, especially the rim of the drum.

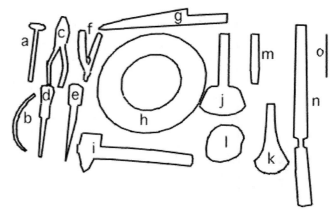

Figure 2.7. Tools of the Tablawala

o) *Tar ka Suva* (तार का सुवा) - This is a very large sewing needle, roughly four inches in length.

These tools will be alluded to frequently in this work. Please commit them to memory.

CONCLUSION

This chapter aquainted us with the craftsmen who make *tabla*. A craftsman who makes a *tabla* is known as a *tablawala*. The life of the *tablawala* is similar to other craftsmen in India. Indian craftsmen lead a life that could be described as lower middle class.

The life and economic situation of the craftsmen is very important in our discussions of the manufacture and repair of *tabla*. The techniques are influenced by the Indian economic conditions. For instance, the tendency to optimise the production practices to conserve materials at the expense of labour is clearly a reflection of larger economic conditions in India. All of these factors will be reflected in the techniques which will be discussed in later chapters.

WORKS CITED

Ganathe, N.S.R.
1983   *Learn Urdu in 30 Days*. Madras, Balaji Publications.

Saletore, R.N.
1985   Visvakarma, *Encyclopaedia of Indian Culture*. Delhi, Sterling Publishers, pvt. ltd.

Srinivasachari, K.
1995   *Learn Hindi in 30 Days*. Madras, Balaji Publications.

Srinivasachari, K.
1992   *Learn Sanskrit in 30 Days*. Madras, Balaji Publications.

CHAPTER 3

METAL

INTRODUCTION

The *bayan,* otherwise known as the *dagga*, is generally made of metal[1]. It is appropriate that we spend some time discussing the nature and qualities of metal, along with a brief overview of the basic principles of metal smithing. We will also show how the shell is made.

METALLURGY IN INDIA

India has an extremely ancient tradition of metallurgy. Metal artifacts are found from the earliest times. Some of these artifacts are simple, yet some show great sophistication.

The early periods of Indian metallurgy are remarkable. By about 500 BC, iron weapons began to come into use. By about 400 AD, Indians were able to construct great iron pillars of gargantuan proportions. Today they may be found in Mt. Abu, Dhar, but the most famous is the great iron pillar of Kumar Gupta in Delhi. This stands over 23 feet tall and is made of solid rustproof iron. As a comparison, it was not until the later part of the 19th century that such feats could be accomplished in the West.

The *Ain-i-Akbari* of Abu Fazal Allami (1598) presents an amazing glimpse into medieval metallurgy. The *Ain-i-Akbari* could be compared to the Encyclopaedia Britannica of the day. In this work, Abu Fazal goes into great detail as to how various materials are derived from the four basic elements (earth, fire, air, and water). From there it goes into the practical aspects.

If one is looking at metallurgy from a traditional Indian standpoint, it is first necessary to have some familiarity with traditional terms. The incredibly large number of Indian languages make a complete overview impossible, but a brief sampling is shown in table 3.1.

Table 3.1 Common Metals in India			
English	Sanskrit	Hindi	Urdu
iron	ayah (अयः)	loha (लोहा)	loha (لوہا)
steel	munda-loham (मुण्ड-लोहम्)	phaulad (फौलाद)	faulad (فولاد)
copper	tamram (ताम्रं)	tamba (तांबा)	tamba (تانبا)
gold	suvarnam (सुवर्ण)	sona (सोना)	sona (سونا)
lead	sisam (सिसं)	sisa (सीसा)	sisah (سیسا)
aluminium	-na-	alaminiyam (अलमीनियम)	alaminiyam (الومینیم)
brass	pittalam (पित्तलं)	pital (पीतल)	pital (پیتل)
silver	rajatam (रजतं)	chandi (चाँदी)	chandi (چاندی)

---

[1] There are exceptions to the metallic shells. In the area of West Bengal, for instance, they are sometimes made from fired clay. In the Punjab, *bayans* were at one time fashioned from wood; however today this is very rare. In the last thirty years of my dealing with *tablas* I think that I could count the number of times that I have seen either of these on one hand.

METALS

There are a number of metals used to make the shells for the *bayan*. Brass, iron, steel, aluminium, and copper are the most common. Let us look at these metals in greater detail.

Brass - Brass is the most common material used to make *bayans*. Brass is an alloy of copper and zinc. Other metals may also be added to give special properties. Brass imparts a very identifiable tonal colour to the *bayans*. This tone can be best described as bell-like. Such colouration is acceptable but not really desirable.

In antiquity the word brass was not precisely defined. Throughout history, the term has been applied to many different alloys of copper. The distinction between brass and bronze was not commonly recognised in the classical world.

However, the distinction between brass and bronze was very well known by the time of Akbar. The *Ain-i-Akbari* mentions bronze as *safidru* or *kusi*, and being composed of four parts copper to one part tin. Brass on the other hand is known as *pital* (पीतल) and was also discussed in great detail in this early work.

There are a number of different types of brasses mentioned in the *Ain-i-Akbari*. It is surprising that this work discusses brass in surprisingly modern terms. For instance, Abu Fazal talks of three different classes of brass. If one mixes 2.5 parts copper to one part *ruh-e-tutiya*, then one obtains an alloy which is malleable when cold[2]. On the other hand, two parts copper to one part *ruh-e-tutiya* produces an alloy which is malleable when heated. Finally, the third type of brass is two parts copper to one part *ruh-e-tutiya,* however this brass is cast rather than beaten. These last two types of brass are interesting because they show very clearly the different qualities that are produced when a metal is cast instead of forged.

Today we divide brass into two classes, the *alpha* and the *beta*. *Alpha*-brasses have a very high percentage of copper with a rather low percentage of zinc. The major characteristic of the *alpha*-brasses is that they lend themselves very well to cold annealing. On the other hand, there are the *beta*-brasses. These tend to have lower percentages of copper. The *beta*-brasses are extremely hard and good for industrial applications, but do not lend themselves well to cold working.

India has always had a very vibrant brass industry. However, unlike the West where such activities are done in large factories, India has a lot of cottage industries. These are small affairs, often no more than two or three people. Usually there is one master and several apprentices. These cottage industries make cooking vessels, utensils, various fixtures, and traditional brass works of art.

Indian brassworking relies very heavily on recycling. The consequence of brass recycling is that it becomes difficult to make definite statements concerning the compositions of the metal. Scrap is constantly being melted and reworked, and in the process, various impurities creep in. Still, we may make a few generalisations.

Indian brasses used in the making of *bayans* are *alpha*-class brasses. *Alpha*-brasses are easily worked by hand without any special equipment. This is particularly amenable to the low levels of technology found in the cottage industries.

Indian brasses have a colour very similar to gold. Although brass may come in a variety of colours, it is the colour of gold that has a special significance in India. Consciously or unconsciously, the industry has grown up around these alloys of the "Dutch metal" or "Mannheim gold" class.

Brass has a number of desirable qualities for the *bayan*. First, it is very heavy. This is a desirable quality in the metal because it is not just the skin that will vibrate, but the whole drum. Therefore, a heavier shell will produce a deeper tone. Another desirable quality of brass is that the tarnish does not harm rawhide. I often do head replacements and one may find a slight blue-green colour on the inner surface of the *pudi*. There appears to be no ill effect of this tarnish on the rawhide.

---

[2] There appears to be some dispute over the exact definition of *ruh-e-tutiya*. According to some it is pure zinc while others suggest that it may be an alloy such as pewter.

Brass does have some undesirable characteristics. The most notable disadvantage is its high cost. Since copper is the major constituent of brass, the high cost of copper translates to a high cost of brass.

All things considered, brass is the most popular metal for making the *bayans*. The tone is acceptable, there is a well developed infrastructure for manufacture, and the cost is not prohibitive. One is not likely to go wrong with a brass *bayan*.

Iron and Steel - Iron and steel have been in use in India since the earliest times. The great iron pillars such as found in Delhi, are testament to the advanced level of iron working in India. The Urdu / Hindi word for iron is *loha* (लोहा) and steel is *faulaad* (फौलाद).

Steel and iron are a class of iron alloys. Typically one finds iron mixed with various amounts of carbon, manganese, chromium, or a variety of other substances. Although terms such as iron, steel, steel alloy, etc. are in common use, there is really no clear separation. For instance, one of the oldest steels known to man is the simple carbon-steel. This is primarily iron with a small amount of iron carbide. However, cast iron is also a mixture of iron and iron carbide. Therefore, the distinction between carbon steel and cast iron is based more upon the difference in malleability rather than the actual constituency.

Iron and steel are often used to make *bayans*. Iron / steel *bayans* have been popular for student grade *tablas* for many years. There are a number of advantages to the steel / iron shell. The biggest advantage is the ease of fabrication. They may be made by virtually any blacksmith in India. Another advantage of these shells is cost; iron and steel are much cheaper than copper based alloys such as brass. The sound of iron / steel shells is also very good; this is due to the relatively neutral sound quality of these shells and the heavy weight.

However, there is one major disadvantage; they rust. It turns out this is such a major disadvantage that it reduces these shells to being some of the least desirable shells in India. The reason that rust is so bad is that it destroys rawhide. When any part of the rawhide remains in contact with rusted steel it causes it to disintegrate as thoroughly as if it had come in contact with acid.

There have been a number of attempts to address this issue. The most common is plating the shell with chrome, nickel, or some other material. Although plating is very common in India, it has historically not been good enough to prevent rusting. There is no acceptable level of rust; any rust will destroy rawhide. It is this zero tolerance for rust, combined with the poor quality of plating, that makes this an impractical solution.

One would think that stainless steel could be used in making shells. There is a very active stainless steel industry in India, so it is a very accessible technology. Yet I have never encountered one. Perhaps it is the considerably higher cost of stainless steel that is responsible.

It is possible that cultural reasons are partially responsible for the low utilisation of iron and steel. Only stainless steel has a good reputation in India; iron has a very bad reputation. It is associated with the planet Saturn, which in Indian astrology is considered to be the unluckiest planet. Even the word *"Shani'* not only means the planet Saturn, but it also means "bad luck". Any major purchase of iron, such as a new car, should be accompanied by a religious ceremony to ward off the effects, otherwise it is believed that one will bring bad luck home with the purchase.

The bottom line is simple; although steel and iron have the potential to produce high quality shells, technical and cultural reasons have relegated this to the least desirable status.

Aluminium - Aluminium is very commonly used to produce cheap, low quality shells for the *bayan*. In the last few years it has superseded iron and steel in popularity for low cost, student-grade *bayans*. This is remarkable considering how recently aluminium fabrication has been introduced into India.

Aluminium is one of the most curious of metals. It is the most abundant metal in the Earth's crust, yet it does not exist in a metallic form anywhere on Earth. It somewhat resembles silver, yet unlike silver, it is one of the cheapest metals available to man. It resists traditional methods of welding and fabrication, yet it is one of the most used metals in our modern civilisation. It does not form alloys as easily as more traditional metals, yet its alloys are among the most useful. If one were to look back upon the last hundred years, it could almost be called the aluminium age!

Aluminium is present in nature only in a chemically combined form. It is commonly found in such various minerals as feldspars, mica, and the soils that are derived from them, such as clay. It is also found in rubies, sapphires, topaz, and garnets. The most common commercial source for aluminium is bauxite.

Aluminium is produced in an interesting manner. Aluminium is so active that it resisted ordinary chemical means to reduce it until 1825 when Hans Christian Ørsted was able to isolate a crude sample by reducing aluminium chloride with a potassium amalgam. Over the years a number of other people used various chemical means. These were slow steps aimed at creating a commercially viable process. Perhaps the first commercial process for the production of aluminium was in the mid 19th century. This was when it was first introduced to the public at the Paris Exposition in 1855. Unfortunately, it was still extremely expensive. It was only with the availability of cheap electricity that it was possible to bring the cost down. Today, commercial aluminium production is based upon the electrolysis of alumina dissolved in molten cryolite.

Given the widespread availability of aluminium technology, it is no surprise that this metal should be used to make *bayans*. In the last thirty years, it has pushed out iron as the preferred metal for inexpensive, student grade *bayans*.

Aluminium has several advantages over more traditional metals. Aluminium is economical; it has fallen in price where copper based alloys such as brass have skyrocketed. Although aluminium is historically a hard metal to work with, the rise in popularity of aluminium for kitchenware has created an infrastructure for the fabrication of *bayan* shells. Aluminium shells are visually attractive. Aluminium does not tarnish, but it does develop a thin oxide patina; unlike rust, this patina does no harm to rawhide.

There is however, one major disadvantage of aluminium shells. It is inherently very light; yet *bayan* shells should be as heavy as possible. Furthermore, the chemical peculiarities of aluminium are such that it is virtually impossible to augment the weight of the shell with lead as one may do with copper or steel shells. (This is important and will be discussed later.)

Copper - Copper shells are considered to be the Rolls Royces of the *bayan* shells. They are expensive, virtually indestructible, rustproof, and have the finest sound.

Copper is a reddish coloured metal which is found both in chemically combined forms as well as a naturally occurring metal. Copper may be found in chalcocite, chalcopyrite, bornite, cuprite, malachite, and azurite. Commercially, copper is usually obtained by chemical leaching or smelting, followed by electrolysis.

Copper has a long tradition. It is one of the most used metals of antiquity. The Latin *cuprum* is a corruption of *cyprium,* as in *aes Cyprium* which means "metal of Cyprus". It was so named because Cyprus was the supplier of copper for Rome. In India, a copper industry has existed since the earliest times. In Sanskrit, copper is known as *tamram* (ताम्रम्). In Hindi it is known as *taambaa* (तांबा) (Ganathe 1983).

Copper does not corrode but it does develop a deep dark patina. Sometimes it forms a greenish compound that may discolour the inner surfaces of the drumhead. Such discolouration is harmless to the shell.

This last section discussed the various metals used in the manufacture of the *bayan* shells. With a clear understanding of these basic metals we may now look at some of the processes that the Indian metal smiths engage in.

ACTIVITIES AND PROCEDURES

There are a number of activities that metal smiths are required to perform. Although an in-depth description is beyond the scope of a simple book on *tabla*, it is still appropriate for us to make a brief overview of them.

Annealing - Annealing is the process of heating the metal to restore malleability. This is necessary because the process of hammering the metal creates stress within the metal. These stresses tend to reduce malleability. Heating the metals to high temperatures allows the crystalline structures to reorganise so that these stresses are reduced. In a sense, annealing is part of hand forging because the metal must be heated until plastic before it may be worked.

Forging - Forging is the repetitive process of heating and beating metal with the purpose of forming it into the desired shape. Forging accomplishes two things. The primary function is to beat the metal into the desired shape. However, it also serves to increase the hardness of the metal.

Bayan shells are forged in a process that is extremely old. One simply beats the metal with an iron hammer against an anvil. However, the form of the anvil in India is very different from the one that we are familiar within the West (fig.3.1). It consists of an iron bar between 1-2 yards in length that has a small bend at the end. Both ends may be used according to the size and dimension of the object being forged. The desired end is used to rest the object being forged on. The entire iron bar is placed in a wooden frame that is roughly reminiscent of a large "A". The worker then sits against the bar/ wood assembly and hammers away at the metal until the object assumes the desired shape (figure 3.2).

Rivets, Nuts & Bolts, and Other Fasteners - Over the years a number of fasteners have been invented for joining metal pieces together. With the exception of rivets, these fasteners have no place in the manufacture of metallic shells for the *bayan*.

The rivet is basically just a small metal rod with a head on both ends. One head is made during the time of manufacture and the other head is formed during the process of joining the pieces together.

Rivets are occasionally used in the fabrication of cheap iron shells for student grade *bayan*. Other than this, they have no place in the making of *tablas*.

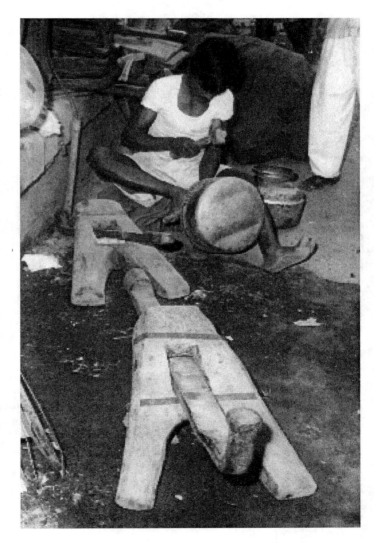

Figure 3.1. Anvil

Welding, Brazing and Soldering - These are the processes involved in joining two pieces of metal together. Some examples are forge welding, arc welding, gas welding, resistance welding, and thermit welding, soldering, and brazing. Brazing is the most used technique, but the others may be found occasionally. Before we discuss brazing in some depth, let us make a quick overview of some of the other techniques.

Forge welding is where the metal is heated and then simply hammered together.

Arc welding uses metallic rods attached to a source of electricity.

Gas welding is done by using the high temperature of a torch, usually using a mixture of acetylene and oxygen.

Resistance welding uses the electrical resistance at the weld joint to generate sufficient heat to weld the joints together.

Thermit welding uses a mixture of aluminium dust and iron oxide. At high temperatures, the aluminium ignites and removes the oxygen from the iron oxide, in the process creating a molten steel. This in turn fuses with the adjacent parts creating a strong bond.

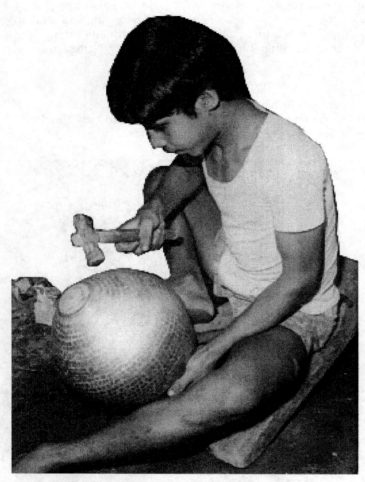

Figure 3.2. Forging the Bayan Shell

Soldering is the process of joining metals together using alloys of lead. The most common alloy is a mixture of tin and lead. This alloy is curious because the melting temperature of the final alloy is even lower than the melting point of either of its two constituents. Although soldering is one of the most accessible technologies, it produces the weakest joints.

Brazing is the preferred process for making *bayan* shells. It is a process which is very similar to soldering in that it requires an alloy which melts at a temperature well below that of the metals being joined. However, brazing alloys melt at considerably higher temperatures than solder, usually in excess of 800° F (430° C). Brazed joints are considerably stronger and more reliable than soldered joints. Furthermore, it is a much more accessible technology than many of the other welding techniques.

We will discuss the specifics of brazing the shell later. But for now let us step back and make a few general observations concerning the joining of our metallic parts.

<u>General Considerations in Welding</u> - Regardless of what welding techniques we use, there are some general considerations for making a good joint. These considerations involve some curious dichotomies. For instance, for a joint to be strong, the surfaces must be clean; however forges are very dirty places. For a joint to be strong, the surfaces must be free of oxide; yet the high temperatures used to make the metals malleable invariably produce oxides. For a joint to be strong the surfaces must be free from flaws, unfortunately the act of forging produces discontinuities in the metal. With these conditions in mind we can better appreciate the skill of the Indian craftsmen.

CONSTRUCTION OF THE METAL SHELL

Let us now look at the construction of the *bayan* shell. There are variations that may be found, but the following technique seems to be the most common.

We have already discussed the various metals that may be used; however for the remainder of this chapter we will presume that the material will be brass. This is because brass is the most common metal used to make the *bayan*. If other metals are used, the procedure will be basically the same.

We have also discussed the various welding techniques available; but for the remainder of this chapter we will presume that brazing will be used. This too is the most common technique.

The process of crafting the *bayan* shell is illustrated in figure 3.3. The construction begins when a disc of brass is cut so that it has a diameter of roughly eight inches. This is then forged into the shape of a bowl. Next, a rectangular piece of brass is cut and joined together so that a cylinder with a diameter of approximately ten inches is formed. The two ends are joined by crimping, then the process of rounding it off by beating it with a mallet begins. It should assume the rough shape of a barrel.

Once it has been rounded enough, it is joined to the bowl-shaped bottom. For this, two slits are cut every half-inch around the bowl so that it may be crimped and welded. This is done by applying a mixture containing a metallic powder called *dag* (दाग़), then heating the whole to a red heat.

The *dag* is the brazing compound; this is crucial to the welding process. I enquired what *dag* was and was told that it was a mixture that contained powdered metal and other things. Although the actual constituency is not known, it is clear that it is a brazing compound. It is safe to say that this mixture contains two types of ingredients. There is some substance to chemically reduce the surface of the metal to allow the weld to form (e.g., borax,) and a metal that has a melting point below that of the brass. I have no way of knowing the exact content.

The rim must now be made. For this, one takes a strong iron ring of about nine inches in diameter and starts folding the brass rim over it. One may rarely find shells of low calibre that do not have this iron ring. Such shells should be avoided.

Now is the time for the final shaping to be done. It is in this stage that the raised disk at the bottom is made (fig. 3.4). It is also in this stage that the entire shell is rotated and beaten all over so that the entire surface is dented (fig. 3.2). The result is a shell which has a fish-scale-like surface. It is this final forging that reduces the malleability and imparts strength.

Now the surface must be prepared. The shell is put on a lathe and polished until all the dents are gone (fig. 3.5). It is then plated with chrome, nickel or some similar metal.

The *bayan* shell is now complete.

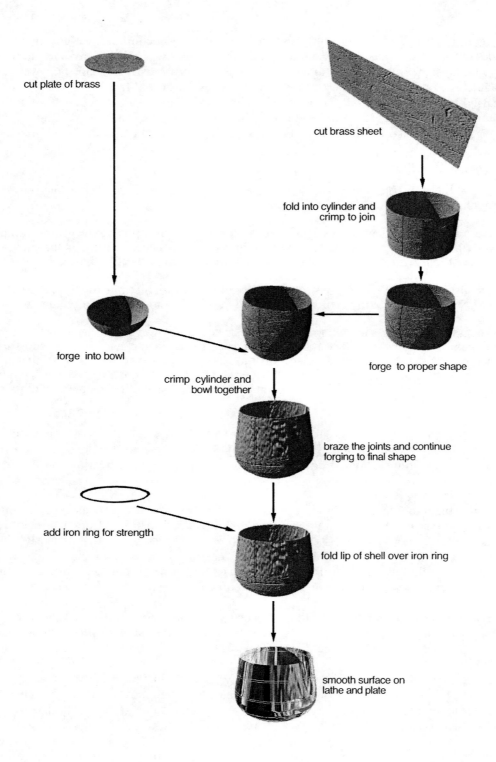

cut plate of brass

cut brass sheet

fold into cylinder and
crimp to join

forge to proper shape

forge into bowl

crimp cylinder and
bowl together

braze the joints and continue
forging to final shape

add iron ring for strength

fold lip of shell over iron ring

smooth surface on
lathe and plate

Figure 3.3. Making the Bayan Shell

Figure 3.4. Raised Bottom of Shell

Figure 3.5. Turning the Shell on the Lathe

Lead Weighting - The addition of lead weight to the shell is an optional stage. Throughout this chapter we have mentioned that the shells should be as heavy as possible. The ideal is to have a very heavy gauge metal that is of a naturally heavy alloy. However, one may further increase the weight by the addition of lead. A kilogram of lead seems to be a reasonable amount to add for most *bayans*.

There is an advantage to adding extra lead that goes beyond merely increasing the weight. Brass has a slight problem in that it tends to impart a bell-like colouration to the tone of the instrument. This is not necessarily a desirable thing. One may dampen the resonance of the shell, thus reducing this colouration, by adding lead to the instrument.

The procedure for adding the extra lead is simple. The inner surface should be clean. There should be no oils, dirt, or scaling. One then takes the shell and heats it up. It should be heated to just under a red heat. Anything more runs the risk of melting the brazing compound in the joints. During the heating process, the inner surface should be well fluxed. Any of a number of fluxes are available; however, the easiest thing to do is to continuously "tin" the inner surface with acid core solder. One next places clean scrap lead into the shell and melts it. One should be careful to keep the temperature above the melting point of the lead but well below the melting point of the brazing alloy. Allow the shell to cool.

This finishes the lead weighting. Ideally it should be done before the shell is plated. The process of heating the shell generally causes a discolouration on shells that are already plated.

Figure 3.6. Relief-work on Bayan

When the shell has had its weight enhanced in this manner it improves the sound considerably.[3]

Relief - One sometimes finds metal shells that are executed in relief or repoussé (fig. 3.6). These seem to be more popular from instruments that come from Pakistan.

There is a very simple process to making this type of decoration. There are steel moulds which have the desired decoration. The metal shells are laid against these moulds and beaten from the inside. This causes the metal to assume the desired shape.

These *bayans* are very attractive but unfortunately never professional quality. This process requires that the sheet metal from which the *bayans* are made to be a fairly light gauge. Unfortunately a good *bayan* needs to be made from as heavy a gauge metal as possible. This type of shell invariably causes us to make some compromises.

These *bayans* are more for the tourist/student market than for the professional market.

CONCLUSION

The manufacture of the metallic shells for the *bayan* is part of an ancient tradition of metallurgy and metal smithing. It is a craft which involves procedures and techniques that have not changed much in the last 2000 years.

We have seen that virtually any metal may be used but the most common is brass. Still, copper is considered the finest. There is a very refined and skillful way that the shells are forged by hand to assume the proper form.

The shells are not simply utilitarian in nature, but may have their looks enhanced by various means. The most common way to enhance the beauty is to plate it with nickel, chrome, or a variety of other metals. On occasion, it may be decorated with patterns in relief.

Weight and strength of the shell are probably the most important considerations. Both may be addressed by using extremely heavy gauge metal when forging the shell. However, the weight may be artificially enhanced by the addition of lead.

---

[3] If you are purchasing a new, finished *bayan*, it is good to know if the shell has had the weight augmented. This is easy to tell. Simply turn over the *bayan* and strike the very bottom. If it is a brass shell and is unaugmented, it will ring like a bell. If it is augmented, then it will have a dull sound. Now sharply rap on the side of the shell. The sound will give you an idea as to whether the shell is made of a heavy gauge metal. You wish the shells to be made with very heavy gauge metal and lead weighting. Sometimes makers will use a very light gauge metal, then augment the weight. Although I will not call this a deceptive practice, it does fool the novice into thinking that it is a higher quality shell than it actually is. Remember, you want lead augmentation *and* heavy-gauge metal, not lead augmentation *instead* of heavy gauge metal.

WORKS CITED

Alami, Abul Fazal
1598   *Ain-i Akbari*. Translated by H. Blockmann. Delh: 1989. Reprinted by New Taj Office.

Encyclopaedia Britannica
1952   "Brass" *Encyclopaedia Britannica*. page 40-42 Encyclopaedia Britannica Inc. Chicago, London, Toronto.
1952   Aluminium, *Encyclopaedia Britannica*. Volume 1, page 713 Encyclopaedia Britannica Inc. Chicago, London, Toronto.
1997   "Copper" *Encyclopaedia Britannica*. Volume 3, page 612 Encyclopaedia Britannica Inc. Chicago, London, Toronto.
1997   "Forging" *Encyclopaedia Britannica*. Volume 4, page 882 Encyclopaedia Britannica Inc. Chicago, London, Toronto.

Ganathe, N.S.R.
1983   *Learn Urdu in 30 Days*. Madras, Balaji Publications.

Keller, Charles
1994   "Invention, Thought, and Process: Strategies in Iron Tool Production", *Ancient Technologies and Archaeological Materials*. page 59-70: Amsterdam, Gordon and Breach Science Publishers. Edited by Sarah U. Wisseman and Wendall S. Williams

Srinivasachari, K.
1995   *Learn Hindi in 30 Days*. Madras, Balaji Publications.

Srinivasachari, K.
1992   *Learn Sanskrit in 30 Days*. Madras, Balaji Publications.

CHAPTER 4

THE RAWHIDE

INTRODUCTION

This chapter will discuss the various characteristics of rawhide. Rawhide is the most common animal product used in the manufacture of *tabla*. We will also discuss the related topics of living skin and leather. To make matters complete, we will also look at the fundamental chemicals which make skin, rawhide, and leather.

Why do we bother to look at these things in such depth? The answer is simple; the characteristics of the finished drum are going to depend upon the characteristics of the skins that go into it. These skins are some of the most complex materials that the *tabla* maker has to deal with.

THE ANIMALS

Several animals supply the skins for *tabla* (unwillingly of course). As a general rule, the buffalo hide or cowhide is used for the lacing, and the goat skin is used for the vibrating membranes.

The water-buffalo is very important in making *tablas*. This is the *bubalus bubalis,* which has been domesticated in Asia from the earliest of times. It is a very large, sturdy animal that thrives in tropical climates. In Hindi it is called *bainsa* (बैंसा)(male buffalo) or *bains* (बैंस)(female buffalo)(Ojha 1969).

There are two domesticated varieties of buffalo in the world. There is the swamp-buffalo, which is common in China, Philippines, South-East Asia, and Indonesia. They have broad, wide horns, large hooves and a chevron on the chest. In these countries, they are mainly used as beasts of burden. There is also the river-buffalo, which is common in India and Pakistan. They are mainly used for dairy production; however the meat is also eaten by many castes. It is the river-buffalo which is used in most *tablas*. Its hide is very thick and very strong and is ideal for the lacing. However, the hide is too thick to be used for the vibrating membranes. For this, goatskin is preferred.

The goat (*Capra hircus*) is very popular in India. It is estimated that there are approximately 100,000,000 goats in India. Mahatma Gandhi referred to them as "the poor man's cow". In Hindi the goat is called *bakara* (बकरा)(he-goat) or *bakari* (बकरी)(she-goat). Some common Indian breeds are the *Barbari, Beetal Chapar, Kamori,* and *Nachi*. Goats are

Figure 4.1. Indian River Buffalo *(Bubalus bubalis)*

the preferred source of red meat in India. They are also raised, to a lesser extent, for their milk. A few varieties are even raised for their hair.

The skins of both the buffalo and the goat are used in very specific ways. Their usage is determined by their mechanical and acoustic characteristics. This brings up the basic question of where these characteristics come from. Ultimately, the characteristics of rawhide are derived from phenomena which are occurring at the molecular level.

THE MOLECULAR VIEW

The characteristics of rawhide, leather and skin are traceable to the way that their molecules behave. Therefore, a working understanding of these molecular structures gives us a clearer idea of why we use certain parts of the skin, why we do not use others, and why these materials behave the way they do.

Figure 4.2. Goat (Capra hircus)

The chemical constituents of rawhide may be broken down into four classes: proteins, lipids, salts, and water. We will now look at these classes in greater detail.

Proteins - Proteins are probably the most important chemicals in the skin. Proteins are a class of compounds that perform wide varieties of tasks for the animal when it is alive. Most importantly for us, proteins are used as the basic building blocks for the body.

The chemical composition of proteins varies widely. In their simplest form, they are extremely long chains of amino acids (fig 4.3). If they are composed only of amino acids, they are known as simple proteins. Common examples of simple proteins include albumin and insulin. Sometimes, proteins include things other than amino acids; these are referred to as conjugated proteins. Examples of conjugated proteins are haemoglobin and the nucleoproteins

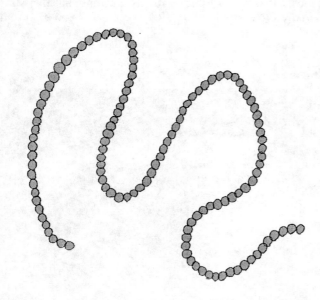

Proteins are extremely large molecules. They are so large that they may bend and fold into virtually any shape imaginable. It is this ability to be made into different shapes that controls both their chemical as well as mechanical properties.

If proteins bend back upon themselves repeatedly, they are often referred to as a globular proteins (fig 4.4). Globular proteins tend to be water soluble and are commonly used to regulate chemical activities. Unfortunately, globular proteins are usually useless as structural elements.

Proteins that are long and stretched out are referred to as fibrous proteins (fig 4.5). These fibrous proteins have very poor solubility, so they are not very useful in regulating biological activities, yet they are ideal for building up large mechanical structures.

Figure 4.3. Protein - Proteins are long chains of Amino Acids.

Therefore, it is the fibrous protein that is the basic mechanical building block. Its relative insolubility, their strength, and the wide variety of materials that may be made from fibres, make them ideal for mechanical purposes. Fibrous proteins may be thought of as the brick and mortar of the living animal.

Lipids - Lipids are oils and fats. They serve a number of metabolic purposes for the living animal. Although they are very important to the living animal, they are of only limited concern to the *tabla* maker.

Salts - There are a number of salts in skin. These salts are very important in creating the proper chemical environment in which skin may live. However, in the process of making *tablas* they tend to be leached from the hides and are of very little concern to the *tabla* maker.

Water - Water is extremely important both to the living organism as well as the *tablawala* who uses rawhides. It has a tremendous effect on both the mechanical and acoustic characteristics of the rawhide.

We showed in this section that there are four main chemical components to skin; proteins, water, salts, and lipids. However, the only class that is really important to the *tabla* is the protein, specifically the fibrous protein.

FIBROUS PROTEINS

The fibrous proteins are the key to the mechanical characteristics of skin and rawhide. Let us look at them in greater detail.

We can easily see how useful fibres are by looking at day-to-day materials. This will help us to visualise what happens at a molecular level. We have ropes made from hemp or other vegetable fibres. We have cloth which may be made from a variety of fibres. There are also less obvious uses of fibres. Boats for instance are commonly made from fibreglass. Aeroplane parts are commonly made from carbon fibres. Integrated circuits are made from glass fibres and epoxy. We could

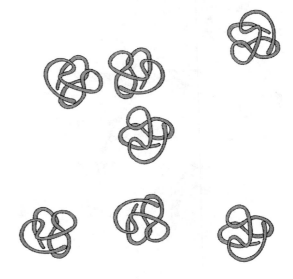

Figure 4.4. Globular Proteins

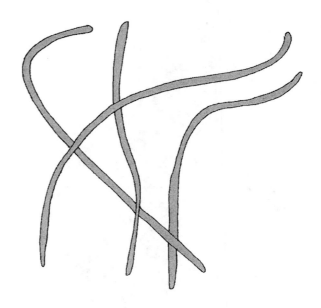

Figure 4.5. Fibrous Proteins

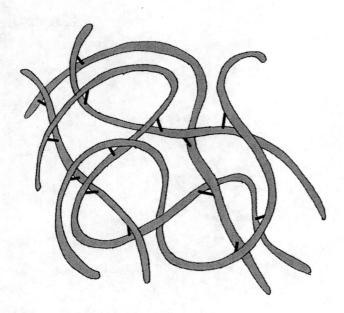

Figure 4.6. Disulphide Bonds - These bonds are a glue which binds proteins together.

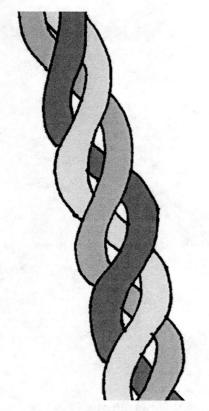

Figure 4.7. Section of Collagen Triple-Helix

think up examples all day long. Day-to-day life shows us that fibres may be used to produce materials with a surprising range of characteristics.

Many day-to-day products require a glue to hold them together. Fibreglass boat hulls and aeroplane parts are just a few common examples of the extremely strong materials that can be made when we add a glue to bind the fibres together. The body too makes use of "glue" to bind its own fibres together.

There a number of ways that the fibres of the body may be glued together. The most powerful is the disulphide bridge, sometimes referred to as a disulphide-bond. The power of these bonds comes from sulphur's amazing ability to bind with itself in many different ways (Kremlin 1996). The way that proteins may be glued together with disulphide bridges is illustrated in figure 4.6.

Let us look more closely at the body's fibres. As mentioned earlier the body uses fibres made of giant proteins. These proteins may be found in a variety of arrangements. They may also be "glued" together to produce a variety of different characteristics. So far we have been discussing these fibres in the most general terms. At this point we should look at specific fibrous proteins in greater detail. The most important ones for our purposes are collagen, keratin, and elastin.

<u>Collagen</u> - Collagens are very important proteins for the *tabla* maker. They are the most common proteins found in the skin. They are also found in bone, cartilage, and connective tissue. In all, about a quarter of the protein in mammals is collagen.

Collagens are fibrous proteins in the scleroprotein class. They are rather whitish, inelastic, and form fibres of great tinsile strength. It is rather insoluble in water, but hydrolyses to gelatine in boiling water. They are especially rich in the amino acid glycine.

The basic unit of collagen is the fibril. This contains three molecules of the collagen protein which spiral around each other (fig 4.7). Furthermore, these fibrils themselves tend to twist about each other to create even larger fibres.

The most obvious question which comes to mind is "how do you wrap proteins around each other?" The answer is found in an amino acid called proline. Proline, or to be more precise its derivative, hydroxyproline, induces a sharp bend when incorporated into the protein chain. Collagen contains a very large amount of this amino acid, about 21%. Therefore the tendency to coil is very natural.

Collagen is very important because it may be made into massive sheets. These sheets form the basis for skin and other membranes. These sheets of collagen are easily visualised. They are somewhat analogous to felt or other non-woven cloths.

Collagen is probably the most important protein for establishing the mechanical qualities of the *tabla's* skin. However, there is another class of proteins that comes in at a close second. This is keratin.

Keratin - Keratin is a tough, fibrous protein that is found in hair, horns, hoofs, fingernails, etc. It is not actually one protein but a class of proteins which make up the basic structural units of cells. Keratin is made up of long helixes. These helical strands then twist around each other to form long filaments, known as intermediate filaments. These are then built into an extremely strong lattice.

Keratin is an example of a substance that has great strength and hardness due to the disulphide bonds which bind adjacent proteins together. Keratin contains large amounts of a sulphur containing amino acid, known as cysteine. When large amounts of keratin are present the proteins link up these sulphurs atom to form an extended hard mass. A turtle shell is a very good example of the strength and hardness of keratin.

Elastin - Elastin is a protein that is found in skin. It allows the skin to be stretched and still return to its original form. Elastin is very stable. The elastic quality is derived from a moderate amount of cross linking in the proteins. It is obvious that if there is too little cross linking the material will be devoid of physical strength. Conversely if there is too much cross linkage the material will be rigid (e.g. keratin). Elastin imparts an elastic quality that is essential for the proper operation of the *tabla*.

This section looked at the common proteins which are found in living skin. Let us look at the next step up, the skin itself, to get a better idea as to what we will be dealing with when we make a *tabla*.

LIVING SKIN

Living skin is useless as a material for everyone (except the animal that is wearing it). Its major flaw is that it will quickly putrefy, and return to the elements. However, an understanding of skin is necessary because the qualities that are present in skin will determine the characteristics of rawhide and leather.

We must not forget that skin did not evolve for humans to make *tablas*. Skin evolved to perform necessary physiological functions such as respiration, elimination of wastes, maintenance of proper body temperatures, and as a sensory organ. However, it is the function of skin as a protective layer which has had the greatest impact on skin as a building material. This great strength has translated into useful substances such as rawhide and leather.

Skin is composed of three layers; epidermis, dermis, and subcutaneous tissue. Each of these has its own characteristics (fig. 4.8).

Epidermis - The thin outer surface is the epidermis, this is the strong outer layer of the skin that is visible on the living animal. Its major function is to protect the animal. It has a number of qualities. The epidermis contains the pigmentation that gives the characteristic skin colour. It contains neither blood vessels nor nerves. The major portion of it is composed of dead cells that have been converted into a strong covering.

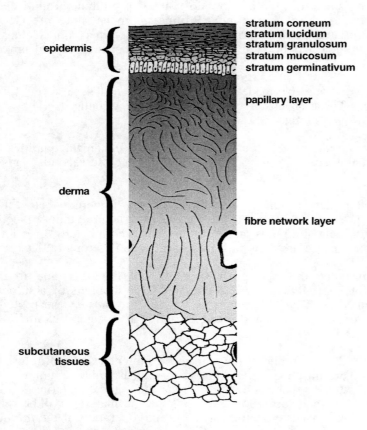

epidermis { stratum corneum
stratum lucidum
stratum granulosum
stratum mucosum
stratum germinativum

papillary layer

derma

fibre network layer

subcutaneous
tissues

Figure 4.8. The Layers of the Skin

Epidermis is composed of five layers. The outermost layer is called the *stratum corneum*; this is composed of a layer of flat dead cells. These cell-remains have been converted into a hard strong keratin rich material. Below the hard outer *stratum corneum* lies the *stratum lucidum*, this too is a layer of flat scale like cells, but it does not have the hard keratin. The next layer down is known as *stratum granulosum*; these cells are not so flattened and have a strong showing of a substance known as eleidin. The next layer down is the *stratum mucosum*, also known as the *stratum malpighii*. This layer is characterised by the presence of polygonal cells. The lowest level of the epidermis is the *stratum germinativum*. This layer is composed of a single layer of columnar cells.

The function of the epidermis in the animal translates to some interesting mechanical characteristics for the drum maker. It is strong and hard. It is so hard, that it is usually removed when making leather. Epidermis is usually undesirable for a leather maker because the high keratin content makes it impossible to make soft and supple. However, for the *tabla* maker, the strong keratin rich epidermis makes the hide extremely strong and produces a very durable playing surface.

Derma or Corium - The thickest portion of the hide lies just below the epidermis; this is known as the derma. The derma, otherwise known as the corium, is composed of living cells which perform most of the physiological functions for the animal. The derma is actually composed of two layers, the outer most is referred to as the papillary layer. It is this papillary layer which is responsible for the characteristic texture of most leather. Below this is the fibre network layer. This layer is composed of numerous collagenous fibrils which are oriented in a roughly perpendicular fashion to the skin.

Subcutaneous Tissues - The third and lowest layer of the skin is the subcutaneous tissues, variously known as adipose tissue, or simply as the "flesh" in the leather industry. These are primarily fat deposits. Although these subcutaneous tissues are very important to the animal they are useless for the *tablamaker* and are removed.

Let us review what we have seen concerning living skin. It is a multilayered covering that performs a variety of physiological functions for the animal. However, as makers of *tabla* we are most concerned with its mechanical properties. It has extreme tinsile strength because of the collagen layers that make up most of the skin. However, the thin keratin rich epidermis also makes a hard surface suitable for playing.

MATERIALS DERIVED FROM SKIN

Our world is filled with many materials which are made from skin. The gelatine in ones dessert or candies is one material that people seldom think about. Other more obvious ones are leather and rawhide. These last two are the only ones important to *tabla* making. We may look at these in greater detail.

Leather - Leather is made by a very complex process of soaking the skins in baths of plant extracts and/or mineral salts. However, since tanned leather is used to such a limited extent in the manufacture of *tabla* we will not go into the topic any further. Interested readers are requested to check other sources of information on the subject.

Rawhide - Rawhide, sometimes incorrectly known as untanned leather, is the most used material in the construction of the *tabla*. Basically it is just the skin, minimally treated, which has been removed from the animal. However, the quality of rawhide, even from the same species of animal, may vary considerably. This may be due to a number of reasons.

One difficulty comes from the concept of "minimal" treatment. Sometimes the treatment is nothing more than the addition of salt. This is added to remove the moisture and keep the skin from rotting. Sometimes rawhide is exposed to solutions of lye to help in the removal of hair. This will cause the lipid content of the rawhide to be lower, thus changing its acoustical and mechanical characteristics. Even if there is no treatment at all, the putrefaction that can occur between the time the animal is slaughtered and the time that the skin arrives at the *tablawala* will alter the mechanical characteristics of the rawhide. These uncertainties force us to be a bit vague when we talk of rawhide. For the rest of this book whenever we refer to rawhide it means a minimal of processing, but do not forget the complex issues which may be masked by this simple definition.

The structure of rawhide reflects the nature of natural living skin (fig. 4.8 and fig 4.9). However, many of the finer physiological details have been rendered irrelevant by the killing of the animal and the drying of the skin.

Rawhide may be viewed as being two layers. This is shown in figure 4.9. In this illustration we see that there is the outer, keratin rich epidermis and the inner collagenous derma. It is interesting to note the things which are not present. First of all, we notice that it has been dehaired. This is a very important step. Notice too that the subcutaneous tissues have been removed. This is generally simply scraped off by hand. In the West, defleshing machines (curiously enough referred to as "fleshing machines") are used, however such machines are generally rare in India. Notice that a nap has been left behind by the process of defleshing. This nap may be reduced by sanding. However, the inner surface of the rawhide will always be nappy to some degree.

THE HIDE

The hide is a basic unit of rawhide and is a fundamental material that the *tablawala* must deal with. So far, we have discussed rawhide in the most general terms. However, the actual hides give some real-world challenges which must be considered.

The first issue of the hide is the matter of how to obtain it. Many times the *tablawala* will obtain the finished hides from the *chamars* (tanners). When this is the case, the hide may already be dehaired and defleshed as shown in figure 4.10. Although this introduces an added cost, this saves a considerable amount of work.

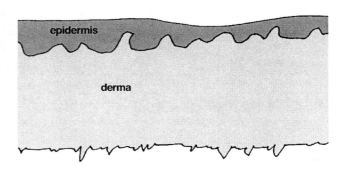

Figure 4.9 - The Layers of Rawhide

page 41

Sometimes the skins are obtained directly from the slaughterhouse. A slaughterhouse is referred to locally as a *kasaikhana*. When the hides come directly from the *kasaikhana* they are much cheaper, but they require considerable work.

Generally two types of hides will be used; there is the goatskin, which is known as the *bakari ki khal* and the buffalo or cowhide.

<u>Bakari ki Khal</u> - The term *"bakari ki khal"* literally means the "hide of a she goat".[1] This is used to make the resonating membranes and is the most critical material that a *tablawala* must deal with. It is so critical that we need to look more closely into this.

A typical hide is shown in figure 4.10. This example is roughly three feet long and about two-and-one-half feet wide. We see instantly from its proportions that it may make the drumheads for several drums . (The particulars of which must wait until Chapter 6.)

The thickness of the hide is not consistent. This is shown in figure 4.11. We find that the areas of the goat which receive the maximum abuse tend to be thicker, while the areas of the goat that receive minimal abuse tend to be thinner.

The thick areas of skin have some interesting characteristics. One thick area is at the top of the neck and spine. There is another thick area at the apex of the shoulder. Finally there is a thickening of the skin at the two sides of the hips where there are boney protrusions. In this example, the thick portions are roughly .020-.025 inch.

The thin areas are also interesting. It is no surprise that the belly and the inner portions of the thigh are the thinnest portions of the hide. Curiously enough, there is also a thin place at the hollow of the rump. This actually makes sense because a hollow receives very little abrasion. In the example shown in figure 4.11, these areas run between .015-.018 inch

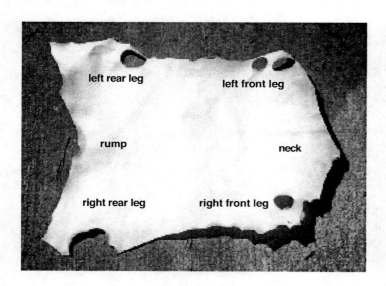

Figure 4.10. The Goat Hide

The fact that hides show inconsistencies in thickness is certainly natural from a physiological standpoint, yet from a material science's standpoint it presents interesting challenges. Different parts of the hide have different mechanical and acoustical characteristics. The practical ramifications of this are staggering.

<u>Cowhides and Buffalo Hides</u> - The hides from the larger bovines are considerably thicker and heavier than the goatskin. These are generally used for the lacing.

The hides from these animals show similar inconsistencies as the goatskin. However, since they are used for mere mechanical functions, such inconsistencies do not seem to pose many problems. We do not need to go into this subject any deeper.

---

[1] Indian Languages are inherently gendered. We must not presume that only the she-goat will be used for making *tabla*. It is just that Hindi/Urdu forces a gender to it. This is very much like the gender implied by the English words "repairman" or "chairman". Obviously we may have a female, "Chairman of the Board", but the English language tends to steer us into the masculine designation. In the same way, one should not associate a gender with the skins.

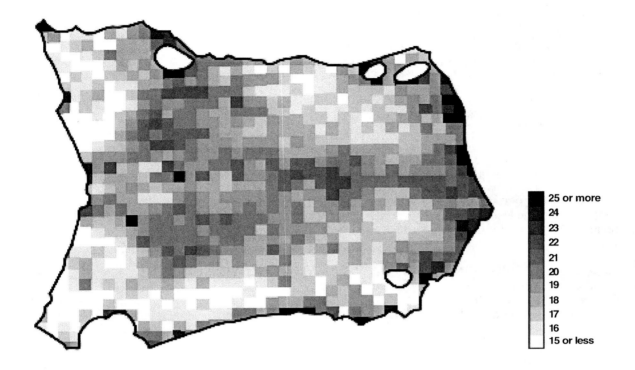

Figure 4.11. Thickness of the Hide (in thousandths of an inch)

SCARS

Scars are the single most problematic flaw that are derived from the living skin. Just as the knothole is the most serious and ubiquitous problem for wood, the scar has the same devastating effect on the rawhide.

The cause of scarring is interesting. When there is a wound, fibroblasts in the adjacent tissue begin to produce large amounts of collagen-rich connective tissue. This tissue does not have the same characteristics as the original skin. It is higher in collagen content, devoid of elastin, does not have hair follicles, nor does it have oil and sweat glands. They do however, have a capillary blood supply. Scars sometimes become tumours after some years.

Ticks seem to be one of the most common causes of scarring on Indian goats. They leave a very typical white spot on the hide, usually no more than a few millimetres in diameter. Although they are very small, and almost unnoticeable, they tend to open up and form a hole in the finished *tabla*.

The bottom line is simple; scars introduce discontinuities that affect the mechanical and acoustical characteristics of the skin. Great attention must be paid to isolate these and keep them out of the finished instruments.

WORKING WITH RAWHIDE

Working with rawhide is a very skilled endeavour. However it deals with only a few extremely simple principles. In a nutshell, it is the understanding of the differences between wet and dry rawhide.

<u>Wet Rawhide</u> - Wet rawhide has some very interesting characteristics. Wet hide may expand tremendously. All hide is wet to some degree. It is so extremely hygroscopic that it has the ability to capture the random molecules of water that it encounters in the air.

Wet hide is very supple. It may be folded, stretched, cut, and manipulated with the greatest of ease. Therefore, almost any time we need to work with hide, it will be wet. This is usually accomplished by placing the hides in water and soaking them for an appropriate length of time.

<u>Dry Rawhide</u> - You will probably never encounter a totally dry hide. Since rawhide has the ability to take water out of the air, the only way to obtain a totally dry hide is to place it in a desiccator. Therefore, we will define dry rawhide as hide which has attained equilibrium with the surrounding air.

Dry rawhide has interesting qualities. It may be as hard as wood. It is not supple; it is very strong and resists being worked. Its volume is considerably less than that of a soaked hide.

The most important and useful quality of dry rawhide is its ability to contract. Drums need to be very tight, and the use of rawhide for this application is natural. As the hide dries, it will contract and make a very nice, tight playing surface.

TECHNIQUES OF WORKING WITH RAWHIDE (MAKING THE LACING)

We would like to discuss some of the techniques that the *tablawala* uses in dealing with rawhide. Actually the majority of the work that the *tablawala* does is dealing with rawhide. This is so extensive that it will be described in detail in a later chapter. However, it is appropriate for us to at least touch upon the topic here. We will uses as a simple example, the making of the lacing (*tasma*). This is an extremely mundane job, but a good introduction to basic techniques.

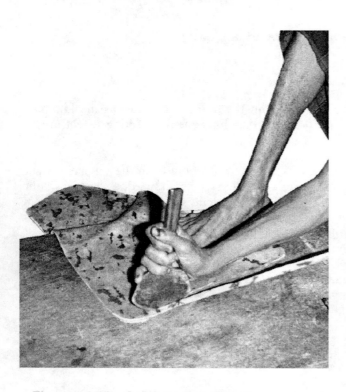

Figure 4.12. Cutting the Tasma

The highest quality lacing starts with a good, heavy hide. This will usually be the rawhide of the buffalo. In some parts of the country it is the rawhide from cattle. It is first made supple by soaking it in water. This may take anywhere from half an hour to two hours depending upon the thickness of the rawhide.

It must now be cut. One holds the hide in place with the feet, then takes a *rampi* (cutting blade) and starts to spiral down to the centre (fig. 4.12 and fig. 4.13). This will produce a rough *tasma*.

The *tasma* must now be finished, this involves trimming and straightening. One trims the *tasma* by holding the *rampi* firmly between the big toe and the middle toe of the right foot. One then cuts away the excess by pulling the soaked hide with the hands across the blade (fig. 4.14). The *tasma* is straightened by pulling the moistened *tasma* over a ring or other object. It is then wrapped around an extra drum shell or similar object, and allowed to dry. This will yield a high quality lacing. During this process it may be beaten with a hammer to help straighten it.

This was just the making of the *tasma*. However, it clearly represents the skills and techniques which will be used for much more complicated jobs, such as the making of the entire drumhead (*pudi*).

CONCLUSION

This chapter has gone into great detail concerning the nature of rawhide. We have seen that most of the mechanical qualities of the rawhide are derived from characteristics of the living skin. This in turn is ultimately derived from the type and arrangement of the molecules.

Rawhide may be thought of as a double layered sheet of interlaced proteins. The uppermost layer is rich in a hard protein known as keratin, while the lower and thicker sheet is composed of fibres of collagen. There is also a large amount of another protein known as elastin.

The rawhide has been shown to vary considerably in thickness. This is a reflection of the different amount of protection which must be given to the underlying tissues on the living animal. Such inconsistencies pose a constant challenge to the craftsman.

Rawhide is extremely hygroscopic; it has the ability to attract and hold an amazing amount of water. The amount of water in the hide greatly affects the mechanical characteristics. When it is wet, it is soft, supple and able to be stretched to a considerable degree. Upon drying it contracts and becomes very hard. The *tablawala* is able to work with the hides by continually wetting, working and drying them.

Figure 4.13. Cutting the Tasma

Figure 4.14. Trimming the Tasma

page 45

WORKS CITED

Kremlin, Richard J.
1996   *An Introduction to Organosulfur Chemistry*. Chichester: John Wiley and Sons.

Encyclopaedia Britannica
1997   Collagen, *Encyclopaedia Britannica*. page 451, volume 3, 15th edition, Chicago, Encyclopaedia Britannica.

Ganathe, N.S.R.
1983   *Learn Urdu in 30 Days*. Madras, Balaji Publications.

Ojha, Gopesh Kumar
1969   *Universal Hindi Self Teacher*. Delhi, Universal Publication.

Srinivasachari, K.
1995   *Learn Hindi in 30 Days*. Madras, Balaji Publications.

Srinivasachari, K.
1992   *Learn Sanskrit in 30 Days*. Madras, Balaji Publications.

CHAPTER 5

WOOD

INTRODUCTION

The wooden shell is one of the most important parts of the *tabla*. It is the basic framework around which the *dayan* is made. There are many issues that arise when dealing with wood. Many of these issues are dealt with in this chapter. However, the serious reader is strongly urged to look into Appendix 2 to get a stronger background into the nature of wood.

Wood is a very interesting substance. It is the dead vascular portion of the tree trunk. This is basically just a series of small tubes made of a combination of cellulose and lignin. These tubes are filled with water. Furthermore there is a lot of water locked into the molecular lattice that makes up these cellulose/lignin tubes. Before the wood may be used it must be dried. This drying is referred to as seasoning. Seasoning is very important because it imparts strength and durability to the wood.

There are some very specific characteristics which the wood must possess to make a good *tabla*. It is important that the wood be as heavy and as dense as possible. It is also important that the wood be resistant to insects. Over the years, local availability has also been an important issue. This has caused there to be a number of different woods from which *tablas* may be made.

Many woods may be used for the *tabla*. These include rosewood, *sal*, jackwood, teak, *tun, babool, khair, bija,* and mango. Many of these woods are very good, but some are very bad. Today the Indian rosewood has emerged as the wood of choice for the *tabla-dayan*.

Indian rosewood is very interesting (fig. 5.1). It is not really one, but two different species of woods. There is the *Dalbergia sisoo*, and the *Dalbergia latifolia*. Both of these trees are referred to as Indian rosewood, locally known as *shisham*.

Figure 5.1. Indian Rosewood (Dalbergia Sissoo)

TECHNIQUES OF WORKING WITH WOOD

There are a number of techniques that have been developed over the millennia for working with wood. Some of the more relevant ones are discussed here.

Hewing - Hewing is the process of chopping away with an axe, adze or similar instrument. It is used in the logging industry; but it is generally too imprecise for use with finished and seasoned woods. Therefore, we will not go into the subject any further.

Sawing - Sawing is a much more precise way of cutting wood. It may be used for crude applications such as felling a tree, yet it may also be used for such fine work as cutting wood into desired shapes for musical instruments.

The precision of the cut is a function of the size of the teeth. Larger teeth produce a rough cut; however, they allow one to cut very fast. This is typically used to fell a tree or make initial cuts on the logs. Smaller teeth produce a fine cut; this allows one to do much more precise work. Unfortunately, small teeth are very slow at cutting. Fine teeth are used in later stages of making musical instruments.

Sawing is common in the initial stages of crafting the shell. Invariably it will be used to take logs and cut them into lengths that are appropriate for turning on a lathe. Typically they will be approximately one foot in length for *tabla*, but they may be up to three feet in length for drums such as the *pakhawaj*.

Sawing is very rare in the final stages of making the shell. The only time I have ever seen a saw used was to reduce the length of a shell.

Nails, Dowels, Screws and other Fasteners - Over the years various mechanical means have been developed to hold different pieces of wood together. They include such things as nails, dowels, screws, staples, and a variety of other fasteners.

Such fasteners introduce anomalies which affect the propagation of sound waves in the wood. It is undesirable for any musical instrument. It is very important that the *lakadi* of a *tabla-dayan* be of a single piece of wood. Therefore, these techniques have no place in the manufacture of *tabla*. I have only seen them used to salvage otherwise unusable shells so that they may be made into substandard, student grade *tablas*.

Gluing - Gluing wood together is one of the most difficult tasks that the woodworker has to perform. In this process, one takes two different pieces of wood and unites them into a common mass. Again since it is important that the shell be of a single block of wood, these techniques have very little place in the production of *tabla*.

In practice, gluing is used in the fabrication of the lowest quality *tablas*. During the process of seasoning the wood, it is common for shells to split, sometimes even in two. The broken sections may be glued and a marginally usable shell will result.[1]

Chiselling and Gouging - Chiselling and gouging are the processes of removing inner material from any particular piece of wood. For this one takes a tool called a chisel or a gouge, and uses it to gouge out material. This is usually done for more artistic work. However, in the case of the *tabla* it is for the more mundane job of creating the cavity for the drum. When one is chiselling out the cavity there are really no major problems. One merely chisels out the cavity until the desired inner volume is produced.

There is really very little difference between a chisel and a gouge. A chisel has a flat blade while a gouge has a rounded blade. However, as the name implies, a gouge is much better suited to removing large volumes of wood from confined areas, where the chisel is not. Generally in India, they do not make a distinction between a chisel and a gouge.

---

[1] Ideally such shells should be eliminated entirely. Unfortunately, this is the real world. I have seen such shells glued together and used. The remaining gaps filled with *lakadi massala*, sanded, painted, and then made into finished *tablas*. Such *tablas* will never be of high quality. Invariably they were laced with substandard lacing and skinned with substandard skins. I wish that I could say that such substandard merchandise was then only disposed of for the local student market. Unfortunately, at least one US distributor is dealing in such shoddy merchandise.

Wood-Turning - This is one of the most interesting processes that can be done with wood. For this, one takes a block of wood and turns it on a lathe. The lathe revolves the piece of wood at a very high speed. One then takes a sharp chisel or gouge and gently removes portions of the wood until the desired shape is obtained. It is the lathe that is responsible for the very symmetric proportions of the *lakadi*.

Every wooden part of the *tabla* has been turned on a lathe. Therefore, this is a very important process. These pieces are the *gatta* and the *lakadi*. However, it is not very likely that the same lathe was used for each piece. The lathe used to turn the *lakadi* must be large and heavy; these lathes are generally used to make such items as the hubs for bullock carts. The lathe that is used for the *gatta* is generally a lighter weight; these are used for items such as table legs.

Painting and Varnishing - Most people have an incomplete picture of varnishing and painting. Most people think of these processes purely from an aesthetic standpoint. Although varnishing and painting do add a lot to the aesthetic appeal of wooden articles, one of the main purposes is practical. Painting and varnishing are essential to the treatment of the outer surfaces of the wood. This protects it against moisture.

In India, one does not simply go and buy paint or varnish. The *tablawalas* make their own. This will be discussed in greater detail in Appendix 3.

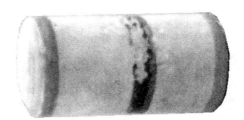

a.

GATTA

The *gattas* are the simplest wooden items for *tabla*. They are also the easiest components to fabricate. The *gatta* is shown in figure 5.2. The *gatta* are nothing but wooden dowels that are turned on a lathe and cut to the desired length.

b.

Figure 5.2.a is probably the most common form of *gatta*. It is merely a wooden dowel roughly one-and-half inch in diameter that has been cut to a length of about two inches. The wood is generally untreated except for three bands of paint which adorn it. *Gattas* of this variety are found throughout most of India, but they are especially common in western India.

Figure 5.2.b shows a slightly different style. This one has a small raised area at each end which is very desirable and makes the *tasma* less likely to slip off. It is especially good when four or more lengths of *tasma* pass over it. This style is much less common, but it may be found throughout much of north India.

c.

Figure 5.2. Wooden Gatta

Figure 5.2.c is a *Bengali* style of *gatta*. This style is almost nonexistent outside the area of Bengal. It is smaller than one normally finds in the rest of India. Its most distinguishing characteristic is a series of decorative grooves which are added while it is being turned on a lathe.

The *gatta* is a humble object that is generally not very demanding. It does not have to be made according to any precise specifications. Mixing *gatta* of slightly different sizes is common and produces no major problems. Wood of almost any condition may be acceptably used.

There is just one caveat; it is very desirable to use woods that resist insects. One often finds mango wood *(aam)*, or other inferior woods used. Although the instruments still function normally, there is a tendency for these woods to be reduced to dust after a few years.

INDIAN DRUM SHELLS

The drum shell *(lakadi)* is the most demanding wooden item in the *dayan*. Great care must be given to each stage of crafting or the final instrument may not be up to standard.

The wood passes through a number of hands before it will start to assume the form of a drumshell. It will be handled by the loggers who fell and transport the logs from the forests. It will be taken to the seasoners, where the logs will be dried. Next, it will pass to the woodworkers for initial work.

Initial Work - The initial work is performed by the woodworkers. They produce a variety of products; however, the most important products for the *tablawala* are the shells shown in figure 5.3. These shells are (from left to right) the *nal (dholki)*, the *pakhawaj*, the *dholak*, and the *tabla-dayan*. Depending upon where in India they are, and what kind of wood they are dealing with, the products might also include shells for other drums as well.

Figure 5.3. Wooden Shells for Drums - (left to right) nal, pakhawaj, dholak, and tabla-dayan

The woodworkers may obtain the shells in any state of seasoning. Ideally the wood is already fully seasoned, but it is not unusual for them to be dealing in green wood. Dealing in fully seasoned wood is sometimes cost prohibitive, while dealing in green wood leaves the workers open to many problems. Every worker has his own way of doing things.

The first job is to cut the logs into lengths just slightly larger than the length of the shells. Next, these are put on a lathe and turned to attain the desired shape. Next, the shells must be hollowed out. They will be hollowed out to the proportions shown in figure 5.4.

There are two ways to bore the inside. One of the most common way is to use chisels (wood gouges) to gouge out the inside. This approach is easily recognisable by the longitudinal gouge marks that are left on the inside (fig. 5.5). Another way is to use machines. A machined shell is recognised by the circular scoring on the inside of the shell (fig 5.6).

There is some debate as to whether the hand gouged or the machined shells are better. I have heard people argue either way. In the absence of any clear consensus, we can presume that there is little or no difference between the quality of the two approaches.

I should point out that there are numerous regional variations to the shells. The most obvious variation deals with the selection of woods. There is going to be a preference given to locally available woods. I think that this is so obvious that we really do not need to deal with this point any further.

Figure 5.4. Shells are Hollowed Out

Figure 5.5. Hand Gouged Shell

Figure 5.6. Machine Gouged Shell

There are also regional differences as to size and proportions. Two of the most common ones are shown in figure 5.7. The shape in figure 5.7.a is the most standard form. This particular style is found throughout most of India. In contrast, figure 5.7b shows the proportions of the wooden shells that are made in the Bengal area.

At this point the shells should complete the seasoning process. Ideally they should be allowed to sit for months, or even years, in a controlled environment to make sure that the shells are completely dry. Sadly this is seldom the case today.

The shells are now ready to leave the wood workers and pass to the *tablawala*

Finishing of the Shell - The shell now passes to the *tablawala* to be finished and converted into a fully playable *tabla-dayan*. This will involve a number of jobs. Perhaps there is no job so important at this point as quality control.

The *tablawalas* grade the wood at the time of purchase; for this they will look at several things. These include: the type of wood, the weight of the shell, the presence of cracks, proper size, pitch pockets, knotholes, and warping of the opening.

Any wood may be used for *dayans*; however, only a few kinds are known to make good ones. These are teak, rosewood and, occasionally, jackwood. The primary characteristics which make these woods good are resistance to insects, extreme weight, and homogeneity of the wood (i.e., no well defined growth rings).

The wood must be the correct size. Non-standard sizes have a certain marketability, but the *tablawala* cannot afford to purchase too many non-standard sizes. Generally, openings that run from five to six inches are the most marketable. The lengths generally run from eight to 12 inches.

Another important aspect to consider in determining the acceptability of the wood is whether or not it has any cracks. Cracks invariably will occur in the direction of the grain and may be caused while the tree is alive or after the tree has been felled. Either case lowers the wood's acceptability.

a.   b.

Figure 5.7. Two Types of Shells - There are regional variation in shells a)standard (Maharashtra / Gujarat) b) Bengal

Cracks and imperfections may be in any of a number of forms. Each has different causes. A few types are the circular cracks, knotholes, pitch pockets, and shakes. Let us look a little more closely at them.

Cracks may be circular. These run circularly around the growth-rings. Theye are referred to as a shakes.

Sometimes a crack starts at the bark and runs radially toward the centre of the tree. This is referred to as a frost shake. This is of course a misnomer because in India, frost shakes are most likely to be caused by extreme drought conditions.

Sometimes cracks are caused after the tree has been felled. These result from a too rapid drying in the seasoning stage. This is what happens: as the outer portions of the wood dries out they contract. However inner portions of the wood are slower to dry out, therefore they tend to remain the same size. As the outer portion tries to contract down upon the stable inner portion, the resultant stresses causes cracks.

All cracks are serious. Depending upon the size and depth of the cracks they can render a shell unusable for the *tabla*.

Pitch pockets, also known as resin pockets, or resin bubbles, are another problem in the wooden shells. These occur when internal cracks have filled with resin and solidified. In a living tree this is usually caused by wind causing the tree to sway. If it bends enough, it can cause the cambium to separate from the xylem (Götz, 1989). (If this does not make sense to you, read Appendix 2). This creates a gap that the tree will fill with resin. This definitely lowers the quality of the wood.

The presence of knotholes in the wood is also a major problem. There is a tendency for knotholes to crack, or even disintegrate during the seasoning process. One may always fill these holes with *lakadi massala*, but this creates an acoustical discontinuity that adversely affects the sound

The weight is probably the most important aspect of the wood in determining the tonal quality of the drum. A light piece of wood will produce a thin sound, while a heavy piece of wood will produce a deep, melodious sound.

Warping is a common problem for wooden shells (fig 5.8). This invariably occurs when improperly seasoned wood is turned on the lathe. The shell was correct when it was turned. Unfortunately, as the wood dries out, imbalances in the shrinkage of the wood causes the opening to warp. This is a major problem that cannot be fixed.

At this point the wood has been graded, so it is time to finish the shells. Some of the shells may have cracks; these cracks must be filled with *lakadi massala*. *Lakadi massala* is a mixture of white glue and sawdust. This will be discussed in Appendix 3. After the *lakadi massala* has dried, it is filed down with a rasp and put aside.

The whole is then painted. There may be several coats of a home-made paint. This is generally a mixture of shellac and pigment. This will be discussed in Appendix 3.

Finally, the lip must be finished. This is just a question of going over the lip to give it the correct proportions. Strangely enough, there is no single philosophy as to how the lip should be. I have run across three philosophies. Some *tablawalas* bring the opening to a sharp edge, other have a gently rounded edge. Still, others cut it straight across.

Figure 5.8. Warped Shell - This happens when improperly seasoned wood is used

Intuition says that the shape of the lip should be of vital importance to the sound of the *dayan*. The fact that the various craftsmen seem so *blasé* about this is absolutely remarkable. It is so remarkable that perhaps we should be looking at this in greater detail. However, this topic is not within the scope of this chapter.

The wooden shell is now ready for final assembly. This will be discussed in the next chapter.

CONCLUSION

This chapter discussed the wood and the fabrication of the shell. This chapter is based upon an understanding of the nature of wood as put forth in Appendix 2. We saw that well seasoned wood is turned on a lathe until it is the right size. It is then hollowed out to the proper depth.

The wood then passes from the woodworker to the *tablawala*. At this point, there must be a considerable amount of quality control. This involves examining the shells for cracks, pitchpockets, knotholes, warping or other flaws. The *tablawala* will then finish the job that was started by the woodworker. This includes such things as painting / varnishing, and rasping the lip until it has the right shape.

WORKS CITED

Brown, H.P., A.J. Panshin and C.C. Forsaith
1952   *Textbook of Wood Technology*. McGraw-Hill Book Company, New York.

Corkhill, T.
1979   *The Complete Dictionary of Wood*. New York. Stein and Day.

Encyclopaedia Britannica
1997   The New Encyclopaedia Britannica, Vol 11. Chicago:Encyclopaedia Britannica. pp 908.

Fullaway, S.V. and C.L. Hill
1928   *The Air Seasoning of Western Softwood Lumber*. U.S. Dept. of Agr. Bul. 1425.

Ganathe, N.S.R.
1983   *Learn Urdu in 30 Days*. Madras, Balaji Publications.

Götz, Karl-Heinz, Dieter Hoor, Karl Möhler, Julius Natterer
1989   *Timber Design and Construction Sourcebook: A Comprehensive Guide to Methods and Practice*. New York: McGraw-Hill Publishing Co.

Hunt, George M. and George A. Garratt
1953   *Wood Preservation*. McGraw-Hill Book Co., New York.

Rietz, R.C.,
1957   "Importance of Dry Lumber", *U.S. Forest Products Laboratory Report No. 1779*, Madison, Wisconsin.

Rietz, R.C. and R.H.
1971   "Air Drying of Lumber: A guide to Industry Practices". *U.S. Department of Agr. Handbook No. 402*.

Srinivasachari, K.
1992   *Learn Sanskrit in 30 Days*. Madras, Balaji Publications.
1995   *Learn Hindi in 30 Days*. Madras, Balaji Publications.

Thelen, Rolf
1923   "Kiln Drying Handbook", *U.S. Dept. of Agr. Bull. No. 1136*.

Tiemann, Harry D.
1938   "Lessons in Kiln Drying". *Southern Lumberman*. Nashville. pp 110.

CHAPTER 6

CONSTRUCTION

INTRODUCTION
The previous chapters discussed at great length the materials which go into the *tabla*. We should now be comfortable with the characteristics of skin, the metal shell, the wooden shell, and various other parts and materials. Let us now look at exactly how these parts come together.

VARIATIONS IN CONSTRUCTION
There are a countless variations in the construction of *tabla*. There is no way that I will be able to cover them all. However, I will try to give as complete an overview as possible.

The reasons for such variations in construction are as numerous as there are makers of *tabla*. Sometimes these differences are due to the availability of materials; yet often times they are a reflection of regional, cultural, and artistic differences. Sometimes, they are purely idiosyncratic and are tied to nothing more than the whims and personal style of the artisan.

There is a geographic breakdown in these variations; there are many reasons for this. For instance, it is not reasonable to expect a large number of *tablas* to be made of *shisham* (Indian rosewood) in parts of India where the tree does not grow, therefore the availability of raw materials is one factor. Craftsmen in the deep south tend to make a lot of *mridangams*, so, it is no surprise that *tablas* from these parts tend to be made like *mridangams*. Therefore, musical culture plays a part in the geographical variations. Bengal has a technological infrastructure that is geared to the fabrication of terracotta drum shells for the *khol*; this same infrastructure is also used for the production of terracotta shells for the *tabla*. So technological infrastructure also plays a part.

Figure 6.1. Tablawalas at Work

I should make one warning before going into the geographic variations in *tabla*-making. India is changing very fast. India's distribution networks have improved greatly in the last 100 years. One may now easily procure woods that have been grown many hundreds of miles from where the craftsman lives. Therefore, the availability of materials is quickly becoming irrelevant. Finished *tablas* may now be shipped all over the country. When they break and come in for repair, the craftsmen are then able to see techniques that *tablawalas* at the other end of the country are using. This increases the flow of information about construction. TV, radio, and the cinema are creating musical fashions that are national in scope. Since the musical influences are now occurring at a national level, craftsmen in widely separated locations are reacting to the same influences and are responding similarly. We have already seen at least one regional variation of *tabla* disappear in the last century (i.e., the *Punjabi style*). It is possible that in 100 years there may be no more regional variations at all.

Let us look at the regional variations as they exist today. The techniques of *tabla* construction, like the languages of India, show a gradual change as we move from one part of the country to another. There is no sharp dividing line. Therefore, the divisions that are described here have a certain arbitrary quality about them. With this disclaimer in mind let us look into some regional variations.

Standard Tabla - The majority of India produces a style of *tabla* that we may refer to as the "standard" *tabla* (fig. 6.2). This style is present in one form or another throughout the height and breadth of India. It is manufactured in the South. It has replaced the traditional *Punjabi* style in the north. Only the Bengal side has not been taken over by this style.

One often finds these *tablas* referred to as Bombay style. I believe that this is a misnomer. It has always seemed that the epitome of this style of *tabla* is to be found in Gujarat, which is just north of Bombay.

The standard *tabla* has an interesting construction. The lacing is moderately heavy, being surpassed only by some of the *mridangam* styles of *tabla*. The vibrating membranes are moderately thick and the size of the shells tends to have openings that are 5-6 inches in diameter.

There are a number of woods used to make this style of *tabla*. In the Maharashtra and Gujarat they are normally made from *shisham* (Indian rosewood) which is very heavy. In places where *shisham* does not grow, shells may be made of *bija* or any of the woods discussed in Appendix 2.

Figure 6.2. Standard Tabla   (Bombay Style -Maharashtra / Gujarat)

page 58

This style of *tabla* is unsurpassed in durability. I have had them last in excess of 20 years, although 5-10 years of heavy use (and abuse) is the norm.

<u>Mridangam Style and South Indian Tabla</u> - The South has an interesting *tabla* making industry. Many believe that, since the *mridangam* is the preferred instrument for South Indian classical performances, and the *tabla* is historically a North Indian instrument, that there are no south Indian *tablas*. This is false. There is a flourishing south Indian *tabla* manufacturing industry that has been in existence for a long time.

The manufacture of *tabla* in the deep south may be divided into two philosophies. There is the standard style (fig. 6.3), and the *mridangam* style (fig. 6.4).

The standard style of *tabla* in the south is not substantially different from the rest of India. This has already been discussed, so there is no need to elaborate here.

The deep south also has a *mridangam* style *tabla*. This style is extremely rare outside Southern India, and even within the south it is a niche market. In the south Indian film industry, it is very common to find situations where there is the artistic requirement for a *mridangam*, yet for various reasons it is sometimes not practical to use a real *mridangam*. Therefore, *tablas* are manufactured with many of the same qualities of the *mridangam*, and consequently a similar tone. Since there is already an infrastructure in place for the manufacture of *mridangams*, it is no problem to find people who can make this style.

The materials and techniques used to make these *tablas* are very similar to those found in the *mridangam*. They are often made of jackwood. They tend to have very heavy lacing and their heads are generally thicker than found elsewhere in India. They tend to have wide *chats*. If straw, or matchsticks are inserted into them, they produce a sound that is indistinguishable from the *mridangam*. If one listens to film songs from any of the south Indian languages (e.g., Tamil, Telugu, Kannada, Malayalam), very often when one thinks that one is hearing a *mridangam*, it is actually one of these *tablas*.

Figure 6.3. Standard Tabla from the South

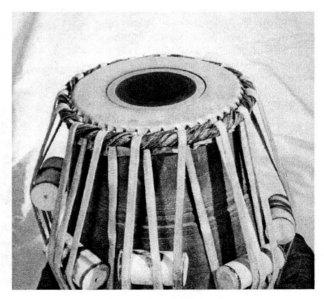

Figure 6.4. Mridangam Style Tabla from the South

Figure 6.5. Traditional Punjab Style Tabla

Figure 6.6. Pakistani Style

<u>Punjab/Pakistan</u> - Some of the earliest *tablas* in India are from this area. There is even some evidence to suggest that the *tabla* was actually developed in the Punjab.

The traditional *Punjabi tabla* is very distinctive. The *dayans* are very large, well in excess of 6 inches in diameter and sometimes over a foot in length. The *bayans* at one time were made of wood, sometimes requiring a temporary application of flour and water like the *pakhawaj*. It is common for them to be brightly painted in greens, reds, and yellows; this is something that one is not likely to see elsewhere in India.

It is curious that in the last 80 years there have been major changes in the construction of *tablas* in the Punjab. This may be linked to the cultural and political problems that started during the partition and continued through the subsequent Khalistan movement. Cultural and political changes tend to be reflected in changes in the musical culture. Today, the traditional Punjabi *tabla* has been almost entirely replaced by the standard *tabla* in India.

The situation is a little different in Pakistan. At one time the Pakistani *tablas* were probably similar to the *tablas* in the Indian Punjab. However today they have taken a slightly different course. The wooden shells still tend to be very large, and have a *pakhawaj* like quality. However, the turnbuckle seems to be particularly popular as a tightening arrangement (fig. 6.6). This is somewhat peculiar because virtually no professional *Pakistani tabla* player will use them. It is likely that these are made just for the export market.

The most distinguishing characteristic of the *tablas* from Pakistan is the very rounded lip of the shell. This makes the head wrap around in a very distinctive fashion.

The *tablas* that come from Pakistan are generally very poor. Many of Pakistan's professional *tabla* players prefer to use *tablas* from

India. The problem seems to be one of workmanship and not design. The overall design seems to be quite sound, but the implementation tends to fail.

Eastern India, Bengal, and Bangladesh - The techniques used to make *tabla* in Bengal and Bangladesh are very different from that found in the rest of India. One can always spot a *Bengali tabla,* even at a distance.

Dayans from Bengal tend to be the smallest in India. The *dayans* average only eight-ten inches in length, with the average opening measuring only about five inches across. The *bayans* have a much more rounded shape than are generally found in the rest of India. Sometimes one finds *bayans* that are made of terracotta; this will not be found in the rest of India.

The most distinguishing characteristic of *Bengali tablas* is their lacing. It is laced in the opposite direction from the rest of India.

The *pudis* from this area, often times referred to as Calcutta heads, are noted for the simplicity of their *gajara,* and the presence of a small pigtail. The skins are very thin, which when made with care, gives them a bright tone. Unfortunately, the thin skin greatly compromises its durability.

The lacing is absolutely abysmal. The *tasma* is so thin that breakage is common. On balance, the *tablas* from Bengal and Eastern India are very poor and should be avoided.

We have made a brief overview of the various regional variations in *tabla* making. This has been necessarily brief and shallow because the details of the differences require a greater knowledge of the construction than we have discussed so far. Therefore, we will go into greater detail concerning the construction. As we delve into the technical *minutia* the subtle differences and variations of construction will be pointed out.

Figure 6.7. Eastern (Bengali or Calcutta) Style

PURCHASING THE MATERIALS

The first step in the construction of the *tabla* is the purchasing of materials. This may seem like a trivial point; but it is not. There are a variety of concerns that must be addressed at this time.

Purchasing anything in India is an adventure, especially something as specialised as the raw materials for making *tablas*. Wooden shells, high quality hides, and the various materials specific to the *tabla* trade, are well outside of the mainstream channels of distribution. Often, various raw materials are supplied by *tablawalas* who over the years have come to specialise in the various components of the trade. Transportation and distribution is usually a question of sending so-and-so's nephew to another city once or twice a year to contact someone else who is known to sell such-and-such. In all, the distribution network is very informal and being "inside the loop" is a professional imperative.

Knowledge of the network is a trade secret. Who sells what, where they work, what the going prices are, all are trade secrets guarded with a reticence that would make the CIA proud. The knowledge of the network is the first thing that the *tablawala* must have.

Quality control is a major consideration in this phase of the business. Shells, rawhide, leather, and wooden components are generally fashioned and made available *caveat emptor*. Wooden shells that are badly split, rawhide which is rotten, metallic shells which are improperly plated, any of a number of flaws are grounds for immediate rejection. Ideally such flawed materials will not enter the complex chain which ultimately leads to the finished *tabla* in the hands of the final purchaser.

All materials are mentally graded. The lowest quality materials, which are grossly unsuitable for *tablas,* should be rejected and not purchased. The finest skins are reserved for the *maidans* of the *dayan.* The best wooden shells are lacquered and made into *dayans,* etc. Still there is also a middle grade for materials. This level is well below prime, but still good enough to be used in some ways. For instance, shells that are moderately cracked may be filled and sold as student grade instruments. Skins that are not prime, may still be useful for less critical portions of the construction without any ill effect. All points are considered at the time of purchasing the raw materials.

This grading is important in negotiating the price. The price is determined by the time honoured tradition of haggling, known as *sauda bazi.*

MAKING THE KUNDAL

The *kundal* (कुण्डल) is the ring which lies at the bottom of the *tabla*. It serves the very important function of providing a mechanical base upon which the head is laced. It is obvious that when the lacing pulls on the drum head, it must be anchored at the other end. The *kundal* is this mechanical anchor.

There is one situation where the *kundal* is dispensed with. *Tablas* that are designed to use turnbuckles as a tightening arrangement do not use them. However, turnbuckles are not common and are certainly not used in professional grade instruments. Therefore, the presence of the *kundal* is the norm.

The word *kundal* is very interesting. Any toroidal (donut shaped) object may be called a *kundal.* Kamal's Oxford Advanced Illustrated Dictionary: Hindi - English (Kapoor no-date) gives the definitions as being an earring (toroidal, not a stud, *jhumki* or similar), a coil, or a halo. The word is probably best known outside of India in the term *Kundalini* (serpent force). This may be derived from the snake's tendency to curl itself into a coil.

There are numerous ways to make the *kundal.* Some are simple, some are complex. Most work very well. We can now look at a few common techniques.

<u>Making the Kundal (Technique #1)</u> - The simplest *kundals* are merely loops of rawhide. A simple technique is illustrated in figure 6.8. We start with a strip of rawhide (fig. 6.8.a). One coils the strap repeatedly. The number of rounds may vary depending upon the desired strength and the thickness of the rawhide. It is then knotted as shown in figure 6.d-6.f.

The quality of these simple *kundals* is generally not very good. If the rawhide is strong, and there are sufficient rounds, it may work acceptably. However, there are two ways that this *kundal* can fail. If the rawhide is too thin, or if there are too few rounds, the *kundal* may break rendering the *tabla* untunable. There is another way that this design may fail. It is readily apparent that there is only one knot holding the *kundal* together. If the knot loosens even the slightest, the *kundal* may slip.

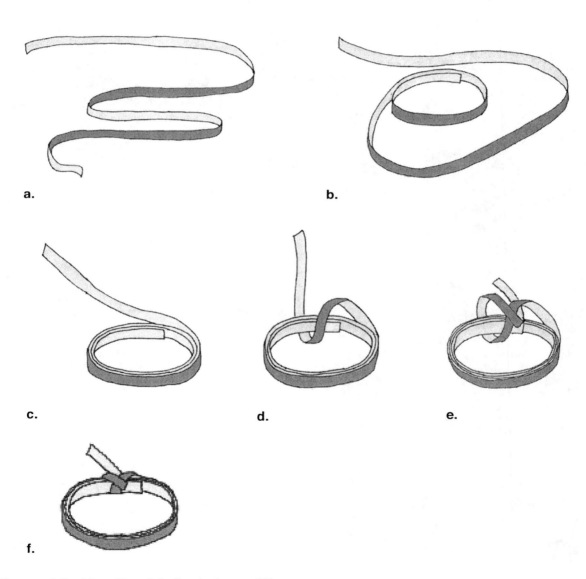

a.

b.

c.

d.

e.

f.

Figure 6.8. The Kundal (technique #1)

Making the Kundal (Technique #2) - This approach is the most common; it is found throughout India. We start with a strip of rawhide (fig. 6.9.a).   This is then lightly soaked in water until slightly supple. It is better if both ends are soft, yet the middle section moderately stiff. We then cut a small slit in one end as shown in figure 6.9.b. Then one takes the other end and inserts it through the slit as shown in figure figure 6.9.c. One bends the strip around and runs it through the slit one more time (fig. 6.9.d). (If the rawhide is thin one may even go through a third time). It is then knotted as shown in figure 6.9.e - 6.9.f.

This technique addresses one of the major problems that was seen in the first technique. We see that the slit and knot arrangement is a much more secure anchor for the two ends of the strap. Therefore, slippage is rare. This style is not without its problems; if the slit is improperly made it may break, thus leaving our *kundal* improperly anchored and susceptible to slippage.   All things considered, if the rawhide is heavy and strong, and the workmanship is up to standard, it is highly unlikely that this *kundal* will fail.

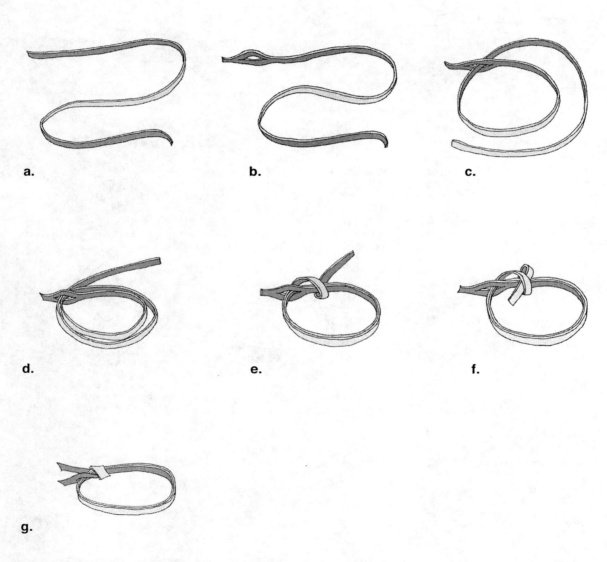

a.   b.   c.

d.   e.   f.

g.

Figure 6.9. Making the Kundal (Technique #2)

<u>Making the Kundal (Technique #3)</u> - This is an approach that seems to be common in *tablas* from the western part of India, especially Gujarat. This too, addresses the problem of how to properly anchor both ends of the strap in the *kundal*.

This technique is very similar to that described in technique #2. Again we start with a length of strap; however this technique absolutely requires that we use the thickest, heaviest, *tasma* that we can find. We cut a small slit in one end of the *tasma*. It is helpful to slightly soak the slit end to make it supple and easy to work with. We then repeatedly loop through the slit. When we get to the end, we make a small diagonal cut in the end of the strap; this will form a small barb that will anchor the end. We then pass the barbed end through the slit. This barb will then connect with the end of the slit and firmly anchor both ends.

This style usually works very well but it is not without its problems. Obviously if the strap is too thin or if there are an insufficient number of rounds, then the *kundal* may break. This is of course possible with all rawhide *kundals*. However there is a problem which is specific to this design. The barb sometimes fails to anchor the end, and slippage may then occur. Another problem comes if the slit is improperly made; it may tear. This too, will allow slippage.

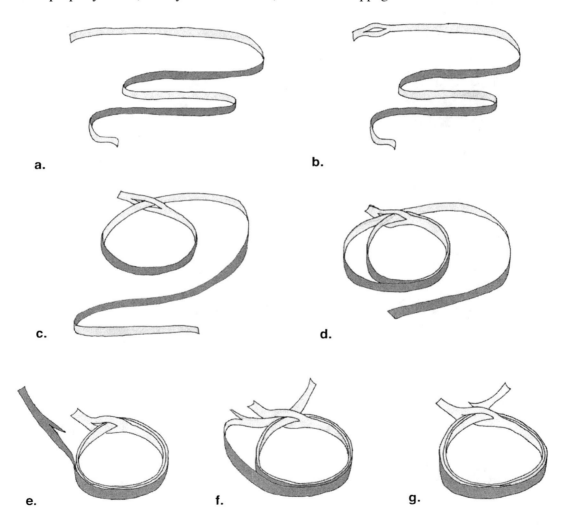

Figure 6.10. Making the Kundal (technique #3)

Making the Kundal (Technique #4) - This is a simple variation upon the previously described techniques. The steps are the same as previously described, except the final *kundal* is tightly wrapped with goatskin or cloth (figure 6.11). If goatskin is used, it should be wet first so it will tighten down upon the *kundal* during drying. This final wrapping is both functional and decorative. It is decorative because it makes for a smoother, more finished look. It is also functional because binding the *kundal* in this manner reduces the chance of slipping and breaking.

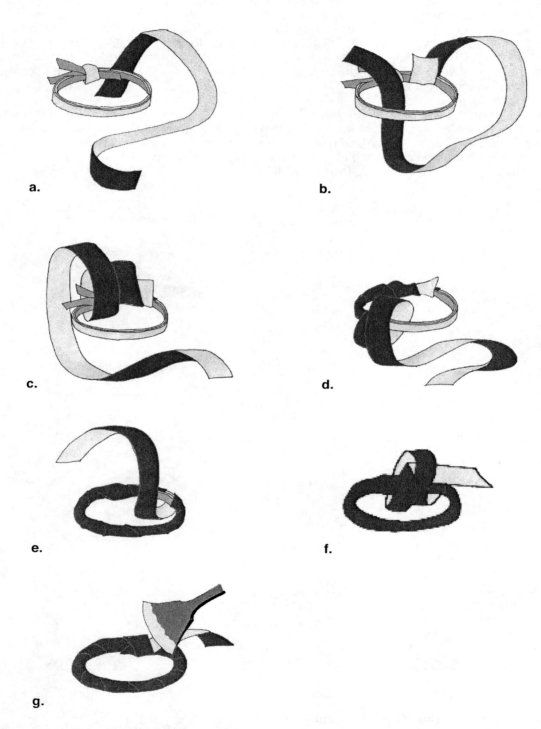

a.

b.

c.

d.

e.

f.

g.

Figure 6.11. The Kundal (technique #4)

Making the Kundal (Technique #5) - Another way to make the *kundal* is shown in figure 6.12. This starts with some simple iron wire (fig. 6.12.a). This wire is very much like the baling wire which was once used to bale hay. We must first take the wire and make it into a coil of the desired size. The ends of the wire are then secured by repeatedly wrapping around the hoop (fig 6.12.b). A piece of lightly soaked goatskin strap is inserted to about one inch between an arbitrary number of wires (fig 6.12.c). This is used to anchor the strap. One then winds the soaked goatskin around the entire length of the coil as shown in figures 6.12.d-6.12.f. When one reaches the end it is secured by passing under the last wrap (fig. 6.12.g). Allow the whole thing to dry. The excess strip may now be trimmed (fig. 6.12.h). The whole is now finished.

It is interesting to note that iron wire is used in this *kundal*. I am sure that brass wire would be better, but iron is used for reasons of economy. We must not forget that iron rusts, and rust will tremendously weaken rawhide. Therefore, the goatskin wrapping is more than mere decoration. If we had left the ring unwrapped and attached the lacing directly to the iron *kundal*, over a period of time it would rust and weaken the *tasma*. This would ultimately cause the *tasma* to break. This goatskin wrapping lies between the iron and the *tasma* and does not have to undergo any real stress. Therefore, there is nothing to break. It serves to insulate the *tasma* from the weakening influence of the rust without any consequence of itself being harmed.

One may note that this style is common in the Deccan and in Pakistan, yet not common in the areas in between. If one looks at a map one easily sees that there is a very great distance between these two areas. I have always suspected that there is an interesting story behind this somehow, but I do not know what it might be.

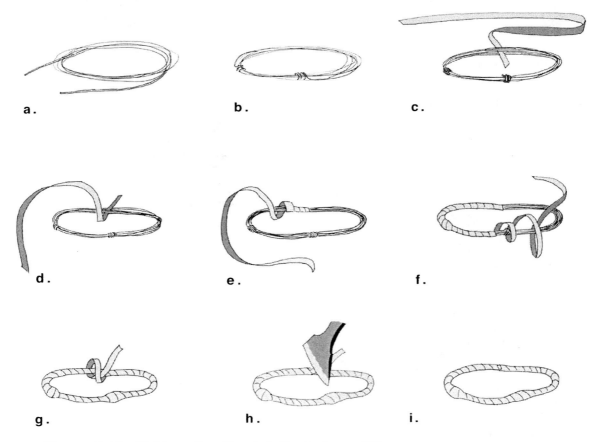

a.   b.   c.

d.   e.   f.

g.   h.   i.

Figure 6.12. Making the Kundal (technique #5)

<u>Making the Kundal (Technique #6)</u> - The most complex *kundals* are the carefully woven hoops found in some South Indian *tablas* (fig. 6.13). Many south Indian *tabla* makers are used to working with *mridangams*. *Mridangam*, like the *pakhawaj*, runs lacing back and forth between two drumheads. This philosophy is reflected in the South Indian *kundal* which is made from a discarded *pudi* (drumhead) that has had the centre cut out.

There are advantages and disadvantages to this approach. One advantage is in the efficient use of materials. Whenever a *tabla* comes in for a head change, the old head is generally unusable and must be discarded. If one simply cuts the centre out, then it can be used as a *kundal*, so it does not have to be thrown away. The disadvantage is that it is much more labour to weave the lacing through the *gajara* of an old *pudi* than it is to simply pass the lacing under a simple *kundal*. It is this extra labour that makes this an unattractive technique.

We have covered several different approaches to making the *kundal*. The function of the *kundal* is very humble yet important. As long as it is strong enough to stand up under the tension, we could use almost any approach.

When we have made the *kundal* we can put it aside until later. Now it is time to make the *pudi*.

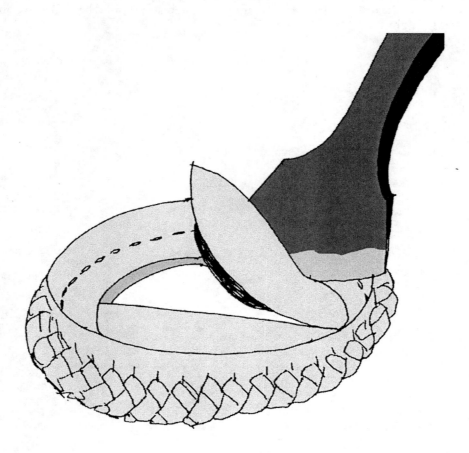

Figure 6.13. The Kundal (technique #6)

MAKING THE PUDI

The pudi (पुड़ि) is the drum head. It is the single most complex part of the *tabla*. It is also the most important part of the *tabla*. If this is made of substandard materials, or if the workmanship is shoddy, then the drum will never have a nice sound.

The origin of the word *pudi* is uncertain. Fallon's New Hindustani-English Dictionary (Fallon 1879) list *pura* (पुरा) for drumhead, *puda* (पुड़ा) is a parcel, and *pudiya* (पुड़िया) is anything that is wrapped in paper, or leaves. We could generally say that the term implies something that is small and bound in parchment.

Making the *pudi* for both *bayan* and *dayan* is similar. In most cases it is just a difference in size. Whenever there are substantial differences they will be pointed out.

Cutting the Goatskin Disks - The *pudi* requires a series of goatskin disks; the *maidan* (vibrating membrane) and the *chat* (outer annular membrane) are the most notable. In some cases a disk is also required for the *bharti*. The initial job of cutting these disks is very important because it may directly effect the quality of the finished drum.

The process begins by marking off the goatskin. This goatskin, known as *bakari ki khal* (बकरी की खाल), has been previously defleshed and dehaired. Templates, known as *jal*, are used to mark off circles of various sizes for use on various drums (fig 6.14). Templates of roughly six-to-seven inches in diameter are used for the *dayan* and roughly 12 inches for the *bayan*.

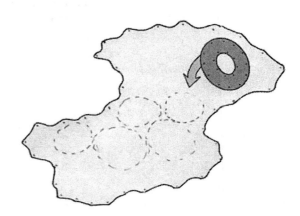

Figure 6.14. Mark the Hide - Circles of skin are marked off with the template (jal)

The skin is carefully examined and graded during the process of marking it off. Great care is taken so that the small scars the goat acquired from ticks and other sources are avoided. The area of the neck and spine is avoided for the *dayan*, but it is considered acceptable for the *bayan*.

This process of marking off the skin involves many complex business and technical decisions. It is possible to maximise the number of circles that may be obtained from a hide; yet this may cause a number of scars and imperfections to be incorporated into the finished *tablas*. Although maximising the number of circles may produce more *tablas* and probably increase profit, the reduction in quality may harm the craftsman's reputation.

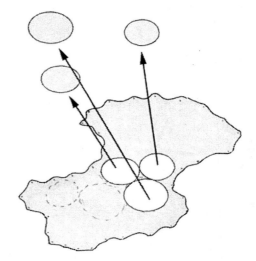

Figure 6.15. Cut Out the Circles

Conversely, if the *tablawala* only chooses the highest quality portions of the skin, this will increase the wastage *(chillar)* and reduce the number of *tablas* that may be made. This may maintain the reputation of the craftsman, but it may force the *tablawala* to charge more than the going rate, thus harming his business.

The normal approach of most *tablawalas* is simple. They go ahead and maximise the goatskin to produce the maximum number of disks, but produce a variety of finished *tablas* in various grades, from student to professional. The prices will vary according to the quality.

When the skin is marked off and graded, the circles are then cut (fig. 6.15). This is usually done with the *rampi*. These small rawhide disks are now put aside for later.

The Bharti - The *bharti* is the internal lining of the *pudi*. Its function is primarily mechanical, but it also serves an acoustic function. There are three philosophies to the *bharti*. One approach has the *bharti* made of numerous small pieces. The second approach has the *bharti* made of a single membrane with the centre removed. The final approach is simply not to have a *bharti* at all. We will look at all three philosophies in greater detail.

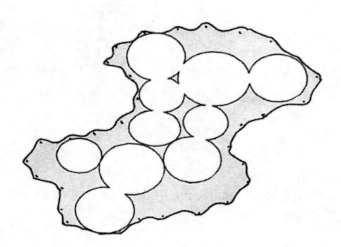

Figure 6.16. Chillar

Figure 6.17. Goatskin Trapezoid

Making the Bharti (technique #1) - A very common approach to the *bharti* has it made of numerous small separate pieces of skin. This is motivated partly by the need to conserve raw materials.

We saw in the previous section that when the circles of skin have all been removed, there are pieces left over; this is called *chillar* (चिल्लर)(fig. 6.16). The word *chillar* variously means "small change", or "leftovers". This usually implies something of very little value. However, we see that much of our *chillar* is prime flank skin. It is only its small size that affects its utility.

It turns out that this *chillar* is choice material for the *bharti*. For the *bharti*, we cut small trapezoids, between two and four inches in size (fig. 6.17). The skins are soaked in water and removed. They are now suitable for making the *bharti*.

Making the Bharti (technique #2) - Another very common approach to making the *bharti* is to have it made of a single membrane. This may be made in the following manner.

The single piece *bharti* starts by taking one of the lower quality skins (previously cut disks)(fig. 6.18.a). It is taken and folded several times to form a triangle (fig. 6.18.b-c). The tip is cut off (fig. 6.18.d), so that when it is unfolded (fig 6.18.e-g), there will be a circle of about two to three inches in diameter that has been removed. This is very much like the paper "snowflakes" we used to make in elementary school

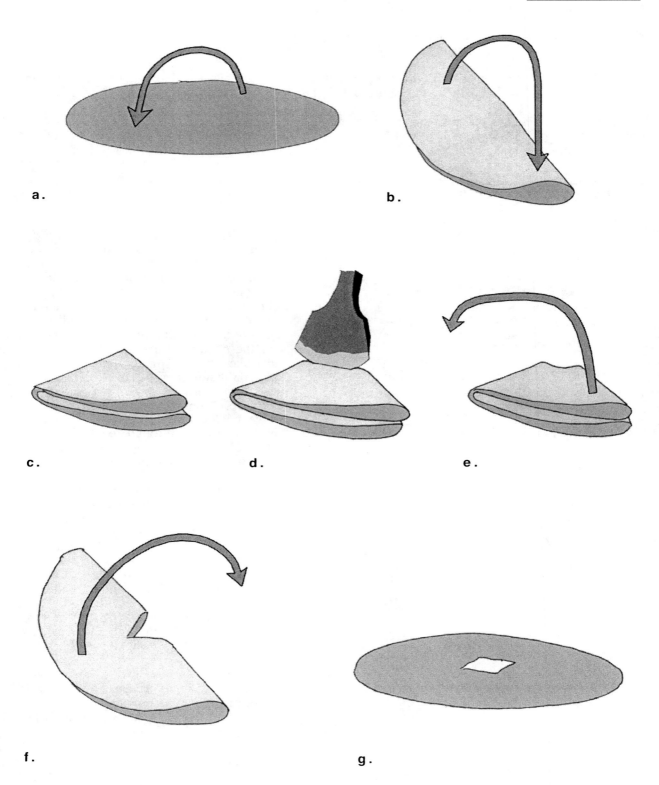

Figure 6.18. Making Annular Membrane (chat or bharti)

Non-existent Bharti (technique #3) - Some makers do not use a *bharti* at all. This approach is not at all recommended because an absence of the *bharti* makes the head less durable.

The Chat - The *chat* is the outer annular membrane. It is extremely important in determining both durability as well as the quality of the sound.

The *chat* is made in exactly the same manner as the single piece *bharti*. Again one takes one of the lower quality disks and cuts the centre out in the previously described fashion (fig. 6.18).

Maidan - The *maidan* is the most important membrane of the *tabla*. For this, you select one of the highest quality rawhide disks. It should be free of scars and imperfections. For the *dayan* the skin should be from the flank, while for the *bayan* it is acceptable to use disks taken from the back.

Temporary Joining of the Chat, Maidan, and Bharti - There must be a temporary joining of the *chat*, *maidan*, and *bharti*. The final joining will come with the weaving of the *gajara*, however a temporary joining is necessary before this can be done.

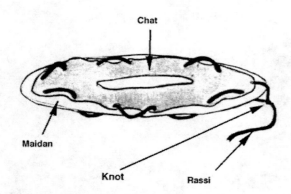

Figure 6.19. Chat and Maidan

The *chat, bharti,* and the *maidan* should be well soaked in water until supple (about 15-30 minutes). The *chat* is laid on top of an intact *maidan* skin so that the outer surfaces (epidermis) of both skins face up. Insertions are made around the edge of the skins with a small chisel (approximately nine for the *dayan* and 13 for the *bayan*). Care should be taken so that the *chat* is slightly bunched up, so that, on the drum, all of the tension will be exerted against the *maidan* (figure 6.19). A piece of cord (*rassi*) is inserted with a large needle (*tar ka suwa*) and threaded back and forth through the two skins as the insertions are made. Finally the two ends of the cord are tied together.

There is an interesting knot used to tie the two ends of the *rassi* (cord) together. (At least it was interesting to me because I had never seen it before.) This is shown in figure 6.20. For this, one separates two plies of the rope (fig. 6.20.a). There may be any number of plies so just divide the plies randomly. Then one passes the needle and cord between two plies (fig. 6.20.b). Then wrap around and through (fig. 6.20.c). Finally one pulls it tight (fig. 6.20.d).

The previously mentioned trapezoids (*bharti*) have been soaking in water (about 15-30 minutes), and are now laid around the rim of the drum shell. The shorter edges face inside (fig. 6.21).

The *chat* and *maidan*, joined previously, are now stretched over the *bharti* and drum shell and tied securely (fig. 6.22).

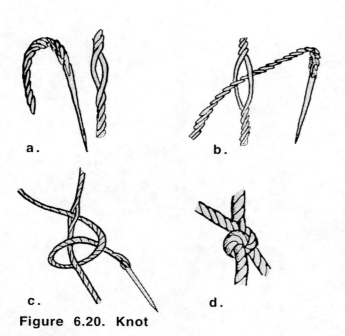

Figure 6.20. Knot

There is no real attachment between the pieces of *bharti, maidan*, and *chat* at the present stage of construction. The attachment will come with the weaving of the *gajara*. This will be described later.

<u>Making Slits for the Gajara</u> - The weaving of the *gajara* requires a series of vertical slits to be made in the various membranes; these run around the edge of the *tabla* (fig. 6.23). Care must be taken that all layers of the skin have been penetrated and that the slits are evenly spaced.

The number of slits is a very good indication of the care and quality of workmanship that goes into a *tabla*. The *bayan* requires 64 slits while the *dayan* requires only 48. If the *dayan* is very small (five inches or less), then 32 slits is acceptable. Numbers other than these are a good indication of shoddy work. For instance, one often finds *bayans* that have only 48 slits. This is a sure indication that the maker was cutting corners. In the same manner, one often finds *dayans* that are well in excess of five inches that have only 32 slits. This too is an indication of cutting corners. One may notice that the number of slits is always a multiple of 16 (32=2x16, 48=3x16, 64=4x16). Occasionally one will find the number of slits to be some non-multiple of 16 (e.g., 60, 58, etc.). Any non-multiple of 16 is a sure indication of the greatest carelessness in the making of the *tabla*.

<u>The Gajara</u> - We must now weave the *gajara*. The *gajara* is the braid which unites the *bharti, maidan*, and the *chat*. It serves the vital function of transmitting the tension from the *tasma* (lacing) to the vibrating membranes.

The importance of the *gajara* becomes clear when we realise that there are two very different types of hide that are used to make the *tabla*. The vibrating membranes are made of goatskin. Goatskin has some very desirable acoustical properties, but it is very weak and ill suited for lacing. Therefore, it is laced with the rawhide of buffalos, or in some cases cattle. The heavier hides from the buffalo are very strong, but acoustically undesirable.

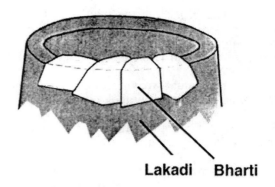

Figure 6.21. Starting the Bharti

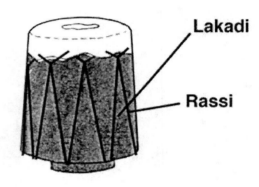

Figure 6.22. Temporary Lacing

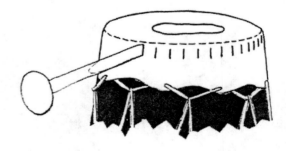

Figure 6.23. Making Slits for the Gajara

If we attempt to directly lace the delicate goatskin with the heavy and unyielding buffalo hide, this would be very bad. Any little imbalance in tension would create a shear force that would tear the delicate goatskin.

The *gajara* forms a buffer. It takes the various forces exerted by the buffalo hide, balances them, and moderates them so that an even tension is conveyed to the vibrating membranes. This buffering action is essential to the proper tuning of the *tabla*. It is also necessary to make the head more durable and less susceptible to breakage.

The actual weaving of the *gajara* may be broken down into three steps; starting, weaving, and finishing. We will now look at the various techniques for these activities.

Starting the Gajara (Technique #1) - Here is a technique that it fairly standard.   The *gajara* is started in the following manner:

1. One starts with two long pieces of buffalo hide. Each thong (*tasma*) is first soaked in water, then lightly covered with oil. The two thongs are inserted into three adjacent holes (i.e., two thongs sharing a central hole) up to their midpoints (fig. 6.24-7.25a, & 6.25b), thereby making four loose ends.
2. Twist in clockwise manner.
3. Go over two slits and insert (fig. 6.25.c).
4. Pull out third slit.

Figure 6.24. Starting the Gajara

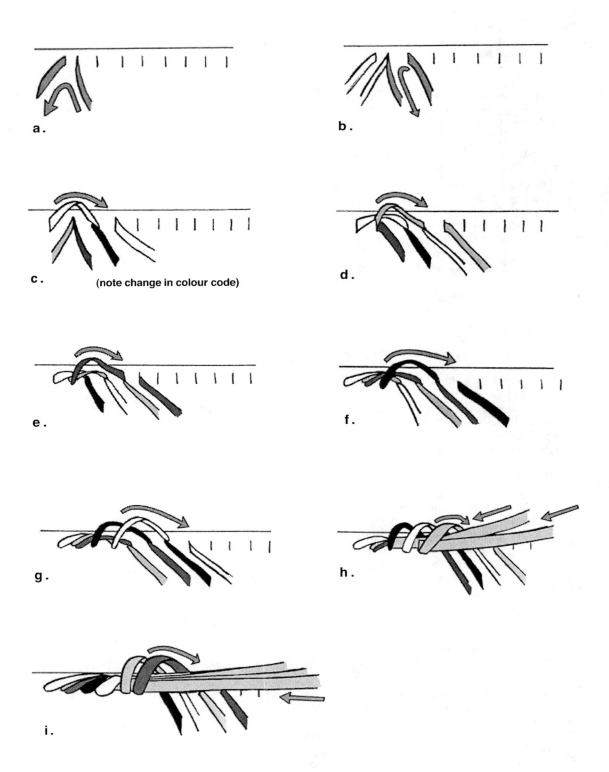

a.

b.

c. (note change in colour code)

d.

e.

f.

g.

h.

i.

Figure 6.25. Starting the Gajara (technique #1)

5. Go to next thong.
6. Repeat steps 2, 3, and 4 (fig. 6.25.d).
7. Go to next thong in same slit.
8. Repeat step 2 (twist).
9. Go over three slits and insert.
10. Pull out from bottom of the fourth slit (fig. 6.25.e).
11. Go to next thong.
12. Repeat steps 7, 8, & 9, but keep loose (fig. 6.25.f).
13. Go to next thong.
14. Repeat steps 7, 8, & 9, but keep loose (fig. 6.25.g).
15. Go to next *tasma*.
16. Repeat steps 7, 8, & 9, but keep loose (fig. 6.25.h).
17. There must be a central core around which the *gajara* is woven. This core thong is made by taking two or three lengths of inferior quality leather strap and wrapping them around the rim. Insert core thong (fig. 6.25.h).
18. Tighten first two thongs.
19. Take next thong.
20. Repeat steps 7, 8, & 9, but keep loose (fig. 6.25.i).
21. Insert last core thong.
22. Tighten last thong.

The *gajara* is now started. One may now continue weaving.

Starting the Gajara (Technique #2) - This is a technique which is common in the Bengal area of India. This is but a slight variation upon the earlier technique.

1. Start with a wide strip of *tasma*.
2. Split it down, nearly the entire length of the *tasma*; however, a small portion should be left uncut (fig 6.26.a).
3. Repeat process with a second band of *tasma* (fig. 6.26.b). There should finally be two such split pieces (fig. 6.26.c).
4. Position the split piece so that both legs are facing up. Take the left most leg and pull it through the first slit (fig. 6.26.d). Remember to place a $\frac{1}{4}$ turn so that it comes out the slit straight.
5. Take the right most leg and repeat the same process in the next slit (fig. 6.26.d).
6. Pull both thongs tight.
7. Take the next slit piece.
8. Apply $\frac{1}{4}$ turn to the left leg and pass through the third slit (fig. 6.26.e).
9. Apply $\frac{1}{4}$ turn and pull out the forth slit (fig. 6.26.e).
10. Pull all thongs tight (fig. 6.26.f).
11. Take first thong and give half turn in clockwise direction (as though one were wrapping it around an imaginary object.
12. Skip two slits and insert in third to leave a small loop (leave loose)(fig. 6.26.f).
13. Take core *tasma* and trim to point.
14. Insert core *tasma* into loop (fig 6.26.f).
15. Pull tight around the core *tasma*.
16. Take second weaving *tasma* and wrap over the core tasma (fig 6.26.g).
17. Skip two slits and insert into third, coming out of the fourth (fig. 6.26.g).
18. Pull tight around the core *tasma*.
19. Take third weaving *tasma* and wrap it around the core *tasma*.
20. Skip two slits, and insert into the third slit, coming out the fourth (fig 6.26.h).
21. Pull tight around core *tasma*.
22. Take fourth weaving *tasma* and wrap around core *tasma* (fig 6.26.i).
23. Skip two slits, insert into the third slit and come out the fourth (fig. 6.26.i).
24. Take the next *tasma* (i.e., the first weaving *tasma* that was previously pulled through), wrap around core *tasma*.
25. Skip two slits, insert into third slit and come out the fourth (keep loose).

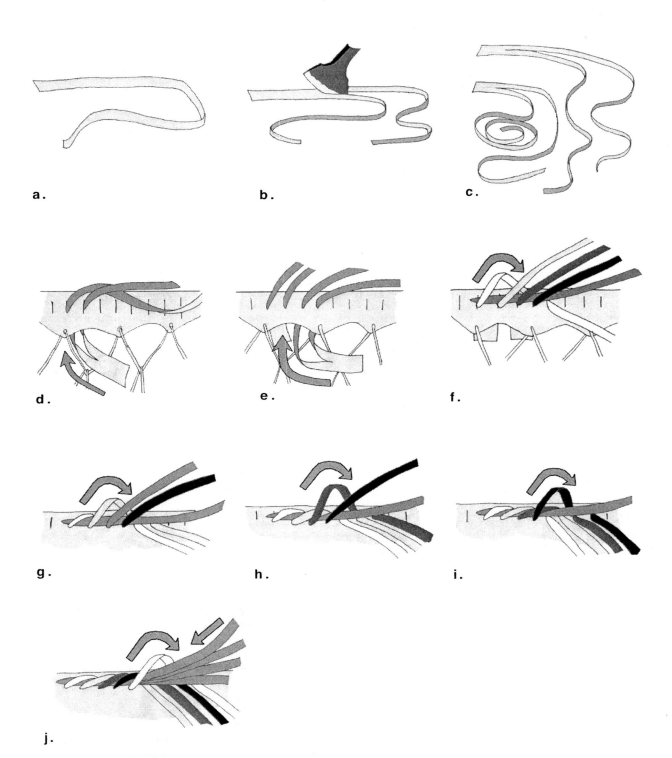

a.

b.

c.

d.

e.

f.

g.

h.

i.

j.

Figure 6.26. Starting the Gajara (technique #2)

26. Insert remaining pieces of core *tasma*. If they are very thin, another three or four may be required. If they are very thick, another two may suffice. The final core should be about a quarter of an inch in thickness.
27. Tighten the last thong around core.

The *gajara* is now started; continue weaving.

Continuing the Gajara - The *gajara* must be woven throughout the entire rim of the *tabla*. This is very simple and it is described below (fig. 6.27):

1. Take thong from bottom.
2. Twist $\frac{1}{2}$ turn in clockwise fashion, this essentially is just wrapping it around the core.
3. Go over two slits and insert in the third slit on top of the core thong.
4. Pull out of the bottom of the fourth slit.
5. Go to next thong and repeat.

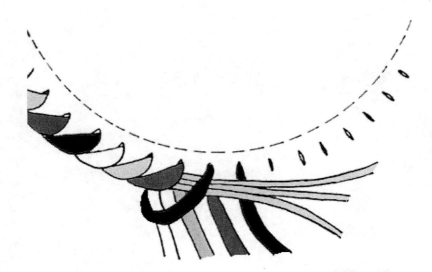

Figure 6.27. Weaving the Gajara

It is interesting to note how incredibly simple the weaving really is. This is in stark contrast to the complex techniques that are involved in starting and finishing the *gajara*.

Ending the Weave - Eventually the weaving must be finished. Basically it is finished in several steps. The first step is to cut the core *tasma* to the required lengths. The next step is the over-weave; in this, one continues weaving past the start. Finally the loose ends must be anchored and trimmed. There are numerous ways to anchor the *tasma*; therefore, we will discuss them separately,

The first two steps (trimming the core *tasma* and the over-weave) are fairly common. They are also fairly easy. These steps are described below:

1. Stop weaving when the thong exits at the starting point (fig. 6.28.a).
2. Cut outer core thong so that it extends $1\frac{1}{2}$ inches over the starting point (fig. 6.28.a).
3. Cut inner core thong so that it just touches starting point (fig. 6.28.a).
4. Cut middle core thong so that it extends $\frac{1}{2}$ to 1 inch beyond the starting point (fig.6.28.a). These cuts in the core are done so that the lengths are staggered. Just as they were staggered when the weaving begins, this overlap is important to making the final weave look smooth. If there are more than three pieces of core *tasma*, they may be cut to proper lengths that will produce a clean finished product.

5. Wrap thong around core.
6. Pull thong over four spaces and insert between *chat* and *gajara* (fig. 6.28).
7. Pull tight
8. Go to next thong and repeat steps 5, 6, 7, and 8, until four over-weaves have been made. This whole thing is illustrated in the various sections of figure 6.28.

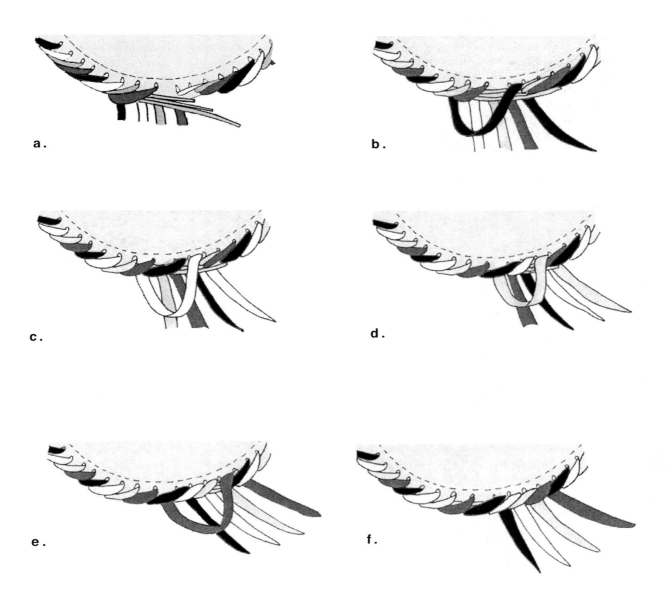

a.

b.

c.

d.

e.

f.

Figure 6.28. End of Gajara

It is useful to make a few observations about the previous process. One will notice that in all of the previous steps (e.g., the starting and continuation of the weave) the *tasma* passed through the slits. This of course was to unite the various membranes (i.e., *chat, maidan, bharti*) into a single unit. This finishing section is unusual in that, rather than passing through the slits, we merely pass between the weave and the outer membrane *(chat)*. This is the defining quality of the over-weave.

There is one more observation that we can make. We see that there are four loose ends. These ends must be anchored in some way, or the *gajara* will unravel. There are numerous ways to anchor these loose ends. Some of the more common ones will be discussed here.

Anchor Gajara #1 (simple cut) - The simplest way to remove the loose ends is simply to cut them off. However, if it were done at the present point it is likely that it would unravel.

This problem of unravelling is solved in two ways. The first is to add an additional round of over-weave. This is shown in figure 6.29.a. The second is the addition of a counter-weave. This counter-weave, known as *bunad*, will keep the weave tight and prevent unravelling.

The procedure in detail is outlined below:

1. Take next weaving *tasma*.
2. Wrap around *gajara*.
3. Go over 3 openings and insert insert in the 4th.
4. Pull tight.
5. Repeat steps 1-4 until the second round of over-weave is complete (i.e., all four *tasmas* have been done).
6. Trim off excess (fig. 6.29.b).

The weaving is now complete.

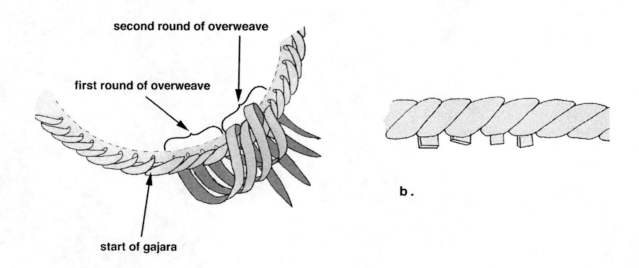

second round of overweave

first round of overweave

start of gajara

a.

b.

Figure 6.29. Anchor Gajara #1 (simple cut)

This approach has advantages and disadvantages. The obvious advantage is that it is quick and simple. It works quite well as long as the *tasma* is thick and strong. It is also very reliable when there is a good, tight *bunad* (cross-weave). It also produces an elegant, clean looking *pudi* when the whole is finished. Unfortunately, this approach is prone to unravelling, especially in the absence of a *bunad*. This can be a serious problem, but fortunately it is very rare.

Anchor Gajara #2 (double braid) - Another approach is a simple double braid. This approach is shown in figure 6.30. It is most reliable if another round of over-weave is performed before this braid. However, sometimes in lower quality *pudis*, this second round is dispensed with.

For the double braid, one takes the four loose ends. One then makes a very small slit, as close to the core of the *gajara* as possible in the second and the fourth *tasma*. The first and the third *tasma* are then inserted into the slits as shown in figure 6.30 and pulled tight. Then the two pairs are wound tightly around each other and the whole is allowed to dry.

There are advantages and disadvantages to this approach. It is very resistant to unravelling. This approach is also quick and easy. The slight disadvantage is that the finished *pudi* may not be quite as clean and elegant as a simple cut.

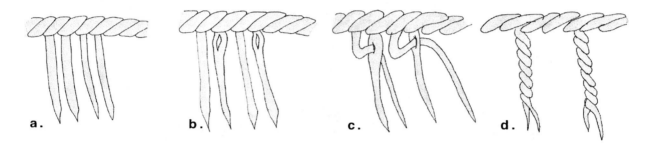

Figure 6.30. Anchor the Gajara #2 (double braid)

Anchor Gajara #3 (double knot) - One occasionally finds a double knot to close the loose ends and anchor the weave of the *gajara*. This is illustrated in figure 6.31. This is probably one of the easiest to do. One simply takes two pairs of *tasma* and ties them as shown in fig 6.31.

This approach has advantages and disadvantages. On the positive side, it is simple and effective. On the negative side, it is inelegant to the point of being down right ugly! Therefore, it is often indicative of shoddy workmanship. If this is found, then one has to wonder about the other shortcuts that may have been taken. The other shortcuts may not be readily visible.

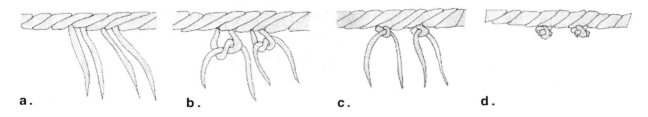

Figure 6.31. Anchor the Gajara #3 (double knot)

Anchor the Gajara #4 (simple pigtail) - This is another simple way to anchor the ends of the *gajara*. It is extremely simple. One need only take one of the thongs and wind it tightly around the other three. Tie it off with a simple knot then trim the excess thong. It is fast and effective.

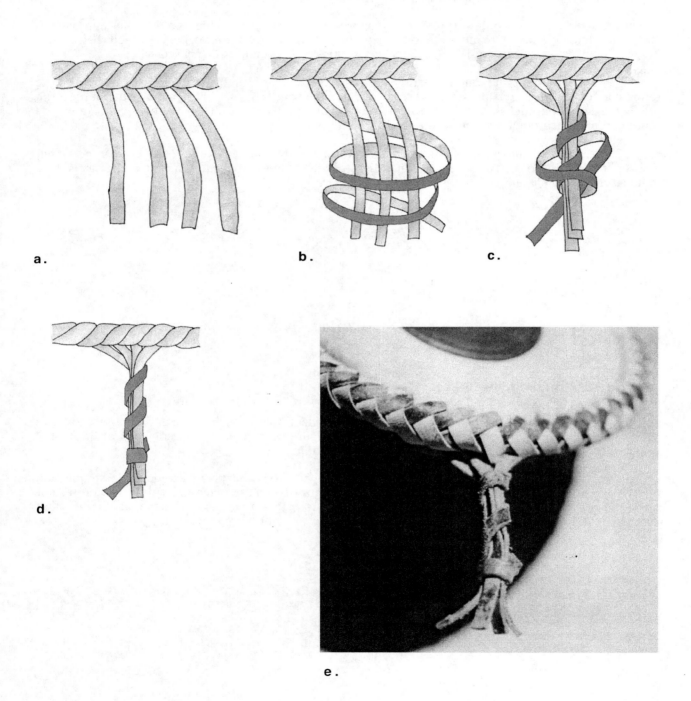

a.

b.

c.

d.

e.

Figure 6.32. Anchor the Gajara #4 (simple pigtail)

Anchor the Gajara #5 (complex braid) - This is probably the most common way that is used in Bengal. The poor quality of *Bengali tasma* absolutely demands that there be great attention paid to the anchoring of the weave, lest the whole *pudi* will unravel.

This method looks to be quite difficult at first glance, but it really isn't. All that we are doing is taking two straps and bunching them together. From here it is braided just like one may braid a little girl's hair. After it is braided a reasonable distance, one of the straps is used to tie it off. The excess is now cut and it is finished.

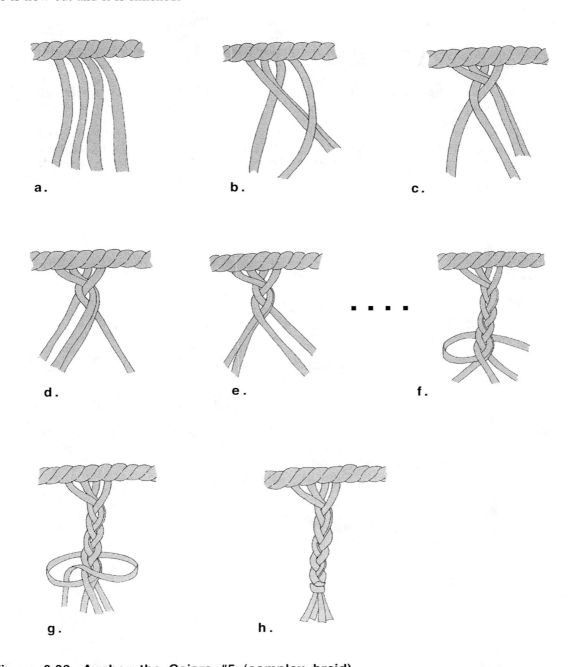

Figure 6.33. Anchor the Gajara #5 (complex braid)

<u>Bunad (technique #1)</u> - The *gajara* is nearly complete at this point; the only remaining step is to weave a crossbraid known as *bunad*. Many craftsmen eliminate the *bunad* entirely. The weaving of the *bunad* goes as follows (fig. 6.34):

1. Pull a strip of dry goathide, Rexene or similar material between the *gajara* and the *chat* (pull up) (fig. 6.34.a).
2. Skip closest thong and pull *bunad* through under the next one (fig. 6.34.b).
3. Pull into correct position.
4. Skip next thong and pull *bunad* through under next one (fig. 6.34.c).
5. Pull down to proper position.
6. Pull tight.
7. Put another piece of *bunad* through the next hole (fig. 6.34.d).
8. Repeat steps 2, 3, 4, 5, & 6 (fig. 6.34.e-6.34.h).
9. Go back and pull the first *bunad* through the next hole.
10. Repeat steps 2, 3, 4, 5, & 6.

This alternating back and forth proceeds until all of the *gajara* is done (fig. 6.34.i). Any excess *bunad* is trimmed away.

There is one thing to note about the *bunad*; it does not have to be made of continuous strips of material. It is common to use strips that are only a few inches in length. If one needs to start a new *bunad*, one simply enters a new strip from the bottom. If there is a decent overlap with two *bunads* going the same path, the friction between the two strips maintains a decent strength. Upon completion of the *bunad*, the *gajara* is finished.

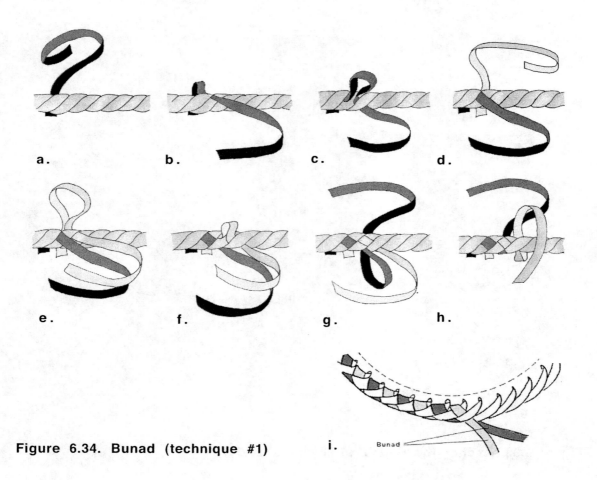

a.   **b.**   **c.**   **d.**

e.   **f.**   **g.**   **h.**

Figure 6.34. Bunad (technique #1)   **i.**   Bunad

<u>Bunad (technique #2)</u> - This style is exactly like the previous *bunad* except there is no effort to put the second weave in.

1. Pull a strip of dry goathide, Rexene or similar material between the *gajara* and the *chat* (pull up) (fig. 6.35.a).
2. Skip closest thong and pull *bunad* through under the next one (fig. 6.35.b).
3. Pull into correct position.
4. Pull tight.
5. Put another piece of *bunad* through the next hole (fig. 6.35.c).
6. Repeat steps 2, 3, 4.
7. Go back and pull the first *bunad* through the next hole.
8. Repeat all steps

Continue until *bunad* is complete.

   It is really difficult to say how valuable this type of *bunad* is. There is no doubt that a well made *bunad* adds to the strength of the *gajara*. But many times, even a fully woven *bunad* (fig. 34) is made in such a way that it is more decorative than functional. It is probably safe to say that a half *bunad,* as illustrated here, is more decorative than functional.

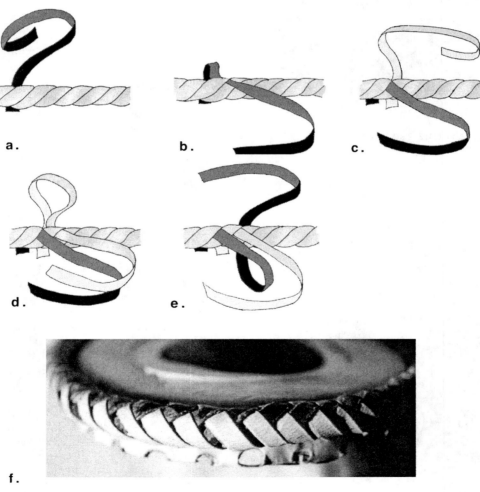

a.　　　　　　b.　　　　　　c.

d.　　　　　　e.

f.

Figure 6.35. Bunad (technique #2)

Figure 6.36. Unfinished Pudi and Temporary Lacing

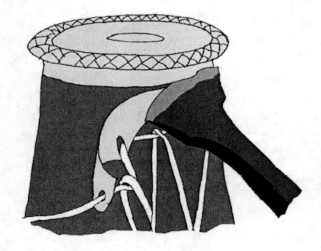

Figure 6.37. Trimming Pudi and Removing Temporary Lacing

<u>Overview of Gajara</u> - It is appropriate that we make a few observations as to the nature of the *gajara*. As mentioned earlier, the *gajara* serves the function of transferring the tension from the lacing to the *maidan*. However, it does so in a manner which is considerably more refined than the hoop found in Western drums. Unlike Western drums, the *gajara* has a strong buffering effect upon this tension. This buffering is important because very little variation in tension is tolerated by the *tabla*. This low tolerance is a natural consequence of the requirement for precise tunability. An interesting feature of this buffering effect is that changing the tension on the lacing functions as a "course tuning" while lightly hitting the *gajara* with a small hammer acts as the "fine tuning". In practice the majority of the tuning is done without any change in the tension of the lacing at all.

The *gajara* also performs the necessary but mundane function of joining all three levels of skin (i.e., *bharti*, *maidan*, and *chat*) together.

FINAL SKINNING OF THE DRUM

The final skinning of the drum involves several steps. The first step is the removal of the temporary lacing. Next the inner and underside of the *pudi* must be trimmed. Finally the *pudi* must be permanently laced to the shell. These steps will be described in greater detail in this section

Presently the *tabla* is as shown in figure 6.36. Here we have a partially completed *pudi* and a temporary lacing.

Trimming of the under portion of the *pudi* and the removal of the temporary lacing may be accomplished in one quick and easy step. One takes a *rampi* and slices around the full rim of the drum (fig 6.37). This circumcision should be about 1/2 inch from the under portion of the *gajara*. The *pudi* and temporary lacing may then be removed from the shell.

The *bharti* must now be trimmed. It is trimmed by taking a flat piece of bamboo (*badda*) and slipping it between the *maidan* and *bharti* (see figure 6.38). The bamboo piece is used to shield the *maidan* from the blade. The *bharti* is trimmed so that there is an even half-inch projecting into the middle of the *pudi*.

There are two functions for the *bharti*. The prime function appears to be mechanical in nature. The *bharti* reinforces the *maidan* and keeps it from tearing under high tension. There is another more subtle function that the *bharti* performs. Along with the *chat*, the *bharti* serves the important function of selectively muting the higher order vibrational modes. This leaves the lower order vibrational modes unaffected. This acts like a tone control. Using this analogy, we can say that the *bharti* and the *chat* work together to cut down the treble. This will be discussed in greater detail in Chapter 10.

A few more words are in order concerning the *bharti*. It is very clear that a single piece of rawhide with a circle cut into it is a superior item to a bunch of leftover scraps that might be woven into the *pudi*. Therefore, a single piece *bharti* has got to be superior to one that is made of scraps of skin, right?

This is not necessarily so.

If one is using a single-piece *bharti* then there is a very real danger that it may tense up. An annular membrane under tension will have very different resonance characteristics from the *maidan* and we do not wish the *bharti* to start vibrating on its own.

This problem has not gone unnoticed by *tablawalas*. Many *tablawalas* make diagonal slits in the *bharti* (fig. 6.39). The function of these diagonal slits is to tear whenever the *bharti* should come under tension. These will tear to whatever extent is necessary to relieve the tension.

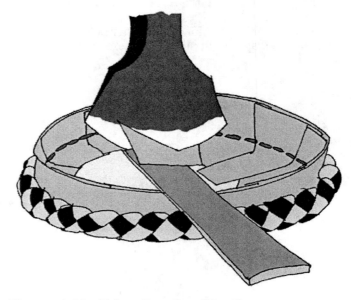

Figure 6.38. Trimming the Bharti

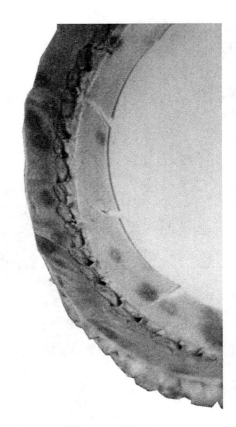

Figure 6.39. Strain Relief Slits in Bharti

<u>Lashing the Pudi Lakadi and Kundal</u> - Before the permanent lacing may be started, the various components must be lashed together. This is to keep them from slipping during the process of lacing. The *pudi*, *lakadi* and *kundal* are all tied together as shown in figure 6.40.

There is one occasion where this lashing is dispensed with. If the drum is destined to use metal turnbuckles as a tightening arrangement this lashing is not necessary.

Figure 6.40. Lashing the Pudi, Lakadi, and Kundal

Overview of Lacing - The final lacing of the drum must now be made. It is this lacing that will be on the drum for many years to come. Therefore, one should use only high quality materials. One may find any number of things used. It is usually rawhide, but on occasion it is rope, or even metallic turnbuckles. These are shown in figure 6.41.

Rawhide lacing is the most common way to maintain tension on the *pudi* (fig 6.41.a). The best quality lacing is made from the hides of water buffalo or cattle. In the Bengal region one finds thin and substandard rawhide which is said to be from goats.

Leather is sometimes used to lace *tablas* (fig 6.41.b). This is usually found in Punjab, Delhi, and Pakistan. If leather is used, it is important that it be top-hide (leather that has not had the epidermis removed). Leather in any form is prone to stretching and breaking and is substandard.

Cord is also used on occasion to lace the drums. (fig. 6.41.c). This is more common on the *bayan* but may also be found on occasion on the *dayan*. There is nothing inherently wrong with cord as a lacing. In fact, the modern nylon cords are really superior to rawhide. However, rope lacing is usually considered the mark of an inexpensive student grade *tabla* and is generally not preferred for professional purposes.

Metal turnbuckles have been found on student grade *tablas* for many years (fig 6.41.d). There are advantages and disadvantages to this style. On the positive side they are easy to maintain and they will hold their tuning for a long time. This

a.   b.

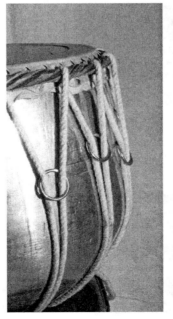

c.   d.

Figure 6.41. Different Tightening Techniques -
a. Rawhide b. Leather   c. Rope   d. Turnbuckle

makes them very desirable for institutional use. On the negative side, they impart a peculiar bite to the sound, especially on the *bayan*. This tonal colouration is considered undesirable. Another problem with the turnbuckle is that the hooks stick out on the *gajara* and hit your hand when used on the *dayan*. This is very uncomfortable.

In the US the biggest problem with the turnbuckle is not in the turnbuckle itself, but what it represents. There is a very major importer in the US who imports large quantities of absolutely terrible *tablas* from Pakistan (fig 6.6). (I shall not name the importer, but anyone in the business will know who I am talking about). This importer then retails to countless well meaning, but ignorant, retailers around the country. The result is that when one is wishing to purchase a *tabla*, the only clue that it is one of these, is the fact that it uses turnbuckles. It is quite unfortunate that this importer has given the turnbuckle such a bad name. In India, I have seen some turnbuckle *tablas* that were really a reasonable quality.

This little overview is not the final word on the topic of tightening the *tabla*. On occasion I have seen some very good *tablas* from Pakistan that use a kind of a nylon *tasma*. I have also experimented with parachute cord with very good results. However, such variations are rare and we need not go into them here.

Orientation with the Pudi - It is very important to maintain proper orientation with the *pudi*. It is very easy to get confused by the complex weaving of the *gajara*. If one becomes disoriented at this phase then the *tabla* will not be laced correctly.

Figure 6.42. Lacing for Good Gajara (dayan)

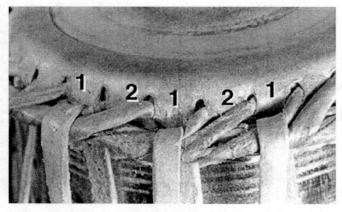

Figure 6.43. Lacing for Bad Gajara (dayan)

We need to know exactly how many gaps there are between the *gajara* and the *chat*. We take the number of gaps, divide by the number 16, and this will give us the ratio of gaps per lacing points. A well made *dayan* will have a ratio of three-to-one (fig. 6.42). Therefore the insertions of the lacing will be made every third gap. Poorly made *dayans* and *dayans* that are unusually small will generally have a ratio of two-to-one (fig. 6.43).

Gap/insertion ratios for the *bayan* will run differently. A well made *bayan* will have a gap-to-insertion ratio of four-to-one while poorly made *bayan pudis* will have a ratio of three-to-one.

If the *pudi* is poorly made, there may be an uneven ratio. In such cases some adjustment needs to be made while the drum is being laced. This is of course a very undesirable situation; fortunately, this does not arise very often.

When we have oriented ourselves to the *pudi* and have a good idea as to how the lacing should be made, we are ready to start.

Standard Lacing of the Tabla -
There are two ways to lace the
tabla. We will describe the most
common one here.

The standard lacing
begins by taking one end of the
tasma and attaching it to the
kundal (fig. 6.44). It is tied so
that the inner surface of the
tasma passes over the *gajara*.
The lacing then begins.

It is laced by passing the
lacing over the *gajara* and into
the gap (fig. 6.45). One then
pulls the *tasma* down (fig. 6.46)
through the gap and then down.
It then turns it around and
passes over the *kundal* (fig
6.44). This process continues
until the *tasma* has traversed the
tabla 32 times.

It will be laced such that
16 insertions between the *gajara*
and the *chat* are made. This
will call upon the correct ratio of
insertions per gaps as was
discussed in the last section.

The lacing continues.
One usually finds that the lacing
will finish before the *pudi* has
been completly laced. One then
slowly takes up the slack. This
will yield sufficient lacing to
finish the job.

It is important to note
that the lacing proceeds in a
counter-clockwise direction.
This is very different from the
way that *tablawalas* in Bengal
lace theirs.

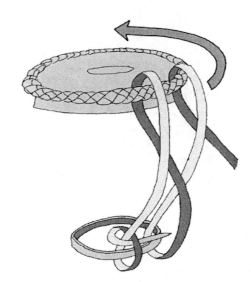

Figure 6.44. Process of Lacing the Tabla

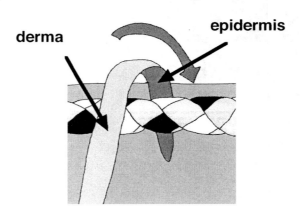

Figure 6.45. Lacing the Tabla (insert over gajara)

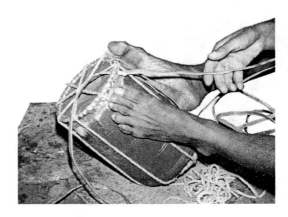

Figure 6.46. Lacing the Tabla (pull down from below)

a.

b.

Figure 6.47. Direction of Lacing - a) Standard b) Bengali

Lacing the Tabla (Bengali style) - *Bengali tablas* are laced in the reverse direction. Other than the direction, the procedure is the same. A comparison between the standard and the *Bengali* lacing is shown in figure 6.47 a-b.

Turnbuckles - Sometimes *tablas* are made using turnbuckles for tuning. This arrangement is shown in figure 6.48. We see that there is a hook which passes through a lug. The opposite end of the hook is secured with a nut. The lug is attached to a threaded shaft. This threaded shaft then passes through the shell, and then through a washer and is secured by a nut on the inside.

We mentioned that the turnbuckle is an easily recognisable sign of the cheap, substandard *tablas* that are often distributed in the United States. The turnbuckle *per se* is not an inferior method of tightening the *tabla*. This brings up the obvious question of how to tell a reasonable quality instrument from the substandard one.

It turns out that counting the number of turnbuckles on the drum is a good benchmark of quality. Turnbuckles sometimes represent a labour saving decision. It is the overly aggressive cutting of corners that is the problem, and not the turnbuckles themselves. If the drum has a large number of turnbuckles, this may be an indication that there was no attempt to cut corners and the instrument may be of a decent quality. A decent turnbuckle *tabla* should have roughly 10-16 turnbuckles per drum. However the substandard Pakistani *tablas* frequently have only 6-8. This is only half the recommended number. Therefore, if you are of the inclination to buy or make a turnbuckle instrument, make sure that you have a sufficient number to do the job.

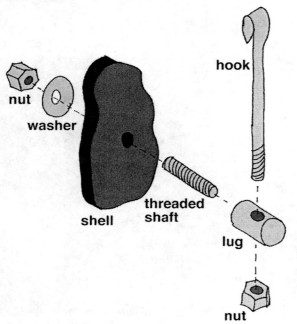

Figure 6.48. Exploded View of Turnbuckle

Rope Lacing - Many *tabla* makers like to make instruments using rope instead of rawhide. This is rare on the *dayan* but relatively common for the *bayan*. Since this is a very inexpensive, yet effective tightening arrangement; it is commonly found on low cost student grade *tablas*.

The overall procedure is illustrated in figure 6.49. We see that it is started with a simple knot on the *kundal*. Then the stringing follows the same basic procedure as the standard rawhide lacing. There is however, one twist. The rope must pass through a series of metal rings (fig. 6.41.c and fig. 6.49). These rings are used to tighten the drum when it gets loose.

This section has gone over the trimming and lacing of the *pudi* to the shell. At this point virtually all of the work on the skins is finished. From here we need to attend to matters that go to give the drum the final sound.

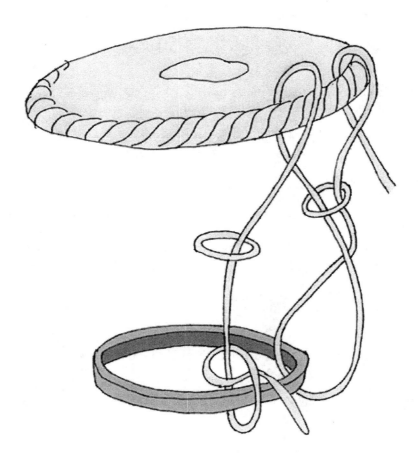

Figure 6.49. Rope Lacing

APPLYING THE SYAHI

The *syahi* is the black spot that lies on the surface of the *tabla*. It is probably the most distinctive visual characteristic of the *tabla*.

The application of the *syahi* is probably the most difficult part of the entire construction. It is a process that really takes a lot of experience. For this reason it is a task which is taken up only by the more experienced workers in the *tabla dukhan*.

The basic form is easily described. It is a number of microscopically thin layers that are built up in a slow tedious fashion until the final shape and form is obtained. Although it is applied in thin layers the final form is actually very different. The final form consists of a number of small, hard particles which articulate with their neighbours, yet are not actually joined anywhere except to the skin at the base. Don't worry if this does not make sense right now; it will become clear as we go along in this section.

The first step is to make sure that we have a large enough work area on the drum. We previously showed how a small portion of the *chat* had been removed. Ideally this gives us a large enough area to work. If we need to enlarge the hole a bit, we simple trim the *chat* with the *rampi* and the *badda*. This procedure is the same as illustrated later in figure 6.58.

A base for the *syahi* must be established. This is done by boiling a small amount of mucilage (called *raal, saresh,* or *suresh*) until it becomes soft and gummy. It is then applied to the exposed surface of the *maidan* to form a circle of approximately $3\frac{1}{2}$ inches for the *dayan* or 4 to $4\frac{1}{2}$ inches for the *bayan*. The circle is then allowed to dry in the sun.

The next step is to actually put the *syahi* on. Key to this is an ingredient known as *syahi massala*.

Syahi massala is a commercially available powder. Its exact ingredients are not known but it appears to be a mixture of soot and metallic dust, probably iron dust (See Appendix 3).

To prepare the paste for *syahi*, a little vessel is filled with a small quantity of water and white flour. This is heated and mixed to make a glue (*lai*). The glue is now mixed with the *syahi massala*. The whole mixing process is done in a rubber mat made from an old inner tube. After a thorough mixing the paste is finished. The application of a layer involves three steps:

Step 1. The *syahi* paste must be applied. This is done by using the first finger of the right hand to take up a small quantity of paste. It is applied with the index finger being supported by the middle finger to give the necessary pressure. It is applied in a circular motion while the drum is rotated. This is to make an even, clean circular application.

Step 2. Excess paste must be removed. This is done by scraping with a curved metallic strip. The *tabla* is rotated during this process so that the application is of uniform thickness.

Step 3. Polishing with a stone is the final step (fig 6.50). Immediately after the excess paste has been removed, a polished piece of basalt is used to rub the *syahi* repeatedly (fig. 6.51). The pressure is very important; it starts gently and builds up to a considerable level. Periodically, the stone is rubbed against the cheek to deposit a small amount of sweat. The polishing is very important because it will determine the density of cracks which are visible in the *syahi*. These cracks will be discussed in greater depth later.

Steps 1, 2, & 3 are repeated for more layers. The diameter of each layer remains full size until four or five layers have been applied. Then the diameters are reduced until the layers are hardly more than half an inch. A few full size layers are again applied, followed by decreasing sizes. This process continues until the desired thickness and shape is attained. This is shown diagrammatically in figure 6.52.

Most of the work in applying the *syahi* is in the actual polishing. Depending upon the humidity, it is not unusual for each layer to take 15 minutes to apply. If we are looking at 35 to 40 layers of *syahi* then we are dealing with an incredible amount of labour. Although labour is very cheap in India this is still too much.

The labour intensive job of apply the *syahi* has been helped by the introduction of polishing machines. A typical polishing machine is shown in figure 6.53.

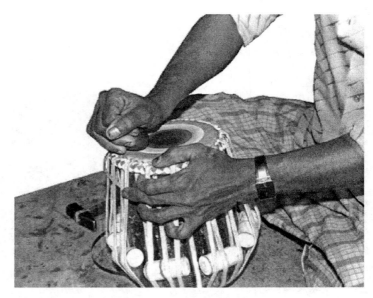

Figure 6.50. The Polishing Stone

Figure 6.51. Applying the Syahi

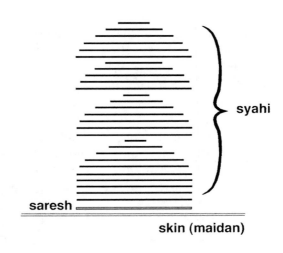

Figure 6.52. Syahi (cross section)

Figure 6.53. Syahi Polishing Machine

<u>Geometry of the Syahi</u> - There is one caveat which must be kept in mind. The shape of the *syahi* is very important. The *syahi* will always be thicker in the centre than at the edge, but by how much? If the geometry is not correct, then many of the resonance modes will not converge in the proper way. The sound will be dissonant with different strokes evoking different pitches. This is unacceptable in Indian music which requires a clearly defined tonal base.

There is a simple rule of thumb that we need to keep in mind. The relationship between the second harmonic and the third harmonic should be as close to a perfect fifth as possible. The second harmonic should be a minor seventh above the fundamental. Strictly speaking, this makes it an enharmonic spectrum, but it is close enough for our purposes.

Applying the *syahi* is not a "fire and forget" process. As we progress in applying the *syahi* we must constantly adjust it. If we make the rim of the *syahi* thicker, it lowers the second and third harmonics more. If we make the centre lower, then it tends to have a greater effect on the fundamental. However this tends to work within a relatively narrow range of thickness of the *syahi*.

The Reticulum - When the *syahi* is all finished, there is one thing which one must notice. There is a reticulum of cracks which covers the entire *syahi* (fig. 6.54). This reticulum is probably one of the most important parts of the *syahi,* yet is one of the least appreciated or understood by the casual *tabla* player.

A cross section of the reticulum shows some interesting things (fig. 6.55). We see that these cracks extend all the way down to the skin.

This reticulum is an absolutely brilliant piece of design. The *syahi* covers a considerable area of skin; and the ingredients of the *syahi* harden to the consistency of cement. Such a hard material covering a substantial area of the skin should hamper the resonance. The cracks are the key to the *syahi* having flexibility, even though it is composed of such a rigid material. Because the particles merely articulate with each other, the overall *syahi* is flexible, even though the individual parts are inflexible.

This raises an obvious question; how did such a complex articulated structure arise from the numerous layers that were applied to the skin? The answer lies in the polishing. This is easily illustrated in figure 6.56. We start off with the *maidan* (fig. 6.56.a). To this, we apply a layer (fig 6.56.b). We then polish it while it is drying. (fig. 6.56.c). A reticulated surface has now been formed (fig. 6.56.d). We then apply another layer (fig. 6.56e). This too, is polished while the layer is drying (fig. 6.56.f). The small reticulum which was started in the first layer now becomes deeper as the latest layer also breaks up (fig. 6.56). The typical *syahi* is around 35 or 40 layers. As each layer is added, the reticulum becomes deeper and wider. This deepening and widening is readily apparent in the cross section shown in figure 6.55.

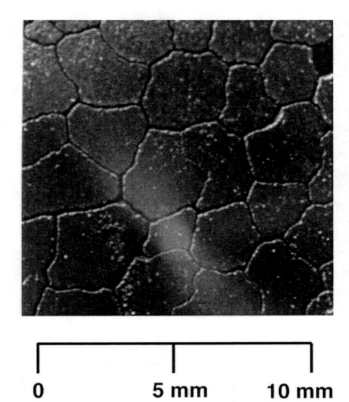

0   5 mm   10 mm

Figure 6.54. Reticulum

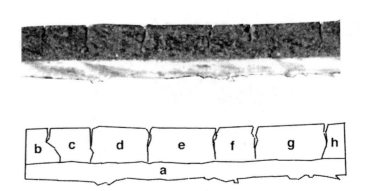

Figure 6.55. Reticulum (cross section)

page 97

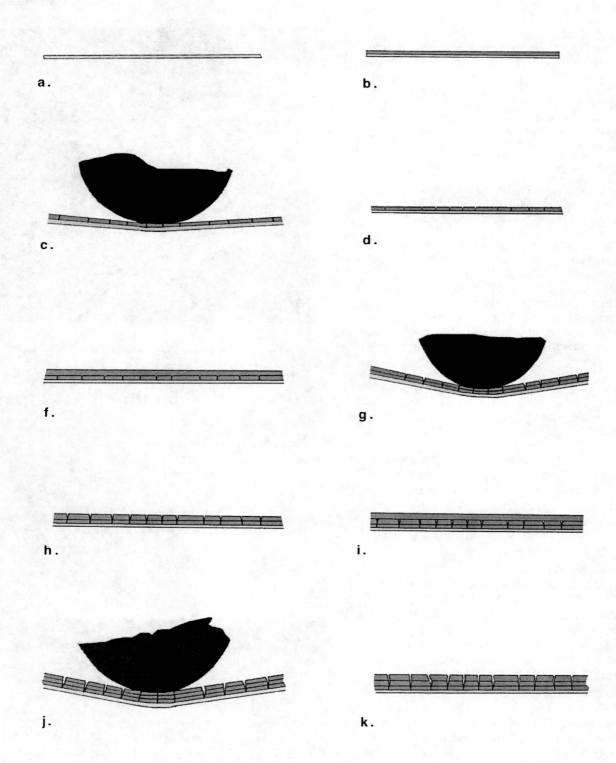

a.

b.

c.

d.

f.

g.

h.

i.

j.

k.

Figure 6.56. Creation of Reticulum

FINISHING TOUCHES

There are a number of finishing touches that need to be performed before the *tabla* is ready to leave the *tablawala*. These touches are in some cases merely aesthetic, but in other cases they do have a significant effect upon either the sound or the operation.

Trimming the Chat - The first of our finishing touches is to trim the *chat*. This must be done on both the *dayan* and the *bayan*. The instrument in its present form, is shown in figure 6.57. At present, the *chat* covers substantially more of the *maidan* than we wish. Trimming it back will open up the sound and make the sustain of the instrument greater. It will also make the sound much brighter.

Large amounts of *chat* were intentionally left intact; this was not an oversight. The process of applying the *syahi*, with its constant rubbing with the stone, takes a great toll on the edge of the *chat*. By leaving a little extra, this damaged skin may simply be cut away.

It will be trimmed to a width of approximately ¹/₂ to ³/₄ of an inch in width. The *maidan* is protected from the blade by the bamboo *badda* in the same way that was done for trimming the *bharti* (fig. 6.58).

Final Tightening and Tuning of the Dayan - It is at this point that the *tabla* usually needs some retightening and retuning. It became loose and out of tune for several reasons.

One of the main reasons that it became loose was from the simple process of equilibration. When the skins and lacing were put on, it took a while before the various forces in the skin and wood reach an equilibrium. During this time the skin relaxes as it gets set into place. This is very much like breaking in a pair of new shoes. This process of equilibration was sped up by the constant polishing with the stone.

Figure 6.57. Unfinished Tabla

Figure 6.58. Trimming the Chat

page 99

This basic principle behind retightening is simple, although the practice is difficult. Conceptually, it is just a process of taking up the slack in the lacing. In practice, it takes a bit of practice to do the job well. The reason for the practical difficulty is that the slack must be taken up in an even manner.

The technique for taking up the slack is illustrated in figure 6.59. In this illustration, we see that we must first identify the beginning of the lacing; this will be the knot as shown in figure 6.59.a. We then grab this length of *tasma* and pull it tight with our left hand (fig 6.59.b). Next we go over and grab the next length with our right hand. Pull both straps tight (fig 6.59.c). We then increase the tension with our right hand while reducing the tension with the left hand. This should cause some of the *tasma* to slip through the *gajara* from the left side over to the right side. We may now remove the left hand (fig. 6.59.d). We now shift the *tasma* from our right hand to the free left hand, without reducing the tension (fig. 6.59.e). Again we move over and grab the next length of *tasma* with our right hand and continue the process throughout the rest of the *tabla* (fig. 6.59.f).

There are several points to keep in mind while retightening the drum. These points are concerned with the manner of lacing and the tension. Let us now look at these in greater detail.

The first point to keep in mind is that the straps must be tight. This is much tighter and much harder physical work than the novice generally expects. In order to make sure that it is very tight without having to work too hard, it is very helpful to use the feet to hold the drum in place. This is shown in figure 6.60.

Another point to keep in mind is that the tension must be uniform. This is where experience is really important. Two areas that are especially problematic are the start and the end of the *tasma*. These are both indicated by the knots. You should make the areas around the knots as tight as possible.

The third point to keep in mind is that *Bengali tablas* are laced backwards. Therefore, they will be tightened backwards.

The final point to keep in mind is to be careful when dealing with substandard lacing. Leather, old lacing, and thin *Bengali* style lacing are especially problematic. Such lacing often breaks while being worked. Should it break, then a repair is discussed in Chapter 8.

Insert Gatta - There is no particular time that the *gatta* will be placed in the *tabla*. They may be added at any time that it is felt that the lacing is getting too loose. However, with experienced craftsmen, it is quite likely that now will be the first time. If it was inserted earlier, then now should be the last and final time.

It is first necessary to orient ourselves to the lacings of the drum. We must not forget that the lacing is inserted between the *gajara* and the *chat* 16 times. Therefore, these 16 insertions will be reflected in 32 spans of *tasma* (16 lengths going into and 16 lengths coming out of the *gajara*) .

Placing the *gatta* in the lacing is conceptually simple, although it does require considerable strength in the fingers. One takes a descending section of *tasma* and brings it over the *gatta* (fig. 6.61). One skips the next three lengths but again places it under the fourth length. Another way to think about it is to place the *gatta* under every alternate descending span. If everything was done correctly, the drum should be tight enough.

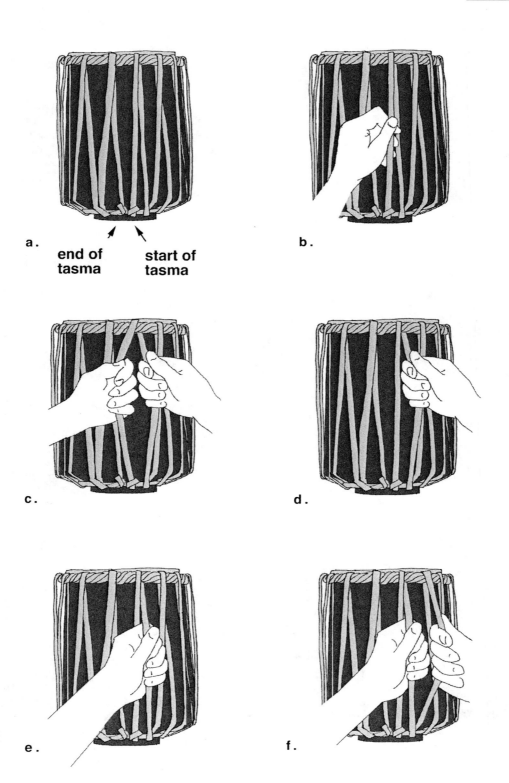

a. end of tasma   start of tasma

b.

c.

d.

e.

f.

Figure 6.59. Tightening the Tasma

Figure 6.60. Using the Feet - Use feet to help tightening the tasma.

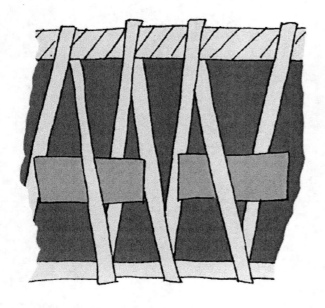

Figure 6.61. Use Alternate, Descending Straps for Gatta

<u>Final Tightening of the Bayan</u> - The process of applying the *syahi*, coupled with the natural process of the skin adjusting to the metal shell causes the *bayan* to become loose. During the process of working with the *bayan*, it may become necessary to tighten it up by the addition of *gattas*. However, the presence of *gattas* on the *bayans* is usually considered a sign of sloppy workmanship, so no *tablawala* wants the instruments to go out in this way (I have never understood this myself; this just causes added inconvenience to the end user who must put in their own *gatta* a few months later). Therefore, it is necessary to retighten the *bayan* before shipping.

The final tightening of the *bayan* is almost the same as the retightening of the *dayan*. There are only minor differences.

One starts the retightening by first wetting much of the exposed portion of the *maidan*. It is very important to keep the *syahi* and its surrounding area very dry so as not to damage the drum. One then tightens the drum in exactly the same fashion as described in figure 6.59.

The *bayan* is then allowed to dry in the sun. When it is dry, then the job is done. There are no *gatta* to be inserted into the *bayan*.

<u>Saf Karna</u> - The expression *saf karna* literally means "to cleanse". This is nearly the final step of the process of making the *tabla*, and is purely cosmetic.

For this, one takes a small piece of fine sandpaper. Its grade should be about 150-220. Then one lightly sands the *maidan* and *chat*. This cleaning action is further enhanced by periodically rubbing the sanded surface with plain white chalk. Attention should also be paid to the edge of the *syahi* to make sure that there is no overflow of *syahi* to the *maidan*. I have even seen workers use a rough wet cloth to remove excess. NOTE - THIS IS POTENTIALLY DANGEROUS TO THE INSTRUMENT AND SHOULD NOT BE ATTEMPTED UNLESS YOU ARE VERY SKILLED! If a wet cloth is in contact long enough for the skin to be moist, the water will wick into the area under the *syahi* and cause permanent damage!

Sometimes whitewash is used instead of simple chalk. Whitewash produces a brighter white skin, but it obviously means that a drying step has been added to the process of making *tablas*.

This *saf karna* is done for many reasons. The main reason is to make the *tabla* more marketable. This is very much like the "new car" scent which is sprayed on the inside of every car in a dealership. Unfortunately, this procedure may also be used to obscure flaws in the skin or nicks caused by poor workmanship. Therefore when purchasing a new *tabla,* be sure and look beyond the superficial cleaning.

OPTIONAL STEPS
There are several optional steps in the manufacture of *tabla*. These steps are usually dispensed with, but still it is good to know of their existence.

<u>Inserting the String</u> - This is the totally optional step of placing string between the *chat* and the *maidan*. This step is indicative of changes in people's expectation of what a *tabla dayan* should sound like. Over the last 200 years the *dayan* has been getting steadily smaller in size and brighter in tone. One of the ways to produce this brighter tone is to trim the *chat* back. However, trimming the *chat* is an irreversible procedure. The insertion of string between the *chat* and the *maidan* slightly lifts the *chat* away from the *maidan*, thus reducing the dampening action. This results is a brighter sound and a better sustain. The beauty is that different tones may be produced by using different types of string placed at different depths. Since there is no permanent modification to the *tabla dayan,* it is very amenable to experimentation.

Here is the procedure for inserting the string(fig. 6.62).

1. Mentally find a portion of the *pudi* that you can use as an index(fig 6.62.a). You will need to know when you have made a complete revolution so some mark is necessary to keep yourself oriented. Usually there is some spot or imperfection on the skin that may be used as an index, but if necessary, make a small mark with a pen or pencil.

2. Place the coin between the *maidan* and the *chat* until it extends to the desired depth (fig. 6.62.b). Midway across the lip of the *lakadi* is an average position.

3. Place the end of the string into the opening (fig 6.62.c).

4. Roll the coin around until a full revolution has been made (fig. 6.62d-f)

5. Cut the string (fig 6.63.a-6.63.b).

6. Roll the end into position (fig. 6.63.c).

7. Remove the coin.

The string is now inserted and the drum should now have a brighter sound.

<u>Tuning</u> - The *dayan* must now be tuned. This will be discussed in greater detail in Chapter 7.

<u>Mounting the Handle</u> - Occasionally the *bayan* has a small rawhide handle. This is a nice addition but one that is not common. This is shown in figure 6.64.

We see in figure 6.64 that this handle is nothing more than a short length of *tasma*. This *tasma* extends from the *gajara* to the *kundal*. It is loose enough so that it presents a readily accessible strap to grab. It is mounted at the *gajara* side with a simple knot (fig. 6.65) and it is mounted at the *kundal* side with a knot very much reminiscent of the knot used to anchor the *tasma*. This is a very simple addition which does not really need any elaboration.

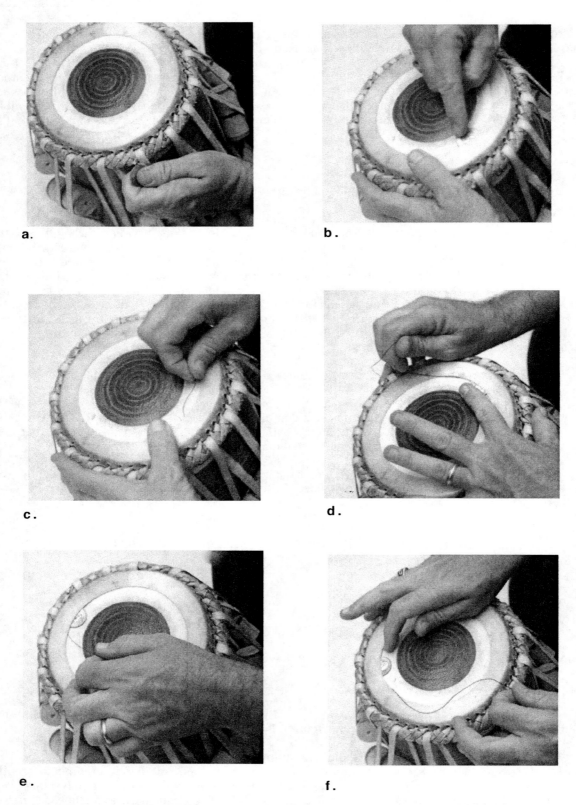

Figure 6.62. Inserting Thread - a. find identifying mark b. insert coin to desired depth c. insert string d-f. roll coin around edge

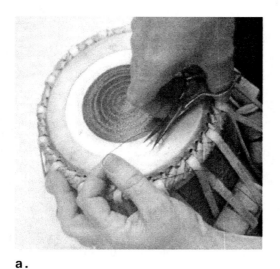

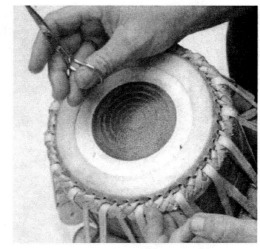

a.

b.

c.

Figure 6.63 Inserting thread (cont.) - a-b. cut string c. push remaining string under chat

CHEATS AND DECEPTIONS

There are a number of activities that are clearly fraudulent. In the years that I was studying under the *tablawalas* in Hyderabad, a number of practices came to my attention. These are not practices that are acceptable. I am discussing them here because the only way that people can guard against them is to know of their existence.

The first step to avoiding such practices is to know what motivates it. In a nutshell, anything that will make the *tablawalas* mad, may cause this. The most common reason is excessive or aggressive haggling over the price.

Reusing old Syahi - One extremely bad practice is to take the old *syahi* from drums, grind them into a powder and reuse them. The overall result of this practice is a *syahi* that has considerably lower density than one that is made with virgin *syahi massala*.

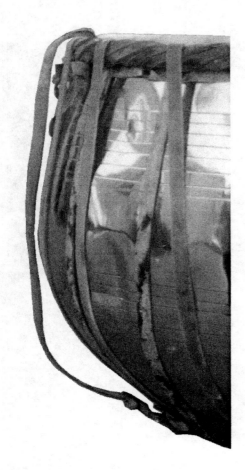

Figure 6.64. The Handle

Figure 6.65. Knot for Handle

This *syahi* may be recognised by a characteristic colour and texture. Virgin *syahi* is a jet black colour; reused *syahi* is greyer with a slightly mottled quality. Virgin *syahi* will polish to a shine, like polished obsidian; reused *syahi* will not have the characteristic lustre.

<u>Bad</u> <u>Wood</u> - *Tablawalas* are supposed to exercise a great degree of quality control when selecting wood. On occasion, I have seen them use wood that was totally split in two, roughly patched and painted and used to make *tabla dayans*. When such substandard woods are also skinned with equally substandard *pudis* and lacing, they may be used as inexpensive, student grade *tablas*.

If these substandard *tablas* are kept within the Indian market it is not really a deception. A professional quality *tabla* in India costs the average of one months salary for a working class Indian. There obviously needs to be some option for the Indian student of limited means.

Unfortunately these *tablas* sometimes find their way into the international market. We must not forget that when a *tabla* is purchased in the UK, Canada, US, or elsewhere in the world market, the actual cost of the instrument is virtually nil. The cost of the *tabla* in the world markets is basically one of shipping, insurance, and other overhead that is part of the complex distribution chain. Therefore, dealing in these substandard instruments does not produce an appreciable savings for the businesses involved, but seriously hurts the final consumer.

The only way that buyers, retailers and consumers can protect themselves is by education. If there are knowledgeable people at every stage of the chain, then these substandard instruments may be intercepted and removed from the distribution network before students are inconvenienced and distributor's reputations become tarnished.

<u>New</u> <u>Maidans</u> <u>with</u> <u>Old</u> <u>Gajaras</u> - This is a rather involved trick. It works only on the *bayans*. For this, one takes the original *pudi*, removes the *maidan*, crudely stitches a new skin in it, and then applies a new *syahi*.

This deception is very easy to detect when the head is removed but very difficult to detect on a finished instrument. The only way is to look very carefully at the underside of the *gajara* and look for a rawhide stitching. This will be noticeable because it is stitched and not woven into the *gajara*.

There are several problems with this deception. The major one is that the skins stretch much faster than a well made *bayan pudi*. They will also break much faster.

CONCLUSION

This chapter described in detail the steps in the manufacture of *tabla*. We have taken every step from the cutting of the hides to the weaving of the *pudis* and the lacing of the drums. We have made every effort to give as many regional variations as possible. However, I am sure that there are many that were missed. India is a very big country and it is not possible to go and check every *tablawala*.

This material is still useful to know. The simple fact that you bought this book means that there is some reason for you to know the material. Perhaps you are a buyer for a music firm. Perhaps you are a musical instrument maker. Perhaps you are simply just a *tabla* player who wishes to learn more about the instrument. Whatever the reason for your purchasing this book, you will probably find that this chapter has the important information you need.

WORKS CITED

Courtney, D.R
1980   *Introduction to Tabla*. Hyderabad, India: Anand Power Press.
1985   "Tabla Making in the Deccan". *Percussive Notes*. Vol 23 No 2: pp 33-34. Urbana: Percussive Arts Society.
1988   "The Tabla Puddi". *Experimental Musical Instruments*. Vol 4 No 4: pp 12-16. Nicasio: EMI.
1993   "Repair and Maintenance of Tabla", *Percussive Notes,* Lawton OK: October 1993; Vol.31, No 7: pp 29-36.

Fallon, S.W.
1879   A New Hindustani - English Dictionary. Banaras, E. J. Lazarus & Co.

Kapoor, R.K.
no-date   Kamal's Advanced Illustrated Oxford Dictionary: Hindi-English. Delhi, Verma Book Depot.

CHAPTER 7

TUNING THE TABLA

INTRODUCTION

Tuning is the process of taking the *tabla* and setting it to the desired tension. In theory, tightening the drum and applying the *syahi* are all just as much a part of the tuning process as the actual hitting with the hammer. However, for the purpose of this chapter, we will exclude all affairs that come under the topic of maintenance or manufacture and simply confine ourselves to the process of the day-to-day tuning. The manufacturing issues were already taken up in Chapter 6 and the maintenance issues will be discussed in Chapter 8.

We may say that tuning is second only to playing in terms of our normal interaction with the *tabla*. It is so basic that the presumption is that the musician will handle it all. The process of tuning requires a considerable amount of skill to relate the sound of the drum to the tension of the head (Courtney 1991).

Tuning really means two different things. It means one thing when dealing with the *bayan* and a totally different thing when dealing with the *dayan*. For the *bayan,* it means setting the tension so that the skin is tight enough to produce a good, strong sound, yet not so tight that it resists our efforts to bend the pitch as we introduce the various modulations. However, tuning the *dayan* is a process that entails identifying ones musical requirements and adjusting the pitch of the head to produce a precise musical tone.

General Issues of Tuning - There are a few main concepts that we need to be comfortable with before we can easily tune the *tabla*. These may easily be grasped by visualising the drum as being somewhat similar to the model that is illustrated in figure 7.1. In this simple model the tension on spring #1 is analogous to the tension being exerted by the *tasma* (lacing). Spring #2 represents the tension on the head, specifically the *maidan*. There is a friction block between them which is resting on a rough surface. This represents the complex arrangement of the *gajara* and *bharti* as it rests against the shell. If none of our parts are in motion, then obviously the various forces are all balanced.

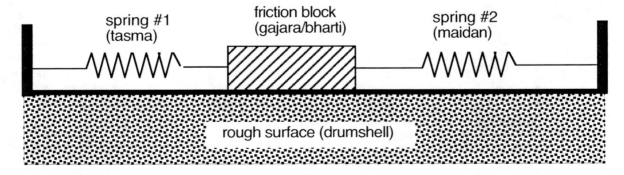

Figure 7.1. Simple Model for Tuning

Let us see what happens as we increase the tension on the *tasma* (spring #1). Let us presume that this model starts out with the tension on the *tasma* (spring #1) being equal to the tension on the *maidan* (spring #2). Let us also presume that the increase in tension was not enough to overcome the force of friction. In such a situation nothing will happen to our system. The block remains in the same position yet both springs are exerting different tensions.

Let us also presume that we continue to increase the tension. Initially nothing may happen, but at some point, the difference between the two tensions will be sufficient to overcome the force of friction, at which point the block will move to some point where the various forces balance out. We may still have the *tasma* (spring #1) with more tension than the *maidan* (spring #2) but the tension on the *maidan* will have increased.

Let us now take this system and reduce the tension on the *tasma* (spring #1) and see what happens. If it is merely a moderate decrease in tension then nothing will happen. Again the forces of friction are moderating the whole system to keep anything from happening. Even when we reduce the tension to balance the two, nothing still happens. It turns out that we have to create a substantial imbalance in the opposite direction before we can again overcome the forces of friction.

A graph of this situation is shown in figure 7.2. It is immediately clear that there is an extremely nonlinear relationship between the tension on the *tasma* and the tension on the *maidan*. This type of nonlinear relationship is known as a hysteresis. We commonly encounter hysteresis in day-to-day life. Imagine the experience of trying to drive a car that has an excessive amount of play in the steering wheel; this can be fatal. Many dead bolts on doors require you to turn past the central position in one direction to open and then again turn past the central position in the other direction to lock. Other less familiar examples of hysteresis are seen in the way that magnetic signals are encoded in cassettes and within computer disks.

At first impression, this large amount of hysteresis is bad. Intuition tells us that this would render the drum untunable. However, over the years Indian drums have been engineered to maximise this hysteresis, and not to try and reduce it. Here is the reason why.

Let us go back to our original model shown in figure 7.1. Now let us not think in terms of changing the tension on the *tasma* (spring #1) as a means to change the tension on the *maidan* (spring #2). Let us just simply strike the block so that it pushes it toward the left. It is immediately apparent that there will be a slight decrease in the tension on the *tasma* (spring #1) but there will be a slight increase in the tension on the head (spring #2). Conversely, striking the block to the right has the opposite effect.

This is exactly what happens when we tune the *dayan*. We strike the *gajara* from the underside to decrease the tension on the *maidan* (fig 7.3). Conversely, we strike from the top to increase the tension on the *maidan* (fig 7.4).

Therefore, this large amount of hysteresis has been converted from a liability to an asset. The large area of nonlinearity

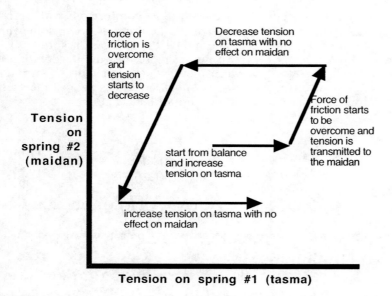

Figure 7.2. Hysteresis

described in the graph on figure 7.2 has been converted from a range of indeterminacy into a range of usable tuning. It is therefore good engineering to maximise the friction to keep the tuning range as wide as possible.

These are the general principles that are to be kept in mind. These principles will be in existence to some degree for both the *dayan* and the *bayan*. Let us now look at the issues which are specific to each drum.

TUNING THE BAYAN

Let us begin our discussion of tuning the *bayan* by looking at some simple issues. As stated earlier, the *bayan* should be tight enough so that it produces a good clear sound, but it needs to be loose enough so that the drum responds to the modulations. As a general rule, if you can press the skin in the centre and it displaces $\frac{1}{2}$ - 1 inch without you having to work too hard, then it is a decent tension.

The *bayan* may be tuned to a certain degree by hitting the *gajara* with the hammer. This was already described so we need not go into detail. However, the constant modulations of our left hand tend to keep the *bayan* continuously at the low end of our hysteresis. Therefore, establishing the low end of the hysteresis will have the practical effect of determining the tension on the head. This naturally must be done by hitting the *gatta*.

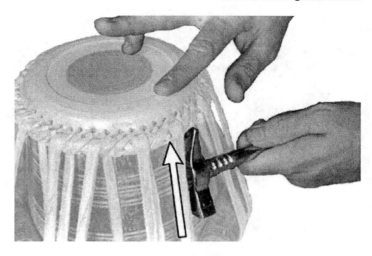

Figure 7.3. Tune Down - Strike from underside to loosen the tension

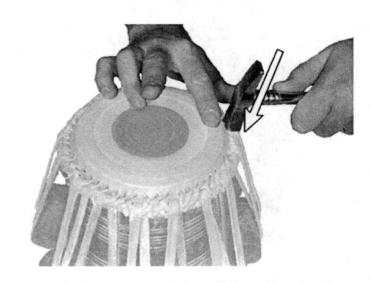

Figure 7.4. Tune Up - Strike from top to tighten

There is just one problem; *bayans* are not sold with *gatta*. Therefore, you will have to make your own.

Virtually anything may be used to make the *gatta* for the *bayan*. In India one common item is the toy dumbbell (fig. 8.5). These are traditionally given to infants when they are teething. Another thing that is commonly used are wooden *"pattis"*. These are long wooden strips used to mount electrical wires. Ordinary wooden sticks work quite well. In the West, wooden dowels are readily available which work very well. Three-quarters of an inch is a comfortable diameter.

Tuning the *bayan* is simple. If the *bayan* is loose, then insert a few *gatta* between the shell and the *tasma* (fig. 7.6). If the *gatta* are already in place, then simply move them up or down to adjust the tension. Move them down to tighten them, or move them up to loosen them. If this still does not take care of the tension, then bring more *tasma* over the *gatta*. If all four *tasma* are over the

Figure 7.5. Teething Dumbbell (actual size)

Figure 7.6. Gatta for Bayan

gatta and it still is not tight, then follow the directions for tightening the drum. This will be discussed in Chapter 8.

These are really all of the issues that we have to deal with for the *bayan*. Let us now look at the *dayan*

TUNING THE DAYAN

The *dayan* has the most stringent requirements for pitch. The *dayan* must be tuned to notes that are musically significant. Before we discuss the technique, it is appropriate that we say a few words about the musical pitch of the *dayan*.

We have made numerous references to tuning the *tabla* in this book. The presumption was that you already know how to tune the drums. However, even many moderately good musicians never really learn how to tune their *dayan* correctly. Therefore, it is appropriate that we spend some time discussing what is happening. Specifically we need to look at what is going on in an untuned *dayan*. This discussion will concentrate on what is happening at the psychoacoustic level.

The Pitch of the Dayan - We discussed at great length the psychoacoustics of a well tuned *tabla* in *Advanced Theory of Tabla*. We should now discuss the psychoacoustics of an untuned *tabla*. Still, a small amount of review of the material in Volume 2 of this series is in order.

The pitch of the *tabla dayan* relies upon the brain's pattern recognition powers. The pitch of the *dayan* is not determined by the fundamental, but by an implied fundamental. The brain takes the pitch of the overtones, most notably the second and third harmonics, and uses these values to extrapolate downward to an imaginary fundamental. It is the pitch of this imaginary fundamental which corresponds to the pitch of the *dayan*.

The various strokes are defined by the proportions of their harmonics. We must not forget that all of the harmonics of the *dayan* are found in all of the pitched strokes; what is different is the proportion and duration of these component frequencies.

There are three important pitched strokes: *Tun*, *Na*, and *Tin*. Let us review these strokes.

Tun is problematic because it is produced by the lowest note of the *tabla*. This is the "real" fundamental of the drum. It causes a problem because it resonates at a pitch which is generally one step above the note that the *dayan* is tuned to. This may be musically very awkward. It is for this reason that it is not used as often as the other pitched strokes.

Tin is a stroke which is characterised by a heavy emphasis of the second harmonic. Conveniently enough, the frequency of this harmonic corresponds to the musical pitch of the *tabla,* but at an octave higher than what the drum is tuned to. Although the second harmonic is not always the loudest, it has one of the longest sustains. From a musical standpoint, *Tin* is one of the most important strokes for providing a musical base. In normal practice the *Tin* provides an unobtrusive drone-like quality to the performance.

Na is a stroke which is defined by a sharp loud expression of the overtones. In modern *tablas*, they are generally expressed by a strong third harmonic. However, in the old days when the *dayans* where much larger than they are today, they showed a strong expression of the fourth and even the fifth harmonics. (Since these large *tablas* are not so common, for the rest of this chapter we will consider *Na* to be defined by a strong expression of the third harmonic.)

So here is the situation in a nutshell; when the brain is listening to the sound of the *tabla* it hears the second harmonic, compares this to the third harmonic, and extrapolates downward to perceive the pitch at the point where the imaginary fundamental resides.

We have briefly reviewed the way that musical pitch is perceived in the *dayan.* Now we need to take this knowledge and apply it to an untuned *tabla.*

Harmonics of the Untuned Dayan - Let us now look closer at the psychoacoustic phenomena that occurs in the untuned *dayan.* This phenomena provides the key for the correct tuning of the *dayan.* It also provides insight into why so many people find this a difficult job.

We see that the untuned *tabla* may be viewed as shown in figure 7.7. The pattern of pitches forms a cross. In this cross, there is a point of high pitch, opposed by another point with an equally high pitch. At 90 degrees from this, is a point of low pitch which is opposed by a point with an equally low pitch. Between these points are sections where the pitch is extremely poorly defined. This is not new. We have been acquainted with this right from Chapter 2 of *Fundamentals of Tabla.* But let us proceed further to see what is going on.

A spectrogram of an untuned *dayan* is shown in figure 7.8. This *dayan* is roughly tuned to A#. In this spectrogram we see the real fundamental, the second harmonic and the third harmonic. It is instantly recognisable that something very unusual has happened to the third harmonic. It has bifurcated into two discrete spectral lines.

This bifurcation of the third harmonic is the key to the inability of many musicians to be able to tune their *tablas* correctly. The psychoacoustic process of comparing the second to the third harmonic to derive the pitch is confounded by the existence of two closely spaced spectral lines in the position of the third harmonic. Experienced musicians are able to hear this as two separate pitches, but most inexperienced musicians are simply confused by this situation.

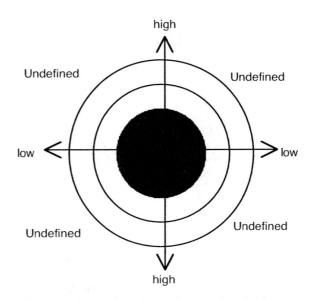

Figure 7.7. Tension Cross for Tabla

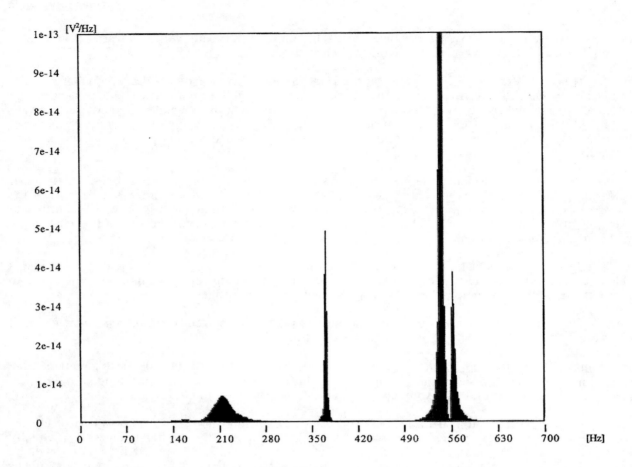

Figure 7.8. Spectrogram of Untuned Tabla-Dayan

Let us see how the spectrum changes as we move around the rim. It is obvious that since the sound of the *tabla* changes, then the spectra should also be different. Figure 7.9 illustrates what is happening.

It is interesting to note that the two components of our bifurcated third harmonic seesaw back and forth as we move around the rim. When we are at a point where the pitch is high, then the upper component is prominent. As we move around, the amplitude of this upper component decreases and the lower component starts to increase. The pitch becomes undefined when both components are present in comparable degrees. As we continue to move to a point of low pitch, then it is the lower component which is prominent and the upper component is deficient. This seesaw motion continues until we return to our starting point.

We have looked at this phenomenon from the standpoint of the frequency domain. We must not forget that what is happening in the frequency domain is a reflection of what is happening in the time domain. Let us now look more closely at this.

Untuned Dayan (Time Domain) - The time domain gives us another way to look at an untuned *dayan*. Our time domain phenomena is most easily heard in the beating of the two portions of the third harmonic. The phenomenon of beating is a basic phenomenon that we all learned in high school. However, if you are like most people, this whole period has been erased from your mind by the years. Therefore, a little review is in order.

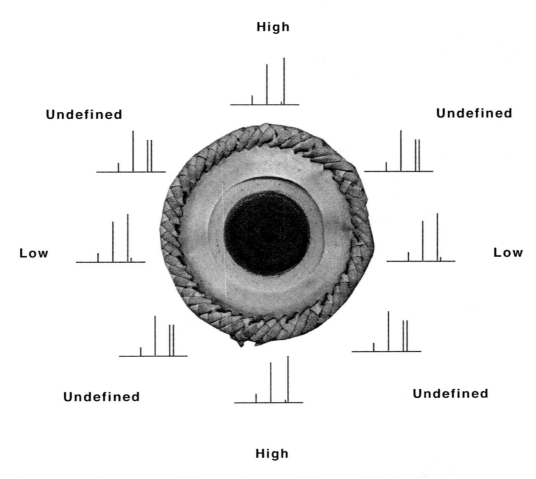

Figure 7.9. Spectra at Different Parts of Untuned Tabla-Dayan

The simplest sound is a sine wave. This is shown in figure 7.10. We can mix sine waves, however, the outcome of this mixing depends upon how the two sine waves relate to each other. Figure 7.11 shows the outcome of mixing two sine waves that are moving in unison. When one wave is moving up, the other wave is also moving up; when one wave is moving down, the other wave is also moving down. When two waves are acting in unison, they are said to be "in-phase". When we mix two waves that are in-phase, they add together producing a wave which has the strength that is equal to the sum of the two components.

There is a different situation when we mix sine waves that are not acting in unison; one case is when the motion is exactly the opposite. In figure 8.12 we see such an example. When one wave is rising, the other is falling; conversely when one wave is falling, the other is rising. These two waves are said to be out-of-phase, specifically they are said to be 180 degrees out of phase. In this case the phase is exactly the opposite, and the amplitudes are the same, so they exactly cancel each other. This yields the flat line illustrated below. Many times the phase is not exactly opposite (180°), yet not exactly in phase (0°). In such situations the phase will be described in terms of degrees. However, a further discussion of this is beyond the scope of this book.

There is one situation which is very important to this chapter; what happens when the frequencies are not exactly the same? This is illustrated in figure 7.13. In this case, we find that sometimes the crests and troughs come into phase; this will have an additive effect. At other times they move out of phase; this will have a subtractive effect. This continuous alternation between additive and subtractive effects produces a beating action.

The rate at which the beats occur is indicative of the differences in the two frequencies. As the frequencies of the two sine waves becomes closer, the rate of beating slows down. As the frequencies become further apart, the beating action speeds up.

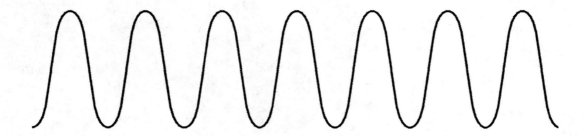

Figure 7.10. Sine Wave

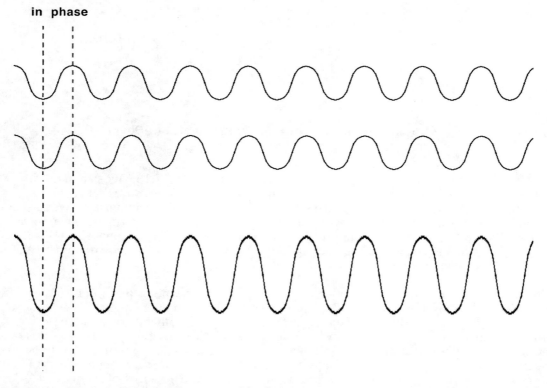

Figure 7.11. Mixing Sine Waves #1 - Mixing sine waves that have the same phase will increase the amplitude.

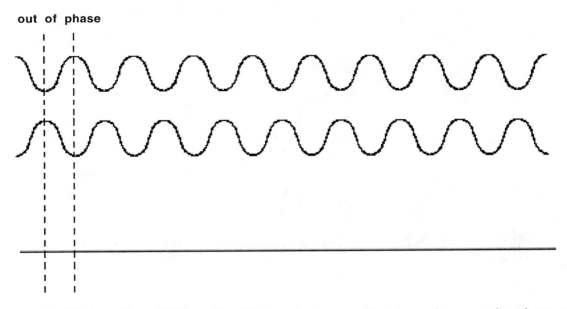

Figure 7.12. Mixing Sine Waves #2 - Mixing sine waves that have the opposite phase will decrease the amplitude.

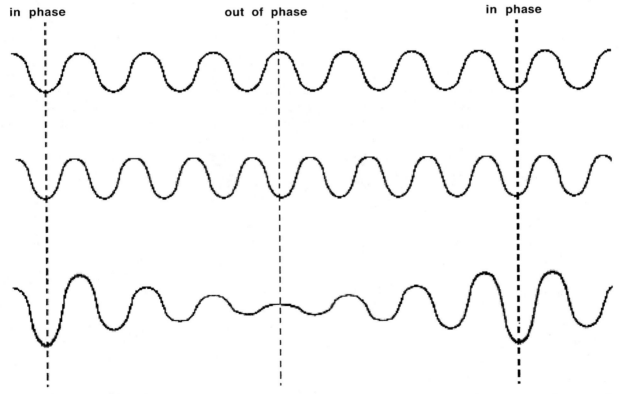

Figure 7.13. Mixing Sine Waves #3 - Beats are produced when two sine waves of unequal frequencies are mixed together.

This phenomenon is not simply confined to sine waves in the laboratory; it is clearly displayed in the untuned *dayan*. The two portions of the bifurcated third harmonic interact with each other to produce this same beating action. This is shown in figure 7.14. In this illustration, we see a beating action that results from the interaction of the two components of the third harmonic. This beating action is most easily heard when playing on the undefined portions of the rim of the *dayan*.

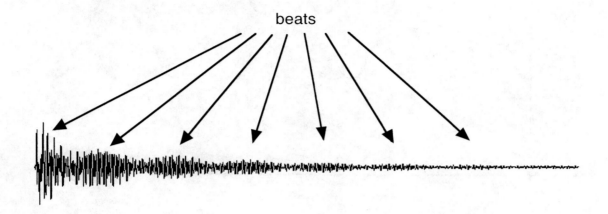

Figure 7.14. Beats in the Sound of Tabla

This section illustrated how certain phenomena in the untuned *dayan* manifests itself in the time domain. Specifically we saw how the two closely spaced frequencies that make up the third harmonic start beating as they interact with each other. Furthermore the rate of beating is an indication of how closely the *dayan* is coming into tune. The rate goes down as the *dayan* begins to come into tune, while the rate goes up as the *dayan* gets more out of tune. This beating action is very useful in learning to tune the instrument.

RANGE OF TUNINGS

The *tabla-dayan* is certainly not indefinitely tuneable. Normally a *dayan* really sounds good at only one pitch, but it is functional over about a two step range. If you attempt to go higher than what your drum is designed for, you may split your *pudi*, thus necessitating expensive repairs. Conversely, if you attempt to tune your drum too low, it will sound dull and lifeless.

Many of you reading this wish to have some more concrete information. Table 7.15 shows a rough breakdown of the tuning range of *dayans* as a function of the size of the head. THIS IS A ROUGH GUIDE ONLY! Your particular *tabla* may be higher or lower depending upon such factors as the thickness of the skin and the thickness of the *syahi*.

There is however one piece of information that we may glean from this chart. It is clear that the usable range is far wider for the large *dayans* than for the smaller *dayans*.

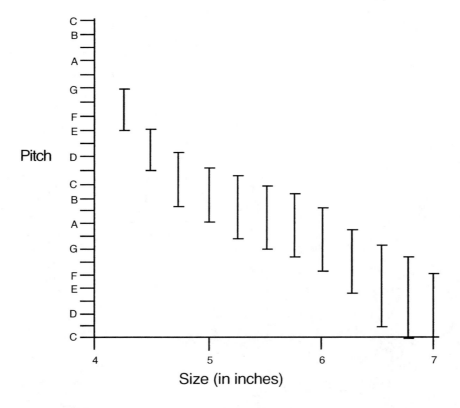

Figure 8.15. Approximate Range of Tunings

CONCLUSION

This chapter has gone into great detail concerning the tuning of both drums of the *tabla*. However, this material must be seen as merely a supplement to the more visceral "feel" for the instrument. Just as it will never be possible to teach someone how to drive a car, or walk or any similar day-to-day activity, in the same way this chapter cannot teach anyone how to tune a *tabla*. However, this material will at least give us an appreciation for the process that otherwise we may not have.

WORKS CITED

Courtney, D.R
1991 "Tuning the Tabla: A Psychoacoustic Perspective". *Percussive Notes*. Vol 29 No 3: pp 59-61. Urbana: Percussive Arts Society.

CHAPTER 8

REPAIR OF TABLA

INTRODUCTION

The repair of *tabla* is a topic that strongly overlaps with the manufacture of *tabla*. However, it is convenient to have this as a separate chapter. In this chapter we will confine ourselves to techniques and approaches which are purely Indian. This is to satisfy readers who are interested in this topic from an ethnographic or an anthropological standpoint. References to Western approaches will be found only as a comparison. Purely Western approaches will be discussed in Chapter 9.

This chapter will be divided into two sections. The first section deals with common procedures. The second section describes common problems.

COMMON PROCEDURES.

There are a number of common procedures that one must be familiar with if one is going to repair *tablas*. These are retightening the *tasma*, unlacing the *tabla*, cleaning, patching broken parts, and replacing the *pudi*. We will look at these procedures in greater detail.

Unlacing a Tabla - It is often necessary to unlace a *tabla*. This procedure is necessary anytime that there is damage to the shell. It is also necessary anytime one must replace either the *tasma, pudi*, or *kundal*.

Unlacing the *tabla* is trivial. Still this does requires a certain degree of physical strength, especially in the fingers and hands. Otherwise, it is quite simple.

Here is the basic process for unlacing the *tabla*. One first removes the *gatta*; the *tabla* immediately becomes loose. One then unties the *tasma* at the place where it ends (fig. 8.1). Please note that for *Bengali tablas*, the start and end points are reversed (refer to Chapter 6). It is then unlaced by starting at the end and working backwards to the beginning. This unlacing is simply the reverse of what was illustrated in figure 6.59. When one reaches the end the drum will be entirely unlaced.

One should note that it is not always necessary to completely unlace the *tabla*. For instance, if one is merely wishing to work on the shell then one need only partially unlace the drum. This is usually enough to allow the shell to be removed without damaging the rawhide portions of the *tabla*.

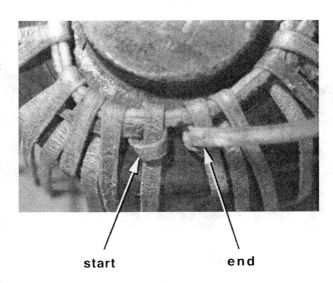

start   end

Figure 8.1. Start and End of Lacing

<u>Tightening the Lacing</u> - Loose *tasma* is one of the most common problems with the *tabla*. In normal use the heads and lacing will stretch; this is normally compensated for by hammering the *gatta* down. After a while the *gatta* may no longer be hammered down without them slipping. It is at this time that more straps are brought over the *gatta*. This will then bring the *tabla* to proper tension.

There will come a time when manipulating the *gatta* will no longer restore proper tension; we must then retighten the *tabla*. This is a major job and previous experience is helpful. In India, the drum is usually sent back to the *tablawala* for retightening. An experienced *tablawala* can retighten the *dayan* in about 15 minutes. This may be done while the client waits. However, retightening the *bayan* sometimes requires wetting the head and allowing it to dry. Therefore, the *bayan* may be left at the *tablawala* for the job to be done and picked up later.

The actual retightening of the lacing is conceptually very simple. One simply starts at the starting knot and tightens the *tasma*. Then one moves around as shown in figure 6.59 until one gets to the end. One then reties the knot.

Although retightening the *tabla* is conceptually simple, it is a very strenuous job. An average male can do it, all-be-it by working up a considerable sweat. However, if you do not think that you have the strength, then you probably should not try this job.

<u>Identifying and Gluing Loose Particles in the Syahi</u> - Occasionally one finds particles of *syahi* that have become detached. This causes a buzzing noise when the *tabla* is played.

The buzzing occurs when the normally attached particle breaks inside and is no longer joined to the *maidan*. Although the particle is detached from the skin, the internal geometry is such that the particle may not be able to fall out. Though it cannot fall out, there is usually enough space for it to rattle about, hence the buzzing noise.

It is often possible to fix a loose particle without resorting to major work. Unfortunately, one must find the particle first.

One way to locate the particle is to hold the drum upside down under a strong light, then strike it (strike the drum, not the light!). If the drum is struck in this position it is often possible to see the loose particle with the naked eye. A good particle is seen in figure 8.2.a while a detached particle is seen in figure 8.2.b. This is a very good approach because you can see exactly where the loose particle is. Unfortunately, it doesn't always work.

There is another way to help you find a loose particle, but one which only works on the *dayan*. Lightly strike the drum with a *"Tin"* stroke. Now slightly rotate the drum. Repeat the process. If one moves around the rim in this manner, it will be seen that in one rotation there will be heavy buzz, light buzz, heavy buzz, light buzz. Now pay very close attention to the last two fingers during

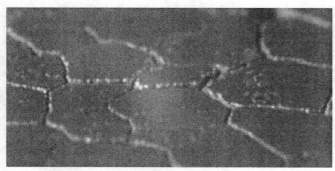

a.

b.

Figure 8.2. Detached Particles - a) normal b) detached

this process. These two points where there is minimal buzz describes a line which bisects the *tabla*. The loose particle will be somewhere on this line. A minimal buzz occurs when the particle lies on the vibrational node.

In practice, both of these techniques may be used together to isolate the particle. One may use the vibrational node technique to get a rough idea then one may visually inspect to localise the particle.

When the loose particle is found, one simply has to place a tiny drop of white glue (or super glue in the US) to bind it to an adjacent particle. The buzz often disappears.

Cleaning the Pudi - It is frequently necessary to clean the *pudi*. Over time dirt, excess powder, and oils from the skin combine to coat the *tabla*, sometimes to the extent that the sound is choked and unclear.

There is no single approach to cleaning the *pudi*. It all depends upon whether the cleaning is preventative maintenance or whether there is already major build-up to the point that the operation of the *tabla* has been impaired. Let us look into this in greater detail.

A simple preventative cleaning is the easiest to do. For this, one simply rubs the face of the *tabla* firmly with a clean dry cloth. This may be done weekly or monthly. It is surprising how much junk, especially caked on powder, comes off in these cleanings.

If the build-up is to the point where the sound is compromised, a much more aggressive approach is indicated. A simple cleaning with a dry cloth is able to remove the build-up on the *maidan*, however this build-up also works its way into the reticulum and under the *chat*. In order to clean the reticulum, it is necessary to re-polish the *syahi* with the stone. For this, one does not apply anything new. There are no chemicals and no new *syahi massala*. One simply takes the polishing stone and rubs the surface repeatedly. This is often able to work out some of the build-up so that it can be removed with a dry cloth.

Cleaning the build-up under the *chat* is much more difficult. Take the *badda* (bamboo blade), and gently work out whatever is under the *chat*. If the *tabla* has a string in it, it is good to remove it at this time. One can always put in a new one later. One then gently scrapes the inner surface between the *maidan* and the *chat*. It may also be helpful to lightly wrap the *badda* with fine cloth to facilitate this process.

The most extreme case of cleaning involves repeating the *"saf karna"* phase that was described in Chapter 6. This involves sanding with light sandpaper and chalk. This is obviously very rough on the *maidan* so, it is not a procedure which is to be done often.

Changing the Pudi - The head-change is probably the most drastic repair that a *tabla* is likely to see. The *pudi* represents more than half of the man-hours that goes into the *tabla*. One may also argue that about half the materials cost is also tied up in the *pudi*. Therefore, replacing the *pudi* is very close to starting with a new drum. Conceptually it is simple; one takes off the old *pudi* and puts on a new one. There are several stages to the process.

The first decision is whether to build another *pudi* around the shell, or to replace it with an existing *pudi*.

In India, about half the time one will go ahead and make a new *pudi* from scratch. This is probably the best from the standpoint of sound. Still it does have the disadvantage of being the longest process. If this is the desired approach, then we need not reiterate the process here; this has already been discussed in Chapter 6.

Very often one will decide to replace the *pudi* with one that has been made for a different shell. This is very often the case in India, and it is virtually always the case in the West.

Using a prefabricated *pudi* brings up an important issue. You are not fabricating it yourself, so you have to be able to evaluate the work of whoever did make it. Here are some points to be considered:

The skin should be smooth and even. This may be checked by holding the *pudi* up to the light to check for inconsistencies. If the skin has fragments of flesh dangling from it, then the skin was improperly cleaned. Look to see if there are any scars, for this will create problems. The *maidan* should be neither too thick, nor too thin. If it is too thin, then it will likely break prematurely. If the *maidan* is too thick, especially on the *dayan*, then the drum may have a choked sound. It is interesting to note that a heavy skin is quite acceptable for the *bayan*.

Be certain that the *pudi* has *bharti* (inner annular lining). A lack of *bharti* indicates shoddy workmanship and such a *pudi* should not even be considered. The style of *bharti* is usually not an issue.

The *syahi* should be rather thick with a reasonable contour (i.e., thicker in the centre and thinner towards the edges). It should also have a slight shine to it. It is especially important that it have a tight grain on the reticulum (the network of cracks) (figure 6.54).

The *gajara* is very important in determining the quality of the *pudi*. Here are several things to look for.

The main consideration is the number of penetrations. If one looks closely at the *gajara* one will see that it weaves the *bharti, maidan,* and *chat* all together. In order for this to happen there must be holes to allow the lacing to penetrate. It is this number of penetrations which affect how evenly the tension is going to be distributed. If the head is 5' or less, 32 penetrations is usual, otherwise the *dayan* uses 48 penetrations. For a *bayan*, 64 penetrations are the optimum. A lower number is an indication of shoddy workmanship. This was discussed in Chapter 6.

See that the weaving fully penetrates all three membranes (i.e., *chat, maidan, bharti*). Sometimes the weaving does not; this may be seen as missing segments of braid (fig. 8.3). Although an occasional miss does not positively mean that the *pudi* will sound bad, it is an indication of carelessness. Such carelessness may show up in other ways that one may not be able to see.

The *bunad* is sometimes an indicator for quality. *Bunad* is a light goatskin or Rexene which is cross woven into the heavier buffalo hide. Many areas of India do not use *bunad*, therefore the presence or absence is not necessarily significant. However, if a *pudi* without *bunad* comes from a shop or locale which normally uses them, then it is a hint that the *pudi* was rushed and may not be of the highest calibre.

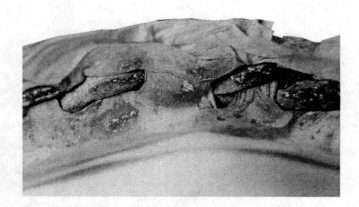

Figure 8.3. Incomplete Weaving of the Gajara

These are the basic points concerning the *gajara*. Let us move on to other factors.

The size is probably the most important consideration in selecting the *pudi*. The *bayan* has a broad tolerance, typically $\frac{1}{2}$ inch. In a pinch, one can oversize the *pudi* even more without affecting the sound. However the *dayan* has a tolerance of only $\frac{1}{4}$ inch at most. There must also be some room to work. It is easy to forget that the *tasma* takes up considerable space. A good rule of thumb is that if you place the *dayan pudi* on the shell you should be able to feel the wooden lip from the top side *(chat)* without having to press the *pudi* down. Additionally one should be able to slip the little finger in between the *bharti* and the shell yet still feel a snug fit. This usually gives the proper latitude in which to work.

The *pudi* must now be prepared. This is essentially a process of carefully wetting part of the *maidan* to make it supple thus allowing it to break in faster.

The procedure for wetting the *dayan pudi* is shown in figure 8.4. Take your finger and carefully moisten the *bharti* and part of the *maidan* with water. Be sensitive to where the *syahi* is. There must be no water under this area. Very little water will be used on the *dayan*. One may even leave it dry, although this will cause the *dayan* to take a little longer to break in.

The procedure for the *bayan* has only a few differences. There is a much greater area to be moistened, and it should be moistened to a greater degree of suppleness than for the *dayan*. The moistening is especially important for the *bayan pudi* so that when it dries, it will shrink and provide the necessary tension.

In both the *bayan* and the *dayan*, the moistening must be done with the greatest of care. Even a slight amount of water under the *syahi* will permanently damage the head. One should leave about one inch between the area where water is applied and the area where the *syahi* starts.

We begin lacing the *tabla* by first lashing the shell, *pudi*, and *kundal* together with a rope (fig. 8.5). Attach the new *tasma* to the *kundal*. The lacing must proceed around the drum so that the *tasma* passes over the *gajara*; through, and then over the *kundal*. This was shown earlier

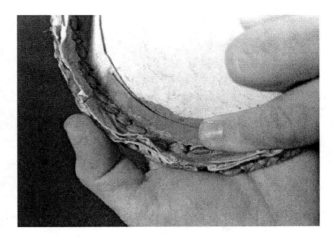

Figure 8.4. Moisten the Pudi Before Mounting

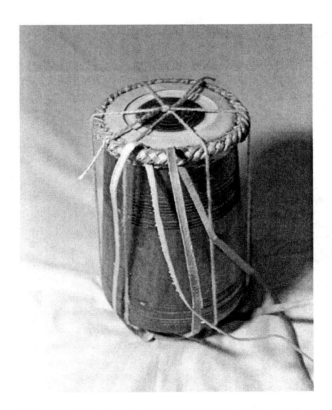

Figure 8.5. Lash the Pudi, Kundal, and Shell Together

page 125

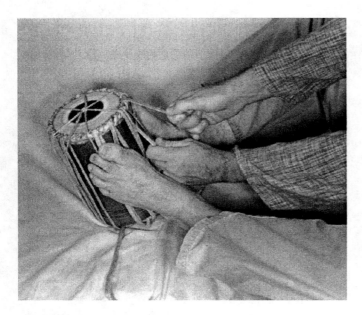

Figure 8.6. Use Feet to Get More Force

in figure 6.44. One should keep in mind that the *tasma* should not be pulled tight at this time. Wait until the lacing is finished then go back and gently take up the slack.

When the slack is taken up, remove the rope and continue tightening. This should continue slowly and evenly with the same considerations which were mentioned in the section dealing with retightening (e.g., keep the *pudi* straight, etc.). This requires a considerable amount of strength and it is helpful if we brace the *tabla* with our feet (figure 8.6). This allows both hands to do the strenuous job of tightening.

We must now tune the drum. This procedure was amply described earlier. However, we have an additional breaking-in step which is part of the tuning.

The "breaking in" requires a finely polished stone. One should rub the surface of the *pudi* with the stone. Initially the pressure is light, but as we rotate the drum the pressure should increase. This breaking in works by two methods. First, it allows the rawhide to settle onto the shell. Finally it acts upon the *syahi*. Humidity and disuse can cause the particles of the *syahi* to bind together. The polishing action of the stone separates the particles so that they no longer bind, thus restoring the *syahi* to its original flexibility.

There remains one final step: cleaning the drumhead. In the course of replacing the *pudi* it sometimes gets dark and dirty. Although this in no way affects the sound, it is good business to give an attractive product to the client. One merely has to use a fine grade sandpaper (approximately #200) and sand the *chat* and *maidan*. Optionally, one may work some chalk into the hide during this process. One other optional step is the insertion of string into the *pudi*.

This completes the process of reheading the drum. One will notice that we really did not go into great detail over the last few stages of the procedure in this chapter. This is because it is insubstantially different from the procedures described in Chapter 6. I strongly urge interested readers to review Chapter 6 in greater detail.

We have covered extensively the basic techniques of *tabla* repair. The basic procedures of tuning, tightening, and head replacement are the most common tasks which need to be performed. We will now discuss specific problems and their recommended repairs.

COMMON PROBLEMS

This section will deal with the problems that one will normally encounter in the repairing of *tablas*. These are the various breaks and damage that occurs with use.

Broken Kundal - This is a problem that is due to shoddy workmanship. There is no way that any *tabla* should suffer a broken *kundal* under normal use. Unfortunately, I have seen this problem too many times. In most cases it was poorly made *tablas* from either Bengal (India) or Bangladesh. This entire region is known for the poor quality of rawhide in the *tablas*. A broken *kundal* is shown in figure 8.7.

There is only one course of action for a broken *kundal*; the entire *tabla* must be unlaced, a new *kundal* must be fashioned and the *tabla* relaced. If one has to do this, I recommend making a small reference mark on the *pudi* and drum so that the head may be reassembled in the same position. There are fewer problems if the head goes back in the original position. Instructions for making a new *kundal* are located in Chapter 6.

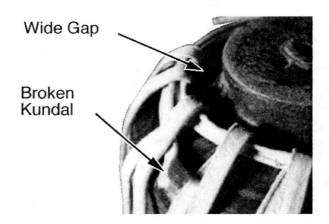

Figure 8.7. Broken Kundal

Major Damage to Syahi - Figure 8.8 shows a *tabla* that has large portions of the *syahi* coming off. This type of damage may come from several sources, but it is most often associated with water damage. If the *syahi* has become wet from any source, this type of damage may occur.

A *syahi* that is damaged to this extent cannot be repaired. In India it is often possible to simply remove the old *syahi* and apply a new one. This approach is not cost-effective in the US, where the only recourse is to replace the entire *pudi*. Even in India, applying a *syahi* is such a strain on the head that it is seldom possible to do it more than two or three times.

Smeared Syahi - Sometimes one may find that the *syahi* smears (fig. 8.9). This is due to playing with wet or sweaty hands. It is only seen on the *tablas* of inexperienced players, because an experienced musician will always use enough powder to keep this from happening.

Although this smeared *syahi* is visually unappealing, it is seldom serious enough to degrade the sound of the instrument. Repair is a simple matter of sanding the skin with a very fine grade of sandpaper. See the section entitled *"Saf Karna"* in Chapter 6 for a complete discussion.

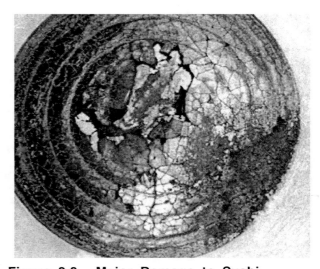

Figure 8.8.   Major Damage to Syahi

"Terrible Two" Tabla - Figure 8.10 shows a *tabla* whose *maidan* has torn with small gashes that are roughly a centimetre in length. Such tears are surprisingly common and result from one thing; children hitting the head with the tuning hammer.

It seems that children get about two years of age and they see their father tune the *tabla* with the hammer. The first time the children get an opportunity, they go and grab a hammer, and.......you can guess the rest.

Figure 8.9. Smeared Syahi

Figure 8.10. "Terrible Two" Damage

Figure 8.11. Missing Particle

Figure 8.12. Damage to Chat

There is only one repair for this problem. The entire drum must be unlaced and a new *pudi* mounted.

Missing Particles - Sometimes a particle may pop loose and be lost (fig. 8.11). This problem may be visually unappealing but it in no way affects the playing or the sound.

However, missing particles are often found in association with loose particles. As mentioned earlier, loose particles produce a major degradation in the quality of the sound.

Damaged Chat - The *chat* may be damaged due to any number of reasons. The *chat* performs a simple function and has a fairly broad tolerance. Therefore, damage to the *chat* may often be ignored.

One common problem is a *chat* which is damaged by being struck with the hammer. This is shown in figure 8.12. If this type of damage is seen, it is important to find out if the underlying *maidan* is also damaged. If the *maidan* is damaged, then it is just a matter of time before you find your whole head split. There is no repair possible short of replacing the entire head.

Sometimes one may find that it is only the *chat* which is damaged and that the underlying *maidan* is intact. If this is indeed the case, then the problem may simply be ignored. It should probably not hurt either the sound or the playing of the drum.

Major Damage to Maidan - Damage to the *maidan* is very serious. Major damage to the *maidan* may instantly render a *tabla* useless.

There are many possible causes for this type of damage. Common ones are mishandling, poor workmanship, over tightening, excessive heat, or a combination of these factors.

A split head is one of the most extreme problems that the *tabla* is likely to face (fig 8.13). The only repair possible is to completely replace the *pudi*.

I have mentioned that a slit head is sometimes due to poor workmanship. It is appropriate that we look and see how this may happen.

This problem sometimes comes when the insertions are made for the weaving of the *gajara* (figure 6.23). Sometimes the cuts are not clean, too big, or too close to the rim. Any of these conditions can create weak points that, in time, will tear right across the drum. This type of poor workmanship is easy to see after the *pudi* has torn, but it is almost impossible to detect while purchasing a new instrument.

Sometimes the cause of a tear is traceable to the final cleaning of the skin. In this stage, excess *syahi* is scraped away with the *rampi* to make it a nice round shape. Unfortunately, the *maidan* is sometimes nicked in the process. This nick is a weak spot that, given time and abuse, may tear.

Another place where poor workmanship may cause this type of problem is in the final stages of construction where the excess *chat* is trimmed away (fig. 6.58). Ideally the bamboo *badda* is used to protect the *maidan* while the *rampi* makes the cuts. Sometimes the *rampi* can slip and nick the skin. Again this nick becomes a weak point and may lead to tearing.

I would like to make it clear that the majority of cases where the *maidan* has torn are not due to poor workmanship, but due instead to mishandling or simply age.

Dented Bayan - This is a very common problem (fig 8.14). The easiest thing to do is absolutely nothing. A dented *bayan* may be aesthetically undesirable, but it rarely effects the sound quality. Sooner or later the *bayan* will be due for a head replacement, and the shell may be fixed at that time.

Removal of a dent is easy. When the shell has been separated, one simply has to beat it from the inside. It is necessary that the shell be cushioned while

Figure 8.13. Split Head

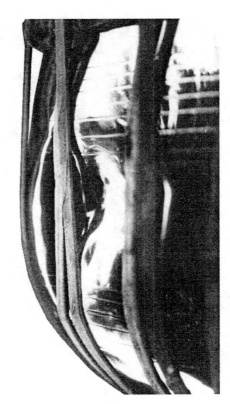

Figure 8.14. Dented Shell

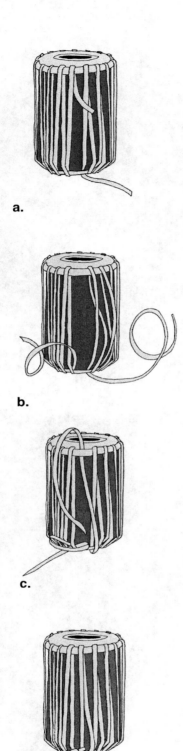

a.

b.

c.

d.

Figure 8.15. Repairing Broken Tasma

page 130

it is being beaten or the surface will be further damaged. If it is properly cushioned, it tends to pop back into its original shape with minimal denting.

In the West, the ideal tool is a rubber mallet. However, I do not recall ever seeing an Indian *tablawala* using one.

Broken Tasma - Broken *tasma* is a very common problem. It is especially a problem with *tablas* from Bengal. However, any *tabla* that uses leather instead of rawhide is also prone to this type of problem. Fortunately, leather is rare and only found in only a few *tablas* from Pakistan and the Punjab.

There are two approaches to the repair; one approach is to patch the two ends of the *tasma* at the point where they broke. Another approach is to attach the loose ends to the *kundal*.

The preferred approach is to attach the two loose ends to the *kundal*. This is shown in figure (fig 8.15). We see that one takes the broken ends and moves them back as far as necessary to be able to tie them to the *kundal*. Any excess *tasma* is then cut off. From there it is tightened in the normal way.

This may be the preferred approach but it has one great difficulty. There is seldom enough extra *tasma* to accomplish this. Therefore, one is forced to either add more *tasma* to the drum or abandon this technique entirely and go with the second technique.

The second, but less elegant technique, is to simply tie the two loose ends together. Although this produces a very ugly *tabla*, it does have the advantage that it requires no more than about three inches of extra *tasma*. One almost always has this much to work with.

One way to join the loose ends is shown if figure 8.16. We see that we are really just tying the ends together.

CONCLUSION

We have covered all of the common problems and their repairs. With these techniques there is no reason for any *tabla* to be left abandoned, unrepaired, or otherwise unused.

WORKS CITED

Courtney, D.R
1985 "Tabla Making in the Deccan". *Percussive Notes*. Vol 23 No 2: pp 33-34. Urbana: Percussive Arts Society.
1988 "The Tabla Puddi". *Experimental Musical Instruments*. Vol 4 No 4: pp 12-16. Nicasio: EMI.
1993 "Repair and Maintenance of Tabla", *Percussive Notes,* Lawton OK: October 1993; Vol.31, No 7: pp 29-36.
1995 *"Fundamentals of Tabla"*. Houston TX: Sur Sangeet Services.
2000 *"Advanced Theory of Tabla"*. Houston TX: Sur Sangeet Services.

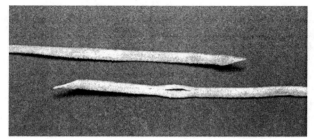

a.

b.

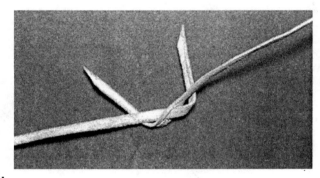

c.

d.

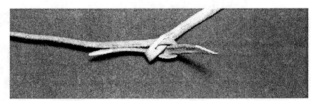

e.

Figure 8.16. Patching Broken Tasma

CHAPTER 9

NON-INDIAN APPROACHES

INTRODUCTION

I would like to use this chapter to describe some non-Indian approaches to maintenance and manufacture. There is no particular focus or order. We will show how you can fashion your own *chuttas*, hammer and covers. We will also look at maintenance as it will typically be done in the US, Canada, or the UK. In short, this chapter deals with miscellaneous issues from a completely Western perspective.

There is one question which is undoubtedly in your mind; why should the approach to the topic be different in the West? It is reasonable to assume that since India has had several hundred years experience, that this should naturally be the best approach. At first this appears to be a reasonable position, but it fails to recognise that conditions in the West are fundamentally different from those in India.

The differences between India and the West may be seen in two basic areas: economic conditions, and infrastructure. Although the two areas overlap, it will make the job of discussing them easier if we draw this separation.

The infrastructure is the complex system of production and distribution of materials. We may illustrate the differences quite simply. Walk into any grocery store in the US and ask for a pint of water-buffalo milk. You will probably look a long time and never find it. However, buffalo milk is readily available in India. This simple example shows that the United States does not have a well developed infrastructure for the production and distribution of buffalo milk, while India does. Therefore, since we are dealing with different infrastructures, it is only reasonable that materials that are available in India may not be available in the West and *visa versa*. This will naturally be reflected in repair practices.

Economic conditions also play an important part in theses maintenance practices. In the West, labour is expensive while materials are cheap. In India, labour is cheap and materials are expensive. This fundamental difference is the most important reason why maintenance practices are different. In India it is very common to use techniques that may require 10 man hours of work simply because it saves a couple of dollars worth of material. This is impractical in the West where economic conditions force us to take a disposable approach. Things will be thrown away and replaced rather than repaired. For instance, nobody will repair a $20 tape recorder in the West because labour charges far exceed the cost of a new one. However, the same tape recorder in India will be repaired indefinitely.

This basic overview sets the stage for the rest of this chapter. We have seen that the procedures outline in this chapter are sometimes a reflection of economic conditions. Sometimes they are a reflection of the nonavailability of certain materials. With these points in mind we can procede with our discussion.

OBTAINING REPLACEMENT PUDIS

A perennial task in *tabla* repair is obtaining replacement *pudis*. This may be problematic outside of India. Let us discuss some of the issues that will arise.

The ideal situation is when you can walk into a shop and purchase the *pudi* of your choice. In this case, one simply checks the size and looks at the quality of the head. The various indicators of quality have been discussed in great detail in the previous chapters, so there is really no need to go into them here.

Unfortunately, most people outside the Indian subcontinent will have to buy a *pudi* by mail. This creates obvious problems for quality control and obtaining a proper size. Here are some points to keep in mind.

The Supplier - When dealing with anyone by mail, it is first important to have an idea who you are dealing with. This will help avoid many problems.

Is your supplier trustworthy? The best indication of the trustworthiness of your spplier is the length of time they have been in business. In the West, if you are not honest, you will not be in business for long. The system is very good at eliminating dishonest people. However, the system takes years to really cleanse itself of such people. In the meantime, new people come along, some of whom will also be dishonest. Therefore, if you look at how long someone has been in business, it is a good indication of the quality of people that you are dealing with.

It is very important that your supplier is knowledgeable. Most people in the retail business are not familiar with the arcane aspects of *tabla* manufacture, and are totally at the mercy of their buyers abroad. These buyers are sometimes no more knowledgeable than the retailers themselves. Furthermore, even the most diligent and honest dealers occasionally get in a bad supply. It is very common for a bad *pudi* to be sold to an unsuspecting customer in very good faith. This situation is less likely to arise with a knowledgable supplier.

Correct Size - The correct fit of the *pudi* is probably the single most important issue. This is especially an issue for the *dayan*. There are really two issues here. The first is determining the size that you need and the second is the ability to communicate this to your supplier.

The common approach is to simply measure the lip and then send the measurement to your supplier. Although this generally works well for the *bayan*, the success rate for the *dayan* is usually only about 50%.

This is a high failure rate, but it is not obvious why this should be a difficult task. Let us look at some of the difficulties.

One of the biggest problems stems from a slight warping of the shell. An example was shown in Chapter 5 in figure 5.8. That illustration was of course an extreme example, but in the real world almost all shells will display some degree of warping. Usually the warping is not visible with the naked eye, but will be evident when you carefully measure the shell.

This is how warping may confuse the measurements: If you measure the shell from the wide side, but the *pudi* is measured from narrow side, this can give you a *pudi* which is far larger than acceptable. In a similar way, if you measure the shell from the narrow side, and the *pudi* from the wide side then your head may turn out too be to small.

The problem of measuring the shell and *pudi* may be further complicated by a slight rounding of the edges. Furthermore, this rounding is not consistent from shell to shell or *pudi* to *pudi*.

Even if you know exactly what you want, there is still one problem; how do you communicate this to the supplier?

Here is the best way to get around this problem. Simply disassemble the *tabla* and lay the shell down on some paper, then trace around the lip with a pen (fig. 9.1). Cut it out and send the tracing to your supplier. The supplier then lays it on the inside of various *pudis* until the right one is found. It may then be sent to you for further work.

Tasma/Pudi Matching - The issue of matching the *pudi* to the *tasma* is a consideration in the West, but not generally an issue in India. In India, most *tablas* tend to be manufactured, sold, used, and repaired in the same geographic area. However, when you are in the West, shells, *tasma*, and replacement *pudis* may come from anywhere. This sometimes creates problems when the *tasma* does not match the *pudi*. Let us look at how this can be a problem.

Figure 9.1. Tracing the Lip - Trace the lip . onto paper to assure a correct fit

The biggest problem comes when we try to use a standard *pudi* (i.e. "Bombay style") with *Bengali* lacing. The standard head is made of heavy hides and *gajara*, while the *Bengali tasma* is weak and thin. The drum may start off fine, but very quickly becomes loose. You go through all the steps of hammering the *gatta*, bring more *tasma* over the *gatta*, and it just keeps stretching. At some point, the *tasma* starts stretching so thin that it starts to break. Even under the best circumstances, *Bengali tasma* is problematic, but it fails much faster when trying to lace a standard head. The bottom line is simple; *Bengali* (i.e., "Calcutta style") lacing is simply not strong enough to lace a standard (i.e., "Bombay style") head.

BAD SYAHI

The contrast between Indian approaches and Western approaches is most visible in the approach to repairing a bad *syahi*. In India, a reasonable approach to repairing a bad *syahi* is simply to remove the old one and put on a new one. This requires an average of 10 man hours to accomplish. However, if we try to do the same thing outside of India the cost for 10 man hours exceeds the cost of a new drum. This is clearly not a practical solution. Therefore, the universal approach in the West is to replace the entire head. An experienced repairman can do this job in about one-to-two man hours.[1]

MAKING THE CHUTTA

You will probably want to make your own cushioned rings. I generally do not recommend people taking half a day to make something that costs so little, however Indian *chuttas* are often inadequate. An inadequate *chutta* is more serious than one may think. If the *chutta* is not able to hold the *tablas* in the correct position, this will affect your ability to play. You can probably make better ones than you can buy, even if you are not particularly good with your hands.

There are several reasons why you may wish to make your own *chuttas*. One reason is that very few of the people who make them in India are musicians; they are usually tailors. Since they do not really know what a good size is, they tend to be the wrong size. You, on the other hand, will

[1] Please note that this does not mean that a head can be replaced in two hours. One must add the appropriate drying time for the skins. Drying time adds time to the job without adding man hours.

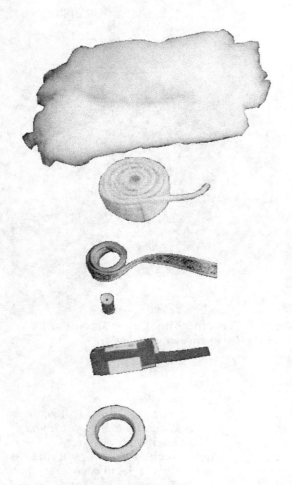

Figure 9.2. Materials Chutta - kapok, rope, brocade, needle, thread, bias tape, adhesive tape

instantly know how your *chuttas* should be. There is another reason; every *tabla* is a different size. Something that will work for one *tabla* may not work for another. Again, you will be the best judge. These are the reasons why you can make better *chuttas* yourself.

It is not hard to make them. Here is the technique.

The materials that we need are shown in figure 9.2. We see that (from top to bottom) there is kapok, rope, brocade, needle and thread, bias tape, and adhesive tape (e.g., duct tape).

Start with some rope. Plain old manilla hemp is probably the cheapest and best. Roll it into a ring of approximately 10 inches in diameter; this may be larger or smaller according to your preference (fig. 9.3.a). Roll the coil until you have one whose thickness is about one-and-a-half inch in diameter. It is not really necessary to fix the ends; simply loosely hold it in position.

Wrap the coil with tape (fig. 9.3.b-9.3.c). Any tape will do. It may be duct tape, ordinary cellophane tape, packing tape, or masking tape. It is not important. It just needs to be held together while you work with it. If you wish, you can use string as a substitute for tape, but this will add a bit of labour as you have to think about securing the ends of the string.

Next you wrap the *chutta* with kapok (fig. 9.3.d-9.3.e). Kapok is a cotton-like material which is available in any fabric store. This will build up the thickness at the same time it is forming a cushion.

Next, one must wrap it in cloth strips (fig. 9.3.f-9.3.g). It is easiest to use bias tape. You can cut your own strips of cloth, but be sure to cut the cloth along the bias. (Look into Appendix 3 for a discussion of warp, weft and bias.) If you do decide to cut your own, you may wish to hem the edges to prevent fraying. Wrap the coil as shown in figure 9.3.g. When you have completely wrapped it, simply take a needle and thread and sew it just enough to hold it in place (i.e., tack it). This is shown in figure 9.3.g.

Next, one takes some decorative ribbon, brocade, or similar band of cloth (fig. 9.4.a -9.4.b), and stitches around the *chutta*. This will have to be done by hand (fig. 9.4.c). This ribbon serves two functions. The first is decorative, for this provides a very nice touch. The second is functional, because it is this ribbon that will hold the whole thing together.

As an optional step one may stitch around the inner portion of the *chutta*. This will give extra strength.

The *chutta* is now finished (fig. 9.4.d). You will probably wish to make several of varying sizes. You will certainly find yourself buying numerous *tablas* of different sizes and it is good to have different size *chuttas* for your drums.

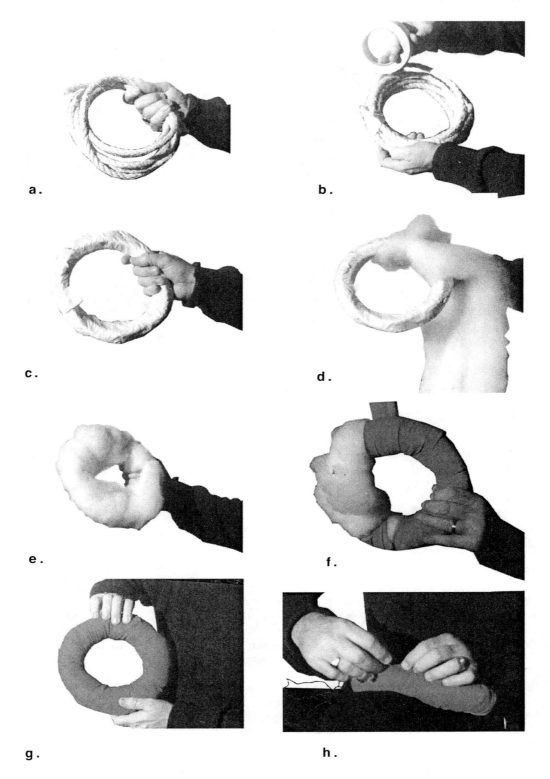

Figure 9.3. Making the Chutta - make coil of rope, wrap with adhesive tape, wrap with kapok, wrap with bias tape, tack

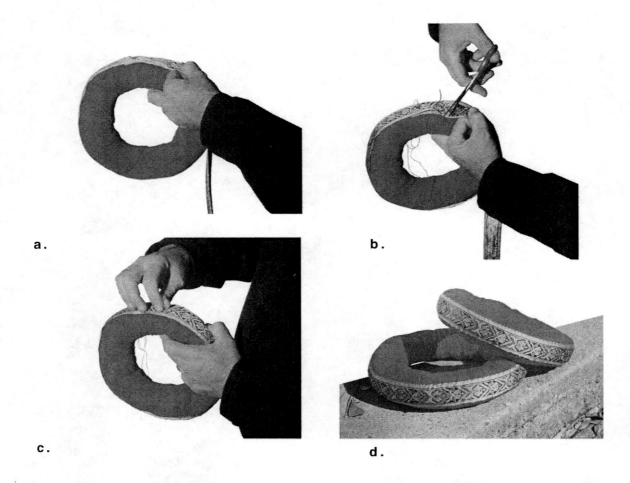

a.

b.

c.

d.

Figure 9.4. Making the Chutta (cont.) - a. wrap with brocade   b. tack & trim   c. stitch   d. finished chuttas

MAKING THE COVERS

You may wish to make your own covers. Those that are made in India are generally poor quality, so you will probably be able to do a better job yourself. Here is one way to do it.

Figure 9.5.a shows the materials for making the covers. From left to right we have outer cloth, inner cloth, and nylon cord. The outer cloth is chosen for strength and looks. In the example shown, we are using duck cloth. This cloth is an extremely heavy cotton and is amazingly durable. This cloth is in the family of denim or canvas. The inner cloth is chosen for the qualities of moisture absorption and the ability to cushion and protect the head. In this case, plush-felt is chosen, but it could just as easily have been a machine made quilt or any similar material. The lacing is nylon cord.

First determine the diameter that you will need. An easy thing to do is make a pattern with paper. To make the pattern, simply lay the drum face down upon the paper and carefully trace around the drum the size that you wish the cover to be. Next you allow for the hem; generally this means adding a band of about $3/4$ inch around. Therefore, the diameter will be $1\frac{1}{2}$ inch larger than the final desired size.

Cut out two circles of this size. One circle will be the outer cloth and the other will be for the inner cloth. Since there are two drums, then this will come to four circles; two of each size. These are shown in figure 9.5.b.

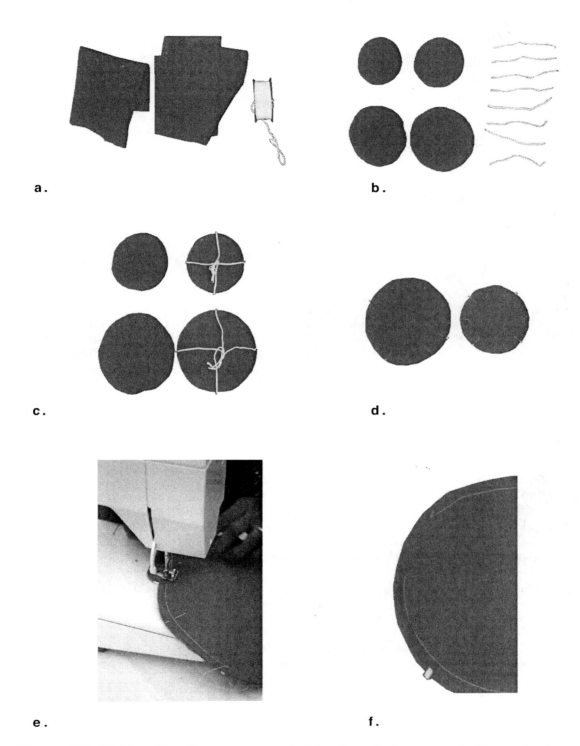

a.

b.

c.

d.

e.

f.

Figure 9.5. Making the Covers - a. materials, b. cut pieces   c. pin laces   d. pin top/bottom   e. hem f.   leave two inches unstitched

Cut eight lengths of nylon cord. There are four straps per cover. They should be about one inch longer than what you want the final length to be. These straps are shown in figure 9.5.b.

Pin the lengths of straps to the disks as shown in figure 9.5.c. It really does not matter whether you are pinning them to the upper cloth or the lower cloth. Just remember to pin them in such a way that they will be accessible.

Pin the pairs of discs together as shown in figure 9.5.d. Please note that you are assembling this inside out. Therefore, if there is any part of the cloth that you wish to be facing outward, it should actually be facing inward at this time. In the same way, the straps are sandwiched between the two cloth disks.

We now sew them together (fig. 9.5.e). This is typically $\frac{1}{2}$-$\frac{3}{4}$ of an inch in from the edge. When you are stitching it, remember to stop and leave about three inches unsewn. This opening will be necessary because you will have to turn the cover inside out.

The cover is now turned inside out. This is very much like turning a glove or a sock inside out. This is shown in figure 9.6.a. When it is turned in this manner, the lacing now comes back to the outside and it has a neat hem. This is shown in figure 9.6.b. Notice too, that the hole is still present.

One must now make a temporary closure to the hole. For this one carefully folds the hem back in to itself and temporarily pins it into place.

The final stitching must now be done (fig. 9.6.c). First, one comes in from the edge about half an inch. This should correspond to a position that will just stitch the hem on the inside. It is now sewn around the entire perimeter. One more line of stitching is necessary; this is just barely inside the edge. When the entire thing is finished, there will be two lines of stitches visible as shown in figure 9.6.c.

The covers are now finished. These are shown in figure 9.6.d.

There are any number of variations to this basic theme. One may decorate it with appliqué, decorative fringes, or brocades. One is limited only by ones imagination.

ALTERNATIVE LACINGS

There may be times that the *tasma* needs to be replaced. This is a rare occurrence in most *tablas* because a good *tasma* will usualy last 10-20 years. However, inferior *tasma* (e.g., Calcutta style, or leather lacing) will go bad very quickly and need to be replaced. It is certainly possible to get on the internet and find a supplier of traditional rawhide lacing; however, the West does provide some nice alternatives. The most practical are a variety of nylon lacings that are on the market

Nylon lacing is available in various forms; the three basic classes are webbing, parachute cord and rope. Webbing is flat and does not stretch. Parachute cord is flat and does stretch, while rope is like any other rope except the fibres are made of nylon.

Nylon webbing is a flat ribbon. Like cloth it has a warp and a weft. The warp runs the entire length of the cord while the weft is very narrow. The webbing used for *tabla* should generally be around $\frac{1}{4}$-$\frac{3}{8}$ of an inch wide. The most distinctive feature of webbing is that it does not stretch.

The fact that it does not stretch is a very desirable quality for the novice. It is easy to estimate what the final length will be from the initial state.

Parachute cord is another form of nylon lacing. This is available in many places that sell mountaineering equipment. Parachute cord looks very much like thick boot lacing. However, the similarity ends there. Unlike standard webbing, parachute cord is woven so that the length of the

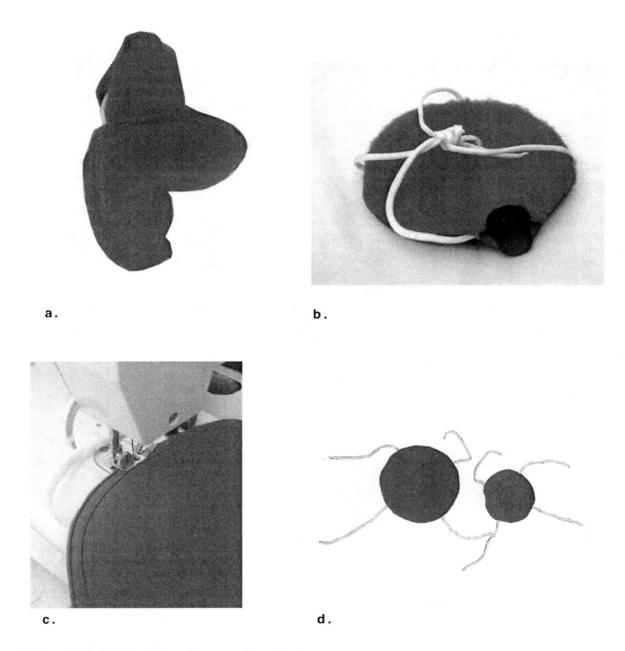

a.

b.

c.

d.

Figure 9.6. Making the Covers (cont.)

cord runs diagonally to the weaving. This gives it an interesting characteristic. It quickly stretches to a final length and then stops. I must emphasise the word STOPs. From that point on, you will not be able to stretch it any more, nor will you be able to break it.

The fact that parachute cord stretches so much has some interesting ramifications. When not under tension, it contracts to a fraction of its final length. Therefore, when you are manipulating all of this lacing, you do not have to wrestle with unmanageably long lengths of cord. This is very convenient for an experienced repairman. However, it does take some experience to know what the final length will be from its initial length.

Nylon rope is another viable alternative to rawhide. This is certainly the cheapest and most accessible alternative. Unlike either the parachute cord or the webbing, the rope is round instead of flat. Different types are available, each with their own strength, size, and degree of stretching.

There are a few common characteristics to all of the nylon replacement lacings. They are all relatively inexpensive, extremely strong, and will last a lifetime. They are all rather easy to work with too.

MAKING A HATHODI
The hammers from India are inexpensive and good quality. There really is no need to have to make your own. However, if you want to, here is an easy and inexpensive way to do it.

Go to a hardware store and get a tack hammer. Cut the handle so that its length is about seven inches. Sand the end so that it is smooth. This is easy and cheap; it has a nice weight and a nice balance.

PATCHING A HOLE IN THE BAYAN
If the *bayan* has a small hole in it, it is possible to patch it without having to replace the entire head.

A split head has many causes. Physical impact, exposure to high ambient temperatures, and defective workmanship are only a few common reasons. When this happens to the *dayan* the only solution is to replace the head. If it happens to the *bayan* and the hole is small, there is another option.

I must stress that the procedure outlined here is far inferior to simply replacing the head. I am placing this information before you as a last possible recourse for people who are not in any position to obtain a replacement head.

Here is the procedure. First remove the *pudi*. Take a small piece of goatskin (perhaps some excess cut from the *bharti*) and soak it for a few minutes in water to soften. Glue it firmly to the inner surface with ordinary white glue. The glue that you use is very important. It should be flexible; glues that are sandable are not acceptable. Plain old flexible "Elmer's" white glue works very nicely. Clamp it firmly and allow it to dry for 24 hours as shown in figure 19.7. Remove the clamp and allow to dry for a few more hours. The head may then be replaced. If this approach is used, remember to keep the patch dry and not to moisten it during replacement.

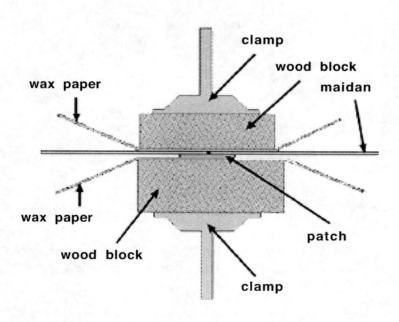

Figure 9.7. Patching a Hole in the Bayan

NEW APPROACHES TO CONSTRUCTION

Construction is linked to culture. As *tabla* is beginning to move out of pre-independence Indian culture into the 21st century global culture, we are starting to see the first changes in construction techniques. At the time of this writing, the most ambitious experiment seems to be the "minitabla" (fig. 9.8).

I have very little information on these drums. It appears that these drums are made of synthetic materials, and the developer is a man named Juerg Wuethrich who lives in Switzerland. (It seems that these are no longer in production)

One thing is certain: we will see many more variations in construction. We will see the increased use of artificial materials. We may see the introduction of large scale mass production. In short, the next 50 years will probably see more change in construction techniques than have been seen in the last 250 years.

Figure 9.8. Minitabla

WORKS CITED

Courtney, David
1993   "Repair and Maintenance of Tabla", *Percussive Notes,* Lawton OK: October 1993; Vol.31, No 7: pp 29-36.

CHAPTER 10

PHYSICS OF THE TABLA

INTRODUCTION

This chapter deals with the physics of the *tabla*. We will start with a simple overview of physics. This reacquaints us with basic concepts, most of which we learned back in our school days. We will next move into the topic of the modes of vibration. These will be for membranes in general and the *tabla* in specific.

So what do we mean by the physics of the *tabla*? In a nutshell, we are talking about how the *tabla* works. Volume one and volume two of this series discussed how the *tabla* was played. This particular volume concentrates on how the *tabla* is put together. Here it is appropriate to discuss how it works.

Unfortunately, our knowledge of how the *tabla* works is very incomplete. It has been a neglected field for a long time. Even the early pioneers such as C. V. Raman were forced to make only a quick overview of the *dayan* and then move on. We know almost nothing as to how the *bayan* works. With this apology given we will now proceed.

GENERAL OVERVIEW OF THE PHYSICS

Let us now start with a general review of a little physics. We will review the concepts of resonance modes, nodes, and frequency.

Simple Vibrational Mode - The concept of a vibrational mode is very important. Many of you are musicians, so the concept of vibrational modes may be a little vague. We may clarify these concepts by reviewing what we learned in our our high school physics classes.

We were acquainted with the concept of vibrational modes through the vibrating string. This is illustrated in figure 10.1. Figure 10.1.a illustrates the first vibrational mode of a string. Figure 10.1.b illustrates the second vibrational mode. Figure 10.1.c illustrates the third mode. This series continues indefinitely.

These vibrational modes are really standing waves in a string; as such, there are two things that we need to be familiar with. There is the node and there is the anti-node. Let us look at them in greater detail.

The node is the portion of the string that does not move. The two endpoints are inherently nodes; this is because they are held firmly in place by the two bridges. From here on, the only possible vibrational modes are those that have nodes on each end. We see in figure 10.1.b and 10.1.c, that there may be other nodes in the middle as well. The second mode for instance, has a node in the dead centre of the string, while the third mode has two nodes in between. If you have ever seen anyone play a guitar by harmonics, they always place their fingers at the points of the nodes which correspond to the desired note.

The anti-node is another important concept. The anti-node is the place where there is maximum vibration. In our illustration, these modes may be evoked most effectively by striking at the points of the anti-nodes.

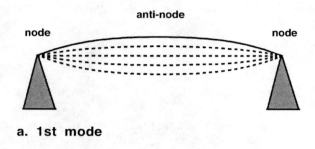

a. 1st mode

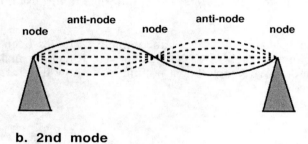

b. 2nd mode

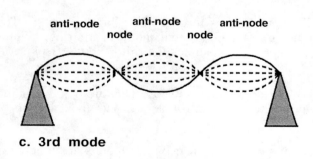

c. 3rd mode

Figure 10.1. Resonance Modes of String

We may return to a practical example for this. A guitar will produce a mellow sound, deficient in upper vibrational modes, by strumming closer to the centre. Conversely, it will produce a brighter sound, one that is richer in overtones, by striking closer to the bridge.

We have described common ways that a string can vibrate; however we have not discussed the frequencies at which these modes operate.

It turns out that there is a very simple relationship between the modes and the frequencies of the sounds they produce. The first order vibrational mode will have a frequency that is f. This is by definition; it is called the fundamental and serves as a point of reference. The second vibrational mode has a frequency of $2f$, the third vibrational mode has a frequency of $3f$, etc. This very simple and convenient arrangement is summarised in figure 10.2.

When the various frequencies are laid out along with their amplitudes, they form what is known as a spectrum. Remember, in volume two of this series we went into great detail to describe the spectra of the strokes of *tabla*. When the frequencies show a simple integral relationship (i.e., f, $2f$, $3f$, $4f$, etc.), then the spectrum is referred to as a harmonic spectrum. When the frequencies do not show this simple relationship, then it is known as an enharmonic spectrum.

We have now reviewed what most people learned about frequencies and vibrational modes back in high school. As we move through this chapter, it is important to remember that the node is the point that does not move in the standing wave, while the anti-node is the point that moves the most. The various ways that something can vibrate are called modes. Also remember that modes vibrate with a particular relationship to the lowest frequency. If the relationship is in simple multiples, then the resultant spectrum is called a harmonic spectrum. If the resultant spectrum does not show this simple relationship, then it is known as an enharmonic spectrum. These are the points that must be understood before we move along.

VIBRATIONAL MODES AND NODES

Let us now look at the various modes, anti-nodes, and the frequencies of drum skins. It is not very likely that drums were discussed in your high school physics classes. They are considerably more complicated than strings. However, easy or not, we are going to jump in.

We saw that the vibrational modes of strings were, in great measure, defined by their nodes. Fortunately this is also true for vibrating membranes. However, the nature of the nodes is considerably more complex on a flat surface.

There are three possible nodes for vibrating membranes. There are nodal circles, nodal diameters, and nodal points.

Nodal Circles - The simplest nodal circle is shown in figure 10.3. This single circle represents the boundary conditions of the membrane. This vibrational mode has only a single nodal circle running around the drum where it is anchored at the shell.

The movement of the skin in this mode is very simply visualised. The skin will at one point move downward as shown in figure 10.3. After a very brief period the skin will then move back up, however it passes through the resting position and continues up until it resembles a hill. Again, after a brief period the membrane moves back and down to its earlier condition. This simple back and forth motion continues indefinitely.

There is an easy way to portray this vibrational mode. It is common to schematically represent it as a simple circle. This is shown in figure 10.4.

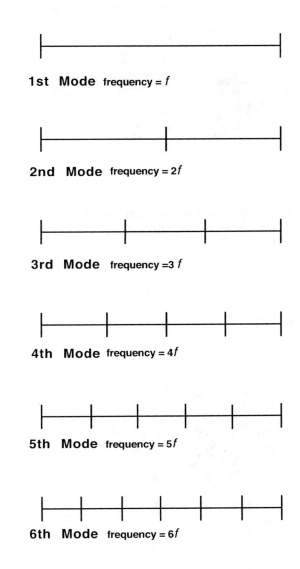

1st Mode frequency = f

2nd Mode frequency = $2f$

3rd Mode frequency = $3f$

4th Mode frequency = $4f$

5th Mode frequency = $5f$

6th Mode frequency = $6f$

Figure 10.2. Resonance Modes of a String

Let us look at another example; figure 10.5 shows a vibrational mode that has two nodal circles. This mode is considerably more difficult to visualise. In this example we see that when the inner portion of the circle moves upwards the outer portion moves downward. Conversely, when the inner portion moves downward then the outer portion moves upwards. Again, this motion continues indefinitely. The vibrational mode that uses two nodal circles is schematically illustrated in figure 10.6.

It is possible to have other nodal circles for a membrane. However, the practical limit for the *tabla* appears to be three.

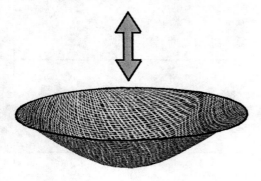

Figure 10.3. Movement of Membrane for Single Nodal Circle

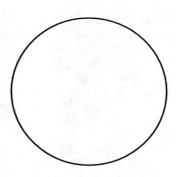

Figure 10.4. Schematic Representation of Simple Nodal Circle

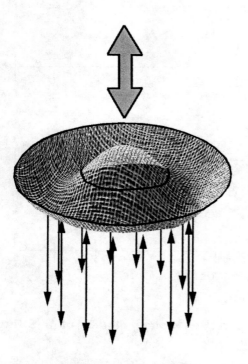

Figure 10.5. Movement of Membrane for Two Nodal Circles

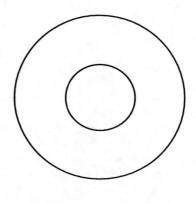

Figure 10.6. Schematic Representation of Two Nodal Circles

<u>Nodal Diameters</u> - Nodal diameters are nodal lines that bisect the drumhead. The simplest real world example is shown in figure 10.7. Notice that this is not just a nodal diameter, but it also contains a nodal circle. This is after all, a real world example and in the real world, the skin is locked into the drumshell, therefore there will always be at least on nodal circle on a drum.

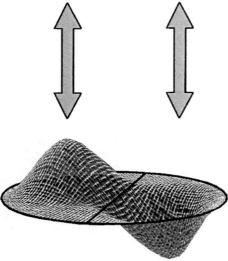

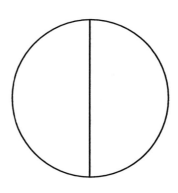

Figure 10.7. Movement of Membrane with One Nodal Circle and One Nodal Diameters

Figure 10.8. Schematic Representation of One Nodal Circle and One Nodal Diameters

Figure 10.7 shows how the nodal diameter behaves. We see that when one side of the membrane rises, the other side falls. Conversely, when the first side falls, the opposite side rises. This is not too hard to visualise.

The vibrational mode with one nodal diameter and one nodal circle is schematically shown in figure 10.8.

Nodal Points - A nodal point is a single point that remains stationary in a vibrating membrane. This is not relevant to the *tabla*, therefore we will not discuss the topic here.

NORMAL VIBRATIONAL MODES

Table 10.1 shows a list of normal vibrational modes for a circular membrane.[1] Let us look at this chart in greater detail.

The first column shows a schematic of the arrangement of the nodes. At this point we should be very comfortable in visualising the modes of vibration from their schematic representation (e.g., fig. 10.3-fig. 10.8).

The next column is the standard designation of the modes. This is expressed in the form of (*m,n*). In this form we see that *m* represents the number of nodal diameters while *n* represents the number of nodal circles. For example, the vibrational mode illustrated in figure 10.6 has two nodal circles and no nodal diameters. Therefore, it would be expressed as (0,2) and is illustrated by the 4th

---

[1] These vibrational modes are an idealised construct and are derived from theory rather than being derived empirically. Their forms and frequency ratios are derived from the wave equation for a thin membrane written as:

$$\frac{\partial^2 z}{\partial t^2} = \frac{T}{\sigma} \nabla^2 z = c^2 \nabla^2 z$$

where T is the tension, σ is the mass per unit area, and c is the wave velocity. For our purposes, the solutions are usually expressed as Bessel functions of order m, and the zeros of these functions give the frequencies of the various vibrational modes. The m and n of table 10.1 correspond to the nth zero of the Bessel function of order m (Rossing 1991).

schematic	mode	rel. freq.
	(0,1)	1.000
	(1,1)	1.594
	(2,1)	2.136
	(0,2)	2.296
	(3,1)	2.653
	(1,2)	2.918
	(4,1)	3.156
	(2,2)	3.501
	(0,3)	3.600
	(5,1)	3.652
	(3,2)	4.060
	(6,1)	4.154

Table 10.1. Resonance Modes of an Idealised Drumhead.

entry in table 10.1. For another example, the vibrational mode illustrated in figure 10.7 would be referred to as mode (1,1) because it has one nodal diameter and one nodal circle; this is the second entry in table 10.1. With these examples, the significance of the first and second columns should be very clear.

The third column represents the relative frequencies. For instance, let us say that the membrane has a vibrational mode (0,1) that has a frequency of 100 Hz (cycles per second), then the frequency of (1,1) will be 159.4 Hz, the frequency of the mode (2,1) has a frequency of 213.6 Hz, etc.

If we look at the frequency values that are derived from table 10.1 something becomes very clear. These values are definitely enharmonic. The frequencies produced by our idealised drumhead do not show the regular, simple ratios that something like a vibrating string would show.

The fact that membranes tend to exhibit enharmonic spectra is musically very significant. Indian music has very stringent requirements for pitch. A drum producing this type of sound would probably not find much favour among classical Indian musicians.

It turns out that there is a way around this enharmonic quality. The key to this may be seen by comparing our idealised model to the real world.

In the real world, factors such as air loading, skin stiffness, and a host of other variables may change the frequency values of these modes. This is very significant because if random factors can influence the frequency values, then conscious design considerations may be even more effective. Therefore, it should be possible to tame the vibrational modes and make them behave in a manner which is much more harmonic.

This is exactly what goes on with the manufacture of *tabla*. It is made in such a way that various modes are coaxed into producing frequencies other than those predicted from our idealised membranes. We may now see how this happens.

HARMONICS, VIBRATIONAL MODES, AND NODES OF THE DAYAN

Let us now look at the resonance characteristics of the *dayan*. So far we have reviewed the basics of nodes, anti-nodes, and vibrational modes. Armed with these concepts we can see how things really work.

The first thing to recognise is that the sound of the *dayan* is said to be harmonic in nature. This means that the various overtones have simple, even relationships to the fundamental. (We will see later that this is an oversimplification, but for now we will accept this view).

Another point to keep in mind is that for every harmonic, there must exist at least one resonance mode to support it. However, we may have several modes working together to create a particular harmonic.

Earlier we discussed vibrational modes and then mentioned the relative frequencies of their vibrations. It is appropriate in the next section for us to take the reverse approach. We will look at the harmonic structure and then look at the vibrational modes that support it.

Harmonics of Tabla - The first question to be addressed is, "How many harmonics are there in the *dayan?*" This is a very good question; unfortunately, we do not have a good answer.

First of all, how do we define our harmonic spectrum? If we require a strict integral relationship (i.e., 1*f*, 2*f*, 3*f*, etc.), then the *tabla* clearly fails. The numerical relationship between the frequencies only approximates a harmonic series. If we take a strict definition in this matter, then there are no harmonics at all! Few people would accept such a strict definition.

Let us look at the spectrogram in figure 10.9 to see how many harmonics we may find. In this graph the intensity is denoted by how dark the line is. The frequency is denoted on the vertical axis and the time is denoted in the horizontal axis. We see a number of spectral lines clearly illustrated; we have labelled 11. One may even argue the existence of 12 and 13, although admittedly this is stretching things a bit. Clearly the higher harmonics are weak, very unstable, and have very poor numerical relationships to the fundamental. We can safely discount the upper harmonics as being insignificant. But this still does not tell us how many harmonics there are.

It turns out that the easiest thing to do is to fall back upon convention. Conventionally, five harmonics are considered. We will bow to convention. But remember, this is a mere simplification and one should really say that there are five "significant" harmonics.

But where did this convention come from? This convention goes back to the pioneering work of C.V. Raman (Raman 1920). Raman had only the crudest scientific equipment, and five harmonics were all that he was able to see. Today, we have very sensitive spectrum analysers which can measure things that were unthinkable in Raman's day. But one thing does not change; Raman was not able to see these other harmonics because they were very weak and insignificant. Even looking at these harmonics with our new equipment, we still find that these upper harmonics are weak and insignificant. With that being said, let us now look at the five "significant" harmonics.

The Fundamental - The fundamental is the lowest frequency that is generated in a harmonic series. In the *dayan*, this is the sound that is produced by the *Tun* stroke. One lightly and quickly strikes the centre of the drum with the index finger to elicit this harmonic.

The resonance mode that creates the fundamental is very simple. It is the (0,1) mode; this has a single nodal circle (i.e., the rim of the drum) and no nodal diameters. This mode is very easy to visualise. It was graphically illustrated in figure 10.3-10.4. It is also the first mode shown in our series in table 10.1.

The Second Harmonic - In a harmonically correct tone, the second harmonic is an overtone that has a frequency of twice the fundamental. In the case of the *tabla* we can only say that it is approximately twice the frequency of the fundamental.

The second harmonic in the *tabla* is generated by the (1,1) vibrational mode. This mode has one nodal circle and one nodal diameter. This mode was described earlier in figure 10.7-10.8; it is also the second mode shown in table 10.1. Although this mode is a bit more complicated, the illustration should make it clear to the reader.

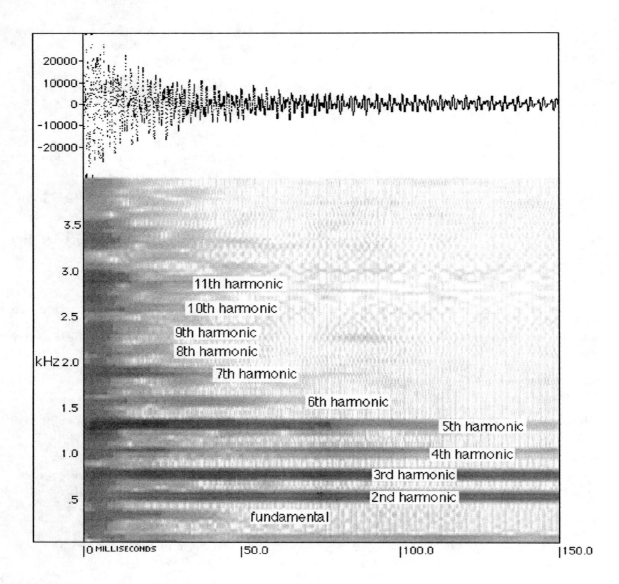

Figure 10.9. Harmonics of Tabla

Third Harmonic - The third harmonic is considerably more complicated than either the fundamental or the second harmonic. There are five vibrational modes that have been shown to be responsible for this harmonic. These are illustrated in figure 10.10.

The vibrational modes responsible for the third harmonic are mixed; there are both normal modes and combination modes. One of the normal modes is the (0,2) mode. This was described in great detail in figure 10.5-10.6; this is also the fourth entry in table 10.1. Another normal mode that is responsible is the (2,1) mode which is the third entry in table 10.1. Curiously enough there are a number of other modes responsible for the third harmonic which are not predicted by our Bessel functions and not normally found in simple drums. These combination modes are the last three shown in figure 10.10.

(0,2)   (2,1)

Figure 10.10. Modes of the 3rd Harmonic

Fourth Harmonic - The fourth harmonic introduces a higher level of complexity in the vibrational modes. The vibrational modes responsible for this harmonic are shown in figure 10.11. Two of the normal modes are described by our mathematics and are found in other drums. These are the (1,2) mode and the (3,1) mode. These correspond to the sixth and fifth examples in table 10.1, respectively. There are three more combination modes; these are shown in the last three examples in figure 10.11.

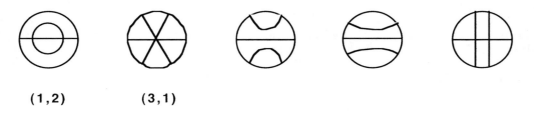

(1,2)   (3,1)

Figure 10.11. Modes of the 4th Harmonic

Fifth Harmonic - The fifth harmonic introduces an even greater degree in complexity of vibrational modes. These modes are illustrated in figure 10.12. The first three modes are normal modes and similar to what we have found in other drums. However, the last mode is a combination mode and is not found on most drums.

This section showed that the *tabla* is able to take a membrane whose spectrum is very enharmonic, and alter the vibrational modes to produce a spectrum which approximates a harmonic spectrum. However, we did not discuss how this happens. We find that the most important process to altering these vibrational modes is a process known as loading.

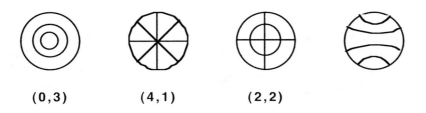

(0,3)   (4,1)   (2,2)

Figure 10.12. Modes of the 5th Harmonic

page 153

LOADING

Loading has tremendous influence over the way that the skin vibrates. Loading is the process of artificially increasing the mass of the resonator. This increase in mass translates to a lowering of the frequency at which the resonator vibrates.

Let us start with a very simple analogy. As a child we used to play with a simple toy made by passing kite string through a button and making a loop. One loop of the string would go in to one hand and the other length would go into the other. The button would be set spinning while we alternately pulled and released the string. The button would spin one direction, then stop, then spin in the other direction only to stop and return once more. This simple little toy could thus be made to spin indefinitely. I think that every one of you has done the same thing, so it should be easy to imagine this. We called them whirligigs, but I imagine that they were known by a host of other names. As would so often happen, we would make different sizes and different weight buttons. Heavier disks would operate much more slowly than the smaller, lighter ones. This example is a very accessible example of loading.

Loading reduces the resonance frequency by increasing the mass of the resonator. This is really not much different from the way that heavier guitar strings will vibrate at a lower pitch than smaller, lighter ones.

The same process of loading is seen in the *tabla*. The *syahi* is a very massive application that loads the skin and thus lowers the frequency. This is represented by the simple model shown in figure 10.13. In this model we see that a mass is stretched between two springs. These springs act to bring the mass back to the resting position. As we increase the mass, the resonance frequency decreases. This is exactly what happens with the *tabla*.

The brilliant thing is that the different vibrational modes are not affected equally. By adjusting both the thickness and the contour, certain modes may be affected more than others. It has been empirically observed that making the centre thicker than the edge affects the fundamental more. Conversely, making the edge thicker affects the higher harmonics.

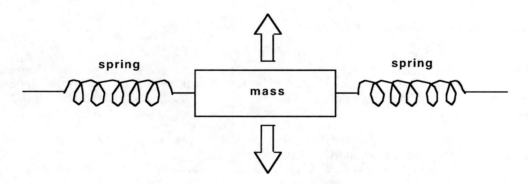

Figure 10.13. Simple Model of Loading

DAMPENING

Dampening is another important factor that influences the way that the head vibrates. Dampening is the process of introducing some type of mechanism to mute the vibrations in some way and drain off the energy. If one sets a pendulum swinging, it will not swing forever, but will eventually die down. It dies down because the pendulum is dampened by such factors as air friction and mechanical effects in the string.

There are a number of dampening factors in the *tabla*. The friction of air is one. Wood porosity and mechanical forces in the skin are also factors. All of these are nearly random and are common with other drums. However, there is one dampening factor that is engineered into the *tabla* that is absolutely brilliant. This is the way that the main resonating membrane *(maidan)* is sandwiched between two annular membranes (the *chat* and the *bharti*).

This is a brilliant scheme because its dampening characteristics are not felt equally across the spectrum. The upper order vibrational modes are significantly more affected than the lower order modes. Let us look at the spectrogram in figure 10.9 to see this in greater detail. In this spectrogram we see that initially many of the higher harmonics are quite strong. This may be seen even up to the 11th harmonic (the strength is indicated by the relative darkness in the graph). Even though they are initially strong they are not able to sustain. One very important reason for this lack of sustain is the dampening action of the *chat* and the *bharti*. This reason for this is illustrated in figure 10.14.

Figure 10.14 shows why the upper order vibrational modes are dampened more than the lower order modes. A lower order mode is shown in figure 10.14.a. We see that the anti-node is located at a considerable distance from the *chat* and the *bharti*. However, as we move into progressively higher modes, the anti-nodes shift towards the edge. At some point, the anti-nodes may even be under the *chat*. It is obvious that the dampening effect on these higher order modes will be extreme.

There is a simple musical reason that necessitates this dampening. The higher order modes produce overtones which give a much sharper, more indistinct musical tone. It is felt by many Indian musicians that the dampening of these modes gives a tone which is more musical.

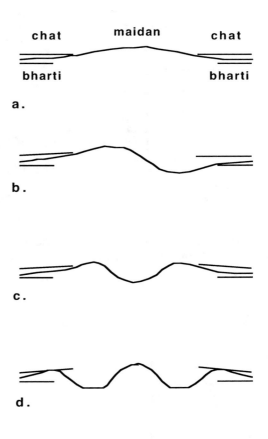

Figure 10.14. Dampening of Higher Order Vibrational Modes

The Enharmonic Qualities of the Dayan - A close examination of the harmonics of the *dayan* very clearly shows that it is not really a harmonic series. We must remember that the *tabla* is based upon the vibrating membrane, so it is no surprise that there are enharmonic qualities. This is very much like the dancing bear in the circus. It is not a question that it dances badly; it is remarkable that it dances at all. The same is true with the *tabla*. It is not surprising that it shows enharmonic qualities; it is remarkable that it shows any semblance to a harmonic series at all.

Let us actually measure the frequencies of the various harmonics and see how they compare to an ideal harmonic spectrum. The typical *tabla* produces frequencies with ratios shown in figure 10.15. In this case, we are taking all of the frequency ratios and comparing them to the fundamental. We quickly see that the spectrum falls way short of being considered a harmonic spectrum. The

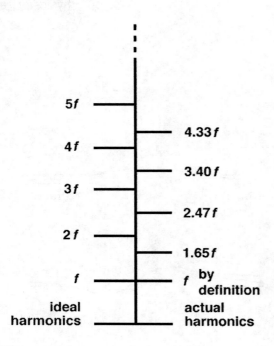

5f

4.33f

4f

3.40f

3f

2.47f

2f

1.65f

f   f by
                        definition

ideal   actual
harmonics   harmonics

Figure 10.15. Ideal and Actual Harmonics of Dayan (reference = fundamental)

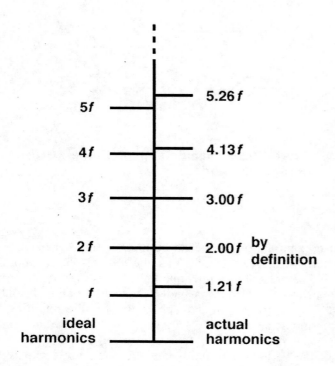

5f   5.26f

4f   4.13f

3f   3.00f

2f   2.00f by
                        definition

f   1.21f

ideal   actual
harmonics   harmonics

Figure 10.16. Ideal and Actual Harmonics of Dayan (reference = 2nd harmonic)

numbers do not come anywhere near the ideal values.

The spectrum is not really as enharmonic as it may at first appear. In order to see this we need to re-evaluate our point of reference. In figure 10.15 we used the lowest frequency as the reference point: This is largely a question of convention; it is not a reflection of the way the *tabla* works in normal performance situations. We can get a totally different, but more relevant picture by shifting our point of reference to the second harmonic.

Figure 10.16 shows the same arrangement of frequencies, but with the second harmonic as our reference point. For this we take the frequency of the second harmonic and simply define this to be $2f$. This then gives us a frequency for f that does not correspond to any actual vibration. When we compare the other frequencies to this imaginary fundamental f, then we see that we have a much better approximation of a harmonic spectrum.

The psychoacoustics of this is quite profound. We find that the pitch of a well tuned *tabla* corresponds to a nonexistent vibration. *Tabla* is not unique in this respect because the same phenomena is seen in many bells.

One may note that there is a slight stretching of the spectrum with our 4th and 5th harmonic. This too is not unusual because stringed instruments also tend to exhibit this behaviour. This is one reason why piano tuners tend to slightly stretch the octave when tuning a piano.

We could discuss these matters at great length, but we will not for two reasons. The first reason is that this is a topic that we already discussed at great length in Volume two of this series (*Advanced Theory of Tabla*). Another reason is that this really takes us in to the realm of psychoacoustics which is a different field from physics. Psychoacoustics is therefore not within the topic of this chapter.

However, it is very appropriate for us to briefly discuss the practical and technical ramifications of the physics.

PHYSICS AND THE TECHNIQUE OF THE DAYAN

The physics of the *tabla* is reflected in the performance technique in two ways. It is reflected in the muting of the (0,1) mode by the last two fingers of the right hand, and it is reflected in the emphasis of other modes by the striking of the drum in particular fashions. We may look at these in greater detail.

Suppression of the (0,1) Mode - The suppression of the (0,1) mode is probably one of the most profound reflection of how the physics of the *tabla* influences the technique. We have seen in our previous examination of the spectra that the lowest frequency component is particularly problematic. Although the rest of the spectra shows a strong harmonic quality, the "fundamental" is sharp.

The sharp quality of the (0,1) mode is easily demonstrated without any equipment. One simply has to take a well tuned *tabla* and compare the musical pitch of *Tun* and the *Tin* and *Na*. Convention says that the *tabla* will use *Tin* or *Na* to tune to. However, when we play the *Tun* we find that it is approximately one step higher than the tonic. Therefore, if the *tabla* is tuned to *Sa* then the *Tun* stroke produces the *Re*.

The way musicians deal with this problem is to simply mute the lowest vibrational mode (i.e., the 0,1 mode). This is done by placing the ring finger against the skin of the drum.

The consequence of this finger position is profound. Only the vibrational modes which have nodes running under the ring finger will be present. A few examples are shown in figures 10.18-10.22. These are only a few examples; one can no doubt see many more.

Striking Positions and the Anti-Nodes - It should be no surprise that the most efficient way to evoke particular harmonics is to strike as close to the anti-nodes as possible. This is most apparent in strokes which emphasise the lower order modes such as *Tun* or *Tin*. As a practical matter, the positions of the the anti-nodes are less well defined in strokes which

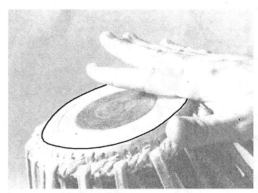

Figure 10.17.   (0,1) Mode

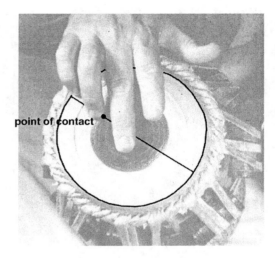

Figure 10.18.   (1,1) Mode

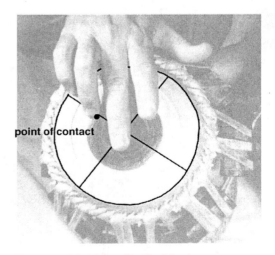

Figure 10.19.   (2,1) Mode

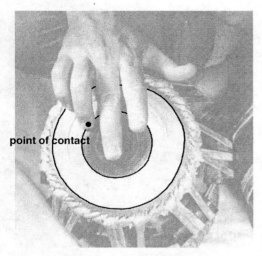

Figure 10.20.   (0,2) Mode

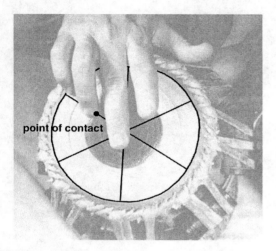

Figure 10.21.   (3,1) Mode

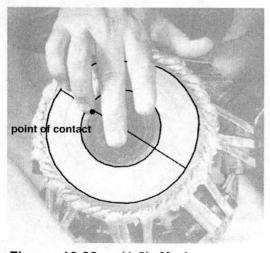

Figure 10.22.   (1,2) Mode

emphasise the higher order vibrational modes (e.g., *Na*). For this, one simply strikes at the rim very forcefully. This has the "shotgun" approach of exciting the upper order vibrational modes with considerably less specificity than one finds in the lower order modes.

It is not appropriate for us to proceed further in this area. Interested readers should review the various spectrograms in the chapter on timbre in Volume Two *(Advanced Theory of Tabla)* for more information.

HARMONICS, VIBRATIONAL MODES, AND NODES OF THE BAYAN

At this time, the physics of the *bayan* is not well understood. I am aware of only one work that was intended to address the issue. This was the work of B.S. Ramakrishna in 1957.

The basic problem seems to be that early investigators were using analysis approaches that had been worked out for the *dayan*. Vibrational modes of a circular membrane create a workable model for the *dayan,* but they just don't seem to work well for the *bayan*. So much of the physics of the *bayan* depends upon what is happening with the air inside the drum, and much less on what the skin is doing.

I have always felt that the closest analogue to the *bayan* is the passive radiator speaker design. Even this seems very remote sometimes. Perhaps one of you will take up the challenge and fill in the gaps.

CONCLUSION

We have briefly reviewed what is known of the physics of the *tabla*. In the final analysis we find that we really do not know very much. Large parts of what we know have essentially been imported from other common drums. The *tabla* is clearly not a common drum and this process has left a lot of loose ends.

WORKS CITED

Cohen, Hirsh and George Handelman
1957   "On the Vibration of a Circular Membrane with Added Mass", *Journal of Acoustical Society of America.* Vol. 29 No 2, pp. 229-233

Courtney, David R.
1999   "Psychoacoustics of the Musical Pitch of Tabla", *Journal of the Sangeet Research Academy.*Calcutta, India, Vol 13, No1 October.

Fletcher, N.H. and T.D. Rossing
1991   Physics of Musical Instruments. New York: Springer-Verlag: New York

Ramakrishna, B.S. and M.M. Sondhi
1954   "Vibrations of Indian Musical Drums Regarded as Composite Membranes", Journal of Acoustical Society of America. Vol 26 No 4. pp. 523-529.

Ramakrishna, B.S.
1957   "Modes of Vibration of the Indian Drum Dugga or Left-Hand Thabala", *Journal of the Acoustical Society of America.* Vol. 29, Number 2, 234-238

Raman, C.V.
1935   "The Indian Musical Drums" *Proc. Indian Academy of Science.* Vol. A1 pp1 79.

Raman C.V. and S. Kumar
1920   "Musical Drums with Harmonic Overtones", *Nature* (London) vol 104, pp 500.

Rossing, Thomas D.
1991   "Musical Instruments", *Encyclopedia of Applied Physics (Vol 11).* New York: VCH Publishers (pp 157).
1992   "Acoustics of Drums", *Physics Today.* New York. American Institute of Physics. March 1992 vol. 45, no 3, pp.40-47.

T. Sarojini and A. Rahman
1958   "Variational Method for the Vibrations of the Indian Drums", *Journal of Acoustical Society of America.* Vol 30 pp. 191-196.

CHAPTER 11

HEALTH ISSUES

INTRODUCTION
Every field has certain health issues associated with it. People quickly think of the occupational hazards involved for miners and firefighters. However, every field has its own occupational hazards and health issues. The manufacture and repair of *tabla* is no exception. Let us look at some of the issues.

GENERAL ISSUES
There are a number of concerns which should be common sense. Still for the sake of producing a comprehensive work, we shall discuss a few.

<u>Cuts</u> - The tools which the *tablawala* uses will cut wood and rawhide with ease. It should be no surprise that they will also cut your fingers. Use care and common sense.

There is another issue which is less obvious. Cutting yourself with the same tool that you have been using to cut rawhide is comparable to injecting yourself with whatever microbes the animal happened to have. We will discuss this in greater detail later in this chapter.

<u>Strains</u> - Lacing and tightening the drums requires a lot of work. Use care to guard against aggravating scrotal hernias or developing back strain.

Now we should discuss issues which are not so obvious.

EXPOSURE TO DISEASE
There are two very important points that should never be forgotten:

1) If you work with *tablas*, it is the same as handling dead carcasses.

2) If you work with rawhides on a regular basis, especially rawhides from India, at some point you will contract some infection.

These last two statements are not intended to cause fear or discourage anyone. They are merely points that must be kept in mind so that basic precautions can be taken.

Let us now put things into some type of perspective. I could just as easily have said, "If you spend a lot of time in libraries, you will at some point get sick!" We all know that any public place is a likely place to contract colds, flues, or or other common diseases. However, it is part of our culture that we have a clear understanding of both the likelihood of catching diseases, as well as an understanding of the types of diseases that we are likely to catch. We do not automatically have a similar understanding of the health issues associated with working with animal products. Therefore, some discussion is in order.

The term disease is rather a vague term. Sometimes it is applied to disorders that result from infection. Colds and flues are common examples. Sometimes diseases are caused by some internal imbalance; cancer and diabetes are common examples of this. In this chapter we will only concern ourselves with diseases that result from an infection.

Some germs that we pick up from animals cause diseases and some do not. Most germs are specific to a particular species. Therefore, we are not likely to get sick from most of the germs that we encounter while working with the hides of animals. However, there are other diseases that are freely transmitted from animals to man. These diseases are known as zoonotic diseases (Britannica 1998). In the rest of this chapter we will discuss some of the zoonotic diseases that may be contracted from goats, water buffalo, and cattle. These of course, are the principal sources of rawhide for the *tabla*.

The incidence of zoonotic diseases is very high in India. India is an agricultural economy where people and livestock live and work together. There are ample opportunities for disease to spread back and forth between them. Furthermore, hygienic conditions are abysmal; this too, adds to the incidence of infection. Another contributing factor is that the Western practice of giving frequent injections of antibiotics to livestock is extremely rare in India; therefore, the incidence of bovine diseases are very high. All of these factors contribute to the high incidence of zoonotic diseases.

These conditions are further exacerbated by the lack of regulation in the slaughter of animals and distribution of meat, hides and other animal products. Where the West is very aggressive in separating the dead and dying animals from the healthy ones, there is no workable system in India[1].

Therefore, when you are dealing with rawhide, you never know what the conditions of the animal were. It may have been a healthy animal slaughtered and processed in a sanitary fashion, or it may have died of rabies or anthrax, and simply been disposed of in whatever manner that was expedient. Always exercise caution.

ZOONOTIC DISEASES OF GOATS, WATER BUFFALO AND CATTLE
Here are a number of zoonotic diseases that are of concern to the *tablamaker*.

Anthrax - Anthrax is caused by the bacterium *Bacillus anthracis*. It is endemic in the bovine populations in India. In Hindi it is known as *Tili ka Bukhar*.

We must make a distinction between anthrax under normal conditions, as opposed to specially processed anthrax for biological warfare. The normal exposures that a craftsman is likely to encounter are a mixture of living bacteria and low concentrations of spores. However, anthrax for biological warfare are the spores in much higher concentrations than one would normally encounter.

Usual exposures that the *tablawala* encounter seldom produce any clinical signs. If signs do occur, they are likely to reflect a cutaneous transmission (Turkington & Dover 1996). This usually starts as an itchy bump that resembles an insect bite. This then forms a painless ulcer, approximately 1-3 centimetres in size. It will usually subside without treatment. However 20% of such cases may result in death, so it is still to be taken seriously.

Rabies - Rabies is a virus that is found in livestock in India. World-wide, rabies kills 50,000 people a year, of which India accounts for roughly 20,000-30,000. India is considered one of the highest risk countries for this disease in the world. A significant percentage of the livestock population shows the presence of the disease.

---

[1] Laws and regulations do exist in India, however they are usually ignored. The only time that there is any effort to enforce them is when the officials are out fishing for bribes. At such times, violators are found and threatened. However, after payment of the appropriate bribe (known as *bakshish* or *mamul*), the dead and dying animals continue their journey through the distribution network.

The symptoms of the disease vary according to the stage of the infection. The initial symptoms are fever, headache, muscle aches, loss of appetite, nausea, vomiting, a general malaise, and a tingling in the area where the disease entered the wound. After that, the symptoms resemble encephalitis. Finally, there is coma and death.

The level of risk posed by handling the skins is not known. This is certainly not the normal way in which the disease is contracted. But we must remember that airborne transmission has been documented, and there is even evidence to suggest sexual transmission. In light of this evidence, we should not be lulled into any sense of security.

Brucellosis - Brucellosis, also known as undulant fever or Bang's disease, is extremely common in bovine populations in India. It is caused by a bacteria. Symptoms include intermittent fevers, headache, weakness, sweating, chills, and generalised aching.

Streptococcus Zooepidemicus - This is a form of streptococcus that is found in livestock. As with other streptococcus infections, it is characterised by fever, chills, and general malaise. However the streptococcus can attack specific areas of the body and thus produce specific symptoms resembling pneumonia, endocarditis, and a host of other diseases. Left untreated it can be fatal[2].

Staph Infections - This is probably one of the most common infections that the *tablawala* must contend with. These infections are caused by any of several forms of the *staphyloccus* bacteria. Staph infections are caused by bacteria entering the skin, usually through cuts and abrasions. This forms puss filled boils or other swellings. Sometimes the staph infections can enter the bloodstream and cause problems in other parts of the body.

Staphyloccus bacteria live everywhere. Therefore, the staph infection is not considered a zoonotic disease. However, the *tabla dukan* is an environment that is particularly suited to promoting these infections. The *staphyloccus saprophyticus* even has a special propensity for living off dead tissue (Sankaran 2000). Therefore care hould be taken to keep all cuts as clean as possible

Leptospirosis - Leptospirosis is found in water buffalo and goats. It is caused by any of a variety of strains of leptospira. The symptoms are varied. In some cases it is asymptomatic. In other cases there is high fever, chills, headaches, jaundice, red eyes, or any of a number of other symptoms. If left untreated it may result in damage to the liver, kidney, meningitis, or other permanent damage.

Zoonotic Tuberculosis - This is a form of TB that is caused by the bacterium *Mycobacterium bovis*. Tests on Indian water buffalo (similar to the human TB test) show between 1%-25% of positive reactions. In India, zoonotic tuberculosis contributes to a very significant number of human cases.

Salmonellosis - Salmonellosis is caused by any of a variety of salmonella bacteria. This causes severe diarrhoea.

Q-fever - Q-fever is found in goats and cattle (Laskin 1977). It is caused by a bacterium known as *Coxiella burnetii*. In many livestock it produces no symptoms. About half of the humans who contract the disease show no symptoms. When there are symptoms, they typically are the usual non-specific symptoms of high fever, headache, sore throat, vomiting and a host of other symptoms.

Giardiasis - Giardiasis is a form of diarrhoea. It is caused by a one-celled microscopic parasite, known as *Giardia intestinalis*. It is found in the intestines of animals and humans. Although it is normally caused by contaminated food and water, it may be found on fecally contaminated skins from the slaughterhouses.

---

[2] I picked up a case of streptococcus infection in India in the early 80's. I neglected to get prompt medical attention and things got bad. I actually thought that I was going to die! It took me months to recover. This is nasty stuff!

Campylobacteriosis - Campylobacteriosis is a form of diarrhoea. It is commonly found in goats. In rare cases it enters the bloodstream and causes a general infection. It may be contracted by handling fecally contaminated skins.

Cryptosporidiosis - This is also a form of diarrhoea. It may be contracted from handling fecally contaminated skins. It is a microscopic parasite that can survive for a long time outside of the body.

Yersinia enterocolitica - *Yersinia enterocolitica* is a bacterium that causes diarrhoea. Again, it may be contracted by handling fecally contaminated skins.

Foot and Mouth Disease - Foot-and-mouth disease is a virus which is common in all hooved animals in India. This disease may be recognised by ulcerations that occur in the area of the mouth. It is extremely virulent, although in cattle it tends to be fatal only to very young or weak animals.

There is evidence that man can contract this disease. However, it produces no symptoms and is believed to cause no harm. However, humans can transmit the disease to unaffected bovine populations with disastrous economic consequences.

PRECAUTIONARY MEASURES

There are really very few precautionary measures that can be taken. Exposure to livestock diseases is an unavoidable occupational hazard. However, there are a few steps which are common sense.

Wash Your Hands - Remember to wash your hands after working with any rawhide. This is especially important before eating. This is a simple routine and it greatly reduces the incidence of gastrointestinal diseases that are spread by fecally contaminated skins. This also reduces the chance of spreading infections to other members of your family who are not directly involved with the hides.

Keep Cuts and Abrasions Clean - This is very easy to say but extremely difficult to do. If you are in the middle of a job and a knife blade that you have been using to cut water buffalo hide slips and cuts your skin, it is very much analogous to injecting yourself with whatever pathogens were present in the hide. Be as careful as possible.

Wear a Mask - Although some zoonotic diseases are spread by breathing the spores of bacterium, this does not really seem to be an issue for the *tablawala*. Unless you feel that you are particularly sensitive to this sort of thing it is not likely that this will help much.

Prompt Attention to Infected Wounds - This is the most practical thing. It is especially important given the high incidence of staph infections.

CONCLUSION

This chapter discussed many of the health problems that may concern the *tablawala*. There are the obvious cuts and strains that come with the craft. However, there are the more important, and potentially dangerous, zoonotic infections. These diseases may be contracted in the normal course of working with rawhide.

WORKS CITED

Encyclopaedia Britannica
1998   "Zoonosis", *Micropaedia*. Encyclopedia Britannica.

Laskin. Allen I
1977   *CRC Handbook of Microbiology*. Cleveland, OH: CRC Press.

Sankaran, Neeraja
2000   *Microbes and People*. Phoenix: Oryx Press.

Turkington, Carol and Jeffrey S. Dover
1996   *Skin Deep: A-Z of Skin Disorders*. New York: Facts on File.

CHAPTER 12

CONCLUSION

This completes the third volume of this series. We have discussed the various issues surrounding the construction of the *tabla*. These naturally concentrated on the actual construction. However, we also discussed the various other issues that relate to the craftsmen, their profession, their health issues, etc.

This volume has an important position within the overall series. The first two volumes concentrated on the techniques and the theoretical issues in *tabla*. This volume will in turn be followed *(inshalah),* by other volumes which deal with compositions and history. Therefore, when everything is taken together, we will have a clearer understanding of this fascinating field.

APPENDICES

APPENDIX 1

GLOSSARY

ain-i-akbari - A *magnum opus* written by Abu Fazal Allami, chronicling the period of the emperor Akbar (late 16th century).

alloy - A mixture of two or more dissimilar metals.

annealing - The modification of the characteristics of metal by exposure to heat.

annual rings - See growth rings.

anti-node - For any particular mode, the portion of the skin that moves the most.

arranged marriage - A marriage that is determined by the elders with limited input on the part of the people getting married.

atta - A mixture of whole-wheat flour and water.

avanaddh (अवनद्ध) - The traditional classification of musical instruments that contains the drums.

babool - A tree (*Acacia tortilis, A. raddiana, A. heteracantha,* or *A. spirocarpa*), which produces a wood which is sometimes used to make the drum shells.

badda (बद्दा) - A flat section of bamboo used to protect the *maidan* when the *chat* is being trimmed.

baddhi (बद्धी) - See *tasma*.

badhai (बढ़ई) - A carpenter or wood worker.

bakari - A she-goat

bakari ki khal - Goatskin

bayan (बांया) - 1) lit. "left" 2) The metal left hand drum of the *tabla*. 3) The left hand face of *pakhawaj, dholak* etc.

beating - A tremolo which results from the mixing of two similar, yet slightly different frequencies.

Bengal - A state in northeast India.

bengali - Anything from Bengal, the Calcutta style *tabla.*

bharti - The inner lining of the *pudi.*

bias - In cloth, it is the diagonal to both the warp and the weft.

bija - A wood from the *Pterocarpus marsupium.* A very good wood for making *tablas.*

black money - The opposite of white money. Black money is not properly accounted for, and the appropriate taxes are not paid.

blue-stain - A fungus which attacks wood during the seasoning process, so named because of the blue colour.

bol (बोल) - The mnemonic syllables of *pakhawaj* and *tabla*

Bombay style - A style of *tabla* that is found throughout most of India, but is most represented by *tablas* from Maharashtra and Gujarat.

bonded labour - A system whereby a lump sum of money is exchanged for labour over a specified number of years.

bovine - Pertaining to cattle, buffalo, and similar large, hooved animals.

brazing - The process of joining two pieces of metal by the addition of a binding alloy, similar to soldering but with different alloys.

brown rot - Any of a variety of cellulose attacking fungi.

buffalo - The Indian water-buffalo (*bubalus bubalis*).

bunad - The crossbraid in the *gajara.*

Calcutta style - A style of *tabla* manufactured in Bengal, Bangladesh, and north-east India.

cambium - A microscopic layer of living cells that lay just under the bark. This layer is responsible for laying down new wood in the tree.

caveat emptor - "Let the buyer beware!"

cell cavity - The lifeless cell wall that is left behind when the cell dies. This is the basis for wood.

cell wall - A rigid, cellulose rich matrix in which plant cells live.

cellulose - A white chemical made of many small units of sugar strung together to create gigantic chains. This is the most common component in wood.

chamada (चमड़ा) 1) Rawhide 2) The *pudi.*

chamar (चमार) - Tanner.

chanti (चांटी) - See *chat.*

chat (चाट) - The outer annular membrane of the *pudi.*

chati (चाटी) - See *chat.*

chenda - A drum from the South Indian state of Kerala, much used for the *Kathakali* and *Mohini Attam* dance forms.

chillar - 1) Leftovers. 2) Small trapezoidal scraps of goatskin used to make the *bharti*.

chini (चिनी) - A carpenter's chisel.

chisel - Generically, any small blade that comes of perpendicularly to the handle used to remove wood. Specifically, it is one that has a flat blade as opposed to a gouge.

churi (छुरी) - A large knife, similar to a kitchen knife.

chutta - The cushioned rings upon which the *tabla* is placed.

collagen - The most important protein in rawhide.

cowhide - The rawhide from a cow or bull.

daf (डफ़) - A large Indian tambourine.

daffali - See *daf*.

dagga - The *bayan*, the left hand drum.

damaru (डमरु) - A common hourglass drum in India.

dampening - The artificial reduction in the sustain of a vibrating body.

dapphu - See *daf*.

darzi (दर्ज़ी) - A tailor.

dayan (दांया) - 1) lit. "right" 2) The wooden right hand drum of the *tabla*. 3) The right hand face of *pakhawaj, dholak* etc.

deccan - Present day Andhra Pradesh, Karnatika, Maharashtra

deciduous - Opposite of evergreen. A tree which sheds its leaves every year.

deel - Low quality wood, normally used for packing crates but occasionally used for *tabla*.

derma - The major portion of the skin and rawhide lying just under the epidermis

dholak (ढोलक) - A two faced folk drum of northern India.

dholak massala - A black tar-like application that is found on the inner surface of the left hand side of the *dholak* and the *dholki*.

dholki (ढोल्कि) - See *nal*.

disulphide bridge - A chemical bond that connects adjacent proteins together in rawhide.

dori (डोरी) - Lacing.

dry weight - The weight of wood in a fully desiccated state.

dukan (दुकान) - A small shop.

earlywood - The inner portion of the growth ring, so named because it is laid down at the beginning of the growing season.

enharmonic spectrum - A spectrum in which the various harmonics lack a simple relationship with each other.

epidermis - The outermost layer of skin and rawhide.

fell - To cut down a tree.

fibre saturation point - The point where the xylem has been voided of water, but there is still water locked in the cell walls.

fibril - A sub-microscopic fibre made of varying numbers of molecular chains.

film music - An extremely popular, mass produced music for popular consumption. It is so named because it is popularised through the Indian films.

filmi - Pertaining to Indian films.

filmi sangeet - See film music.

flesh - The subcutaneous tissue that adheres to the inner surface of the rawhide.

forging - The process of beating metal into the desired form.

frequency - The rate at which something happens. In acoustics it is usually expressed in Hertz or cycles-per-second.

frequency domain - Looking at acoustical phenomena from the standpoint of spectra, frequencies etc. The opposite of time-domain.

fundamental - The lowest frequency in a spectrum.

gab (गाब) - Black spot on the centre of the *tabla*.

gajara (गजरा) - Rawhide weaving on the *pudi*.

gatta (गट्टा) - Wooden tuning blocks.

ghorta (घोटा) - The *ghorta* is a rounded highly polished stone used to apply the *syahi*.

goatskin - The skin of the goat.

got (गोट) - See *chat*.

gottuvadyam - A south Indian instrument, very similar to a *vina*, except it has no frets and it has sympathetic strings.

gouge - A chisel with a curved blade.

green weight - Wood in a natural state before it has been seasoned.

growing season - The time of the year in which new wood is laid down in a tree. In temperate climates this is usually spring and summer. In India this is usually the monsoon period.

growth ring - The wood which is laid down in one growing season.

gurudakshana - A gift, usually including money, that is made to the teacher.

harmonic - A component frequency in sound.

harmonic spectrum - A spectrum in which the harmonics have an integral (i.e., 2x, 3x, 4x, etc.) relationship with each other.

hathodi (हथौड़ी) - The hammer used to tune the drum.

heartwood - The hard, dense, insect resistant centre of a mature tree trunk.

Hertz - Unit of measurement for frequency. 1 Hertz = 1 cycle-per-second.

Hindi - The most used language in India.

hygroscopic - The propensity to attract and hold water.

idakka - An hourglass drum from South India.

Indian Rosewood - see *shisham*.

inharmonic - See enharmonic.

inverse domains - Two mathematical domains that may be interchanged by way of a fourier transform.

isomer - Different forms of a molecule, formed by rearranging the atoms.

jack - See jackwood.

jackwood - The wood of the jack or jackfruit tree (*Artocarpus heterophyllus*).

jal (जाल) - Literally a "net" 1) Round, metal templates used to layout and mark the skin. 2) The rope lacing of the *dholak* or *nal*.

kanjira - A small lizard skin tambourine from South Indian music.

Kannada - The language of the south Indian state of Karnatika.

kapada (कपडा) - Cloth.

kath (काठ) - The wooden shell.

Kerala - A state in southern India.

keratin - A hard, insoluble protein, found commonly in horn and nails. It provides a hard surface for the outer portion of the rawhide.

khol (खोल) - A folk drum of northeast India.

kiln - 1)An oven for firing clay. 2) A chamber for seasoning wood.

kiloHertz - One thousand cycles-per-second.

kinara (किनारा) - See *chat*.

kudi (कुड़ी) - Metal shell of the *bayan*.

kundal (कुण्डल) - Ring for lacing the *tabla*.

lab (लब) - See *maidan*.

lakadi (लकड़ी) - The wooden shell upon which the right hand drum (*dayan*) is made. The wooden shell of any drum such as *pakhawaj, nal,* or *dholak*.

lakadi massala - A mixture of sawdust and white glue. It is used to fill cracks and knotholes.

Lanka - Sri Lanka, formerly known as Ceylon.

latewood - The outer portion of the growth ring, so named because it is laid down at the end of the growing season.

lav (लव) - See *maidan*.

leather - The highly processed skin of various animals. Leather has very limited usage in the making of *tablas*.

lignin - A brown substance made of many alcohols joined together to make one massive molecule. This is a very common component of wood.

loading - The reduction of the resonant frequency due to the addition of mass.

loha - Iron, steel.

macromolecule - A huge molecule composed of hundreds, or thousands of atoms.

Maharashtra - A state in Western India. The largest city in Maharashtra is Bombay (Mumbai).

maidan (मैदान) - Main resonating membrane of the *tabla* or *pakhawaj*.

Malayalam - The language of the south Indian state of Kerala.

mango wood - The wood of the mango tree (*Mangifera indica*) which is commonly used to make inexpensive, student grade *tablas*.

metallurgy - The scientific study of metal and metal-working.

mode - The manner in which the skin vibrates.

modulation - The process of bending the pitch of the *bayan* for artistic purposes.

monomer - A single functional unit of a polymer.

mridang - A generic term that is applied to a variety of Indian drums. The basic characteristic is that they are barrel shaped drums, often with a permanent application on the right hand side and a temporary application on the left hand side.

mridangam (मृदंगम) - *A* South Indian version of the *pakhawaj*.

nagada - A pair of Indian kettle drums.

nal - A barrel shaped drum.

node - portions of the skin that do not move in a particular vibrational mode.

Odissi - 1) A dance from the East Indian state of Odissa. 2) The music from the East Indian state of Odissa.

pakhawaj (पखावाज) - A two faced barrel drum, believed by many to be the progenitor of the *tabla*.

palir (पलिर) - Pliers.

parachute cord - A form of nylon lacing.

patina - A light, protective oxide layer on the surface of aluminium, brass, or other metals.

patti - Literally a "thin leaf". 1) A metallic ribbon used to scrap off extra *syahi massala*. 2) A strip of wood designed for the electrification of old houses, but also used to make the *gatta* for *bayans*.

phloem - The vascular area in the bark that is involved in transporting nutrients.

pital (पीतल) - 1) Brass. 2) The metal shell of the *bayan*.

pitch pocket - A crack in a living tree that becomes filled with resin. This is a major flaw in many woods.

polymerisation - The process of stringing simple molecules together to make larger chains.

polysaccharides - Macromolecules made of large numbers of sugars strung together.

pudi (पुडि) - The drumhead.

pung (पुंग) - A barrel shaped drum from the north-east Indian state of *Manipur*.

Punjab - A region in north-west India and Pakistan.

Rajasthan - A state in northern India.

rampi (रम्पि) - A blade on a perpendicular handle.

rasp - A type of file used to remove wood.

rawhide - Untreated or minimally processed skin as it is removed from the animal.

rays - Small radial channels that run from the centre of the trunk outward to the cambium at the bark.

resin - A dark pitch-like substance composed of congealed sap and metabolic byproducts of the tree.

reticulum - The lattice of cracks in the *syahi*.

rosewood - A hard resinous wood in the genus of *Dalbergia*.

saf karna - The final cosmetic steps to make the *tabla* look nice in preparation for sale.

sal - A tree used to make wood in north India. The *Shorea robusta*.

sapwood - The porous wood that holds the sap. Sapwood is located between the bark and the heartwood.

seasoning - The process of drying wood to make it suitable for working.

shisham - Indian rosewood, the preferred wood for making *tablas*. This is sometimes *Dalbergia sisoo* but it is also sometimes *Dalbergia latifolia*.

Shiva - The Hindu god associated with destruction.

shuddha madalam - A drum from the South Indian state of Kerala, much used for the *Kathakali* and *Mohini Attam* dance forms.

spectrogram - A chart showing the amplitudes and frequencies of the various frequencies in a sound.

spectrum - The proportion and arrangement of the various frequencies in the sound of the *tabla*.

stump site - the place in the forest where trees are cut.

sur (सुर) - See *maidan*.

suva (सुवा) - A awl with a a broad flat point. Sometimes a very large needle. (i.e.,*tar ka suwa*).

syahi (स्याही) - Black spot on the centre of the *tabla*.

syahi massala - A black powder used to make the *syahi*.

tabla (तबला) - A pair of hand drums.

tabladukan - A shop that makes and sells *tabla*.

tablawala (तबलावाला) - A craftsman who makes *tablas*.

tamasha - Street performances that are popular in Western India.

Tamil - The language of the south Indian state of Tamil Nadu.

tannin - Dark organic material rich in tannic acid.

tar ka Suva - This as a very large sewing needle, roughly 4 inches in length.

tasma (तस्मा) - The rawhide lacing of the *tabla, pakhawaj,* or similar drum.

tavil - A South Indian drum with a roughly spherical shell played in weddings.

taxonomy - The scientific approach to organising things.

teak - A tree (*Tectona grandis*) that produces an amazingly durable wood.

Telugu - The language of the south Indian state of Andhra Pradesh.

terracotta - Simple fired clay.

time-domain - Looking at acoustical phenomena from the standpoint of waveforms. It is the opposite of frequency-domain.

tun - A wood (*Cedrela toona* or *Toona ciliata*) which is sometimes used for making the *tabla dayans*.

turnbuckle - The screw arrangement for tightening *dholaks, tablas* and similar drums.

udaku - An hourglass drum from South India.

Urdu - The national language of Pakistan, but also very common in India.

vadi (वादि) - 1) The important note of the *rag*. 2) The *tasma*.

vascular - Having tubes for the transmission of liquid. (e.g., blood, sap).

Viswakarma (विश्वकर्मा) - The Indian god who protects craftsmen and artisans.

warp - 1) An alteration of the geometry of wood, usually due to changing moisture content. 2) In cloth it is the long direction of the cloth.

water buffalo - A large black bovine (*bubalus bubalis*).

webbing - A flat nylon cord that is used as a substitute for *tasma* in lacing *tablas*.

weft - The weave.

white money - This is the opposite of black money. White money is properly accounted for and the applicable taxes are all paid.

white rot - Any of a variety of lignin attacking fungi.

xylem - wood.

zoonotic disease - A disease which may be contracted from animals or animal products.

APPENDIX 2

MORE ON WOOD

INTRODUCTION

Wood is an extremely complicated material. The chemistry, structure, mechanical properties, as well as the issues involved in the harvesting and processing of the wood, are a challenging field of study. These are all issues that directly affect the quality of the wood, and consequently, the sound of the *tabla*.

The material in this appendix could not be placed within the body of the book without compromising the readability. Therefore we have placed it here. This does not mean that the information is unimportant; anyone with a serious interest should be familiar with this.

<u>Important Concepts</u> - There are a lot of concepts which must be fully grasped before we can proceed. These are rather fundamental from an engineering and scientific standpoint. However, for the practising musician, it is not something that comes up every day.

Just as geographers must rely on terms such as north, south, east and west to discuss directions, in the same way we need to be able to discuss the directions in reference to wood. Traditionally these are expressed by four terms; transverse, radial, tangential and longitudinal.

Figure 2.1 shows a transverse section. This is basically a cross section. A transverse section is the best way to view the growth rings.

The term longitudinal refers to the perpendicular of the transverse plane. This is indicated by the arrow.

Figure 2.2 shows a radial section. This is a longitudinal slice that passes through the axis of the tree.

Figure 2.3 shows a tangential section. This is a longitudinal slice that does not pass through the axis of the tree.

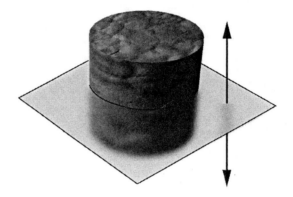

Figure 2.1. Transverse Section and Longitudinal

Figure 2.2. Radial Section

Figure 2.3. Tangential Section

Dry weight is another important concept. This is basically wood that has no water in it at all. We must not mistake the concept of dry weight for wood that has been seasoned and ready for use. Wood has such an affinity for moisture that it will take water right out of the air. Therefore, the only way to really obtain dry weight measurements is to completely dry the wood in a kiln or similar desiccator.

Green weight is another important point of reference. This is a fully saturated condition. It more nearly approximates the conditions of a living tree in real world conditions.

The importance of these concepts may be illustrated with a simple example. Imagine a glass of water with a gram of salt in it. Now imagine that it is left outside in the elements. Sometimes it rains and the glass starts to fill with water. Sometimes it is sunny and the water starts to evaporate. If we track the percentage of salt in relationship to the water it goes up and down wildly. However, there is still only a gram of salt in the glass; this has never changed. Therefore, it is more practical to use a standard point of reference to make all comparisons. Dry weight is the most common.

These concepts and terms will recur frequently in this appendix. Let us move on to the topic of wood.

CHEMICAL FUNDAMENTALS

The mechanical characteristics of almost everything is traceable at some level to what is occurring at atomic and molecular levels. We illustrated in Chapter 4 how the mechanical characteristics of rawhide were a reflection of the proteins that composed it. In a similar way, we will see that the characteristics of wood are a reflection of what is going on with its component chemicals.

It is interesting that both plants and animals have fallen back upon the fibre as the fundamental unit of structure. When animals need "brick and mortar" to create the living tissue, they rely very heavily on the fibrous protein. Plants, when faced with similar challenges, have strung sugars together to form gigantic fibres.

There are terms that we should be comfortable with before embarking upon this section. Many of the terms relate to these gigantic molecules. Any unusually large molecule is known as a macromolecule. Many times these macromolecules are simply long chains of simple units. This process of stringing units together is referred to as polymerisation. For example, long chains of vinyl chloride are known as polyvinyl chloride (PVC). Many of our macromolecules are made up of long strings of sugars and are therefore known as polysaccharides. A single unit of a polymer is generically known as a monomer. The list of macromolecules that plants use is very large, but one of the most important is a polysaccharide known as cellulose.

Cellulose - Cellulose is the most important structural chemical for wood. It may be thought of as the basic brick from which the tree is made. Wood is roughly 50% cellulose by dry weight.

If cellulose is the basic brick of the plant, then glucose is the material from which the bricks are made. Glucose ($C_6H_{12}O_6$) is a sugar that is found in both plants and animals and is essential for life. It has many names in industry. Dextrose is one common term. Corn syrup is merely a commercial grade of glucose. Other terms for specific forms include levulose, manilose, galactose, and a host of others.

There are various ways to represent the glucose molecule. Although it is sometimes represented as a simple chain (i.e., the Fisher projection), its form is more accurately shown as a simple ring; this reflects the form that it takes in a solution. It is shown in figure 2.4. This a ring of five carbon atoms folding in upon itself around a single atom of oxygen. There is an aldehyde projecting from one side (CH_2OH).

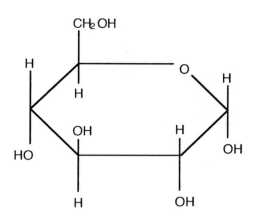

Figure 2.4.   Glucose (α-D-glucopyranose) - a basic building block of wood

The atoms of glucose may be arranged in different ways. These are referred to as isomers. The form shown in figure 2.4 is known as α-D-glucopyranose. The topic of isomerism is a very vast topic and is clearly beyond the scope of a book on *tabla*.

Just as bricks may be put together to form such diverse things as stores, houses, and barbecue pits, so too can glucose be put together to form many different types of chemicals.

Maltose for example, is a simple molecule made up of two units of glucose strung together (fig. 2.5). Maltose is referred to as a disaccharide, meaning that it is a sugar composed of two simpler units of sugar. (The ordinary sugar that one finds in every kitchen is also a disaccharide known as sucrose). Maltose is a product of the breakdown of starches and is extremely important in the making of beer.

We do not have to stop with combinations of two units; we can construct larger molecules from these simple units. For instance, starches are also constructed by stringing large numbers of glucose together. From the standpoint of *tabla*, the most important macromolecule made from glucose is cellulose.

Cellulose is a truly massive molecule. It may reach a length of up to 4 microns. The molecule is composed of several thousand units of glucose strung together to form a long fibre. Cellulose may contain as amany as 25,000 units of glucose (Brown 1996). The basic arrangement is shown in figure 2.6.

It is interesting to note the alternating arrangement of the glucose units. Therefore, the aldehyde projects from both sides in an alternating fashion. This causes cellulose to assume a ribbon-like form and is responsible for many of the chemical qualities of cellulose.

The form of cellulose is such that it has a strong propensity to form crystals. In fact, cellulose molecules are never found in isolation in nature, but in the form of crystals known as microfibrils. These microfibrils are formed when molecules of cellulose line themselves up side by side. The smallest microfibrils are approximately 36 molecules and the largest ones are up to 12,000 molecules (Brown 1996).

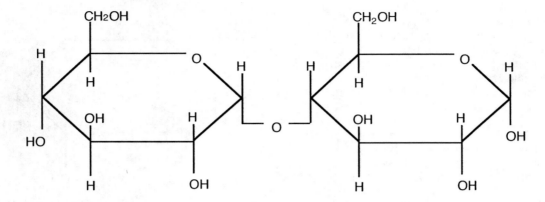

Figure 2.5.   Maltose

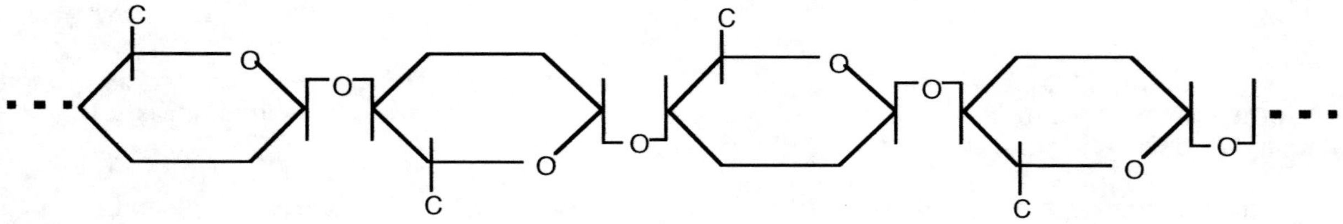

Figure 2.6. Cellulose - The most common chemical in wood

Cellulose is certainly the most common and most important chemical in wood; however, it is not the only one. There is another one known as lignin.

<u>Lignin</u> - Lignin is a complex substance that is important in binding the cellulose in wood together. If cellulose is viewed as the bricks of a plant, then the lignin may be viewed as a mortar. Lignin makes up 20% -30% of wood by dry weight.

Lignin is a complex polymer made of a variety of aromatic alcohols. The most common are *p*-coumaryl alcohol, coniferyl alcohol, and sinapyl alcohol. Their structure is shown in figure 2.7.

The way that the various monomers come together to form lignin is one of the biggest unanswered questions that we have today. The overall form of lignin is illustrated in figure 2.8. The polymerisation proceeds in three dimensions, in an apparently random fashion. There are an unfathomable number of chains, side chains, and cross linkages. The molecular weight of lignin is highly variable. This indicates that sometimes the molecules are very big and sometimes they are smaller.

There are two schools of thought concerning the synthesis of lignin in nature. One school holds that it proceeds in a random fashion. Another school maintains that there is a structure and form, but we simply do not know what it is. At the time of this writing, there does not appear to be any answers to these important questions.

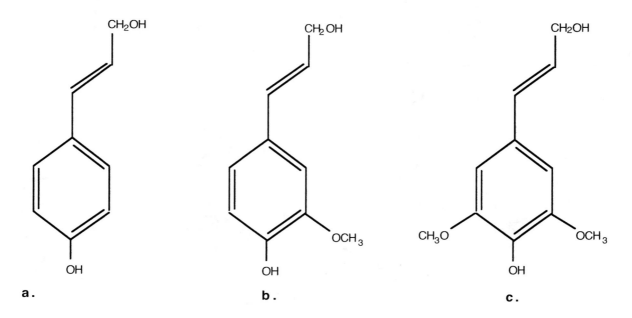

Figure 2.7. Common Monomers of Lignin - a. p-coumaryl alcohol b. coniferyl alcohol
c. sinapyl alcohol

Other Chemicals - There are a host of other chemicals that concern wood. Let us take a brief look at some of them.

Pectin is a water soluble polysaccharide that is found in plant cell walls and intercellular (interstitial) fluids. It is important in giving firmness to plants and fruits. It also plays a part in cementing the cellulose together in the formation of wood.

Hemicellulose is a macromolecule that may be thought of as a regulator in the formation of wood. It is composed of long glucose chains, as in cellulose, but it also has side chains. Hemicellulose binds with cellulose and helps regulate the formation of cellulose fibrils.

Proteins are not directly responsible for the mechanical properties of wood; their content in cell walls is simply too small. However, they do play major roles in regulating the growth of cells and the formation of cell walls.

We have gone over the molecular components of wood; let us now recap it very simply. The structure of wood is very similar to composite materials that we use in day-to-day life. Composites are essentially fibres with a bonding agent. Aeroplane parts may me made of carbon-fibres while fibreglass boat hulls may be made of glass-fibres. These fibres are then locked in a matrix of a binding agent such as epoxy. In the same way, wood may be visualised as cellulose fibres that are bound together in a matrix of lignin, hemicellulose, and a host of other chemicals.

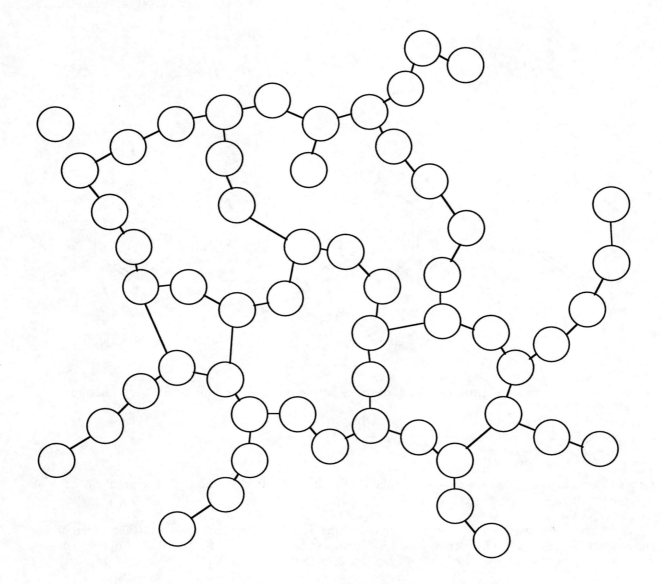

Figure 2.8. Arrangement of Monomers in Lignin? - Lignin is the second most common chemical in wood

PLANT CELLS AND CELL WALLS

Plant cells and cell walls are crucial to the development of wood.   Let us review some basic biology so that we may put things in some type of perspective.

A basic model of living tissue is illustrated in figure 2.9.   This model is so general that it could be found in almost anything, either plant or animal. The nucleus is a DNA rich structure that controls most of the cell functions. The cytoplasm is actually a combination of countless subcellular structures, such as ribosomes, mitochondria, chloroplasts, and endoplasmic reticulum, etc.   The cytoplasm is where most of the basic process of the life of the cell takes place.   The membrane is the gatekeeper between the extracellular and the intracellular environment; it controls numerous functions such as the concentration of ions, nutrients, and water content. The interstitium is what is of real interest to us.

The interstitial areas are the areas between the cells. If your high school biology was anything like mine, this was largely ignored and deemed to be not very important. However, from the standpoint of wood, it is of prime importance.

Wood is essentially just the lifeless interstitium of the tree. The interstitial areas of the plant are occupied by something known as a cell wall.

Cell Walls - The cell wall is one of the defining characteristics of plant tissue[1]. Animals do not have cell walls.

The cell wall serves many functions. The major function is structural. Since plants lack bones or shells, they depend upon the rigidity of the cell walls to maintain their shape. This is especially important in land plants. However, the function of cell walls is not purely mechanical. It is also important in warding off plant diseases and maintaining a proper environment for the metabolic process of the plant.

The chemical composition of the cell wall is very complex. Essentially we may view the cell wall as a thick, watery mixture of cellulose that is thickened and hardened with polysaccharides and glycoproteins.

The cell wall is not homogeneous, but is instead divided into sections. There is the primary cell wall and in many cases there is a secondary cell wall. These sections have very particular functions and properties.

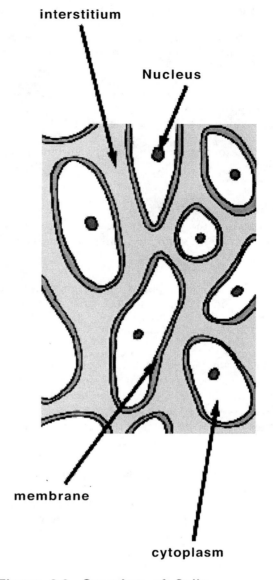

Figure 2.9. Overview of Cells

Types of Cells in Wood - The varieties of cell types in plants is vast. In this work we will only concern ourselves with the cells found in the trunks of trees. These are the only types that concern us in our discussion of wood. The types that we will discuss are the tracheide, vessel members, fibres, and parenchyma.

The tracheide is one of the most primitive cells found in the trunks of trees. It is a simple tube-like cell that is closed on both ends. The walls overlap and are perforated so that fluids may flow unhindered in the tree.

---

[1] In most of the biological sciences the terms "cell" is usually applied to the living cell. However when dealing with wood, the term is often applied to the empty space that was left behind as the cell died. This point should be kept in mind so that there should be no confusion.

Vessel members are another type of cell. They are believed to have evolved from the tracheides. They come in a variety of sizes. Lengths may run anywhere from 0.3 to 1.3 millimetres and with diameters that range between 0.01 to 0.5 millimetres.

Fibres too are believed to have evolved from the tracheides. They tend to be shorter than tracheides, usually only 1-2 millimetres in length. They have narrower diameters, closed ends, and thick cell walls.

Parenchyma are the smallest and simplest cells found in wood. They are only about 0.1-0.2 millimetres in length. Parenchyma usually have a large central vacuole (a small sack used to store waste products, food, or other chemicals).

These various types of cells are not living an independent isolated existence. They are part of a large living organism. This is of course the tree. Let us now turn our attention in this direction.

THE TREE

Understanding the nature of the tree is the next step towards understanding the nature of wood. This may appear to be a simple matter; yet, upon closer examination even the exact definition of a tree is complex.

Here is what a tree is. It is a perennial plant; that is, one that renews its growth each year. It is genetically linked to the shrubs, vines, and herbaceous plants. Trees belong to various divisions and subdivisions of the pteridophytes; they include such diverse plants as tree ferns, gymnosperms, and angiosperms (Britannica, 11, 908).

So what does all this mean? Not much really! It basically means that there is very little genetic difference between trees and the other common plants that are likely to come to ones mind. Where a flower might produce a stem, its not too distant relative might produce a mighty trunk. So we may ask ourselves, why are trees derived from so many different types of plants? The answer becomes clear when we look at their evolution.

Millions of years ago plants began to make their way out of the oceans. It is the very nature of life that it seeks to expand and occupy all possible environments. Therefore, plants found the land to be a vast unoccupied space suitable for their purpose. Millions of years elapsed and plants became very successful in occupying the land. Some lived in rocky soils, some lived in clay or loam. Some could survive the blistering heat of the tropics and others adapted to live in the driest deserts. Yet there was one environment yet to be conquered, the air!

The various plants all started to fill this new environment in a similar way. They started to force themselves up, first on small stalks and then later upon mighty trunks. In some cases these new plants could force themselves hundreds of feet into the air. Thus were the trees born.

If we wish to couch this in scientific terms we may say that the tree is defined by morphology. It is the form of the tree which defines it, not the family of plants that it is derived from. Just as the nature of the water has caused the porpoise and the fish to assume a similar morphology, in the same way, the requirements of an aerial existence have forced a similar morphology on vastly dissimilar types of plants.

The majority of wood comes from two classes of trees; the gymnosperms and the angiosperms. These produce wood with interesting characteristics.

Gymnosperms - Gymnosperms contain some of the oldest trees in the world. This group consists entirely of trees and woody shrubs. Their major characteristic is that the seeds develop exposed in the form of cones. Gymnosperms are usually evergreen, meaning that they remain green all year round.

The earliest known forests on earth were gymnosperms. During the Carboniferous period (280,000,000-345,000,000 years ago), vast forests of fernwoods covered the earth. Today, these fernwood forests are known only by their fossil remains.[2]

The most common gymnosperm trees alive today are the conifers. These are known commercially as the softwoods. Firs, spruces, cedars, junipers, hemlocks, sequoias, and pines are some of the more common examples.

The wood (xylem) of the gymnosperms is very simple and primitive. It has a characteristic cellular structure that is made of only tracheides and parenchyma.

Angiosperms - Angiosperms are the most common plants in the world today. They are characterised by the use of flowers for reproduction. Unlike the gymnosperms where seed production occurs in the open, the angiosperms produce the seeds within an ovary. Fruits such as apples, mangoes, and coconuts are merely the enlarged ovaries of these angiosperm trees. Angiosperms also include a very large number of plants that clearly are not trees.

Trees come from two groups of angiosperms. There are the monocots and there are the dicots. Monocots are represented primarily by palm trees and bamboo. The wood is characterised by an absence of rings. Dicots are somewhat higher on the evolutionary ladder. These are often referred to as the broadleaves, or the hardwoods. These include the oak, walnut, and maple.

The hardwoods have a much more complex cellular structure. There are vessel members, fibres, and parenchyma.

We have briefly looked at the types of plants that form trees. Let us look much more closely at the nature of the wood from these trees.

THE TRUNK AND WOOD

The trunk of the tree is nearly synonymous with wood. This is for the very obvious reason that most wood is derived from the trunk of the tree. You may ask yourself, "But what happens when the tree is cut down? Doesn't that change the characteristics?" The answer is surprisingly no! There is very little change in the characteristics of the wood of a living tree and the wood that we use for making things. The reason for this is because wood is just as dead in the living tree as it is when it is cut down.

Lifeless Tissue - The trunk is a massive amount of dead cells. There are very few living cells in the trunk of the tree. It is actually necessary that the majority of the tree be dead! Let us look at some of the reasons why.

One reason why the tree trunk is dead, is due to plant metabolism. A tree is a truly massive thing. If it were all living, it would require a tremendous expenditure of the plant's metabolic resources just to keep it alive. This is an unacceptable waste. The trunk's major job is simply to transport food and water. The wood (xylem) is so hygroscopic that it is able to raise water and minerals to a very great extent simply by capillary action. This requires no expenditure of energy on the part of the tree. Therefore, it is more efficient to allow it to be dead.

Another reason why the major portion of the tree is dead is mechanical. Plant cells that are living must be highly porous. Water must be able to enter and leave; food for the cells must be able to enter. This is the nature of life. This necessitates porosity. However, such porosity can compromise mechanical strength. One may gain considerable strength by taking old cells, resin, etc. and compressing them into a hard strong mass. This extremely hard mass of dead cells is strong enough

---

[2] It is not really correct to say that they are entirely extinct. Of the entire order of Ginkgoales, one species survives today. It is the ginkgo, otherwise known as the maidenhair tree. It has long since become extinct in the wild and exists today only because it is cultivated in Buddhist temples in Asia.

to support branches high in the air and still stand up to storms, winds, and other environmental factors.

Let us take a closer look at a cross section of a tree trunk (fig. 2.10). This will allow us to identify the parts of the trunk. Essentially there are only three sections: the xylem (wood), the bark, and there is a microscopic layer known as the cambium.

Bark - Bark is extremely important for the tree. It is the most biologically active portion of the tree trunk. The base of the bark is the cambium (described later), the next layer out is composed of the phloem. The phloem is a series of sieve elements and companion cells whose job is to transport food. Beyond the phloem is the cortex. The outermost section of the bark is the periderm; this is essentially a protective layer, but it is also involved in food storage and gas exchanged with the air.

Cambium - The key to the production of wood is in the cambium. The cambium is the microscopic layer of cells that surrounds the wood, but lies just under the bark. This layer of living cells is responsible for the growth of the trunk. At the beginning of each new growth cycle, a layer of soft wood is deposited.

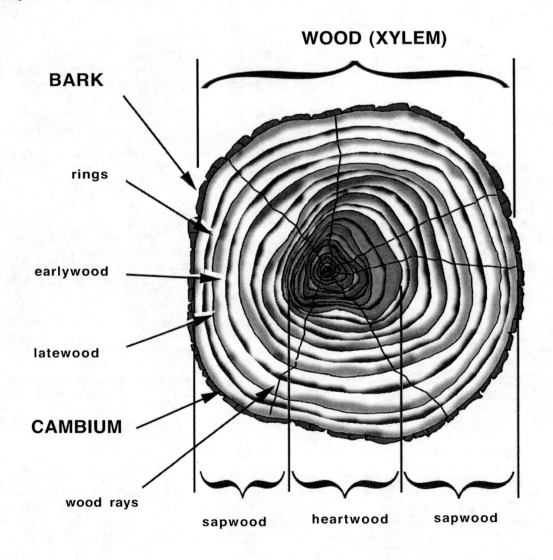

Figure 2.10. Anatomy of a Tree Trunk

page 180

<u>Xylem</u> - The xylem is the major portion of the trunk. These are lifeless cell walls that have been voided of living material. They then become capillaries for the flow of water and minerals. They carry them from the roots to the leaves, fruit, flowers, or other elements in the crown. We may divide the xylem into two sections, there is the heartwood and the sapwood. The sapwood is vascular while the heartwood has been clogged with congealed sap and resin. Both the heartwood and the sapwood show growth rings. Each ring is itself divided into two. The innermost section is known as the earlywood or the springwood. The outer section of the ring is known as the latewood or summerwood.

The heartwood lies at the very core of the tree. It is a mass of compressed dead cells and disused xylem that have become filled with solidified resin. It is nonporous, and is incapable of transmitting fluids. Although this is the deadest part of the tree it is also the strongest.

The tree must have an abundance of active xylem before heartwood may form. This generally takes 20-40 years. When the tree has sufficient xylem that some may be sacrificed, various substances such as tannin, resin, fats, and rubber-like materials are transmitted through the wood rays to the core of the tree where they are deposited. These chemicals are generally toxic to both the tree and potential parasites.

The heartwood serves several functions for the plant. One function is as a repository for toxic wastes from the bark and cambium. Remember that unlike animals, the tree has no real excretory system. Something must be done with metabolic waste products lest they accumulate and kill the tree. Therefore, one of the functions is to act as a repository for these wastes. Another function of heartwood is to make the tree strong. Heartwood has an incredible density and great strength. There is still a third function of heartwood. Plants do not have highly developed immunological systems; xylem is dead tissue, so it effectively has none. Depositing toxic materials in superfluous heartwood makes it resistant to insects and decay.

A look at any part of the xylem will show a series of rings. These may be referred to as growth rings or annual rings. The biological key to the production of these rings may be found in the perennial nature of the plant. A perennial plant keeps on growing each year. This does not mean that the growth is continuous; usually it is not. It merely means that each new cycle of growth will lay down a new layer of cells over the old ones and continue growing.

The initial layer of xylem laid down by the cambium is different from the later layers. The first deposits are variously referred to as "springwood" or "earlywood". As the growing season continues, the deposits begin to be much harder. The last wood to be deposited is the "latewood", or "summerwood. During winter in temperate climates, the tree remains dormant until the start of the next growing season. This constant cycle between the two types of wood is the cause of the rings.

The terms "springwood", and "summerwood" may be very misleading. In India, the growing cycle is regulated not by winters and summers, but instead by monsoons and dry seasons. Therefore the terms "earlywood" and "latewood" are much more accurate terms.

<u>Wood Rays</u> - Wood rays are small, barely visible channels which run from the outside of the tree in towards the centre. We alluded to them earlier. These rays are used by the tree to transmit resin and metabolic wastes from the cambium to the centre of the tree.

Let us review the important parts of this last section. Wood is almost entirely lifeless tissue. It is lifeless for several reasons. One reason is to conserve metabolic resources. Another reason is that it is much easier to make a strong support structure out of dense lifeless tissue, than porous, living tissue. This fact makes it very easy to maintain the mechanical characteristics of the wood long after the tree has been felled.

MECHANICAL AND OTHER CHARACTERISTICS OF WOOD

The characteristics are very important in determining the uses for wood. These characteristics include such diverse properties as weight, compressibility, and strength under a variety of conditions. There are several considerations when dealing with the mechanical qualities.

There is no such thing as good characteristics or bad characteristics. It is all just a question of using the right wood for the right job. For instance, one would never attempt to build a house with balsa-wood or pith. By the same token, one would be ill advised to try and build model aeroplanes from the heartwood of an oak.

It is even difficult to measure these characteristics. Trees are very inconsistent; within the same species they vary from tree to tree. The qualities even vary widely from one part of the tree to another. With this caveat in mind, let us look at some of the basic qualities.

Dimensional Stability - One extremely important characteristic is dimensional stability. Dimensional stability is a difficult term for a very simple concept. If we cut a cube of wood that is exactly one–inch square on all sides, can we come back later and measure it and still find it one inch? At first glance this may seem like a silly question, but it is not. This one-inch cube of wood is likely to be slightly different every time we measure it.

The dimensional instability of wood is essentially due to variable water content. As the tree absorbs water it will expand. As it dries out the wood contracts. This reflects the extremely hygroscopic nature of cellulose coupled with the high porosity of the wood. The hygroscopic nature of cellulose is the fundamental affinity for moisture, while the porous nature of wood provides a large area by which moisture can enter or leave the cellulose / lignin matrix.

Stiffness - Stiffness is another mechanical characteristic. This characteristic is sometimes difficult to assess because the stiffness varies tremendously according to the relationship with the grain. Stiffness does not seem to be a significant factor for the *tabla*.

Density - Density is the relative weight of the wood. Given an identical volume of wood, there may be a tremendous variation in the weight. This varies from species to species. Woods like oak are very heavy and very dense. Woods like balsa are very light and have a low density. The density also varies within the same species of tree. The same variety may produce different densities of wood depending on factors such as age and the nutrition of the tree. To make matters even more complicated, the density of the wood varies even within the same tree. The heartwood of a large, old tree is going to be much denser that the wood from outer portions of the trunk (sapwood).

Insect and Fungus Resistance - Resistance to insects, fungus, and other biological factors are another important consideration. This is especially important in determining the life of *tablas* made of inferior quality woods, such as mango (*aam*). Parasitic insects can reduce a musical instrument to dust within a few years in the warm Indian climate. Fungus is especially damaging to woods before they are properly seasoned. (We will discuss seasoning in greater detail later.)

Acoustical Characteristics - Acoustical characteristics are the way that sound interacts with wood. Sound is essentially a vibration, and wood has the ability to vibrate just as most other substances. The two major considerations are acoustical absorption and acoustical transmission.

The ability of the wood to transmit sound is very important for musical instruments. If we apply an acoustical vibration at one end of a piece of wood, what is the wood's ability to transmit this vibration. This is not really one factor but several factors. Let us briefly look at some of these qualities.

The speed at which wood may propagate an acoustic vibration is one factor. Wood is heterogeneous, therefore it should surprise no one that the propagation speeds are also variable. For instance, propagation speeds for an ultrasonic signal are in the range of $1 kms^{-1}$ against the grain while they run around $5 Kms^{-1}$ along the grain (Beall 1986).

It seems that the most important acoustic factor in determining a good wood and a good *dayan* shell is attenuation. When one puts an acoustic signal into the wood, how much does it reduce the intensity? It is hard to give an exact value because the attenuation actually increases exponentially with frequency. Experiments with ultrasonics (100-200kHz) have shown that while the attenuation along the grain is only about 30dBm^{-1}, when one attempts to propagate a signal across the grain the attenuation increases to 200 dBm^{-1}(Beall 1986). These numbers of course are just examples. Geometry of the wood, frequency, and any number of variables may bring it up or down.

We can recap these points very simply. Sound travels very easily in the direction of the grain, but very poorly across the grain. Hardwoods transmit sound better than soft pithy woods. For *tabla dayan,* we want to use the hardest, heaviest woods that we can find.

INDIAN WOODS USED FOR TABLA

It is now time to take a closer look at the various woods used to make *dayans*. We find that there are a number of factors which influence the decision as to what woods will be used. Certainly the previously mentioned mechanical and acoustical characteristics play a major part. Also, the ability to resist insects plays a major part. However, we must not forget that mundane considerations, such as cost and availability, play important roles. Let us look at some common Indian woods with these various considerations in mind.

Indian Rosewood (*Dalbergia latifolia* and *Dalbergia sissoo*) - The Indian rosewood is the preferred wood for making the *dayan*. Rosewood has peculiar characteristics. It is a deep dark colour, but it does not accept varnish very well due to it very resinous character. It is very dense, very heavy, and very hard and is therefore very difficult to work with. The name "rosewood" is derived from the fact that freshly cut wood has a rose-like fragrance.

The very characteristics which make it a difficult building material make rosewood ideal for musical instruments. The very heavy, hard quality is very good acoustically. It resists insects. It is also fairly homogenous; it is almost lacking in growth rings. Rosewood was once in great demand for making pianos, but dwindling sources have made it cost-prohibitive. It is still used extensively for making marimbas, claves and a variety of instruments, both Indian and non-Indian.

There are not one, but two varieties of Indian rosewood. There is the *Dalbergia latifolia* and there is the *Dalbergia sissoo*. Within the Indian timber trade, there does not appear to be any distinction between the two species. They are both commonly referred to as *shisham* or Indian rosewood. Let us look at both of these varieties.

Dalbergia sissoo is a remarkable tree (fig. 2.11). It is variously known as Indian dalbergia, Indian rosewood, *shisham, sisoo*, and a host of other local names. It grows to about 60 feet in height and about two-to-three feet in diameter. It produces a very irregular wood with many suckers. The leaves are clustered with anywhere from three to seven leaflets per cluster. Each leaf is approximately three inches in length. Its seeds are flat and brown, roughly one-half-inch long.

Figure 2.11. Indian Rosewood (Dalbergia Sissoo) - This is a good wood for making dayan shells.

Dalbergia latifolia is also interesting. It too, is called *shisham* or Indian rosewood, but it may also be referred to as *sitsal, beete,* or Bombay blackwood. It may reach a height of 60-120 feet at maturity, and a diameter of approximately two-to-three feet. Leaf clusters are alternate with five to seven leaves of unequal size. It produces white flowers, and has a grey bark (Troup 1921). In India, it may be found from the foothills of the Himalayas all the way down to the southern tip. The most important commercial forests are found in the Western *ghats* which extend from Tamil Nadu into Kerala and Karnatika.

The wood of *Dalbergia latifolia* is very valuable. The sapwood is pale yellow to white, while the heartwood varies from brown with purple streaks to being dark purple-brown with black streaks. As the heartwood ages, it darkens and becomes extremely dense. Most importantly for makers of musical instruments is that it shows no visible growth rings. In a sense, the heartwood resembles one monolithic mass of dense, heavy wood. This is very desirable from an acoustical standpoint.

Sal (*Shorea robusta*) - *Sal* is also known as *shala, salwa, sakhu, sakher, kandar, sakwa,* and a host of other names (fig. 2.12). It is one of the most prized timbers for construction. In India, *sal* forests are found in Nepal, Madhya Pradesh, Uttar Pradesh, Himachal Pradesh, Orissa, and Bihar. *Sal* is also found in Bangladesh.

Sal has some interesting characteristics. It is a large sub-deciduous tree that grows well in moist sandy loam. It is very gregarious and usually forms the dominant composition in the forests where it occurs. It has whitish flowers. *Sal* is fairly slow growing, but it may attain great size. It can grow to approximately 100 feet in height with a diameter of around $2-2^{1}/_{4}$ feet in about 100 years. It grows straight and tall; this makes it ideal for timber.

The trees are commonly tapped for their sap. This is an oleoresin which contains triterpenoids, the derivatives of ursonic, oleanane, and triterpene acid. This resin is used in the indigenous systems of medicine as an astringent and detergent. It is taken internally as a treatment for diarrhoea and dysentery. It is also used externally in ointments for skin diseases and in ear troubles. One also finds it burned in Hindu homes as incense.

The wood is very dense and hard. Typically it is around 25-30 Kg per square foot. This great weight and density makes it a very difficult wood to work with. However, it is well suited to the making of *tablas*. Its great strength, large dimensions, and straight growth, also make it a suitable material for beams used in construction of buildings, bridges, and similar structures.

Jack (*Artocarpus heterophyllus*) - Jack, jackfruit, or jackwood, is also known locally as *panasa, lakuchi,* or a host of other names (fig 2.13). This wood is very suitable for making *tablas,* but its use is not really that common. One is more likely to find jackwood shells in the deep south.

This is a very interesting tree. It grows 30-70 feet high. It has alternate, glossy, and somewhat leathery leaves that are quite large, sometimes nine inches. It has sticky white sap that is sometimes used as a glue. The jackfruit is very unusual in that it attains a monstrously large size. A single fruit may be up to three feet long, 20 inches wide, and weigh up to 110 pounds! The fruit has a somewhat banana-like flavour and a somewhat pineapple-like aroma; it is widely eaten in south India.

Figure 2.12. Sal Trees

Although common in south Asia and the tropics, the range is somewhat restricted. It does not tolerate droughts and frost may decimate the young populations.

The wood has a number of interesting qualities. It ages to a deep dark brown colour and polishes very well. It is very resistant to insects. As is typical of other woods used to make *tabla,* it is hard, dense, and very difficult to work.

Teak (*Tectona grandis*) - Teak is a deciduous tree found in the tropics (2.14). It grows tall and straight and is buttressed at the base. It reaches a height of about 100-150 feet at maturity. It produces clusters of small white flowers. These will in turn ripen into a small fruit somewhat reminiscent of cherries. The leaves are very large, about one foot in length, and resemble tobacco leaves.

The wood of the teak is very dense and hard. The sapwood is white while the heartwood is a yellowish brown. The wood is dense, yet it is fairy easy to work. Furthermore it has a remarkable dimensional stability.

Teak is an amazingly durable wood; there are recorded instances of teak surviving over 1000 years! In India there are a number of cases where teak beams are still in use in buildings after over 200 years. It resists insects and decay. It is weatherproof in all conditions. It even resists acid!

India has a long history of dealing with teak. In Sanskrit, teak is known as *saka.* As early as 600 BC, India was exporting teak to China. Ancient Phoenicians and Arabs used Indian teak in the making of their ships. Under British rule, massive amounts of teak forests were cut and exported to the rest of the British empire.

However, centuries of commercial exploitation have nearly destroyed the Indian teak forests. India has turned from a teak exporter to a teak importer. Today teak is imported into India from Mayanmar (Burma), Nigeria, and elsewhere, simply to satisfy local demands. Therefore, the cost of teak has become prohibitive and teak *tablas* are today very rare. In the last 30 years of my association with the *tabla,* I think that I can count the number of teak *dayans* that I have

Figure 2.13. Jackfruit Tree

Figure 2.14. Teak Tree

encountered on one hand. These were invariably antiques. It seems that the near elimination of the local teak forests essentially removed teak from the list of viable woods from which to make *tabla*.

Tun (*Cedrela toona* or *Toona ciliata*) - *Tun* is only a modest quality wood for *tabla*. In English, *tun* is variously known as Indian mahogany, red cedar, or Australian red cedar. It is a deciduous tree with a thin grey bark. It may be found in the higher elevations anywhere in south Asia. It is normally found mixed with *shisham* (Indian rosewood), acacias, fiscus, bombax, and a host of others (fig. 2.15).

There appears to be some disagreement as to the classification of *tun*. Traditionally, *tun* was categorised under the genus of *Cedrela*, hence the scientific name *C. toona*. However, there are a large number of scholars who are of the opinion that it deserves its own genus, hence the scientific name of *T. ciliata*. Obviously a book on the manufacture of *tabla* is not the best place to get involved in such esoteric controversies.

Tun is a fast growing tree, generally reaching maturity in 70-80 years. At maturity it is about 50-100 feet tall. The trunk may be several feet in diameter. It may be buttressed and fluted at the base.

Tun has well defined growth rings. Although this gives an attractive grain when used for general applications, this is not the most desirable quality for making musical instruments. Still it is very often used to make a variety of musical instruments including *sarangi*, *sitar*, and *tabla*.

There is a substantial difference between the heartwood and the sapwood. The heartwood is red in colour, quite dense, and acceptable for making *tabla*. The sapwood in contrast, is much lighter in colour and lighter in weight; this is obviously much less desirable.

Tun has some problems in the area of dimensional stability. This is especially seen in the drying stage. Shrinkage of 10% by volume is normal.

All in all, *tun* is not the best wood for musical instruments, including *tabla*. The heavy, well defined growth rings introduce discontinuities in the propagation of acoustical waves. The dimensional instability means that *tun* shells have a strong propensity toward warping. Furthermore, *tun* is susceptible to insects. Still, its widespread availability and ease of working have made it a popular wood for musical instrument builders.

Figure 2.15. Tun

Babool (*Acacia tortilis*, also *A. raddiana*, *A. heteracantha*, or *A. spirocarpa*) - The *babool* is a moderately acceptable wood for *tabla* (fig. 2.16). On the positive side it is a heavy, dense wood. However, it is susceptible to insects. One sometimes finds *tablas* made from this wood in Rajasthan (India) and parts of Pakistan.

The *babool* thrives in extremely arid regions. It requires very little water. It grows well in sandy dunes and rocky soil. It prefers alkaline soils and will tolerate high salt and gypsum contents. It tolerates extremes in temperature where the sun bakes the soil in the day and the night plunges to near freezing.

It was introduced into India from Israel at the time of Independence; this was done in an attempt to aid the development of desert areas such as Rajasthan. It has thrived in these regions and is often the only source of wood.

There are several species and subspecies of *babool*. Academia is not in agreement as to what constitutes the species and subspecies. This explains the various scientific designations such as *Acacia tortilis*, *A. raddiana*, *A. heteracantha*, and *A. spirocarpa*. Again, this is not a place to go into the various academic debates.

Babool has some interesting qualities. The wood is red in colour. It is very dense. However, the tree is loaded with thorns. This makes the harvesting somewhat difficult.

All things considered, the *babool* would never be the first choice of wood for the *tabla*. Unfortunately, in many parts of India it is the only wood which is locally available. Therefore, one will occasionally find *tablas* made of this wood.

Figure 2.16. Babool Tree

Khair (*Acacia catechu* or *Catechu nigrum*) - *Khair* is known by many names. Some common ones are *khairbabul, khoria, koir, kagli, cachu, kugli, kaderi, khoiru,* and *sandra* (fig. 2.17).

It is a medium sized, deciduous tree found in India, Nepal, Pakistan, as well as many other tropical countries. It has a rough, dark grey-brown bark. It matures in about 50-60 years. It is not a particularly tall tree; it attains heights of about 25-35 feet, and a trunk of about one-to-two feet in diameter. It seldom grows straight, but usually grows in a twisted, gnarly fashion. It produces flowers that vary from yellow to creme colour.

The wood is very good for *tabla*. The wood is red in colour, and grows darker upon exposure to air. It is extremely hard. It is also extremely heavy, approximately 61 pounds-per-square-foot. It is extremely durable. As with many other woods that make good *tablas*, it is very difficult to work owing to its hardness. Although the sapwood is subject to insects, the hardwood is very insect resistant.

There is an extract of the heartwood known as *katha*. This extract is partly responsible for the red colour of an after dinner leaf mixture known as *paan*.

It is a very valuable tree. The wood is used for lumber, the bark has a number of uses, and the *katha* is very marketable. These

Figure 2.17. Khair

page 187

Figure 2.18. Bija

Figure 2.19. Mango

products fetch very high prices; therefore, there is considerable commercial exploitation of the *khair* tree. Unfortunately, this exploitation is not always legal. There is a major problem of illegal harvesting, and the black market in *khair* wood and *khair* products is extensive.

Bija (*Pterocarpus marsupium*) - *Bija* is also known as bastard teak, Indian padauk, *bijasal, bijasar,* red sandalwood, *piasala, biju, murga, vijayasar,* and a host of others (fig. 2.18).

Bija is a large deciduous tree with a thick yellowish grey bark. Leaves are six-to ten inches long. It produces white flowers. *Bija* is said to be a very good wood for making *tablas.*

Mango wood (*Mangifera indica*) - Mango is also known as *aam, mamidi,* and a host of other names (fig 2.19).

The mango is inextricably linked to Indian traditions and customs. For instance it is customary to hang fresh mango leaves from the door of the house during the south Indian New Year. On special holy days, many Indians brush their teeth with mango instead of the usual *neem* twigs. In the fashion industry, the paisley pattern that was so popular in the 60's is a stylised mango, which even today is called *aam* (mango) in India. (The term "paisley" comes from the town in Scotland that was famous for producing an imitation Indian shawl with this pattern.)

The mango tree grows to be about 100 feet tall. The leaves may even grow to be a foot long. The leaves are slightly yellowish or reddish until they mature, then they become green. The flowers are small and come in clusters. They are usually creme coloured or pink.

The mango is one of the oldest cultivated fruit trees in the world. It is said to have been cultivated for the last 4000 years.

The mango is most famous for its fruit. The skin of the mango may be almost any colour. Although it is always green when unripe, the ripe mango may be green, red, orange, or yellow. Sometimes a ripe mango may show all of these colours on the skin at the same time. The fruit has a single hard, wood-like seed, somewhat reminiscent of a large, flat avocado pit. The flesh clings tightly to this pit. The fruit varies from yellow to orange in colour and is vaguely reminiscent of peach.

Mango wood has been increasing in popularity in India. On its positive side, it is easy to work. It has a light colour which easily accepts paint, stains and other finishes very well. Perhaps most importantly is that it is inexpensive; it costs considerably less than *shisham*, teak, or other Indian woods.

However, it does not make good *tablas*. The wood is not heavy enough. The light, slightly pithy quality of mango produces *tablas* that have a very poor sustain. Another problem is that mango wood is very susceptible to insects. All in all, it is neither strong, heavy, nor is it durable. Still, mango is commonly used to produce inexpensive student grade *tablas*.

We have gone into great detail concerning the trees and woods used to make the *tabla*. Let us now turn our attention to how these trees are actually harvested.

LOGGING

It is obvious that the trees must be cut, processed, and transported to the urban areas before they can be used for any application. *Tabla* makers certainly do not go to the forest and cut and season their own wood. They depend upon a highly developed logging and timber infrastructure. It is to our advantage to understand something about this system.

Logging in India is a two pronged approach. There are legal logging operations and there are illegal operations. The wood for *tabla* is just as likely to come from one as another. Let us look a little closer at both approaches.

Legal logging in India is usually done by private contractors. The logging contracts are generally sold by an auction from the government. However, there are cases where the government itself controls and manages the logging. At one time, all of the legal logging in India was controlled by the government, but this practice has largely been abandoned. There have also been experiments with co-operative societies of forest workers being given government contracts.

The logs and other forest products may be disposed of in a variety of ways. In some cases the logs are sold directly to timber merchants and wood dependent industries. Yet in other cases the wood must be sold back to the government for distribution through government agencies.

Illegal logging is handled quite differently. In such cases there are no contracts or licenses, and no rules are followed concerning the felling of trees. Usually bribes are paid to forest officers or other concerned parties so that they will look the other way. In extreme cases violence may be used to keep the concerned authorities from discharging their duties[3].

Logging operations in India are labour intensive affairs. The timbers are felled and rough cut by hand. The transportation is usually by pack animals and the initial processes are basically manual. Attempts have been made to mechanise logging operations, but these attempts have generally failed.

The reasons for the failure of these attempts to mechanise are complex. The bottom line however is simple; mechanical approaches cost more than manual approaches. Labour in India is amazingly cheap. Mechanical equipment on the other hand is very expensive. Furthermore, the infrastructure necessary to support mechanical approaches is not developed enough to be reliable. Shortages of electricity, diesel fuel, and petrol are common. Furthermore, one may never be sure that

---

[3] The case of Verrapan is an extremely colourful example of an illegal logger. For decades he has been engaged in illegal sandalwood logging and ivory poaching in the south Indian state of Karnatika. He has killed anyone who has stood in his way. Present estimates are that he has killed over 140 people. He finally came to international attention when he kidnapped a famous south Indian movie star. At the time of this writing he is still on the loose.

Figure 2.20. Felling the Trees

replacement parts will be available. When they are available, the quality is often suspect. Strangely enough, there is a widespread system of counterfeit mechanical parts in India. Sometimes they are merely non-original replacements with no deception intended; however, many times they are packaged in such a way that there is a deliberate effort to deceive the buyer. Either way, the quality is usually substandard.

The logging industry uses extremely simple technologies. The basic felling is usually done by axe and/or crosscut saw (fig. 2.20). The limbs are generally removed with an axe. The bark is removed by hand. Depending upon the wood and the purpose, there may be further work at the stump site. A lot of work is done at the stump site in order to lighten the load to be transported out.

Transportation of the logs from the stump site is usually very low-tech. The common means is to simply drag the logs by means of animals. Elephants, buffalo, and bullocks are most often used in these endeavours (fig. 2.21). Once they have been worked into smaller logs and transported to places where the roads are better, transportation by bullock carts, tractors, lorries, or some other means is common.

There are other forms of transportation that are specific to particular terrains. Such specialised means of transportation include gravity ropeways, wet slides, chutes, and earth slides. Floating and rafting are still common in India.

SEASONING
Seasoning is the process of taking wood from its green state and converting it into a usable wood. In its simplest form, it is nothing more than the drying of the wood. Seasoning the wood gives many desirable qualities and reduces many undesirable ones. Seasoning improves the dimensional stability; wood is notoriously bad at maintaining its size and shape. Seasoning reduces biological degradation; insects and fungus can reduce moist wood to dust. Seasoning also improves surface workability. Let us look more closely into this.

Figure 2.21. Elephants Transporting Logs

<u>Hardness</u> - Seasoning increases strength and improves hardness. Green wood tends to be softer and spongier than dry, seasoned wood. One can take a fingernail and easily make an impression on green wood. This is much harder to do with fully seasoned wood.

<u>Workability</u> - Seasoned wood is much easier to work. It is very difficult to sand green wood. A rough cut for green wood may work acceptably but fine cutting is not so easy. Painting or varnishing green wood is an extremely difficult affair.

<u>Strength</u> - Drying of the wood past the fibre saturation point (described later) also increases hardness and strength. As the moisture is driven from the cell walls, the fibres become more compact (Wangaard, 1950). The reduction in water actually causes hydrogen bonds to be created between adjacent cellulose molecules (Wakeham, 1955).

<u>Dimensional Stability</u> - Dimensional stability improves once we take wood to the normal ambient moisture state, however there are considerable changes which occur as the wood dries. Engineering books tend to show these functions in terms of radial and tangential shrinkage rates. Sometimes the overall volume is also indicated. These rates will not just vary from species to species, but also from tree to tree. Furthermore, even within the same tree it varies (e.g., heartwood, vs. sapwood).

<u>Fungus</u> - The most important reason for seasoning wood is to protect against biological degradation. Green wood may simply rot away but, well seasoned wood may be stored and used indefinitely. The most important infection for wood is fungus.

Fungal infections may come from several sources. Sometimes the infection starts with air-born spores. Sometimes the infection starts when wood comes in contact with infected wood. Either way, once the fungal infection starts, it is often hard to control.

There are many classes of infections. Some fungi are more damaging than others. Brown-rot and white-rot are the worst, followed by blue-stain. Moulds are the least dangerous (Rasmussen 1961).

Brown-rot is one of the most serious problems that can affect unseasoned or improperly seasoned wood. These fungi send microscopic root-like hairs which penetrate the wood and use an enzyme to digest the cellulose in the wood. Cellulose is one of the most important macromolecules in the wood. When it is destroyed the wood becomes brittle to the point that it will crumble in your hands.

The name brown-rot is derived from the brown colour of the infected wood. The brown colour is due to the fact that cellulose is white and lignin is brown. When the fungus destroys the white cellulose, it leaves the brown lignin behind.

Another devastating fungus that attacks woods is white-rot. White rot is very similar to brown rot, except that the fungus destroys the lignin, leaving the white cellulose behind. This gives the infected wood a white colour.

Both brown-rot and white-rot are not caused by a single fungus, but by any of a number of different strains having similar cellulose / lignin attacking properties. More information may be found elsewhere (e.g., Duncan and Lombard 1965).

Blue-stain is another type of fungus that attacks wood. It is usually caused by any of several strains of *Ceratocystis*. Blue-stain affects the look of the wood, but does not really weaken the wood significantly. This is not a problem to the *tabla* maker because the common approach it to paint the wood rather than stain it. Since it does not pose a major problem to the *tablamaker,* we need not go into the topic any deeper.

Another type of fungus which affects wood is mould. There are numerous strains of mould; these may be any colour. There is generally not much of a compromise in the strength of the wood because the effects are usually superficial.

The bottom line is simple; seasoning wood makes it more resistant to biological degradation. Well seasoned wood tends to be durable while green wood tends to rot away. The cause for this rotting is generally fungus. There is not one species of fungus, but numerous types which attack the wood in very specific ways.

Other Advantages of Seasoning - The previous points were of particular importance to *tablawalas*; however, there are other advantages. These include such things as improving the ability to take nails, screws, staples, and other fasteners. The thermal and electrical insulating abilities are improved. Also, seasoned wood is better able to be glued than green wood.

Basic Principles of Seasoning - Seasoning is the process of drying the wood. When a tree is felled, up to 50% of its weight is simply water. Water is present in the tree in two ways. First, there is water which is in the cell cavities. This is basically the sap. This is analogous to a glass that is full of water. However, there is also moisture which is locked into the cell walls themselves. Returning to our analogy of the glass, it is as though a large amount of water was actually locked into the structure of the glass itself. This water is referred to as "imbibed" or "hygroscopic".

Seasoning of the wood progresses in two phases. First, the free water is evaporated. At some point all of the free water has been removed, but there is still water locked in the cell walls. This point is known as the fibre saturation point. From here on, any water removed will be removed from the cell walls. For most species of trees the fibre saturation point is 25%-30% moisture (by weight as compared to kiln dried weight). It is easy to see that at the fibre saturation point there is still a lot of water tied up in the wood.

It is not necessary or practical to remove all of the water; ultimately the wood will reach equilibrium with its environment. This will normally be between 4%-12% moisture content. Therefore, if we get the wood to this range, it is considered seasoned.

There are two overall approaches to seasoning the wood. There is air seasoning and there is kiln seasoning. The appropriate process is determined according to what the final application is going to be, what the initial wood is, as well as a number of economic considerations.

Air Drying - Air seasoning allows the wood to dry out at normal ambient temperatures. This has the advantage that it does not consume large amounts of energy as a kiln would. It also has the advantage that the wood is much less likely to develop cracks. Unfortunately, it has the disadvantage that many of your less durable woods tend to degrade before they are properly seasoned; this greatly reduces the quality. There is the further disadvantage that the processing time may take years to accomplish. This may have undesirable economic consequences.

One of the simplest, albeit slowest, air seasoning process was used in the seasoning of teak trees. For this one girdled the tree. Girdling is the process of cutting a band of bark off from the tree. This leaves the xylem intact but denies the tree its phloem, which causes the tree to die. The dead teak tree is then allowed to remain standing for several years as it slowly dries out. This process works for teak because it is an amazingly durable wood; most trees would simply rot with this type of treatment.

Usually air drying is nothing more than stacking the logs or timber in a dry place and letting it sit. They must be stacked in places where they will not be rained upon. Furthermore, they must be stacked in such a way that air may freely circulate.

As a general rule, air drying is extremely gentle and does not damage the wood. However, there are situations where even air drying is too fast and cracking may result. For such situations, the drying may be slowed down by painting the ends with wax, tar, or any similar substance. This will slow down the drying and make the seasoning even gentler.

<u>Kiln Drying</u> - For many commercial operations, kiln drying is the preferred way to season wood. It is fast; it sustains a very large throughput, and it is controllable. Unfortunately, it consumes energy which is very costly in India. Furthermore, it tends to cause large items, like the *dayan* shells, to crack.

There are two overall forms of kilns. There is the progressive kiln and there is the compartment kiln (Thelen 1923).

The progressive kiln is very much like an assembly line. The green wood enters one end and progresses through the kiln until it comes out fully seasoned at the other end. Each section of the kiln maintains the appropriate temperature and humidity for the particular stage of the drying. Some progressive kilns allow for a natural draft of air to dry the wood, while others rely on fans to force the dry air over the wood (Rasmussen 1955).

Compartment kilns operate in a very different manner; they process the wood in batches. In a compartment kiln, the wood is loaded into the kiln and remains there the entire period. Temperature and humidity are varied periodically according to what stage the batch is in. As in the progressive kiln, the flow of air may be by natural convection or it may be forced by fans.

The seasoning technology is a constantly evolving craft. A number of new technologies are being introduced, but have not yet found their way into general usage. Such examples are dehumidification drying, chemical seasoning, high frequency dielectric heating, resistance heating, infrared radiation, and a host of others. These are generally not used in India and are of little interest to the topic of the making of *tablas*.

<u>Economics of Seasoning</u> - Economics plays a major role in the decision as to what seasoning process is to be used. As a general rule, air drying is the preferred method of seasoning, because it requires very little energy. However, the globalisation of the world economies has meant that India has started to have access to technologies that were previously unavailable. Furthermore, wood that is exported must now come up to world standards. These standards are not easily met with air drying because of the vagaries of nature. Furthermore, the slow throughput of air seasoning makes air drying operations unable to respond to rapid fluctuations in the price of wood. Therefore, there are major moves afoot to shift from air drying to kiln drying. Still, India moves very slowly and it appears that air drying will be here for a long time.

<u>Seasoning and the Dayan</u> - The *dayan* presents some interesting twists to the process of seasoning. In many ways, the requirements for the *dayan* run counter to the rest of the industry. For instance, kiln drying generally produces a higher quality of lumber because of the reduced chance of moulds and fungi. However, kiln drying lowers the quality of *dayans* produced because the dimensions are such that there is an increased chance for cracking and warping. The woods that are used for the *dayan* tend to be naturally resistant to biological degradation, so biological degradation is usually not a problem. For these reasons, air drying is the preferred means of seasoning.

We have seen in this section that drying the wood, known in the industry as seasoning, is very important. Unseasoned wood has many undesirable qualities, the most important being that it will simply rot away. When the wood is fully seasoned it may be worked to form the shells used to make the *tabla*.

INSECTS
Wood boring insects are a serious issue to the maker, seller, and purchaser of *tabla*. Although the better woods are resistant to them, the lesser woods, such as mango, are extremely susceptible to infestation. Probably the most common is the false powder-post beetle, often times called simply the "powder beetle". These beetles are any of a number of species belonging to the family of *Bostrichidae*.

What is most dangerous is the fact that it is often difficult to tell how much damage is being done. It is very common for them to hollow out a *dayan lakadi* and just leave the shell. This shell will then crumble when you try and work with it. The only superficial sign that something is wrong is that it may have a bunch of very small holes. Usually the more visible sign is the fine wood dust that has been cast out by the beetles as they leave the shell when they reach maturity.

Many woods are susceptible to the false powder post beetle. These include: mango wood, *sal*, and it has even been reported to attack teak.

CONCLUSION

We have gone into tremendous detail concerning the nature of wood. We have looked into the chemical and the molecular characteristics of wood. We examined the various types of trees and the logging operations. Furthermore, we looked at the seasoning. This is all to clarify the details of the fabrication that were discussed in Chapter 5.

Many will question the necessity of such detail. I admit that there was an incredibly tedious attention to detail, and this certainly does not make for easy reading. But a problem at ANY stage will compromise the quality of the finished *tabla*. Therefore, one stage is not inherently more important than any other. For instance, a compromise in the chemical content of the wood (e.g., brown-rot) is just as problematic as faulty workmanship in the final stages. Poor selection of the species of tree is also just as much a problem as improper seasoning. Since we are unable to point our finger at any one critical area, we have no recourse but to be familiar with wood from every angle. This will of course be a challenge to anyone with a serious interest in the subject.

WORKS CITED

Beall, F.C.
"Wood: Acoustic Emission and Acousto-Ultrasonic Characteristics", *Encyclopedia of Materials Science and Engineering (Supplementary Vol. 2)*. Oxford. Pergamon Press. Edited by Robert W. Cahn (pp 1375-1378).

Bender, F.
1964   *Dimensional Stabilization of Wood*. Canadian Dept. of Forestry Publication 1087, Ottawa.

Boyce, J.S.
1961   *Forest Pathology*. McGraw-Hill, New York.

Brown, H.P., A.J. Panshin and C.C. Forsaith
1952   *Textbook of Wood Technology*. McGraw-Hill Book Company, New York.

Brown, R.M., I.M. Saxena and Kudlicka
1996   "Cellulose Biosynthesis in Higher Plants", *Trends in Plant Sciences*. Elsevier Trends Journals., May 1996, Vol. 1, No.5 (pp 149-156).

Corkhill, T.
1979   *The Complete Dictionary of Wood*. New York. Stein and Day.

Cowling, E.B.
1961   *Comparative Biochemistry of the Decay of Sweetgum Sapwood by White-Rot and Brown-Rot Fungi*. U.S. Department Agr. Tech. Bul. No. 1258.
1963. "Structural Features of Cellulose that Influence its Susceptibility of Enzymatic Hydrolysis", *Advances in Enzymatic Hydrolysis of Cellulose and Related Materials*, Edited by Elwyn T. Reese, Pergamon Press, New York.

Dastur, J.F.
1949   Useful Plants of India and Pakistan. Bombay, India. D.B. Taraporevala Sons & Co. Ltd;

Duncan, C.G. and F.F. Lombard
1965   *Fungi Associated with Principal Decays in the United States*. U.S. Forest Serv. For. Prod. Lab. Rept. No. WO-4.

Encyclopaedia Britannica
1997   The New Encyclopaedia Britannica, Vol 11. Chicago:Encyclopaedia Britannica. pp 908

Fullaway, S.V. and C.L. Hill
1928   *The Air Seasoning of Western Softwood Lumber*. U.S. Dept. of Agr. Bul. 1425.

Ganathe, N.S.R.
1983   *Learn Urdu in 30 Days*. Madras, Balaji Publications.

Götz, Karl-Heinz, Dieter Hoor, Karl Möhler, Julius Natterer
1989   *Timber Design and Construction Sourcebook: A Comprehensive Guide to Methods and Practice*. New York: McGraw-Hill Publishing Co.

Henderson, H.L.
1939   *The Air Seasoning and Kiln Drying of Wood*. J.B. Lyon Co., Albany, New York.

Hunt, George M. and George A. Garratt
1953   *Wood Preservation*. McGraw-Hill Book Co., New York.

Kimball, K.E. and O.W. Torgeson
1959   A Small Lumber Drying Unit Employing a Portable Crop Drier for Heat and Air Circulation, *U.S. Forest Products Laboratory Report 1799*, Madison, Wisconsin.

Kollmann, F.,
1936   *Technologies des Holzes*. Julius Springer Publishers, Berlin.

Lindgren, Ralph M.
1952   Permeability of Southern Pine as Affected by Mold and Other Fungus Infection. *Proc. Am. Wood-Preservers' Assoc.*, Vol. 48.

Markwardt, L.J. and T.R.C. Wilson
1935   Strength and Related Properties of Woods Grown in the United States, *U.S. Department Agriculture Technical Bulletin* 479.

Mathewson, J.S.
1930   The Air Seasoning of Wood. *U.S. Dept. of Agr. Tech. Bul.* 174.
1954   *High-Temperature Drying: Its Application to the Drying of Lumber,* Forest Products Research Society Reprint 553, Madison, Wisconsin.

McMillen, J.M.
1956a. "Special Methods of Seasoning Wood: Boiling in Oily Liquids," *U.S. Forest Products Laboratory Report* 1665, Madison, Wisconsin.
1956b   "Special Methods of Seasoning Wood: Solvent Seasoning", *U.S. Forest Products Laboratory Report* 1665-2, Madison, Wisconsin.
1956c   Seasoning Hickory Lumber and Handle Blanks, *Hickory Task Force Report No. 4*, U.S. Department of Agriculture, Southeastern Forest Experiment Station, Ashville, North Carolina.
1960   "Chemical Seasoning", *U.S. Forest Products Laboratory Report 1665-6* (revised), Madison, Wisconsin.

McMillen, J.M. and W.L. James
1961   "Hi-Frequency Dielectric Heating", *U.S. Forest Products Laboratory Report 1665-7*, Madison, Wisconsin.

Parsons, W. T. and E. G. Cuthbertson.
1992   *Noxious weeds of Australia*. Indata Press, Melbourne:Sydney. p. 472-473.

Peck, E.C.
1955   "Moisture Content of Wood in Use", *U.S. Forest Products Laboratory Report 1655*, Madison, Wisconsin.
1956   "Air Drying of Lumber". *U.S. Forest Products Lab. Rept. No. 1657*. Madison, Wisconsin
1962. "Drying 4/4 Red Oak by Solar Heat", *Forest Products Journal* 12:3:103-107.

Prasad, A.G.D. and M.V. Shilalingadaradhya.
1988.   *Distribution and Economic Potential of Dalbergia in Karnataka*. Myforest 24 (4): 241-47.

Rasmussen, E.F.
1955   "Types of Ventilated Lumber Dry Kilns". *U.S. Forest Products Lab. Rept. No. 1900-2*.
1956   "Need for Uniformity of Temperature in a Forced-Air-Circulation, Ventilated, Compartment Dry Kiln". *U.S. Forest Prod. Lab. Rept. No. 1669*.
1961   "Dry Kiln Operators Manual", *U.S. Department of Agricultural Handbook No. 188*, U.S.G.P.O., Washington, D.C.

Rietz, R.C.
1957   "Importance of Dry Lumber", *U.S. Forest Products Laboratory Report No. 1779*, Madison, Wisconsin.

Rietz, R.C. and R.H.
1971   "Air Drying of Lumber: A guide to Industry Practices". *U.S. Department of Agr. Handbook No. 402*.

Scheffer, T.C.
1973   "Microbiological Degradation and the Causal Organisms", *Wood Deterioration and its Prevention by Preservative Treatments, Vol. 1*, edited by D.D. Nichols, Syracuse University Press, Syracuse.

Shigo, A.L. and E.H. Larson
1969   "A Photo Guide to the Patterns of Discoloration and Decay in Living Northern Hardwood Trees". *USDA Forest Research Paper NE-127*.

Srinivasachari, K.
1992   *Learn Sanskrit in 30 Days*. Madras, Balaji Publications.
1995   *Learn Hindi in 30 Days*. Madras, Balaji Publications.

Stevens, W.C.
1965   "Forced Air Drying Tests", *Timber Trades Journal*, May 1.

Thelen, Rolf
1923   "Kiln Drying Handbook", *U.S. Dept. of Agr. Bull. No. 1136*.

Tiemann, Harry D.
1938   "Lessons in Kiln Drying". *Southern Lumberman*. Nashville. 110 pp.

Troup, R.S.
1921.   *The Silviculture of Indian Trees, Vol. 1*. Oxford, Clarendon. pp.318-325.

Wakeham, H.
1955   "Mechanical Properties of Cellulose and its Derivatives; High Polymers", *Vol. 5, Cellulose and Cellulose Derivatives, Part 3*, p. 1304. Interscience Publication, New York.

Wangaard, F.F.
1950   *The Mechanical Properties of Wood*, p. 183, John Wiley and Sons, New York.

APPENDIX 3

MISC. RAW MATERIALS

INTRODUCTION

The previous chapters and appendixes have dealt with the most common materials used in the manufacture of *tabla*. However, there are a few other materials that just did not fit in elsewhere. Sometimes these materials are vital for the *tablamaker*. One example of this is the black powder, used to make the *syahis*. Sometimes it is a material that is rarely used in making *tablas*; terracotta is one example. Sometimes it is an item which is very mundane; glue and paint for instance. We will use this appendix to discuss these items.

CLOTH

Cloth is not directly used for the *tabla*. However, it is very important for the covers and the cushioned rings. Cloth comes in a variety of materials, textures, colours, and qualities. It is certainly too vast of a subject to cover in any detail here. However, we will cover some of the points that are important to the *tabla* maker.

Moisture Retention - The ability to retain moisture is a very important quality for the cloth accessories. This is especially an issue with the protective covers. All of the rawhide portions of the drum are sensitive to moisture; but the *syahi* is so sensitive that high moisture will permanently damage the the drum. If the covers are made of material that absorbs and retains moisture, this will tend to protect the *tabla*. It does so by keeping water away from the drum. Cotton is one of the best materials for this. The ability of cotton to attract and hold moisture is probably a reflection of the highly hygroscopic nature of cellulose.

Cutting and Fraying - It is important that the cloth be easy to work with. Cottons and cotton mixes are easy to work with. Nylon and many artificial fibres on the other hand present some special difficulties. If you simply cut nylon, it will tend to fray very badly. It is always better to melt nylon. The easiest way to do this is to take a soldering iron and simply trace out the pattern. You do this instead of cutting with scissors.

Nylon is not a good cloth to use for the covers because of its poor ability to retain moisture. However nylon cord is very nice for the lacings for the covers.

Anatomy of Cloth - It is important to understand the layout of the cloth. Understanding this anatomy is crucial to obtaining the proper qualities (fig 3.1).

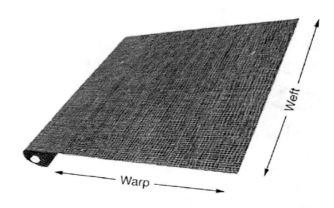

Figure 3.1. Cloth

The threads that run longways to the cloth are called the warp. The threads that form the warp are generally very strong and they have a lot of sizing (a glue like substance used to impart stiffness and strength). If a strip of cloth is cut along the warp, it will generally be stiff, yet strong.

The threads that run across the cloth are known as the weft. The threads that compose the weft are generally of a slightly lower quality. There is considerably less sizing, consequently they are far more flexible. If a strip is cut along the weft it will generally be soft and supple, but not as strong.

Often times it is necessary to cut diagonally to both the warp and the weft. This is referred to as the "bias". If a strip is cut across the bias there is a major compromise in strength, but it has the maximum flexibility. It will have the unique ability to conform to peculiar shapes. Neither strips cut along the warp, nor strips that are cut along the weft have this same capability.

TERRACOTTA

Terracotta is one of the most wide spread materials in the world. The word "terracotta" is Italian and literally means "baked earth". It is generally a brown to deep red fired clay. It is very hard, very brittle, and moderately porous.

Terracotta is found all over the world, and has very similar characteristics wherever it is found. It is an accessible technology that easily lends itself to mass production of low cost items. Historically, it has been used to produce low cost items such as roofing tiles.

Terracotta is a very common material in India. There are an indescribable number of items made from it. Such items as small wooden stoves *(angithi)*, statues, art work, *chillums* (small pipes used to smoke a variety of substances), and roofing tiles are common. Undoubtedly, the most popular are vessels for storage of drinking water[1](fig. 3.2).

Figure 3.2. Terracotta Items

Terracotta is known in India simply as *matti*. *Matti* means "mud", "earth" or "clay". There are a number of clays that have been, or may be used. In India, the most common is the red clay. It is readily available, very plastic, very cheap, and has a very low firing temperature (Clark 1983). It is ideally suited to the simple technological infrastructure that one finds there.

There is an interesting legend concerning the origins of pottery. According to the story, the Gods were churning the oceans to produce *amrit* (ambrosia). They then realised that there was no vessel to put it in. Therefore, it fell to the celestial artificer Viswakarma (see Chapter 2), to produce the first pot (Chattopadhyay 1995).

Terracotta has a religious connotation. Terracotta vessels, and items are generally found as part of

[1] The use of terracotta for drinking water is very interesting. Terracotta is very porous. It is so porous that water vessels constantly exude water. This means that the surface is always wet. In dry climates, such as Hyderabad where I used to live, this "sweat" is constantly evaporating, thus lowering the temperature. Therefore, anytime you get drinking water from it, it is always cold! Not only is the temperature cold, but the terracotta imparts a very subtle, yet very refreshing flavour.

pujas (religious ceremonies). It is common in various parts of India to make small effigies of the Gods out of clay, and then worship them. It is even said that if no effigy is available, then a clay pot may be used (Chattopadhyay 1995).

The surface of these items is generally simple. Sometimes these articles may be glazed, however more often they are not. The majority of terracotta items are utilitarian rather than decorative, therefore glazing and other decorations are considered superfluous.

It is not surprising that such an accessible technology should be used for the production of *tabla* shells. Curiously enough, I have only seen *bayan* shells made from terracotta.

Bayan shells made from terracotta have some interesting characteristics. They are very heavy (a desirable quality in *tabla* shells); they are relatively inexpensive; furthermore, they sound very good. The only quality that keeps them from being widely accepted is that they are very fragile and impossible to repair once broken. The only *bayans* that one finds made of terracotta are from the Bengal area of India.

There is another drum known as *khol* which is traditionally made of terracotta. Its extreme fragility has forced non-Indian players to seek the plastic and fibreglass version that is available in the West.

There are several steps used in making a *bayan* out of terracotta. They are cleaning and preparing the clay, throwing, drying, and firing. These will be discussed in greater detail.

Cleaning and preparing the clay are the first steps. If it is obtained in a dry state, it must be ground and mixed with water. Sticks, stones, and pockets of air must all be removed in this phase. It is also necessary that it be worked until it has an even consistency. This is a very labour intensive process that is somewhat reminiscent of a baker kneading dough.

The next step is to shape it. This is done by turning it on a potter's wheel. It is necessary for the potter to make the shell a little bit larger than he wishes, because as the shell dries, it will become smaller. The degree of shrinkage may vary tremendously from one clay to another.

Next is the drying stage. This takes many, many weeks. It must dry slowly and thoroughly. If the shells are not completely dry, then they will break upon firing.

It is appropriate for us to briefly mention India's seasons: invariably the potters must synchronise their activities to the weather. This is very convenient in India because there are well defined wet and dry periods. We can divide the year into three seasons. September to January is Winter; in this period the weather is dry but very comfortable. Summer starts toward the end of January to June. Traditionally the festival of *Shivaratri* is considered to be the start of summer. This is the best time for the potters because it is predictably hot and dry. The monsoon generally starts in June and runs to September. During this period it is almost impossible for potters to dry their goods.

The final stage is the firing. In this stage there is a great bonfire made with the articles, such as bricks, tiles, pots, and, in some cases, drumshells, such as for the *khol* and *bayan*. These articles are interspersed with various flammable items such as grass, rice husks, and the dung of cows and buffalos. The entire thing is left to burn for days on end.

The firing is the true test of the potter's skill. If there is the least little problem during any of the previous steps, the item will not survive. Even a great potter will not have 100% yield. Invariably, between start to finish there will be a fair number of broken and mis-shapen items. This is a natural consequence of the lack of control that comes from natural materials, dependence on the sun for drying, and other factors of nature. However the potter's business is based upon the fact that there will always be a sufficient yield to keep the potter going.

For the buyer, these last points are cause for caution. Business in India is very much based upon the principle of *caveat emptor*. No one buys a clay item without very careful examination.

The bottom line is simple: if you are interested in Indian percussion, you will eventually run across drum shells made of terracotta. Although they are very heavy and produce a very delightful sound, their extreme fragility makes them impractical for ordinary applications.

SYAHI MASSALA
Syahi massala is probably one of the most important materials used to make the *tabla*. However, it is not manufactured by most rank and file *tablawalas*. It is a specialty item that is purchased through a small, informal distribution network. The method of manufacture is a closely guarded secret. Therefore, whatever I relate is purely hearsay.

One of the ingredients in the *syahi massala* is iron. It is important that the iron be a fine dust. Iron particles such as iron-fillings are generally not considered to be acceptable. Although the process of obtaining iron particles in such a fine powder is a secret, I have heard a story that seems plausible. It seems that boys (referred to as *"chokadas"*) are sent out to the railroad tracks to rub their fingers over the smooth rails to collect the microscopic collection of iron dust that is deposited there. This supposedly is the source of the iron. It is then mixed with soot, and perhaps even other ingredients to make the high quality *syahi massala* that is then sold to other *tablawalas* around north India. I am told that the finest *syahi massala* comes from Gujarat. Since Gujarat produces some of the finest *tablas* that I have ever heard, this is certainly believable.

PAINT & VARNISH (SHELLAC)
This may seem trivial, however, it is not. Indian *tablawalas* do not just go out and buy paint or varnish. They make their own.

Traditional craftsmen use techniques which have not changed much in many centuries. These are based upon the traditional shellac. As a general rule, varnish is made by mixing some brown chips known as *lak* with a small amount of a crystalline substance known as *chandresh* and French polish. Let us look into this more closely.

The *lak* is the key ingredient. It comes in the form of brown chips. *Lak* starts when a small insect *(Laccifera lacca)* feeds on the sap from trees which are indigenous to India. Common trees that support the insect are the *babul* (described in the last appendix), *kusum (Schleicherer oleosa)*, *palas (Butea monosperma)*, *ber (Zizyphus mauratania)*, *Khair* (described in last appendix), and the *arhar (Cajanos cajan)*. The bug then secretes an amber like substance that protects the eggs while they are incubating. This secretion is harvested and then processed into the finished lac *(lak)*.

The term, "French polish", often means something different in India than it does in the rest of the world. To the rest of the world, French polish is a mixture of alcohol, *lak* or resin and perhaps other ingredients as well. However in India, the term French polish has come to mean just the alcoholic solvent that is used to dissolve the *lak*. This typically is any of the butyl, methyl or propyl alcohols.

Chandresh is considered an optional ingredient. It is used to impart a lustre to the surface. Unfortunately, I have never been able to find an English translation for the word.

We have spent a lot of time talking about the shellac that is used to varnish the shells, but what about the paint?

Paint is exactly the same thing, except a pigment is mixed in. Such pigments are generally sold in India in a powdered form. This is how the paint is made.

GLUE

There are three types of glue that are used by the *tablawalas*. These are white glue, *lai*, and *saresh*.

White glue is the commercially available synthetic resin. It appears to be a synthetic resin similar to "Elmer's" white glue. It is probably the best glue that a *tablawala* uses. However, it is very expensive by Indian standards. Therefore, it is used for limited applications.

Saresh is the most traditional glue that a *tablawala* uses. These come in deep brown sheets that are broken into small chips. I believe that it is just mucilage, which is a gelatinous substance produced by the hydrolysis of collagen. Basically just a bunch of leftovers from the slaughter house that are boiled until the mucilage is rendered.

There is a typical way in which *saresh* is used. Chips of *saresh* and a small quantity of water are placed inside the vessel (usually just an old can) and the whole is heated. It is heated and mixed until a deep dark brown gelatinous goo is produced. It is important that the *saresh* be kept hot, therefore it is put on the fire every time that it looks like it is cooling down. It is also important that it be kept from drying out; therefore, water is continually added as needed during the day.

Another version of glue is called *lai*. *Lai* is basically the same type of glue that we give to children in elementary school. *Lai* is made by boiling some water and gently stirring in white flour. When this comes to a glue-like consistency it is ready.

Figure 3.3. Rope and Plies

LAKADI MASSALA

Lakadi massala is a substance that is used to fill the cracks in the wood. It serves the same function as "Plastic Wood" or any of a number of commercially available materials in the West.

Lakadi massala is made by mixing white glue and sawdust. When it has hardened, it may be sanded and painted very much like the original wood.

ROPE AND CORD

Rope and cord are indispensable for the makers of *tabla*. Many *tablas* use ropes as a means of lacing, and all *tablas* will utilise rope at some time in their construction.

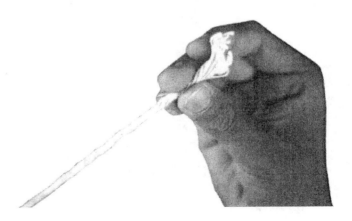

Figure 3.4. Plies and threads

Rope, cord, twine, and similar items are some of the oldest tools known to man. Throughout history, they have been made from a variety of substances. Hair, plant fibre, bark, sinew, strips of skin, or internal animal membranes are common materials from which they were made.

The kind of cord used by the *tabla* makers is usually a soft, cotton based cord. It is not terribly strong as far as ropes go, but it is very soft and will not damage delicate skins and other membranes.

Rope is made of several layers of ply (fig. 3.3. and 3.4). This is very important because each level must twist in the opposite direction from the smaller or larger level. Therefore, as each individual fibre attempts to relax, it actually causes the whole rope to become tighter.

CONCLUSION
This appendix touched upon the various miscellaneous materials used in the construction of *tabla*. We have looked at rope, terracotta, glue, and other items in order to become more familiar with them.

WORKS CITED
Chattopadhyay, Kamaladevi
1995   *Handicrafts of India*. New Delhi. New Age International Publishers Ltd.

Clark, Kenneth
1985   *The Potter's Manual*. Edison, NJ. Chartwell Books.

APPENDIX 4

OTHER INDIAN DRUMS

INTRODUCTION
This is a book on the manufacture of *tabla*; however we can put things in better perspective if we are also familiar with the manufacture of other Indian drums. In some cases, such as the *dholak* or the *pakhawaj*, the manufacture is done by the same craftsmen who manufacture *tabla*. In such cases it is not surprising that techniques and nomenclature are very similar. However, we will also take a close look at the manufacture of the *mridangam*, whose traditions are extremely different. This will provide an interesting contrast.

DHOLAK
The manufacture of *dholak*, like the *tabla*, is a refined art. But *dholak* is a much simpler instrument than the *tabla*, consequently it requires far fewer man-hours to make.

Parts of the Dholak - It is first helpful to become acquainted with then parts of the *dholak*. The parts are shown in figure 4.1. We see that there is the wooden shell, this is known as the *lakadi*. Upon this are two skins. The right hand side is called variously the *dayan pudi* or the *zil*. The large left hand drumhead is known as the *bayan* or the *bayan pudi*. There is the rope lacing, which is known as the *jaal, dori*, or the *rassi*.

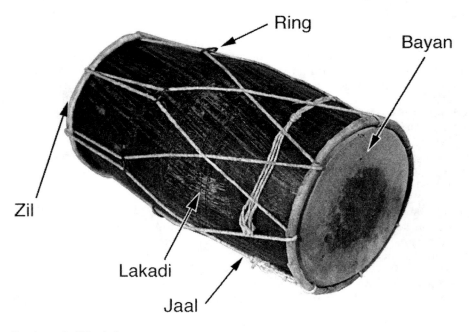

Figure 4.1. Parts of Dholak

The heads are of several parts. The *zil* (right hand head) is a simple membrane that is folded into two bamboo hoops. The *bayan* is merely a larger version of the *zil*, with one exception; the *bayan* has an application which is known as *dholak massala*. It is this application which gives the deep resonant sound of the *dholak*.

Construction of the Dholak - The *dholak* is constructed in an interesting fashion. First, one must make the shell. The technique is virtually identical to the preparation of the wooden *tabla* shell. This has already been discussed in great detail in Chapter 5.

One must prepare the skins. *Dholak pudis* are very different from the *tabla pudis*.

We must first make the hoops upon which the heads will be wrapped. These are known as the *baddha ka kundal*. One starts by making thin strips of bamboo. These are then bent into hoops and tied with string. They should be just slightly larger than the rim of the drum. There will be two hoops, one for each side, therefore the sizes will be slightly different.

One takes a piece of skin and selects a suitable template. A template *(jaal)* is chosen so that it is just larger than the bamboo ring *(baddha ka kundal)*. Circles of skin are then marked off and cut. Then the appropriate skins are soaked until soft. This entire process parallels that which was done for making the *tabla* as was described in detail in Chapter 6.

A skin is placed over the open shell. It is placed so that the epidermis is facing out. A previously prepared hoop is then placed over the skin and pulled down until it is just slightly lower than the lip of the drumshell.

One then takes the bamboo *bunad* (a broad blade of bamboo), somewhat reminiscent of a tongue depressor, and starts to press the thin hoop down so that it is just below the thicker hoop.

The process is repeated for both sides. It is then bound with cord. The whole is allowed to dry.

When the unfinished *pudis* are dry, the cord is removed and the excess rawhide is trimmed away with a *rampi* (flat blade). The right hand *pudis* are now finished.

The left hand *pudi* requires the addition of *dholak massala*. There are several ways to make *dholak massala*, but the easiest, and probably most widespread, is made by mixing clay and old motor oil.

Applying the *dholak massala* on the inside of the left hand *pudi* is critical. The amount, the thickness, and the shape are all important factors. They must all be just right, otherwise the characteristic deep sound will not come. The amount of *massala* to be placed on the *pudi* is dependant on the size of the head. For a small head (approximately eight inches) a tablespoon or two should be sufficient. For a larger head (approx. 16-20 inches) three-to-six tablespoons may be required. The dimensions are critical. As a general rule it should be flat. However, I have seen some applications that have a depression in the centre.

The *pudis* will be mounted on the shells in different ways. Sometimes they are laced with cord and sometimes they are held in place by turnbuckles. It is interesting to note that it will never be glued in the fashion after many middle eastern dumbecks.

The mounting of the heads on turnbuckles is shown in figure 4.2. For this one will take the *pudis* and wet them to soften them slightly. One may soften them by soaking them 5-10 minutes, just to soften them a bit. One then places them over the rim of the shell and then tightens it down. The *pudis* will tighten up on their own accord when they dry.

Things are a bit different when the *dholak* is laced. For this, one takes a large needle called a *suva*. (I had a friend who was disturbed by the sight of them because they were the same needles that were used by undertakers. I am neither able to confirm nor refute this.) One takes the needles and threads the cord through it. There are basically two types of lacing: simple and crossed. The crossed lacing was shown in figure 4.1.

Whichever style of lacing is used it is important to remember to lace through the metallic rings. The rings are used to tighten the drum.

When everything is laced, one then tightens the drum. It should be fairly tight. It will further tighten itself as the skins dry.

Figure 4.2. Turnbuckle Style Dholak

The final step is purely cosmetic. One lightly sands the skin with a very fine grade of sandpaper (e.g., 200). As one is sanding one lightly covers the skin with a thin layer of chalk. When it is finished, the skin has a nice smooth look and feel. This final stage is referred to by the *tablawalas* as *Saf Karna* which literally translates as "to clean".

This is how the *dholak* is assembled. Let us now move on to the *pakhawaj*.

PAKHAWAJ

The *pakhawaj* is generally considered to be the progenitor of the *tabla*; therefore, understanding this instrument is useful in getting a perspective on the *tabla*. The *pakhawaj* is also important because the same craftsmen who work on *tabla* also work on *pakhawaj* (fig. 4.3).

The *pakhawaj* is a north Indian representative of a very ancient class of drums called *mridang*. The *mridangs* are barrel-shaped drums with heads on both sides. Common examples of the *mridang* are the *pakhawaj*, *maddal*, *mridangam*, *khol*, and *pung*. Unlike the *dholak*, the various *mridangs* are characterised by an application on both surfaces. Sometimes the applications are permanent on both sides (e.g. *khol*), but more often the left hand's application is just a temporary mixture of flour and water.

The manufacture of *pakhawaj* and *tabla* are very similar. This similarity is to be expected because it is carried out in the same places by the same people, with the same tools and techniques. It is also not surprising that the nomenclature for the parts is basically the same.

Since there is so much similarity between the *tabla* and the *pakhawaj* it is not necessary to go over all of the points; instead we will just cover the points that are different.

The Dayan Pudi - The *dayan pudi* is indistinguishable from an oversized *tabla pudi*. However, the skins are a little thicker than found in the normal *tabla pudi*. This is to accommodate the low pitches that the *pakhawaj* has to tune to.

The *gajara* is a little different. A normal *dayan pudi* has 48 slits made in the skin to accommodate the weaving. The *pakhawaj pudi*, like the oversized *tabla pudi*, has 64. Therefore when one is lacing the *pakhawaj* one must remember to have a lace for every four insertions instead of the usual one for every three.

The *syahi* is substantially thicker for *pakhawaj pudi*s. This too is to meet the requirement of a very low pitch for the drum.

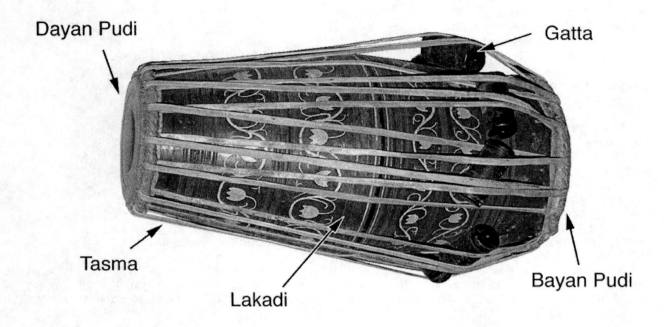

Dayan Pudi

Gatta

Tasma

Lakadi

Bayan Pudi

Figure 4.3. Parts of Pakhawaj

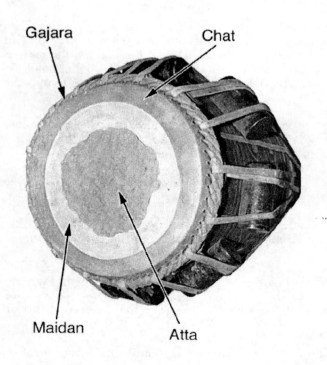

Gajara

Chat

Maidan

Atta

Figure 4.4. Temporary Application

The Bayan Pudi - The *bayan pudi* is identical to the *bayan pudis* for the *tabla*, with one exception. There is no permanent *syahi*. Whenever one wishes to play the *pakhawaj* one must make a temporary application of whole wheat flour and water (fig. 4.4).

The application of the flour and water, known as *atta*, takes some time and practice. For this one must mix whole wheat flour and water until the mixture has a consistency similar to that for making bread. While you are mixing the *atta*, it is good to keep the *pudi* moist. One then takes a very small dollop and carefully applies it to the centre of the *bayan*. Be careful to press it, and knead it into the drum so that it is solidly stuck. One then continues to take small dollops of *atta* and apply them until it covers a fair amount of the head. The figure 4.4 shows roughly the area to be covered. The job of applying the *atta* may take five to ten minutes. You will get a better sound if you let the drum sit for about another ten minutes before trying to play it.

It is very important that the *atta* be removed after the performance. If the *atta* is allowed to dry out, it will ruin the head and the only possible repair is to completely replace the *bayan* head.

page 206

One may take the flat blade of the *hathodi* and and gently scrape off the *atta*. Care should be taken so that the skin will not be damaged.

The constant application and removal of *atta* to the *pakhawaj* takes a big toll. With constant use the *bayan* will simply rot away. Once the *bayan* has been compromised it will split or develop small holes. The only repair for these problems is to replace the head.

MRIDANGAM

Mridangam is a very different instrument from the *tabla* and the *pakhawaj*. There is a tendency for many Indians to lump the *pakhawaj* and the *mridangam* together. They probably share a common evolution, but their present performance practice, tradition, and manufacture, are very different. Although the manufacture of the *mridangam* is a totally different affair from the *tabla,* it is useful to take a brief look so that we may gain a perspective on the subject.

Let us first become familiar with the parts of the *mridangam*. These are shown in figure 4.5.

Kattai - *Kattai* is the wooden shell. This is generally made of jackwood or margosa. However, sometimes coconut wood is used. It is turned upon a lathe until it has the proportions shown in figure 4.6. It is hollowed out with chisels (gouges).

Vaaru - The *vaaru* is a very heavy lacing made of cowhide or buffalo hide. It is laced so that the epidermis always wraps around the weaving of the right hand drumhead *(valantalai)*.

Pullu - The *pullu* are wooden blocks that are placed between the lacing and the shell. They serve to tighten the lacing. The *pullu* will not be present on a good tight drum, but will be added as the drum becomes loose.

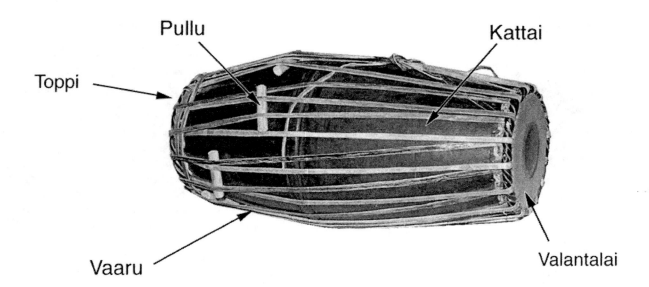

Figure 4.5. Parts of the Mridangam

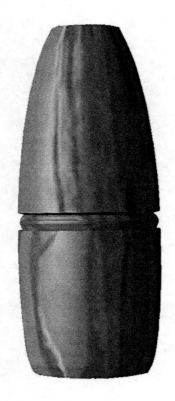

Figure 4.6. Proportions of Shell

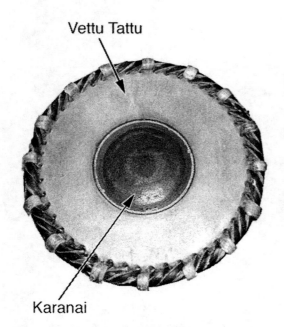

**Figure 4.7. Parts of Valantalai
(right head)**

Valantalai - The *valantalai* is the right hand drumhead (fig. 4.7). It consists of three layers of skin sandwiched together. A semipermanent application, weaving, and a number of small pieces of straw are also part of the construction.

The innermost annular layer of skin is known as the *ukkara tattu*. This serves a similar function to the *bharti* of the *tabla*. The *ukkara tattu* is made of cowhide. This part of the drumhead is only visible by disassembling the drum.

The main resonating membrane is called the *kottu tattu*. This is made of goatskin and serves a function very much like the *maidan* of the *tabla*. This membrane is also known as the *chappu tol*.

There is a semipermanent application on the face of the *kottu tattu*; this is known variously as the *karanai*, *soru*, or *marundu* (Sambamoorthy 1959). This is made of a special kind of *syahi massala* known as *kittam*. *Kittam* is powdered manganese, and iron oxide, all mixed with a paste made from water and rice flour. It is applied with a polished stone in a manner very much like the *syahi* of the *tabla*.

There is an outer most layer of skin. This is called the *vettu tattu* or the *meetu tol*. This serves a function very much like the *chat* of the *tabla*. The *vettu tattu* is made of cowhide.

Sandwiched in between the outer membrane *(vettu tatu)* and the main playing skin *(kottu tattu)* are sixteen pieces of straw. These are known as *kucchi*. These are placed radially running from the edge of the *vettu tattu* to nearly the edge of the drum. These pieces of straw are responsible for the *mridangam's* characteristic sound.

The various parts of the *valantalai* are all held together by a rawhide weaving. This is very similar to the *gajara* of the *tabla*.

Toppi - The *toppi* is the left hand head of the *mridangam*. It is also known as *idantalai* (fig. 4.8). It is made of three pieces of hide woven together. There is a temporary application on the centre of one of these hides
.

The inner most skin of the *toppi* is the main playing membrane. This is called the *Kottu Tattu*. It is made of goatskin.

There is a temporary application on the playing membrane. This is called *ravai*. *Ravai* merely means "cream of wheat". As the name implies, it is nothing more than coarsely ground wheat.

The *toppi,* curiously enough has not one, but two outer annular membranes. This is referred to as *vettu tatu*.

Size and Pitch - Like the *tabla*, *mridangams* come in a variety of sizes and pitches. However for simplicity they are often referred to as being either high pitch or low pitch.

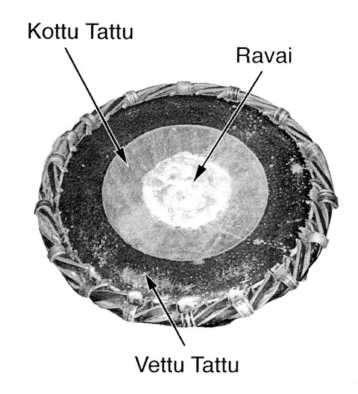

Figure 4.8. Parts of Toppi (left head)

The higher pitch *mridangams* are referred to as *hechchu sruti*. These generally have right hand pitches that run from F to G#. Typically the right hand diameters are about $6\frac{1}{4}$ inches while the left hand diameter is about $7\frac{1}{4}$.inches The overall length is usually about 22 inches.

The lower pitch *mridangams* are referred to as *taggu sruti*. These have a key that usually runs from about C-E. Not surprisingly, the *taggu sruti mridangams* are a bit larger. $6\frac{3}{4}$ inches for the right side and $7\frac{3}{4}$ inches for the left side with a total length of about 24 inches is typical.

CONCLUSION
This appendix gives us a passing familiarity with the construction of several other Indian drums. We looked at the *mridangam*, the *dholak,* and the *pakhawaj*. These three drums, along with the *tabla* represent the most common drums of India.

The purpose of this appendix was to place things in some type of perspective. Obviously we did not go into the same depth as we had with the *tabla*. Still we may at least feel what the differences and the similarities are.

WORKS CITED

Sambamoorthy, P.
1959   *Laya Vadyas*. New Delhi, All India Handicrafts Board.

APPENDIX 5

NON-TABLA APPLICATIONS

INTRODUCTION

Many drums require an application on the skins. Sometimes these applications are temporary and sometimes they are permanent. The *syahi* is the best known example of a permanent application; this was discussed in great detail in Chapter 6. However, totally different applications may also be found. For instance, there is a mixture of flour, or cream of wheat and water; this is found on the *mridangam* or the *pakhawaj*. A different type of application is found on the left-hand *pudi* of the *dholak*. These applications were briefly described in the last appendix. Both have problems that need to be discussed. This appendix will deal with these non-*tabla* applications and the various issues that surround them.

DHOLAK MASSALA

The *dholak massala* is the black, pitch-like material that is found on the inner surface of the *dholak, nal,* and similar drums. Let us first discuss the traditional approach to maintenance and then look at the problems associated with this approach.

Traditional Repair Procedure - This is the procedure for fixing *dholak massala* once it has reached the end of its life. The lifespan is generally only six months to a year. First one removes the head. If it is a turnbuckle type, then one need only remove the left head. However, if it is a traditional rope version, then both heads need to be removed. Please note that if you are using a rope *dholak,* you do not have to completely unlace the drum. You only have to unlace it and loosen it enough so that the heads pop off.

Once the left-hand head has been removed, take a dull knife, spoon, or similar object and gently scrape off the old *massala*. It is then mixed with old motor oil and carefully kneaded. It is kneaded in a manner very similar to the way that one may knead dough. One slowly adds old discarded motor oil until the proper consistency is obtained.

The consistency is critical. It should be as soft as you can get it before it runs. In other words, if too much oil is added, it will not stay fixed on the surface of the drum, but will slowly drip or run as though it were excess paint. This is not acceptable.

The heads are then lightly soaked in water, remounted, and tightened. When the heads have dried, then the *dholak* is ready to play.

It usually takes about an hour for an experienced repairman to perform the whole procedure.

Problems and Solutions - There are several problems with the traditional approach especially outside of India. These problems are the the non-availability of suitable motor oil, the high cost of labour, and the shortage of experienced repair personnel.

Labour is very dear in the West. One neither wants, nor expects, a musical instrument to have to go in for servicing every six months. It is not like a motor car where one is mentally prepared for this sort of thing. It is a major inconvenience and expense for the owner. Although the instrument only takes one man-hour to repair, the drying time for the heads means that it must be left and picked up on a later date. If we consider the time that the repairman takes to repair the *dholak*, and then figure in transportation, this may come to several man hours. If we figure a reasonable dollar value for this, we get a figure that is comparable to the cost of a new drum in India. This is clearly not acceptable. Towards the end of this appendix, we will show new applications that do not require this constant maintenance.

Another problem comes from the shortage of qualified personnel. It is a very difficult job to locate experienced repairmen outside of India. Fortunately, the internet has come along and makes it easier to locate someone. There are any number of search engines and directories out there. However, one possibility is to go to http://chandrakantha.com/suppliers/ and go down the list of establishments that sell *dholaks*. Most of these people should be able to refer you to someone.

The non-availability of a suitable motor oil is another problem. The old, expended motor oil as one finds in India, is not available.

Let us talk about the non-availability of old motor oil. The West has a major phobia when it comes to used oil. Environmental concerns about the proper disposal of used oil has created a very complex system of labelling, transporting and processing of the waste oil. It is designed to keep all used motor oil out of the public, and out of the environment.

The consequence is that used motor oil is almost unobtainable. It would seem at first that new oil should work just fine, but sadly this is not the case. New motor oil is deficient in two areas, viscosity and tack. Many household oils such as those which are used for sewing machines are simply two light. If the oil is too light, it will not stay mixed with the old *dholak massala*. After a period, the skin will act as a sponge and absorb the oil while leaving the old *massala* behind to become hard prematurely. This may be addressed by using the heaviest, most viscous weight motor oil that you can find. 20W-50 does just fine. But there is one other problem.

The other problem with new oil is that it is not as tacky as old oil. Cheap, low-grade motor oils, such as used in India, tend to break down into a thick, black, tar-like substance. This is very tacky. New high-grade oils, such as found in the West, are not nearly so tacky.

Here is a solution to this problem. One simply has to add a small amount of butyl rubber to the *massala*. It is very important that the correct amount be added. If too much is added, the rubber will harden and thus choke the sound. If too little is added, then it will not give sufficient tack. As a general rule, 5%-8% butyl rubber (by volume) is all that it takes to restore the tack.

Now you are probably wondering where you get the butyl rubber. This is no problem. Simply go to a hardware store and look at the various caulks, glues, and sealants. They sell a butyl rubber sealer/adhesive that is designed for gutters. Put only a small drop or two into the *massala*, along with the 20W-50 oil and this will do the trick.

This last procedure comes closest to the traditional Indian approach to maintaining the *massala*. These are all materials that are readily available in the West. However, it is clear that this does not solve the basic problem of having to rework the *massala* every six months. For this, we need a radically different approach. This will be the permanent application. This will be discussed later in this appendix.

FLOUR / WATER APPLICATION

The flour / water application is common on drums such as the *pakhawaj* and the *mridangam*. There are several variations to this. In general the possible applications are based upon white flour, cream of wheat, or whole wheat. Let us look at them in a little more detail.

Cream of wheat is often used for these applications. This is locally known as *suji, rawai,* or a host of other names. It has a very reasonable tack. It is easy to apply, and it sounds good.

Whole wheat is also a good application. This is generally known as *atta* in India. It also has a reasonable tack, and sounds good. Unfortunately, it takes a longer time to apply. This added time can add up if you do a lot of regular practice.

White flour is also used on occasion. This is generally referred to as *maida*. Although it sounds fine, it has the problem of being too sticky. This makes the job of applying it a real chore.

All of these applications suffer from one common problem; they must be put on before playing and removed afterwards. This lowers the life span of the *pudi* and it is a lot of labour. In the next section we will discuss some alternative *massalas* that address this issue.

ALTERNATIVE MASSALAS
It turns out that there are some easy, low maintenance alternatives to these labour intensive applications. We will discuss two of them here.

Alternative Massala #1 - This is an easy alternative. This particular one is well suited as a replacement for the *dholak massala* that is found on *dholaks* and *nals*. For this we need:

    1 teaspoon of bird shot
    1 -2 tablespoons of silicone sealant (used for bathroom repairs)

For this, simply mix the bird shot and silicone rubber and apply it to the inner surface of the skin. That's all there is to it!

There are several advantages to this technique. It is permanent, and made from easily accessible ingredients. This application will last the lifetime of the head.

There are however, several disadvantages. The biggest disadvantage is that once it is put on and dried, it cannot be reworked. Another disadvantage is that it requires a certain amount of experience to do it and get it right. This is because the characteristics of the *massala* when you put it on are going to be very different from the finished product (i.e., it hardens on you). You will need the experience to know what the final characteristics will be.

Alternative Massala #2 - This is another variation. This one is more suited for the *pakhawaj* because it may be put on, reworked. and taken off an indefinite number of times. This is conceptually similar to the flour/water mixture, except it will not dry up on you. For this we need:

(for *dholak*)
    1 teaspoon of bird shot
    1-2 tablespoons of tacky putty (The kind that is in office supply stores)

(for *pakhawaj*)
    3 teaspoons of bird shot
    6 tablespoons of tacky putty

Simply mix the ingredients and apply.

There are a number of advantages to this mixture. The greatest advantage is that the characteristics do not change. One does not need experience to know what the final characteristics will be. Another advantage is that it is not absolutely permanent. If you apply it and later feel that it is too much, too little, or perhaps just not the right shape, you can always remove, add, or remould it. This is very much an advantage when you are learning how to make the applications. Another advantage is that it has a superb sound. The final advantage is that it will not harden up on you like traditional oil-based *massalas*.

<u>Condition of the Skin</u> - Both of these applications require that the skin be free of oil. This is an issue when dealing with the *dholak*. It is not possible to take a *dholak*, remove the old application, apply the new one, and have it work reliably. The oil that has soaked into the skin may interfere with the new application's ability to adhere. Therefore, if one is dealing with a *dholak* it is bette to use virgin skin.

There is no problem with these application for the pakhawaj. A flour / water residue does not seem to interfere with the new applications ability to adhere to the skin.

<u>Birdshot</u> - Both of these applications require birdshot. Throughout these discussions there were certainly many readers who were wondering where to buy birdshot. I live in Texas; here it is not unusual to find people with what amounts to small-arms factories in their garage. It is very easy to get birdshot here. Unfortunately, for many people this may be a much more difficult task.

Here is a way to get a decent substitute. Go to any store that has athletic equipment and get some weights that are strapped to the feet or hands. Cut them open and usually you will find some type of shot. This usually works well.

CONCLUSION

This appendix discussed various non-*tabla* applications from a Western standpoint. We showed how to manage traditional *dholak massala* in the absence of degraded, low-quality motor oil. We also discussed permanent, or at least semi-permanent applications that could be used as a replacement for either traditional *dholak massala* or the flour/water mixture that goes on the left-hand side of the *pakhawaj* and the *mridangam*. Attention to these things will make things much more easier for the musician residing outside India.

INDEX

1

Introduction and terminology

1.1 Introduction

Despite the increased expertise and technology available for treatment in neonatal and intensive care units, there has not been the expected decrease in the numbers of children with severe neurological impairment who are surviving beyond infancy or surviving severe trauma during childhood (Hagberg et al. 1996; Pharoah et al. 1996). There is also an increasing cultural expectation for quality of life despite severe neurological impairment.

Many of the children attending Chailey Heritage Clinical Services have severe neurological impairment, and we have developed an approach to postural management which includes a consistent method of assessing ability for the prescription of treatment and equipment (Mulcahy et al. 1988; Green et al. 1995; Pountney et al. 1999). Both the treatment and equipment are designed to promote normal motor control, improve practical ability and reduce the progression of deformity. We worked with the children on several projects, studying different aspects of postural management including ability in the lying, sitting and standing positions.

This section will explain why normal motor development has been used as the basis for the postural management programme.

keypoint

> **The term postural management is used to describe everything that has an impact on a child's postural ability including:**
>
> - **Positioning and mobility equipment**
> - **Individual therapy sessions**
> - **Active exercise**
> - **Orthoses**

The studies of lying, sitting and standing had two important factors in common: the need to develop a consistent method of analysing posture, and a common language for assessment and communication.

activity

Look at the following six illustrations.

Take about five minutes to write a description of what you see using your current method of analysis.

Figure 1 *Supine lying*

Figure 2 *Supine lying*

Figure 3 *Box sitting*

Figure 4 *Box sitting*

Figure 5 *Standing*

Figure 6 *Standing*

There are many different ways of interpreting and describing what you see. This book will describe the method that we find the most useful.

Take a second look at the illustrations when you have finished reading the book and compare your answers.

The description you wrote down when looking at the pictures may refer to symmetry and posture. You probably found it difficult to describe the detail in an objective way. This difficulty relates to the variety of ways we consider posture and the terminology we use. In a multidisciplinary team this can cause problems, and a common language and standard are required for the purposes of clarity and accuracy.

When looking at data on a subject for which no clear standards exist, scientists establish a theoretical model. This provides a clear reference point, which is used to assess each and every piece of information. Obviously the model used needs to have a close relationship with the data being studied. One technique is to build the theoretical model on the attributes of similar data in a 'normal' situation. This is a recognised scientific approach already used in gait analysis, for instance. Normal motor development provides a good basis for the study of the development of postural ability in lying, sitting and standing in children with cerebral palsy.

A model is a theory, which is proposed in order to organise some of the varied facts and observations made about particular occurrences or situations.

At the beginning of our work on postural ability it was necessary for us to study very young infants because the detailed information required was not contained in the considerable amount of literature available at the time. The figure below gives an example of the stages of normal child development and the gap in our knowledge of what happens between the child gaining some head control and beginning to crawl (Shirley 1931).

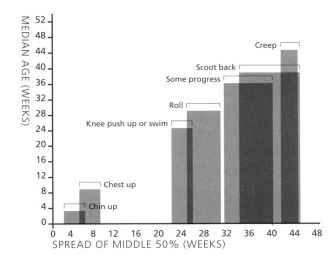

Figure 7 *Diagram illustrating Shirley's work*

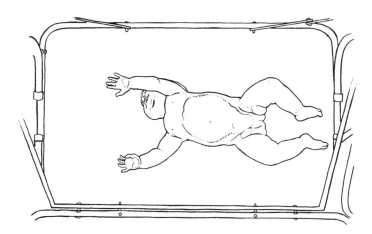

Figure 17 *Lying on a table*

Why do you think this is?

The information gained from this study showed that as motor skills develop, the predominant pelvic and shoulder girdle positions change and the pattern of loadbearing is altered accordingly.

When assessing pelvic and shoulder girdle positions, remember that if the pelvis is posteriorly tilted in prone, it is not touching the surface, and therefore not loadbearing through the supporting surface.

Loadbearing can also be affected by the type of supporting surface. Only the old fakir places his full body weight on a surface of up-turned nails!

> **Loadbearing needs to be evenly distributed over as large an area as possible.**

keypoint

If loadbearing is concentrated heavily in small areas there is always an increased risk of tissue trauma. If a child remains in one position for a long time the loadbearing needs to be evenly distributed over as large an area as possible in order to avoid pressure sores.

If you can't see where a child is loadbearing, place your hand between him and the supporting surface and feel for yourself.

> **Look at the illustration of the child below and describe the areas of loadbearing.**

activity

Figure 18 *Loadbearing in prone lying*

1.5 Symmetry

What exactly do we mean by symmetry?

Let's start with the dictionary definition.

Symmetry: exact correspondence of size, shape, etc. between opposite sides of a structure or object; harmony or proportion; balance between a regularity of parts.

The latter part of this definition is probably the most appropriate for our use of the term symmetry. Our bodies are not symmetrical in any direction, but the term will be used to describe a controlled harmony and balance between body parts.

activity

Take a moment's break from this section to think about the position you are in. Do you think it is symmetrical?

Briefly describe the position. Are your legs crossed? Are you leaning back or to one side?

We think everyone will be asymmetrical.

Now think how long it will be before you move, even a little bit.

Next time you are at a boring meeting, fix yourself into an asymmetrical position and time how long it takes for you to become uncomfortable and to need to change position. Watch how many times your colleagues move. See if they choose symmetrical postures and remain still, or shift between asymmetrical postures.

We do not always choose symmetrical postures. We can at any time move into one. We are not limited to one position.

During normal motor development an infant begins life being unable to adopt a balanced symmetrical posture. As his motor coordination improves he will be able to maintain a symmetrical position, and finally he will be able to move between symmetry and asymmetry in a controlled manner.

Children with a neurological impairment may lack this ability to move. If they are placed in or adopt an asymmetrical position and cannot move out of it, they are likely to become uncomfortable and stiff. If this situation persists then asymmetrical deformities may follow.

To prevent this happening we need to provide symmetry in a variety of positions. These positions should allow movement within certain boundaries provided that a child has some ability to control his movements and change position.

The ability to achieve, and move in and out of symmetry requires control in several directions. Look back at your description of how you were sitting at the beginning of this section. You may have been asymmetrical from side to side, front to back, top to toe, or all three.

Later sections in this book will describe in detail how and why treatment and equipment is used to provide a symmetrical position as part of a postural management programme.

Questions

1 **What are the potential problems that may result if a child consistently adopts asymmetrical postures?**

2 **How can we overcome this?**

1.6 Chailey Levels of Ability

The Chailey Levels of Ability describe a progression of ability based on the components of loadbearing, movement and symmetry as described in the previous sections. Once you have a grasp of these concepts it becomes easier to analyse posture and movement in this way.

The nine components listed below form the basis of the Chailey Levels of Ability and were defined during the study of normal infants. Aspects of components change as a child develops, and indicate the level of ability.

- The parts of the body which are loadbearing when still and when moving

- The ability to change areas of loadbearing: in an uncontrolled and controlled manner, longitudinally and laterally and when moving into and out of position

- The position of the pelvis (posterior, neutral or anterior tilt), and the position of the trunk and legs

- The position of the shoulder girdle (retracted, neutral or protracted), and the position of the trunk and arms

- The position of the head and of the chin (poked, tucked or retracted)

- The lateral profile of the body

- The effect of head movement on the trunk and limbs (trunk follows head movement, trunk moves in opposite direction, ability to move head without associated trunk or limb movement)

- The ability to isolate limb movement from the head, trunk and other limbs

- Predominant positions of the major joints

The Chailey Levels of Ability form a sequence of discrete stages of motor performance that can be observed as a child matures. They provide an explanation for a child's developing ability to control his balance and movement, progressing from positions of asymmetry and uncontrolled movements to symmetrical balanced postures, and on to controlled movement in and out of symmetry.

The Chailey Levels of Ability give us a clear, easily repeatable, reliable and objective method for assessing a child's postural ability. They work equally well with children who have neurological impairment and those who are able-bodied. The abnormal neurological signs are not disregarded, but the emphasis is placed on the biomechanical changes that occur at each stage of development. It is the quality, frequency and range of movement in a child with neurological impairment that may differ from that of an able-bodied child.

The Chailey Levels of Ability are described in Chapter 2.

2

The Chailey
Levels of Ability

2.1 Introduction

This section of the book is a reference section. Read it through; don't try to memorise it. As you use the Chailey Levels of Ability you will become familiar with them.

The Chailey Levels of Ability have been found to be a reliable and valid measure for children with neurological impairment. They are not norm referenced or validated as a screening test (Pountney et al. 1990; Smithers 1991; Carpenter 1998; Pountney et al. 1999).

Based on a normal model of motor development the Chailey Levels of Ability can be used to:

- Assess postural ability

- Plan treatment

- Evaluate change

- Design equipment for postural support and control

- Prescribe postural management equipment

The Chailey Levels of Ability are a recognised reliable and accurate measure for clinical and research purposes.

Remember the activities you did in Chapter 1.2 on pelvic and shoulder girdle position, symmetry and loadbearing? The Chailey Levels of Ability are based on the observations of these four components and the effect of movement on them.

An understanding of the components of the levels and how they can change is essential for planning intervention.

keypoint

> **The analysis of the child's movement is more important than ascribing a level.**

There may be a difference between the level of ability a child can achieve when trying his best and his usual level. The two levels should be separately recorded as best and usual. A child who rests in a consistently asymmetrical position is at risk of developing deformity so the resting position needs to be documented.

The assessment procedure is described in Chapter 5 – Assessment. The separate assessment charts found in the back of this book should be used when recording the Chailey Levels of Ability.

2.2 Levels of supine lying ability

Figure 19 *Level 1*

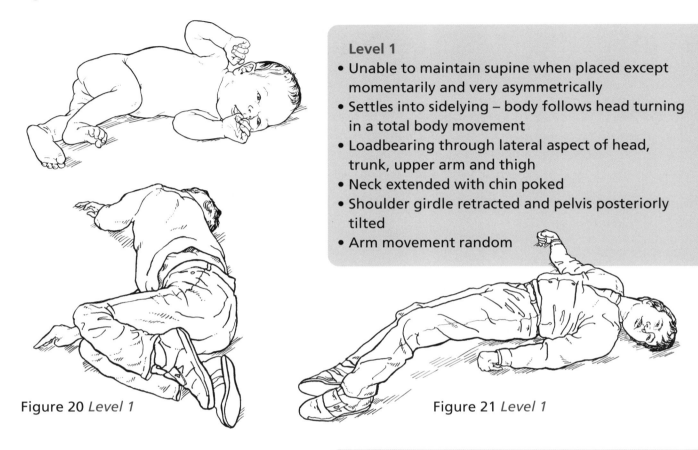

Figure 20 *Level 1*

Figure 21 *Level 1*

Level 1

- Unable to maintain supine when placed except momentarily and very asymmetrically
- Settles into sidelying – body follows head turning in a total body movement
- Loadbearing through lateral aspect of head, trunk, upper arm and thigh
- Neck extended with chin poked
- Shoulder girdle retracted and pelvis posteriorly tilted
- Arm movement random

Level 2

- Asymmetrical posture
- Settles on back when placed
- Loadbearing through head, shoulder girdle, trunk and posteriorly tilted pelvis
- Chin poked
- Shoulder girdle retracted, shoulders externally rotated and abducted
- Arms out to side
- Head to one side, pelvis and legs to opposite side
- Head movement followed by pelvic movement in the opposite direction
- Arm movement random

Figure 22 *Level 2*

Figure 23 *Level 2*

Level 3

- Maintains symmetrical posture
- Loadbearing through head, shoulder girdle, pelvis and feet
- Neutral pelvic tilt and shoulder girdle neutral giving general trunk curvature
- Hips abducted and externally rotated
- Chin tucked but not retracted and head able to turn freely from side to side
- Controlled eye movements possible
- Beginning of unilateral grasp to side of body, takes fist and objects to mouth

Figure 25 *Level 3*

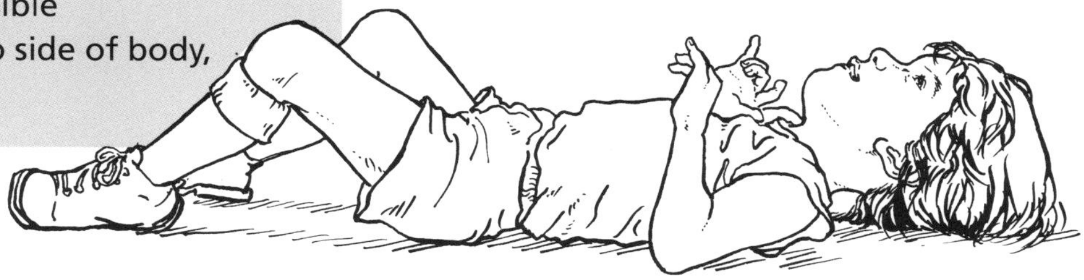

Figure 24 *Level 3*

Level 4

- Symmetrical posture
- Loadbearing through anteriorly tilted pelvis, protracted shoulder girdle and upper trunk
- Ability to change loadbearing to head and trunk only
- Able to retract chin and turn head freely
- Definite lordotic curve
- Shoulders able to flex and adduct allowing midline hand play above chest
- Free pelvic movement beginning allowing child to touch knees with flexed hips or extend hips and knees
- Feet to midline
- Beginning of lateral load shift
- Unilateral leg raise

Figure 26 *Level 4*

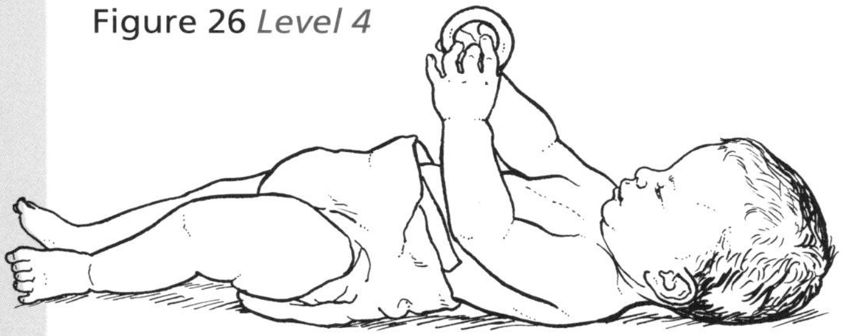

Figure 27 *Level 4*

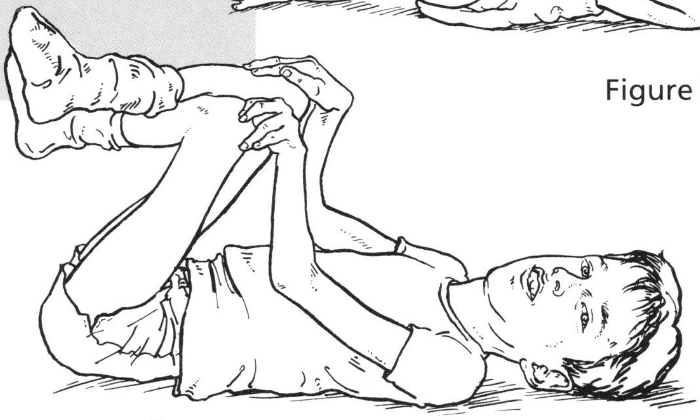

Figure 29 *Level 4*

Figure 28 *Level 4*

Level 5

- Able to achieve standing using support, usually through half kneeling
- Able to move outside of base
- Loadbearing through hands and plantargrade feet
- Trunk upright
- Able to lean backwards and rotate whole trunk
- Free pelvic movement and lumbar lordosis
- Can reach above shoulder height
- Deliberate stepping within position
- Leaves position in controlled way, using support

Figure 77 *Level 5*

Figure 79 *Level 5*

Figure 78 *Level 5*

Level 6

- Moving freely into and out of position using support
- Cruising, initially using three points of support with broad standing base
- Progressing to two points with narrow base
- Free pelvic movement and lumbar lordosis
- Loadbearing through plantargrade feet, occasionally tiptoes
- Decreasing amount of hand support, which is mainly used for balance

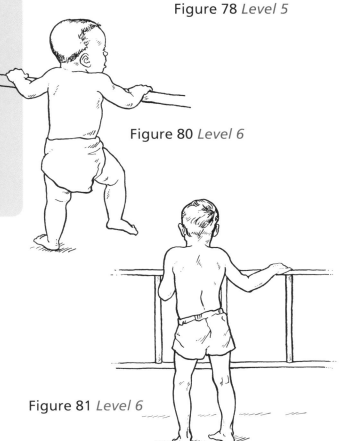

Figure 80 *Level 6*

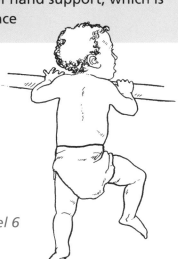

Figure 82 *Level 6*

Figure 81 *Level 6*

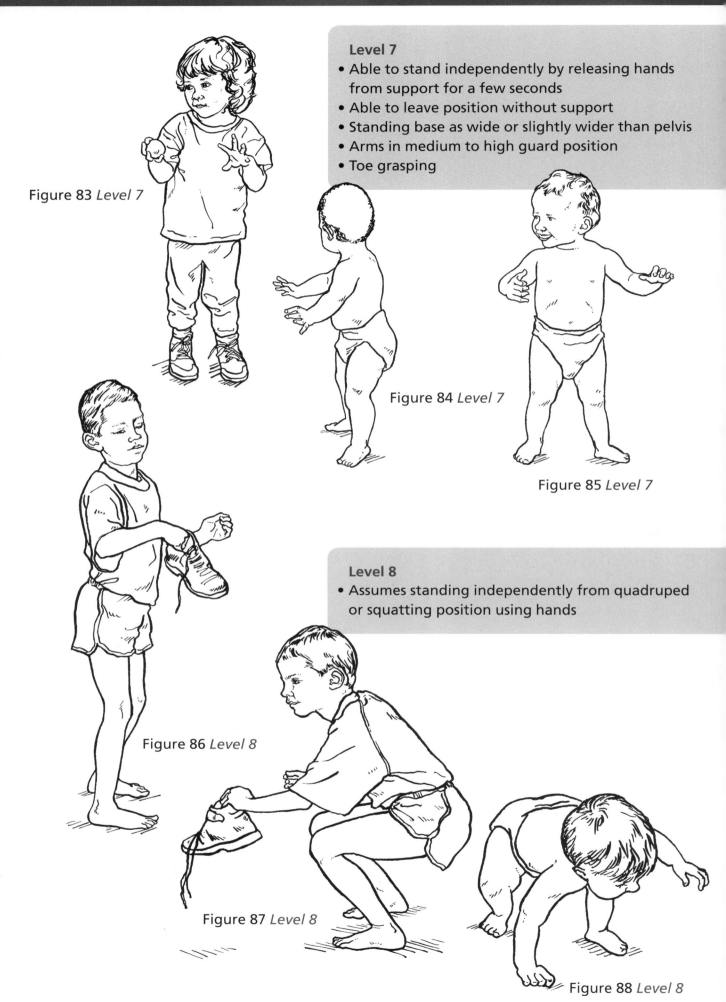

Level 7
- Able to stand independently by releasing hands from support for a few seconds
- Able to leave position without support
- Standing base as wide or slightly wider than pelvis
- Arms in medium to high guard position
- Toe grasping

Figure 83 *Level 7*

Figure 84 *Level 7*

Figure 85 *Level 7*

Level 8
- Assumes standing independently from quadruped or squatting position using hands

Figure 86 *Level 8*

Figure 87 *Level 8*

Figure 88 *Level 8*

3

Postural and practical ability

3.1 The links between abilities in lying, sitting and standing

Studies conducted at Chailey Heritage Clinical Services established the following links between abilities in the positions of lying, sitting and standing:

- None of the children could sit independently (Level 3) until they had reached Level 4 in both prone and supine lying.

- All the children were able to sit independently by the time they had achieved Level 6 lying ability.

- Independent standing (Level 7) was only achieved when Level 6 lying and Level 7 sitting were reached.

The skills needed for independent sitting (Level 3) are first learned in lying. To get to this stage, in both prone and supine, a child has learned to move his pelvis actively from posterior tilt into anterior tilt, turn his head freely without its affecting another part of his body, retract his chin, protract his shoulder girdle and raise his arms against gravity, or use his arms to prop. Once he has gained all these skills in prone and supine lying, he will be able to maintain a sitting position with his pelvis in neutral tilt, shoulder girdle protracted, hands propping and his weight forward over his sitting base.

Figure 89 *Child maintaining sitting but unable to free hands for play*

activity

Look at the picture of the child and use the chapter on the Chailey Levels of Ability to help you identify which components of posture are limiting her ability to use her hands.

A child with motor impairment who can maintain a sitting position but cannot control the tilt of his pelvis to a neutral position is not achieving Level 3 sitting ability. He may be functioning well but his postural ability is still poor.

Sometimes there is a discrepancy between the level of ability in prone and supine. This may be because of an emphasis of positioning or treatment. Many children have no early experience of prone positioning since the 'Back to Sleep' campaign was introduced. Also, children with motor impairment may be more able in some components than others because of the nature of the specific neurological pathology.

Children with motor impairment often rest in an asymmetrical position (Level 2) but are able to achieve a higher level of ability when they are active. It is important to check this at the time of assessment because there is a risk of deformity developing. They may take longer to process information and respond to it, so it is also important to allow them time to move.

In the typical developmental process children will be able to achieve symmetry in lying (Level 3) by the time they are about 3 months old, independent sitting (Level 4) by about 8 months, and standing and cruising at about 10 months. Early intervention for children with motor impairment who are unable to reach the appropriate level of ability at the right time is crucial in order to encourage the developmental process and prevent deformity. It is never too early to start a programme of intervention that aims to improve a child's level of ability.

With a great deal of practice a child's gross motor skills will become more and more competent to the point where they are used automatically. But as he begins to move into a less stable position, e.g. from sitting to standing, he will use the posture in which he is least likely to fall. In standing, for instance, the most stable posture is with the shoulder girdle protracted and the pelvis in a neutral position so that the trunk weight lies just in front of the base. This is the position that we all adopt when learning a new skill in standing (such as skateboarding or skiing) until we reach the stage where the new skill becomes automatic.

Question

1 **Name the postural skills learned in prone and supine lying that will be used in sitting.**

3.2 The link between the levels of ability and fine motor skills

Throughout the day we are continually adjusting our posture to make tasks as easy as possible. In circumstances that require concentration and accurate fine motor skills we find a way of stabilising our bodies, our work surface and our tools. When writing, for instance, we need to be posturally stable and have a solid surface to work on.

Do you find it easier to write a cheque when standing in the queue at the bank or on the counter when you reach the cashier?

A child's highest level of postural ability is his most newly acquired and hence his least practised skill. He can be seen to adopt a more stable base of support, i.e. a lower level of ability that he has previously mastered, when he wants to use fine motor skills such as grasping and manipulating a toy. In order to learn a skill, a child practises it many, many times. As his postural ability improves and he gains shoulder and pelvic girdle control, he will also gain control of fine motor skills. He will gradually refine all these skills until he can use them automatically.

Do you remember trying to reach in front of you with your shoulder girdle retracted?

When a child achieves a neutral position of the shoulder girdle (Level 3) he can bring his arm to his side. With active shoulder girdle protraction (Level 4), he will be able to move his arms and head without compromising his balance. Once a child is able to control his pelvic girdle in a neutral position he will have the choice of making postural adjustments both into a posterior tilt and into an anterior tilt. When he has developed the ability to anteriorly tilt his pelvis he will be able to move his limbs and upper trunk independently of his pelvic girdle.

Protraction of the shoulder girdle (Level 4) allows him to bring his hands to the midline of his body. If he can retract his chin at the same time, his hands will be within his visual field. If he can accomplish this on his back, he will be able to bring his arms up against gravity and play with a toy in the air, at his midline and within his visual field. In prone, his ability to fix his pelvis in an anterior tilt and take the weight off one arm (Level 5) will allow him to manipulate objects and explore his environment. As he learns to control the shift of his weight from side to side he will be able to reach or kick across his midline. In supine, if he can move his shoulder girdle and pelvic girdle independently of his trunk,

4

Knowledge base

4.1 Why should postural management work?

This section will consider the theoretical and physiological reasons why postural management is effective in:

- promoting motor ability

- enabling practical activities

- controlling deformity

It will explore how postural management programmes can overcome some of the factors that limit progress and practical activity in children with neurological impairment.

Postural and motor ability are the result of a combination of factors including:

- the maturational level of a child's nervous system

- sensory processing

- length-associated changes in muscles

- selective control of muscle for posture and movement

- bone and joint formation

- biomechanical forces

- nutrition

- the health of a child

- the close and wider environment

- the activity a child is engaged in

Limits to progress may occur in one or more of these areas for a child with neurological impairment.

Think about a child you know and list all the things that are limiting his ability to progress.

activity

4.2 Neuroplasticity

During the last century knowledge of the nervous system and the control of movement advanced rapidly with the development of techniques to investigate the activity of these systems. The nervous system is now widely recognised as a dynamic structure, which is continuously changing in response to environmental needs and demands placed on the system by learning, development and experience. Leonard (1998) describes activity in the nervous system from conception to two years as a 'Tsunami wave of development and change' which results in structural changes following activity-dependent processes. This plasticity occurs in young children in response to a variety of influences including maturation, growth, myelination and experience. In older children and adults plasticity occurs in response to activity and experience but is largely due to changes in synaptic strength.

Neuroplasticity literally means the adaptability of the nervous system.

Neuroplasticity is the term given to the system's response to change within and outside our bodies. This adaptation itself involves changes to the structure and physiology of tissue at a cellular level (the chemistry is complicated, but if you want to know more we suggest you read the work of Leonard (1998) and Kidd et al. (1992).

Neuroplasticity is a major element of therapeutic intervention that can work for or against us. An understanding of the mechanisms and how they relate to postural management can help us maximise a child's motor ability.

A number of common factors influence neuroplasticity in children, adolescents and adults. These include:

- Practice and repetition – Practice will result in long term changes in neural connections if enough repetitions are performed

- Task related activities – Voluntary activity related to a task is a more effective way to learn movements than guided or passive movements

- Conditions of practice – Movements should be practised under the conditions in which they are to be used

- Competition between synapses – Pruning of synapses occurs through development and synapses that have less activity are more likely to be snipped

Theories now suggest that movement and sensory exploration are vital in the developing nervous system (Leonard 1998). If there is no or little activity in a neural pathway then that pathway is unlikely to survive.

Movement, for example, provides us with internal and external environmental feedback to our nervous system. Persistent patterns of abnormal movements will, therefore, result in our nervous system adapting to and consequently perpetuating these movements. In this instance neuroplasticity is working against us. Therapy can positively affect changes by preventing abnormal movements and encouraging normal movements.

Lawes describes the nervous system as a social group. If you respond to people's conversation they will carry on talking to you, if you ignore them they will stop and go away. Connections in the nervous system will remain open if they receive feedback from being used but will retract if they are not.

For children with a neurological impairment the process of disconnection does not appear to happen as efficiently as it should. The aim of therapy is to get rid of those connections that are not useful and encourage those that are to stay connected.

The way in which we use our nervous system is also important. In order to stay connected, our movements must be active and purposeful. They must be part of everyday activities.

activity

Imagine that you are attached to a special machine, which moves your body for you through all the correct movements in a game of tennis. Do you think that if you used this machine every day for several weeks your game would improve?

Implications

Young children have very adaptable neuromuscular systems. This could be detrimental for those who sustain perinatal insults, as abnormal movement patterns may be established in the early stages of development. A positive effect of this is that children may be able to recover more successfully from neural injury. Early treatment and postural management intervention can take advantage of this adaptability and help establish normal patterns of active movement.

Although changes may take longer in older children and adults, they will still happen.

4.5 The importance of sensory experience

Sensory and motor systems are intimately linked. When we move we are responding to sensation from our own body and from the environment. Before we move, as well as during movement, our nervous system needs to process this sensory information. This information processing is sensory integration, when our brain is selecting, comparing, inhibiting, enhancing and making associations in a flexible way.

Our sensory systems include:

- visual
- auditory
- olfactory
- vestibular
- tactile
- kinaesthetic
- proprioceptive

and we take into account information from all these systems when we move.

keypoint

> **Sensory motor learning is the use of this information to plan and organise sets of responses to incoming information.**

There is no one set way for us to organise sensations. Although there may be a recognisable pattern of moving, we may each vary individually in the way we do the same task in differing circumstances and different people may perform the same task in different ways.

activity

> **Think about the way people write. We all have different ways of holding our pen, just as there are different types of paper and shapes of pen. We all form the letters differently and put varying amounts of pressure on the paper... yet nearly everyone has legible writing!**

In the same way we all have individual characteristics of posture and gait. It is possible to recognise who is approaching by hearing their footsteps or seeing the way they walk.

This is a complex concept. One way to illustrate what is happening is to imagine the job of an air traffic controller at Heathrow. A plane has to land every thirty seconds. It's Tuesday and you are on the same shift as last week but with different colleagues. Business travellers expect the same schedule every Tuesday. Your job is to direct arriving planes not only on to the runway but also into their landing gates. You need to organise the descent order according to future departure plans, taking into account factors of wind speed, weather conditions, visibility, fuel levels, height and loading of the plane. Will your work today be a repeat of last Tuesday's? Our sensory system has even more demands than this placed on it.

If the air traffic controller has access to all the information he needs but his computer is faulty and won't process the information correctly, imagine how the service would be disrupted. This is similar to what might happen if we have a fault in our sensory motor system. If our bodies are to move in a coordinated way an intact sensory motor system is essential. Children with cerebral palsy receive and interpret sensory information correctly but have difficulty in storing it in their sensory memory.

Movement disability in children with cerebral palsy results, in part, from an inability to formulate and communicate appropriate motor commands to muscles rather than from disruption of voluntary movement by spasms and spasticity, i.e. the air traffic controller's computer has a fault (Neilson et al. 1982).

It is therefore important that they receive repeated and consistent sensory experiences to enable them to help build internal models of their environment (Gordon et al. 1997).

activity

> **Imagine that you are playing a game of tennis on an indoor court where the walls and floor do not stay in the same position. How likely do you think it is that your tennis skills will improve?**

A defect in motor planning results in difficulty retrieving the right information for normal movement (Neilson et al. 1990). The area of the brain that directs voluntary contraction has adequate access to the muscles, but limited control over the timing and gradation of their activity. Athetosis, spasticity and spasm do not directly disrupt voluntary movement.

Research has shown that children can learn to self-regulate spasm and spasticity but this is not sufficient in itself to improve functional control of movement (Neilson et al. 1982). Spasm and spasticity are therefore not the only cause of movement disability.

A variety of interactions with our environment gives us the chance to explore and evaluate different responses and how they relate to movement. Children with neurological impairment often do not experience a variety of patterns of movement (Gordon et al. 1997).

Life is multi-sensory. In some situations this may mean reducing the amount of sensory information a child is receiving as it might distract him. A child might concentrate better in a quiet room away from people's conversations and noisy play. In other circumstances a child might benefit from extra sensory input such as being helped physically and verbally with an activity.

Some children with sensory deficits may require a longer time to process and respond to information.

A study by van der Weel et al. (1991) demonstrated that giving a child a concrete task to do rather than asking him to perform a movement with no purpose improved his success. This could be due to added sensory clues.

activity

You are trying to encourage a child to reach out and stretch his arm. Think about things you could do to influence his performance.

When children only have a limited opportunity to experience different positions and movements it is particularly important for us to provide the best experiences possible. Positioning equipment can provide a starting position from which a greater repertoire of movements can develop.

One of the aims of any therapeutic intervention is to enable a child to build internal and external models of himself and his environment in order to improve the efficiency of his sensory-motor responses.

 Question

1 **What is considered to be a contributory cause of movement disability in children with neurological impairment?**

4.6 Biomechanics

Biomechanics was first mentioned in Chapter 1, where we explained how we are going to use the term to describe the areas of the body which are loadbearing, how muscle and gravitational forces affect the body, and methods of controlling these. This section will explore these biomechanical forces in more detail.

The biomechanics of a person's body influences his neurology in terms of sensory feedback and the ease with which movements can be performed. Woollacott et al. (1996) showed that children with and without cerebral palsy who adopted crouch knee positions demonstrated the same muscle activation patterns, indicating that the biomechanics of the posture rather than the neurology was influencing muscle firing. This suggests that correct biomechanical alignment can have a major impact on motor activity.

keypoint

> **Biomechanical forces are imposed on the body by our environment, movement and activity and, in children, by growth and development.**

These forces can either be advantageous, as in normal development, or may result in abnormal musculoskeletal development if a child has a neurological impairment.

There are two aspects of biomechanics that we are concerned with:

• the biomechanical changes that occur during normal growth and development, movement and activity. These form the components of the Chailey Levels of Ability

• the biomechanical forces that we can apply to the body to help it grow in a planned way where there is neurological impairment

The Chailey Levels of Ability describe:

• The parts of the body that are loadbearing when still and when moving

• The ability to change areas of loadbearing: in an uncontrolled or controlled manner, longitudinally and laterally, and when moving into and out of position

• The position of the pelvis (posterior, neutral or anterior tilt) and the relative position of the trunk and legs

• The position of the shoulder girdle (retracted, neutral or protracted) and the relative position of the trunk and arms

- The position of the head and of the chin (chin poked, tucked or retracted)

- The lateral spinal profile

- The effect of head movement on the trunk and limbs (trunk follows head movement, trunk moves in opposite direction, the ability to move the head without associated trunk or limb movement)

- The ability to isolate limb movement from the head, trunk and other limbs

- Predominant positions of the major joints

We have already explored and experienced how positioning can compromise ability and we looked at loadbearing in some detail. For a child with neurological impairment these biomechanical factors are fundamental to his ability to perform motor tasks.

> **The duration and type of biomechanical force will influence the development of bones and joints.**

keypoint

Muscles and bones will have different types of forces acting on them during and after growth. Bone, cartilage, tendons and ligaments all respond to forces in different ways. The types of forces acting on the body are described below.

Tensile force: opposing forces pulling away from each other. A tensile force puts an object into tension.

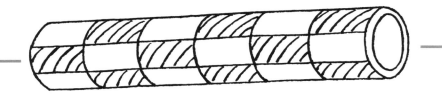

Figure 96 *Tensile force*

Compressive force: opposing forces pushing towards each other. A compressive force puts an object into compression.

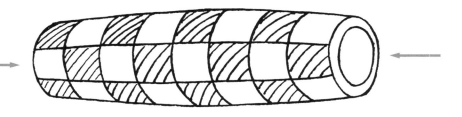

Figure 97 *Compressive force*

Rotational force: forces acting around the axis in opposite directions. A rotational force puts an object into torsion.

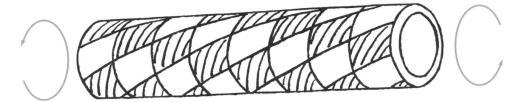

Figure 98 *Rotational force*

Shear force: applied perpendicular to or parallel to a body with an equal and opposite force in the body causing deformation in the body. A shear force puts an object into shear.

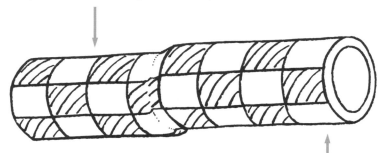

Figure 99 *Shear force perpendicular to a body*

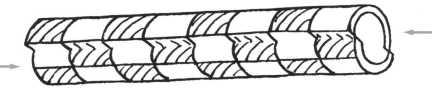

Figure 100 *Shear force parallel to a body*

keypoint

> **If forces are equal and opposite there will be no movement. If they are unequal movement will occur.**

There are a number of other terms we need to know about:

• Friction force occurs when one body moves over the surface of another. Friction can be static (the force which must be overcome to start a body moving) or dynamic (the force required to keep a body moving over a surface). Static friction is higher than dynamic friction

• Reaction force – the opposing forces generated by applying a force

• Gravitational force – generated by the earth which pulls objects towards the ground

• Bending force – the result of at least a three point loading

In lying, sitting and standing, children will experience compressive forces, as gravity acts as a downward force and the supporting surface provides opposing forces. In lying, children without sufficient strength or ability to move against gravity will develop a flattened posture.

Figure 101 *Flattened posture*

In sitting, where gravity cannot be counteracted by a child's postural ability there is a risk of deformity developing e.g. the development of scoliosis or kyphosis.

A child sliding forward in a seat will be experiencing friction and shear forces. This type of situation often results in tissue trauma.

A child lying in an asymmetrical posture will be experiencing torsion around the spine.

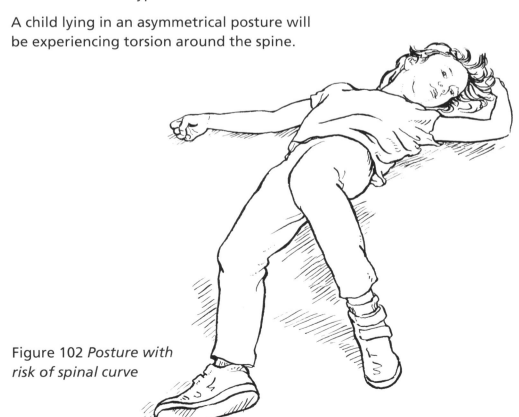

Figure 102 *Posture with risk of spinal curve*

A child in a hip abduction spica will be experiencing tensile forces in his hip adductors. These forces will cause changes in soft tissues such as tendons and ligaments. Stretching will produce a tensile force and this needs to be applied gently over time to prevent tearing of tissues and the resulting formation of adhesions.

A corrective spinal jacket will apply compression, torsion, bending and tension in correcting a scoliosis.

Figure 103 *Spinal jacket*

Children with neurological impairment who are going through a growth spurt are especially vulnerable to the development of deformity, and we know that changes to tissue happen most easily during periods of rapid growth. For this reason we need to apply extrinsic corrective forces to prevent the progression of deformity. Forces applied during these periods of rapid growth can be very effective.

In the following parts of this section we will look in detail at how we use our knowledge of biomechanics to help a child's musculoskeletal system grow and develop in the right way.

Questions

1 **What are the two aspects of developmental biomechanics?**

2 **When is the application of biomechanical force most effective?**

4.7 Muscle adaptation

This section outlines the structure and function of muscle, how it responds to neurological changes, disuse and therapy interventions. We will explore strategies to maintain muscle length and strength and joint range, and to prevent the development of deformity or at least arrest its progress.

The musculoskeletal system produces the biomechanical output of the nervous system, in other words it directs muscle action. However, the reverse can also be true. If the biomechanics of the musculoskeletal system changes, e.g. changes in body size and strength, it will require the body to move in different ways. This will alter patterns of muscle activation and feedback to the nervous system. Muscles are designed to create movement or stability. It is important to remember that muscles work in groups to produce efficient movements. These movements are learnt by exploring different ways of moving and selecting the preferred choice.

Muscles and bones adapt most rapidly in young children, especially during growth spurts, but will adapt in any body at any age. The earlier intervention starts the more successful it is likely to be.

Muscle shape

Muscles come in different shapes and sizes depending on the force they need to generate to cause movement or maintain posture. This variety of shapes can result in opposing muscle groups becoming susceptible to an imbalance of power. For example the hip adductors are short pennate muscles which are designed for strength. These oppose the long hip abductor muscles composed of parallel fibres designed for rapid movements (Newham et al. 1998). The shape of opposing muscles can make the maintenance of the delicate balance of length and strength harder to maintain and lead to the disruption of bone and joint development.

Muscle structure

Muscles are made up of a large number of fasciculi enclosed in the connective tissue sheath or muscle fascia. Fasciculi are bundles of muscle fibres held together and surrounded by connective tissue.

The connective tissue provides support and a lubricating surface over which muscle fibres can move when contracting and relaxing. Connective tissue can affect the function of a muscle if changes occur in its structure due to age, disease or disuse.

Questions

1 **What are fasciculi?**

2 **What happens to muscle fibres when a contraction occurs?**

Within each muscle fibre there are rod-like structures called myofibrils. The number of myofibrils increases with growth.

The myofibril is divided into repeating regions of sarcomeres by 'Z' shaped discs. Sarcomeres are the contractile unit of the muscle fibre composed of actin and myosin filaments. When a contraction occurs the thick filaments of actin at the centre of the sarcomere remain stationary whilst thin filaments of myosin slide inwards over them, drawing the discs closer together (Goldspink et al. 1990). The diagram below illustrates this effect.

Fasciculi are bundles of muscle fibres held together and surounded by connective tissue

A muscle consists of a large number of fasciculi enclosed in muscle fascia

A myofibril is divided into repeating regions of sarcomeres by z-shaped discs

In each muscle fibre there are rod-like structures called myofibrils

Figure 104 *Muscle structure*

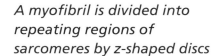

Figure 105 *Sarcomeres, relaxed (left) and contracted*

Fibre types

There are two types of muscle fibre – fast twitch and slow twitch.

The fast twitch fibres are used for rapid power movements, e.g. sprinting, kicking a football, and playing squash. Once we begin to use fast twitch fibres they grow rapidly. Arnie Schwarzenegger springs to mind!

The slow twitch fibres are used for slow postural movements and prolonged low intensity activity, e.g. maintaining a good posture whilst typing or window-shopping.

The number of muscle fibres does not change after birth but fibres are able to change their size and type according to their use. Muscles are made up of a mixture of fibre types allowing muscles to move quickly or act slowly to maintain postures. As a child learns to maintain an upright posture, a balance between slow and fast twitch fibres will develop.

If a child's motor development does not proceed as rapidly as normal there will be an imbalance between fibre types, which may compromise a child's ability to move.

Questions

1 **Give two examples of activities in which fast twitch fibres would be used.**

2 **What type of functions do slow twitch fibres perform?**

Muscle length changes

Muscle need to work at their optimal length to work efficiently.

Muscles working at a shortened length have:

• Fewer sarcomeres

• Decreased muscle fibre length

• Increased resistance to passive stretch due to connective tissue changes

• The stretch reflex stimulated before the muscle reaches its full length

These factors build up a cycle of further shortening, as the muscle never works through full range. When a child walks on his toes his calf muscles progressively shorten and the opposing muscles lengthen (Tardieu et al. 1982).

Muscles working at an increased length have:

• More sarcomeres

• Increased fibre length

• Decreased resistance to passive stretch

• Delayed stretch reflex stimulation

Use it or lose it…

If either type of

muscle fibre is not

used it will atrophy.

These factors make it difficult to generate tension at the mid and inner range of movement. Lengthened muscles work only in their outer range, making them effectively very weak.

An example is a child who has shortening of the elbow flexors. The elbow extensors have gradually lengthened as the flexors have shortened. This lengthening has caused sarcomeres to be added to the fibres so at rest they may already be overlapping. When he tries to straighten his arm the extensors contract but complete overlap of the sarcomeres occurs before the muscle can move far through its range. This means the muscle cannot generate enough force in the mid and inner ranges and the child is therefore unable to fully extend the elbow.

When muscles are short you will notice they are much stiffer, i.e. more difficult to stretch and move. The muscles in the opposite group will have to work much harder to stretch them. In this case the problem is double edged, as the muscles that need to be very strong to stretch the shortened muscle are in fact weaker because they have been lengthened by the shortening!

activity

Think about the child who walks with a crouch gait due to tight hamstrings. What factors make it difficult for him to straighten his knees?

Now think about the effects of shortening in one of the following muscle groups: ankle dorsi and plantarflexors, wrist flexors and extensors and hip abductors and adductors. Write down your thoughts and possible solutions.

Questions

1 What happens to the number of sarcomeres when the muscle is lengthened?

2 Why do increasing numbers of sarcomeres restrict muscle contraction?

3 How can you tell from passive movement if the muscle has shortened?

Muscle strength and weakness

Muscle weakness is now recognised as a major cause of disability in children with cerebral palsy. Studies suggest that muscle strengthening can improve function and does not increase muscle spasticity (Damiano et al. 2002). Conversely weakness of the gastrocnemius muscle has been implicated in muscle shortening as the decreased fibre diameter may shorten the aponeuroses and cause contracture (Shortland et al. 2002)

Muscle length changes, spasticity and tone

Let's begin by defining what we mean by spasticity and tone.

Spasticity is the increase in muscle tone as a result of damage to the nervous system occurring at cortical or spinal levels which results in increased muscle tone and exaggerated tendon reflexes (Lance 1980).

Healthy muscles are all held in a state of slight tension or readiness, which can be described as tone.

Hypertonus is an increase in this level of tension, and hypotonia a reduction.

Tone can be determined clinically by passively stretching the muscle, observing the tautness of the muscle or by palpating its tension. The speed at which muscle is stretched will affect the resistance to stretch. Muscles with high tone will resist fast stretch more than those with low tone.

Four factors contribute to a muscle's tone:

• Intrinsic stiffness – the intrinsic elastic properties of the muscle, tendon, connective tissue.

- Hyper-reflexia – this is another term for spasticity and is present when there is a loss of balance between inhibition and excitation of muscle activity. Hyper-reflexia can trigger muscles to contract very easily when they are stretched. This may make it difficult for a child to control his muscle contractions.

- Muscle contraction – a muscle contracting under voluntary control, or opposing muscles contracting simultaneously (co-contraction), will offer resistance to an opposing force.

- Thixotropy or 'the tomato ketchup effect'– a muscle that has been inactive for a period of time becomes 'sticky'. Movement and stretch will reduce this viscosity. Think about your first few steps in the morning!

Spasticity can either develop slowly or rapidly following a neurological insult.

Fast developing spasticity is usually the result of high brain stem lesions.

Slow developing 'spasticity' may indicate that there is a muscle adaptation to the lesion. Several researchers have suggested that muscle shortening causes the muscle to contract more quickly (earlier in its range) when stretch is applied preventing the muscle moving through its full range. This results in the muscle contracting and sets up a vicious cycle of hypertonia leading to muscle contracture, leading to further hypertonia. Some researchers would say that all chronic spasticity is associated with some muscle shortening (Chapman et al. 1982; Dietz et al. 1983; Carr et al. 1995).

Questions

1 **If a child's spasticity gradually increased over a period of time how would you adapt your interventions?**

2 **Why is it important to recognise the difference between shortened muscle and spasticity?**

3 **Can you list three reasons why muscle length changes might occur in a child with neurological impairment?**

4 **At which stages in a child's life might it be most important to make sure muscles do not shorten?**

> **The link between muscle length and spasticity emphasises the importance of maintaining muscle length and strength.**

keypoint

For treatment to be effective it must be targeted at the cause. If changes in muscle length are causing stiffness, then interventions must aim to change this either by gentle stretch or strengthening. It is possible to confuse length-related changes with spasticity and consequently not provide appropriate treatment

To help identify the difference between muscle shortening and spasticity the following may be useful:

- If the stiffness is variable in different positions, spasticity will be involved

- If stiffness has developed some time after the damage, it indicates that some shortening may have occurred

- If the full range of movement cannot be achieved, muscle fibre changes or connective tissue shortening must be present

Research findings show movement disability is caused more by loss of strength and lack of muscle control than by spasm and spasticity. It is also the result of an inability to formulate and communicate appropriate motor commands (Neilson et al. 1982).

Muscle length changes are a common secondary problem for children and adults with neurological impairment. They can cause pain, make management and handling difficult and affect how much progress is made ... But remember – for every shortened muscle there is a lengthened, weaker muscle opposite to it.

The ideal situation is to anticipate potential risks and prevent length changes occurring.

The main reasons why muscles change length are:

• Immobility, where movement is restricted by their inability to move, or perhaps by splinting or plastering, or is limited or non-existent, will increase muscle weakness

• Disuse, when muscles are inactive because they are immobilised, denervated or not used to their maximum. Inactivity will cause atrophy and muscle weakness, and changes in the connective tissue and bone shape

• Asymmetry, continually adopting asymmetrical postures will cause length changes in muscle groups on both sides of a joint

• Gravity, where an inability to move against gravity will cause the body to adopt asymmetrical or 'flattened' postures e.g. windswept hip deformity and scoliosis or excessively abducted hips

• Abnormal movement patterns tend to lack variety of movement and often result in stereotyped movement patterns or substitutions causing an imbalance of muscle use

• Growth can exacerbate difficulties with muscle shortening. Normally bones grow first and muscles accommodate to this growth by lengthening. If a child is not moving normally then this muscle lengthening may not occur

Interventions to control muscle length, strength and joint range

Therapy interventions are used in a number of ways to promote motor development and reduce the risk of inappropriate muscle length changes. Interventions that affect muscle groups can be categorised as loading or unloading (Lin et al. 1994).

Unloading can be described as preventing the muscle from working. It occurs when a muscle is not being used and produces fast twitch characteristics that contribute to shortening. Interventions that may cause unloading of muscles include prolonged immobilisation and tendon releases (Lin et al 1994).

Loading activities can be described as those activities that encourage the muscle to work. They produce a correct balance between fast and slow twitch characteristics in the muscle and this helps maintain muscle length. Loading occurs when muscles are being used or positioned correctly. Interventions that create loading are stretches, active exercise and using positioning equipment that allows movement (not prevents it).

Opposing muscles need to be loaded equally during a variety of activities.

activity

Read through the following list and decide which activities load muscle groups and which unload, and why.

- **Therapy programmes promoting normal development and providing passive movements and stretching**

- **Postural management equipment which allows movement in the positions of lying, sitting and standing, and mobility equipment**

- **Practical activities e.g. driving a wheelchair, eating, swimming**

- **Immobilisation**

- **Active exercise**

- **Orthoses ranging from simple ankle-foot orthoses to walking frames**

- **Surgery – single or multi-level, soft tissue and bony**

- **Botulinum toxin injections – these are given to selected muscle groups to inhibit muscle activity and last approximately three months**

- **Functional electrical stimulation – a method of electrically stimulating muscle either to strengthen the muscle or activate it during a movement pattern**

Make notes on a separate sheet if you need to.

Active exercise, passive movements and stretching will all load the muscle and increase blood flow, oxygenation and maintenance of joint range. Passive movements and stretching may be effective in warming up muscle and preventing connective tissue contractures. Short periods of stretch will not be adequate to increase muscle length.

Loadbearing with movement contributes to muscle, bone and joint development and loads muscles.

Postural management equipment should provide periods of stretch to a variety of muscles in a variety of positions (lying, sitting and standing). Controlled active and functional movement that will load muscles should be possible within the equipment. All practical activities need to encourage such controlled movement.

Immobilisation will unload the muscle, leading to muscle weakness and decreased bone density.

Active exercise and specific strength training will load muscles and improve muscle activity.

Orthoses can be used to load or unload the muscle. Continuous use of rigid orthoses that prevent muscle movement will unload the muscle, whereas orthoses that allow movement but provide control will load muscle.

Certain types of surgery, such as tendon releases, would generally be considered to unload the muscle, increase fast twitch fibres and lead to increased spasticity. Careful consideration needs to be given to this type of intervention.

Interventions such as surgery and aggressive stretching may lead to increased tendon length rather than muscle length and cause an imbalance in the muscle's length-tension relationship (Lieber 2002).

Botulinum toxin is given to reduce the tension in the muscle and allows stretch to take place. Initially unloading may in this case allow loading by blocking the movement of an antagonist muscle, allowing movement of the agonist.

Functional electrical stimulation provides exercise for the muscle and therefore loads the muscle.

Questions

1 **Explain the effect of loading a muscle group.**

2 **Suggest three activities that induce loading.**

4.8 Bone adaptation

Bone, like muscle, is an extremely adaptable tissue that will change its shape according to how it is used.

Think of the structural changes that occur to the feet of ballet dancers, or the forearms of professional tennis players. We also know that periods of time spent in outer space cause gradual osteoporosis. Our bodies will adapt to the forces placed on them.

> 'Nothing else is necessary to achieve normal or almost normal shape than to make normal or almost normal the stressing of deformed bones.' (Wolff 1986)

keypoint

As long ago as 1892 Julius Wolff outlined his theories of bone remodelling and described how correct loading of the bone could correct deformities without recourse to the knife. He maintained that bone was capable of changing shape according to the load placed upon it.

The internal structure of bone consists of collagen fibres and minerals. The collagen forms bands of supporting tissue, trabeculae, which are surrounded by minerals. The collagen fibres withstand tensile forces and the minerals withstand compressive forces. The structure of bone has been likened to that of reinforced concrete (Low et al. 1996).

> Bone is constantly being formed and removed according to its use. Therapeutic remodelling of bone is best achieved by the smooth, gentle application of force sometimes known as 'creep' (Wolff 1986; Arkin et al. 1956; Dunn 1976).

keypoint

The way a child with neurological impairment develops and uses his muscles affects the development of his skeletal system. At birth his skeleton is the same as that of other children and abnormal bone shapes are largely a result of faulty muscle loading.

Question

1 **How is it best to apply forces to remodel bone?**

Bone responds to:

- Gravity
- Compressive force
- Tensile force
- Shear force
- Rotational force or torsion
- Bending

The type and duration of force will, in the early stages of growth, be a determining factor in the type of tissue that develops. As development continues these forces will affect the amount and direction of growth.

keypoint

> **Compressive, tensile and rotational forces have the greatest impact on skeletal development.**

Let's look at how the different forces affect bone and cartilage. Growth plates in children are vulnerable to forces acting across them. Altered forces can have a dramatic effect on bone growth and shape.

COMPRESSIVE AND TENSILE FORCES

Compression, which is achieved through loadbearing, is required to stimulate normal bone growth. Increased loadbearing results in increased thickness and density of bone. Lack of compression due to limited loadbearing will limit bone growth and cause reduced bone density and can eventually lead to bone atrophy (Stuberg 1992). This is seen in children who do not walk independently.

Excessive compression on one side of the growth plate may cause a decrease in growth on that side and overgrowth on the opposite side leading to a change in the direction of growth. Knock-knees and clubfoot are examples of this (LeVeau et al. 1984).

Constant compression on cartilage leads to its thinning. Intermittent compression allows it to thicken.

ROTATIONAL FORCES

Bone growth responds to rotational forces on the growth plate. Abnormal rotational forces acting across the growth plates will cause bone to grow spirally away from the plate. This deformity is commonly seen in the vertebrae of scoliosed spines and femora of subluxed hips.

Any persistent asymmetric and abnormal force that may be present in children with neurological impairment can lead to deformity. Prevention and control of these forces is important to prevent and control deformity.

Children developing normally achieve a symmetrical posture in lying at around 3 months, begin to sit by about 8 months and walk at about 14 months. These activities produce forces that are vital to bone development. Children who are unable to achieve these activities independently need to be positioned appropriately to enable them to experience these forces.

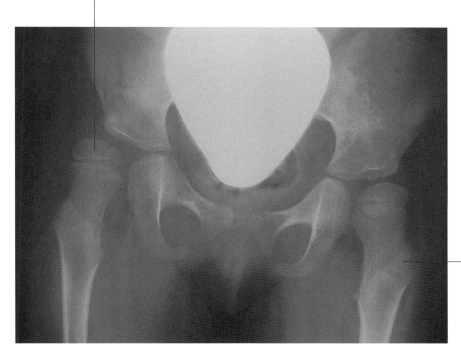

Asymmetric compressive forces across this growth plate has led to an increased growth rate on the medial aspect

Femoral rotation is indicated by the anterior position of the greater trochanter

Figure 106 *X-ray showing effect of comressive and rotational forces*

 Questions

1 **Why is it important for children to stand?**

2 **What occurs at the growth plates if asymmetrical forces are applied to them?**

3 **Give two examples of rotational deformities.**

4.9 Link between ability and musculoskeletal changes

The development of deformity is a complex interaction of neural, muscular, bony and biomechanical mechanisms. Changes to the musculoskeletal system may often be more debilitating to the child than his original neurological symptoms.

A close link exists between a child's motor ability and his risk of developing deformity.

A child who does not progress beyond the early asymmetrical postures of Level 2 lying ability, or who is unable to attain symmetry despite having good function, will be at high risk of developing deformities.

Hip dislocation and scoliosis are the two most common deformities seen in children with cerebral palsy. Between 35 and 40% of children with bilateral cerebral palsy experience hip dislocation and approximately 65% of children with spastic quadriplegia have a scoliosis. In real terms this means that, in this country, approximately 4 out of 10 children with cerebral palsy each year will experience dislocation of the hip for the first time and approximately 6 out of 10 children with spastic quadriplegia will develop a scoliosis (Lonstein 1995; Bernstein et al. 1990; Scrutton et al. 1997). These conditions can cause pain and require surgical interventions and we need to try to prevent their development. The first part of this section will consider ways of preventing deformity by early intervention and the second will consider strategies to reduce existing deformities.

Preventing deformity by early intervention

A child with no neurological impairment will be experiencing:

• a symmetrical lying position (Level 3 lying ability) at 3– 4 months of age

• an independent sitting position (Level 4 sitting ability) at 7–8 months

• a standing and cruising position (Level 5 standing ability) at 10–12 months

This highlights how early we need to begin postural management programmes for children with neurological impairment.

keypoint

> **Chronological age and not developmental age should be used as a guide to when a child should be experiencing different postures.**

Any infant older than 3 months who has not achieved Level 3 lying ability is already predominantly experiencing asymmetrical movement patterns. Think back to the sections on muscle and bone adaptation. Even a child with mild asymmetry might be experiencing changes in his hips, pelvis and spine. Muscles and bones change insidiously, long before any clinical evidence such as limited joint range is apparent.

The process of deformity starts early. Hip X-rays taken when a child is 30 months clearly show if hip dysplasia is present and can be used as an indicator of future hip problems (Scrutton and Baird 1997). This indicates that the process of deformity starts early. To prevent a child developing deformity, therefore, we must interrupt the process before clinical symptoms are apparent.

The types of change typical in the pelvis, hips and spine of a child with cerebral palsy child are:

• Shortening of the hip adductors, internal rotators and flexors

• Lengthening of the hip abductors, making them effectively weak

• Reduced pull by the hip abductors on the greater trochanter and arrested development of the femoral neck

• The direction of growth is altered due to asymmetric forces on the growth plates

• Femoral head is gradually pulled away from the acetabulum

• Biomechanical forces are not placed on the acetabulum, preventing its development

• Pelvic obliquity and rotation, and consequent compensatory scoliosis developing

The X-rays overleaf illustrate the process of hip subluxation and dislocation.

Questions

1 **What should you use as a guide to introducing positioning equipment in the lying, sitting and standing positions?**

2 **When should a child be referred for an X-ray?**

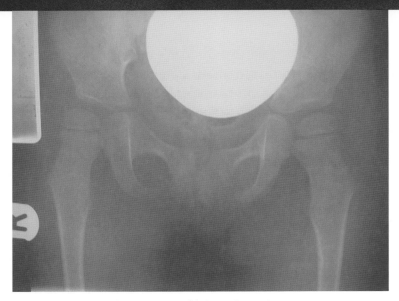

Figure 107 *Early stages of hip migration*

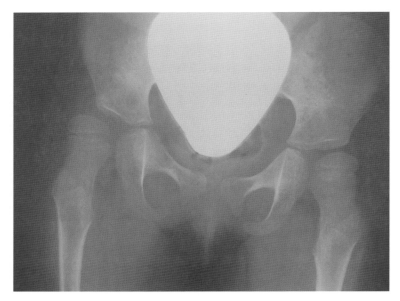

Figure 108 *Hip subluxation*

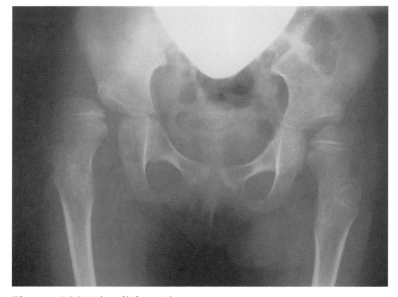

Figure 109 *Hip dislocation*

Scrutton and Baird (1997) have developed an X-ray surveillance protocol for children with cerebral palsy to detect children at risk of hip dislocation. We have modified this protocol to include our ideas of when postural management programmes need to start. This can be found at the end of this section.

Evidence from a retrospective study indicates that children who used the Chailey Approach to postural management prior to hip subluxation had a significantly reduced risk of developing hip dislocation (Pountney et al. 2002).

If we allow deformity to develop it will hinder a child's ability to progress in his motor skills.

> ## Case study
>
> Anna (9 years old and Level 2 lying ability in supine) was on the list for soft tissue surgery 18 months ago. At this time she was supplied with a Chailey Lying Support and used it for about 9 hours every night. Her parents were determined that they would do all they could to avoid surgery. X-rays taken at her 6 monthly review showed that her left hip migration percentage had remained the same. Further follow up at one year showed an improvement of 15% and the surgeon was able to take her off his list.

Reducing existing deformity

There is no quick fix for existing deformity. Once it has developed it becomes a treatment priority that requires careful planning if the treatment is to be successful.

Deformities can appear rapidly during growth spurts and children need to be monitored very carefully during these periods.

Surgery is often thought to be an easy option but, if done in isolation from postural management intervention, it often has to be repeated.

To be effective in preventing contractures and maintaining muscle length, gentle stretch needs to occur for a period of 5 – 7 hours a day (Pountney et al. 2002; Lespargot et al. 1994; Tardieu et al. 1988).

Most growth occurs as we relax during sleep at night and relaxed muscles are more easily stretched.

A deformity that has taken many years to develop will take many months to correct.

Upright positioning often requires a compromise between achieving the best possible posture, comfort, pressure relief and the effect on existing skills. It is often easiest to begin correcting deformity in the lying position both during the day and at night.

Using our knowledge of muscle and bone adaptation, we can devise a plan of management with the child and his family.

Case study

Robert, a boy of 13 with spastic quadriplegia who was Level 2 in supine, had increasing flexion contracture of his right knee due to a persistent posterior pelvic tilt causing hamstring shortening. He was also developing a kyphosis in sitting. He was using a CAPS II seating system and upright standing support and was sleeping on his side with flexed hips and knees and rounded spine. In standing he had flexed knees and was experiencing considerable pressure. It was decided to supply a Chailey Lying Support with raised knee supports in supine. He tolerated the support well after an initial acclimatisation period. The knee support heights were gradually reduced and the knee contracture reduced sufficiently over a period of 3 months to achieve full knee extension.

Measuring musculoskeletal changes

Before we can monitor whether treatment to reduce deformity is effective we need to have baseline measures of deformity. These measures are only useful if they are repeated. It is the changes in these measures over time that are significant. Listed below are some of the methods used.

Question

1 **In which position is deformity reduction most easily achieved?**

HIP X-RAYS

If taken with the child positioned correctly and consistently, these provide the most reliable data on the progression of deformity (Pountney et al. 2003; Parrott et al. 2002). For the measures to be valid it is important that the child's pelvis and hips are in a neutral position as in the diagram below. This can be checked on the X-ray by measuring the degree of hip abduction/adduction and the rotation of the pelvis.

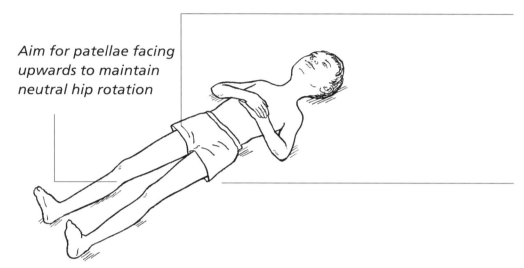

Aim for patellae facing upwards to maintain neutral hip rotation

Position the pelvis as near as possible in a neutral position of anteroposterior tilt, rotation and obliquity

Place the hips in neutral ab/adduction

Figure 110 *X-ray position*

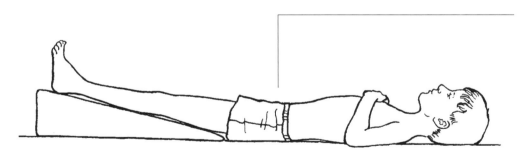

If neccesary raise legs to flatten lower spine to counteract tight hip flexors

Figure 111 *X-ray Position*

The migration percentage is the most commonly used measure and records the amount of the femoral head lying beyond the lateral margin of the acetabulum (Reimers 1980). The acetabular index is also widely used and indicates the distance of the femeral head from the acetabulum (Tonnis 1976). Normal values for this measure are available and the risk of future hip dislocation can be determined from measurements taken when the child is 30 months.

The diagram below represents a pelvic X-ray and illustrates how to measure migration percentage and the acetabular index . Using this approach an accuracy of measurement at inter- and intra-rater levels of between 3% and 8% can be achieved (Pountney et al 2003).

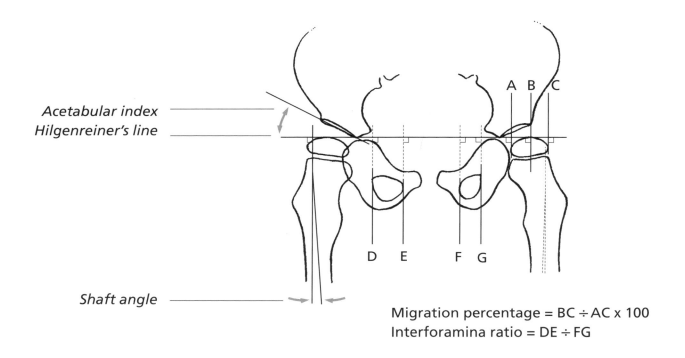

Migration percentage = BC ÷ AC x 100
Interforamina ratio = DE ÷ FG

Figure 112 *Measuring hip migration percentage and acetabular index*

The measurement of migration percentage is only valid if:

• Hips are in a neutral position

• Adduction is less than 15° and abduction is less than 10°, measured using femoral shaft angle

• Pelvic rotation is minimal: The inter-foramina ratio is between 2 and 0.5

keypoint

What is the significance of these measures?

Hips are considered to be:

Subluxed if the migration percentage is greater than 33%

Dislocated if the migration percentage is between 75 and 100%

At risk, if the rate of migration per annum is greater than 7%

When a child is 30 months if the migration percentage is greater than:

15%, there is a 25% to 54% risk of hip problems at 5 years

33%, there is a 100% risk of hip problems at 5 years

(Scrutton and Baird 1997)

RANGE OF MOTION MEASURES

This measurement option is available to all therapists. Measuring the range of joint movement can provide useful information about changes in the musculoskeletal system. The protocol for measurement must be clearly stated for reliability.

Studies have shown that the range of hip abduction does not always clearly reflect the hip migration percentage and can remain unaffected until a 60% migration is reached (Reimers 1980). Range of motion measures therefore cannot be substituted for X-ray measurements.

SPINE X-RAYS

There is no defined protocol for the surveillance of spinal curvature in children with cerebral palsy. The position for the X-ray should be consistent. At Chailey Heritage Clinical Services we usually X-ray the child in his normal sitting position e.g. in his seating system wearing his jacket.

The X-ray is usually taken when the child is either sitting:

• free

• in supportive seating

• wearing a spinal jacket

• suspended

It is important that this is recorded so repeat X-rays can be taken in the same circumstances. A child's usual sitting position is normally best, as this is an indicator of his everyday posture.

Questions

1 **What level of migration percentage at 30 months is an indicator for intervention?**

2 **How should a child be positioned for a hip X-ray and why?**

3 **When is a hip considered subluxed?**

Question

1 At what angle of spinal curvature is bracing recommended?

The Cobb angle

The Cobb angle is the most commonly used measure to determine the degree of spinal curvature. It is determined by measuring the angle between the upper edge of the vertebra at the upper end of the curve and the lower edge of the vertebra at the lower end of the curve. This measurement is best achieved using the Oxford Orthopaedic Engineering Centre's Cobbometer, available from Oxford Orthopaedic Engineering Centre, Nuffield Orthopaedic Centre, Oxford, UK.

The diagram below illustrates the process of measurement. If you don't have a Cobbometer you can draw lines extending from the vertebra at the upper and lower end of the curve and measure the angle at their intersection.

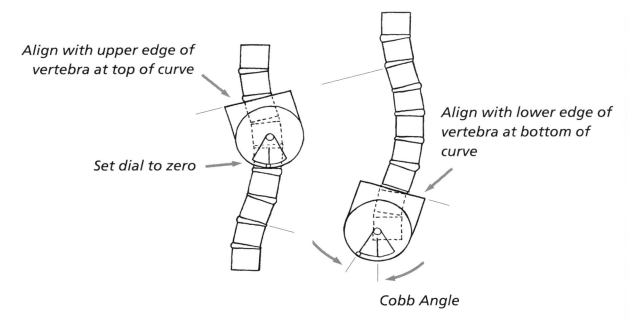

Align with upper edge of vertebra at top of curve

Align with lower edge of vertebra at bottom of curve

Set dial to zero

Cobb Angle

Figure 113 *Spinal measures*

keypoint

What is the significance of these measures? If the Cobb angle is greater than:

15° monitoring is required

at 20° bracing is recommended

at 35–40° surgical correction is indicated

(Staheli 1992)

Surveillance protocol for managing hips at risk of dysplasia in children with neurological impairment

Full motor assessment at referral. Any child who has not achieved a symmetrical lying position (Level 3 lying ability) or independent sitting (Level 4 sitting ability) is:

- assessed and prescribed an appropriate postural management programme with positioning in lying, sitting and standing at the correct chronological age

- referred for radiological examination if there is clinical evidence of a hip problem

- parents and carers are given a clear explanation of the reasons for intervention

  Radiological examination needs to be an A/P pelvic X-ray with the hips in neutral position, patellae vertical and the pelvis in neutral tilt

  It is recommended that all children with bilateral cerebral palsy have a baseline X-ray when they are 30 months

  Any child with a migration percentage of greater than 15% needs to be prescribed positioning equipment to control posture and be referred for an orthopaedic opinion

  Any child aged 30 months who has an annual migration of greater than 7% per annum is at risk of dislocation and should continue to have an annual X-ray

4.10 The effect of surfaces

Surfaces are an aspect of the environment that can have a significant impact on a child's postural ability. This section will explain the effect that different types of surface have on postural ability.

It is summer time and you are at the seaside. You have taken off your shoes and are walking along the beach. Where would you choose to walk, on the sand, or on the pebbles? Which surface would cause points of pressure on your feet? You decide to sunbathe. Would you prefer to lie on firm sand, soft sand or on a wooden sun deck? Would you lie on a towel, a mat or a lilo?

Think about the things that influence your decision.

keypoint

> The type of surface that a child is placed on, and loadbears through, affects the distribution of loadbearing.

A compliant surface that conforms to the body placed on it allows the greatest distribution of load. A hard, non-conforming surface provides a smaller area of contact. A firm surface can benefit a child who has achieved Level 3 lying ability. During active treatment sessions it can enable a child to isolate areas of loadbearing. In contrast this can have a detrimental effect for the child whose ability is less than Level 3 lying ability (Green et al. 1995). His impoverished ability to loadbear will be compromised by a surface that provides only a small area of contact and his consequent lack of security might result in lack of confidence and motivation. In the sitting position the cushion cover, lining and quality of foam will all have a subtle but very important effect on a child's loadbearing.

Question

1 **How do compliant and hard surfaces affect load distribution?**

There are other circumstances such the temperature or type of surface (warm or cold, slippery or sticky, rough or smooth, continuous or discontinuous) that can also affect a child's performance.

activity

> Look at the three pictures on the next page and, using the descriptions of the levels of ability, decide which components have changed to bring about the improvement.

Case study

A child whose preferred lying posture was Level 2 lying ability in prone was placed on a slatted table during a movement group. The child was not happy performing the tasks during the lying group activities and was observed to adopt an asymmetrical top-heavy posture. The instability induced by the hard discontinuous surface only enabled her to achieve Level 1.

Figure 114 *Hard discontinuous surface*

A sheet of Evazote was attached to the table and when placed on this the child was immediately able to adopt her best lying ability, Level 2.

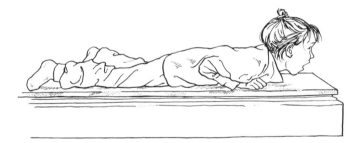

Figure 115 *Soft compliant surface*

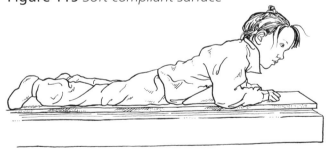

Figure 116 *Soft compliant surface with wedge*

A foam treatment wedge was then placed on the mat, positioned beneath the child's chest, enabling her to prop and lift her head in line with her upper trunk. Gravity assisted her to anchor her pelvis on the surface of the mat and so she was able to experience lying ability Level 4 and participate in the group activity with her peers.

Preventing tissue trauma and relieving pressure in areas that are particularly vulnerable is an issue that must be considered for anyone who remains in one position for more than twenty minutes at a time without being able to move actively. We need to look at the properties of the supporting surfaces in order to achieve the best possible distribution of load. Often the most important factor in reducing the possibility of tissue trauma is achieving even load distribution throughout appropriate areas of the body. When a child is sitting, the ability to bring his trunk forward over his sitting base will also help to take the load off vulnerable areas.

Think about how red an area of your skin can look after a long period of pressure. As soon as your skin is at risk your sensory system tells you it is sore and reminds you to relieve the pressure. A child with neurological impairment might not be able to do this. We need to be alert to potential tissue trauma and follow up any reference to being sore.

Factors that increase the risk of tissue trauma

Factors that increase the risk of tissue trauma are:

- Excessive compressive forces causing tissue deformation and restriction of the blood supply

- Shear or friction forces from maintaining a position or changing position

- Temperature – warm tissues have a better blood supply and therefore have less risk of developing pressure sores

- Humidity – wet skin is more vulnerable to damage

- Anaesthetic areas are at risk because a child will be unaware of the above factors

- Poor health and nutrition will affect skin integrity

activity

Think about children you know who may have an increased risk of tissue trauma and write down why.

Reducing the risk of tissue trauma with postural management equipment:

The risk of tissue trauma can be reduced by:

- Achieving a good position by evenly distributing the load over the supporting surface, which in sitting includes buttocks, thighs, feet and possibly arms.

- Preventing shear forces developing, for example by ensuring the child is not sliding forward in his seat

- Using breathable material helps with temperature control and humidity

- Ensuring that the surface is not hard or slippery, but has a fabric covering with two-way stretch, enabling good distribution of load.

- Discouraging use of incontinence pads

- Not leaving a child sitting on slings after using a hoist

- Encouraging active movement within the postural management equipment

- Regularly checking equipment for wear

- Being aware of changes that occur with growth or altered position of the child

 Question

1 **How do you think a supporting surface can reduce the risk of tissue trauma?**

4.12 The effect of orientation

Let us start with some definitions:

Orientation is the position of the body in relation to the direction in space

A reclined seated position is where the trunk leans back at an angle of more than 90° at the hips

A tilted seated position is where an angle of 90° is maintained at the hips but the whole body is tilted backwards

A seat can be reclined and tilted.

If you look back to the section on the levels of ability you will see that babies develop the ability to sit and stand initially in a position of forward prop and later learn to come to upright. Once this is established they will begin to control the shift of their weight laterally. They will move and reach from side to side and rotate to reach behind before being able to take their trunk weight behind their base and then recover their sitting balance by coming forward.

Being able to recover your balance from a reclined position is a high level of skill. A child who is placed in this position before he has developed this skill will be posturally disadvantaged. A baby placed in a reclined position such as in a hammock or bucket type seat will struggle to sit forward, clear of the backrest.

activity

Imagine that you are sitting in a chair and someone comes along and tips you back. Think about the posture you would adopt. We suspect that you would bring your weight forward to maintain your balance.

Children with neurological impairment who are placed in a reclined or tilted sitting position feel that they are falling and often try to counteract this by bringing their head and trunk forward. This is often interpreted as flopping forwards and the child may be given further restraints or the seat may be reclined or tilted even further in an attempt to stop this. Better results will be achieved by putting the seat on a horizontal base with an upright backrest position.

Reclining or tilting a child with cerebral palsy in sitting has been shown to promote extensor thrust (Nwaobi et al. 1983; Nwaobi et al. 1986). Studies of muscle activity found that both back extensors and hip adductors showed a significant increase in tone in the tilted position.

Tilted seated positions do not allow efficient use of hands and arms (Nwaobi 1987). Often the hands become positioned in high guard with the shoulder girdle retracted. This is not a functional position as it is exceedingly difficult to bring your hands to midline when your shoulder girdle is retracted. This will have an impact on achieving activities such as driving a powered chair or using a communication aid. Look back at the pictures of Jack upright and tilted in his wheelchair (in Chapter 3.4).

activity

Find yourself a biscuit or any other nibble.

Sit down on a chair. Lean slightly backwards so that your trunk is reclined. Take a bite and try to swallow.

Now sit up straight or slightly forward in your chair. Take another bite of biscuit.

Is it easier to swallow in the reclined position or upright?

Most people find it is much harder to swallow in a reclined position. Swallowing is neurologically a flexor activity (Guymer 1986) and the risk of choking is greater in the reclined or tilted position where the chin becomes poked due to change of orientation.

Another activity that is more difficult in the reclined or tilted position is to look straight ahead. Someone in this position may have a good view of the ceiling or the sky but we are sure that they would rather look at what is going on around them. Activities such as driving and using a computer will be compromised.

Children with a neurological impairment may require more postural support when placed in the reclined or tilted position because these positions are inherently unstable even for people with good postural ability. Children with cerebral palsy may not perceive a reclined or tilted position as a position of comfort.

Seven reasons for not placing a child in a reclined or tilted sitting position:

• It is developmentally inappropriate

• It can increase tendency to move into extreme extension or flexion

• Hands become positioned in high guard with the shoulder girdle retracted

• The child may have a feeling of instability, counteracted by coming forward

• It alters the line of vision

• Swallowing is difficult and the risk of choking is greater

• The performance of complex cognitive tasks will be adversely affected (See Chapter 3.4, page 48)

The upright seat position

If we look at the upright seat position, i.e. one that has a horizontal base with an upright backrest, we can see it provides many advantages.

These include:

- The opportunity to develop sitting ability

- Reducing the tendency to move into extreme extension or flexion

- Improved position of the shoulder girdle and arms, enabling improved practical ability

- Postural stability

- A horizontal line of vision allowing improved eye contact and involvement with the world around them

- Allows a normal pattern of swallowing

- Greater ability to achieve complex cognitive tasks, including schoolwork

The tilted seat position

There are several wheelbases that have the facility for tilt-in-space and there is, occasionally, a need to tilt the seat position. Each child should be assessed for this on an individual basis with the reasons clearly identified. For instance, a child who has severe epilepsy that is not controlled may need to be tilted during and after seizures to allow him to recover. A child who is very floppy when the weather is very hot, for example, may also need this facility.

Bearing in mind the information listed above, it is reasonably easy to work out a plan for when the tilt is used and when the seat is brought upright. As far as possible, it should be in the upright position for eating and drinking, schoolwork and using switches or other practical activities.

Using a tilt-in-space base to give an alternative position for rest or relaxation and in order to save the need for a transfer out of the chair is not a valid reason in most circumstances. Children need to have a variety of positions offered to them during the day and should not be expected to stay in one piece of equipment for prolonged periods.

Questions

1 **Is a reclined position a useful solution for a child who flops forwards?**

2 **Is swallowing a flexor or extensor activity?**

5

Assessment

5.1 Introduction

In recent years the importance of having reliable and valid assessment tools has been increasingly acknowledged and a variety of standardised tests are now readily available. Some of these tests are used to determine whether a problem exists and the extent of that problem, to plan intervention and to evaluate what change takes place over time and some to predict future outcomes. The Chailey Levels of Ability do all of these.

Standardised tests give an objective view and help with treatment planning and goal setting. They give useful feedback to providers of the service and therapists, and to parents and children. They can also be used for research purposes and to monitor the effect of different interventions. Measurements and tests need to be capable of detecting true and meaningful changes and be suitable to a child's level of physical and cognitive ability (Ketelaar et al. 1998; Stratford et al. 1996).

The Chailey Levels of Ability are a standardised, valid, reliable test. They provide a framework that details how the progression of postural ability is achieved from birth to the beginning of the ability to walk. It is a sensitive measure that can be used for any age and helps treatment to be targeted accurately.

Different assessment tools are needed to assess functional ability. This book is concerned with how we assess postural ability, and function is considered within this context.

Apart from the Chailey Levels of Ability, some of the assessment tools you may be familiar with include:

- Gross Motor Function Measure (GMFM) (Russell et al. 2003; Russell et al. 1989)

- Gross Motor Function Classification System (GMFCS) (Palisano et al. 1997)

- Movement ABC (Henderson et al. 1992)

- Treatment Evaluation by A Le Roux's Method (TELER) (Barnard et al. 1998)

- Melbourne Assessment of Unilateral Upper Limb Function (Randall et al. 1999)

- Quality of Upper Limb Extremity Skills Test (QUEST) (Randall et al. 1999; De Matteo et al. 1993)

- Pediatric Evaluation of Disability Inventory (PEDI) (Haley et al. 1992)

- Toddler and Infant Motor Evaluation (T.I.M.E.) (Miller et al. 1994)

- Hip migration percentage (Reimers 1980; Pountney et al. 2003) and Cobb angle (Keim 1978)

- Pain scales (Hunt et al. 2003 and 2004; RCN pain guidelines)

In order to justify our interventions we also need outcome measures. An outcome measure is a measure of change from one point in time (usually before an intervention) to another point in time (usually after an intervention). The use of standardised outcome measures will tell us whether our intervention has been effective and give us objective information on which to base further goal setting and treatment planning.

Outcome measures are not comprehensive or universal, so a range of different measures may be used for one child. We use them to measure change over time or after treatment and also to predict future outcomes. Unlike any of the measures listed above, the Chailey Levels of Ability look at detailed information about a child's posture and movement in the very earliest stages of development. This does not mean that they can only be used with children. They can be used for anyone, of any age, who has a motor impairment.

The Chailey Levels of Ability aim to create a naturalistic assessment in which the child is encouraged to move through play while the therapist observes. It can be completed without access to specialised equipment. Research has shown that items on tests that require handling are less reliable than those that the child performs alone (Haley et al. 1986; Miller et al. 1994).

Postural ability, both in and out of equipment, needs to be assessed and recorded objectively as a basis for:

- Defining treatment goals for gross and fine motor development

- Prescribing equipment for postural management

- Providing a 24-hour programme of postural management

- Measuring change

- Predicting the risk of deformity

Remember, a child's reactions may differ in a clinic setting from those seen every day or in individual treatment sessions. Below are some reasons why this may be so:

- Feeling vulnerable

- Concern about being handled by different people

- The timing and situation may be difficult

- Apprehension about the situation

- Wanting to be somewhere else

- The pressure to perform

For these reasons a child's therapists, parents and main carers all need to be included in the assessment. They all have vital information about what happens in the everyday situation including familiarity with the child's method of communication, which can enable him to keep informed and to have his say during assessment. They will know about his ability to attend and respond, and stay still or adjust his posture as and when necessary.

Photographs provide a quick subjective method of recording postures. Although they cannot be used as a reliable indicator of change, they are often useful as a visual record of a child's progress over a period of time in terms of postural ability and equipment changes. They can be taken in a child's normal environment or during the assessment process and will provide an accurate visual record of the best position a child achieves without support, or when using a piece of equipment.

A video recording would be an added bonus, giving a qualitative description of ability during assessment.

 Questions

1 Why is it important to have people who know the child well at the assessment?

2 What is the main advantage of assessments that do not require much handling?

BODY STRUCTURE

A child's body structure will affect his ability to move. The ability to assess biomechanically how a child's skeleton is developing enables us to identify muscle imbalance and asymmetry. Children are particularly vulnerable during intense periods of growth when the potential for deformity through contractures is greatest. Understanding this gives us the ability to predict unwanted change and act to prevent it.

SENSORY SUPPLY

The supply and interpretation of sensory information such as kinaesthetic feedback and spatial awareness, together with a child's understanding of verbal feedback, all influence a child's ability. Orientation during seated activities and positions used in standing frames, are just some areas to consider when trying to improve postural ability.

OTHER CONSIDERATIONS

A child's ability with expressive and receptive language, his ability to express his needs and wishes and whether he is comfortable and happy, need to be taken into account.

The child in context

Having found out all we need to know about a child, the next stage is to consider him in the context of his situation, e.g. his family and their expectations, a child's situation at school, his extended family, respite care, and how this needs to be managed and resourced. Giving parents all the information they need so that they can contribute to the decisions made should make any provision more effective. Understanding how they work as a family will help us to select solutions that will work and not burden them too much. In collaboration with the child's school it should also be possible, within the new Special Educational Needs code of practice, to clarify a child's needs more precisely.

Reflecting on and justifying decisions

This part of the process brings together the information gathered on a child and his life with the knowledge and experience of the professionals to decide the best way forward for a child and family.

Keeping track of current evidence and honing the ability to appraise it critically will help to increase our professional knowledge and understanding of all the issues. We should always be comfortable with the clinical decisions we make, knowing that we have searched out all the evidence, and critically and systematically evaluated it.

Evidence to support this approach to postural management has been referenced clearly through the chapters, and it is worth investigating the papers you are not familiar with in order to form a considered opinion.

Question

1 **Apply this clinical reasoning process to a child on your caseload and try to identify some options for interventions.**

5.5 How to use the assessment charts

keypoint

> **The analysis of the child's movement is more important than ascribing a level.**

To reach a level of ability all components of that level must be achieved.

There may be a difference between the level of ability a child can achieve when trying his best and his consistent level. The consistent level should be identified and recorded, ability at 'best' should be noted separately. A child who rests in an asymmetrical position is at risk of developing deformity so his resting position also needs to be checked.

As we have previously described, a child needs to achieve each component of a level before they can be said to have reached it. The charts will help provide a detailed analysis of areas which may be limiting a child's progress, and where he is doing well.

The following items should be noted on the assessment chart: if the child was assessed in or out of any equipment, and what that equipment was; the type of surface used for the assessment e.g. mat or floor, ramped cushion, and if orthoses were worn.

These charts can be used to record a child's ability in a number of situations. It is important to use each sheet only once. You can photocopy or print them out as you need them.

During the Assessment

• Encourage a child through movement and play to achieve his highest level of ability without assistance

• Observe a child, considering each of the sections on the side of the chart separately

• In each section, mark the items you observe a child achieving consistently by placing a tick in the box under the 'Achieved' heading

• Record any notes or specific observations in the assessment notes section

Scoring the Components Groups

• Score the level for each Component Group separately.

• Match the components achieved with the numbers and record the highest corresponding level of ability. All components indicated by solid black numbers must be present to achieve a level of ability

• Some components, indicated by bracketed numbers, may be observed but are not essential when scoring a level of ability

• Occasionally, the components achieved may not correspond with those required for any level of ability. In this case, place a dash in the box

• Careful analysis of any Component Groups with a dash will be needed to determine the reason

Ascribing an overall Level of Ability

• Record the lowest Level of Ability observed for any Component Group

• This is a child's overall Level of Ability

Points for clarification

Below are some common mistakes and confusions which are made when assessing a child's Chailey Level of Ability. These points may help you with your assessments:

• At higher levels of ability a range of movement, particularly at the pelvis, needs to be present for a child to achieve that level. For example, a child with an anteriorly tilted pelvis who cannot achieve a neutral or posterior tilt would not be able to achieve a Level 4 prone or supine.

• The details of symmetry, position and movement of the limbs are essential in determining the Chailey Level of Ability and identifying the risk of deformity. Functional skills are not sufficient evidence of a level of ability, e.g. independent sitting with posteriorly tilted pelvis does not represent a Level 3 sitting position.

The example shown opposite looks at an illustration of supine lying. It is not possible to make an accurate assessment of a child's ability from a still picture. For the purposes of the example, not all of the sections have been shown. All sections should be completed when assessing the level of ability. The example shows part of an assessment chart that would result in the child achieving a Chailey Level of Ability 2 in supine.

Worked example

1 Observe each Component Group

2 Tick the box to record that you have observed the component and the child has achieved it

3 Record the level achieved of each Component Group

4 Record the LOWEST level achieved from all the Component Groups in this box. This shows the Overall Level of Ability

5 Record other details of the assessment including use of equipment, supporting surface and use of orthoses

Below is an extract from a Supine Lying assessment chart.

COMPONENT GROUP	COMPONENT		CHAILEY LEVEL OF ABILITY 1 2 3 4 5 6	GROUP SCORE
Shoulder Girdle Position	Retracted	☐	1 2 (3) (4) (5) (6)	3
	Neutral	✓	3 4 5 6	
	Protracted	☐	4 5 6	
Pelvic Girdle Position	Posteriorly tilted	✓	1 2 (3) 4 5 6	2
	Neutral	☐	3 4 5 6	
	Anteriorly tilted	☐	4 5 6	
Leg Position	Asymmetrical position and movement	☐	1 2	—
	Hips abducted and externally rotated	☐	3 4 5 6	
	Hips extended, knees straight	✓	4 5 6	
	Hips and knees both flexed at 90°	☐	4 5 6	
	Feet touching midline	✓	4 (5) (6)	
	Hips flexed, knees straight	☐	(5) (6)	
☐ IN EQUIPMENT ✓ OUT OF EQUIPMENT TYPE OF SURFACE: *Mat*			OVERALL LEVEL OF ABILITY:	2

She is achieving Level 3 in her shoulder girdle position as it is in neutral. Her pelvis and leg position, however, are still at Level 2. She has two of the components required for Level 4 as her feet are touching in midline and her hips are extended with the knees straight. She does not have her hips abducted and externally rotated or hips and knees both flexed at 90°.

The dash on 'Leg Position' indicates she does not yet have the variety of movement required to achieve Level 3 or 4 (or it was not observed during the assessment).

The following pages contain the assessment charts. A loose and CD ROM copy are enclosed at the back of this book

Chailey Levels of Supine Lying Ability

LEVEL 1
- Unable to maintain supine when placed except momentarily and very asymmetrically
- Settles into sidelying – body follows head turning in a total body movement
- Loadbearing through lateral aspect of head, trunk, upper arm and thigh
- Neck extended with chin poked
- Shoulder girdle retracted and pelvis posteriorly tilted
- Arm movement random

LEVEL 2
- Asymmetrical posture
- Settles on back when placed
- Loadbearing through head, shoulder girdle, trunk and posteriorly tilted pelvis
- Chin poked
- Shoulder girdle retracted, shoulders externally rotated and abducted
- Arms to side
- Head to one side, pelvis and legs to opposite side
- Head movement followed by pelvic movement in the opposite direction
- Arm movement random

LEVEL 3
- Maintains symmetrical posture
- Loadbearing through head, shoulder girdle, pelvis and feet
- Neutral pelvic tilt and shoulder girdle neutral giving general trunk curvature
- Hips abducted and externally rotated
- Chin tucked but not retracted and head able to turn freely from side to side
- Controlled eye movements possible
- Beginning of unilateral grasp to side of body, takes fist and objects to mouth

LEVEL 4
- Symmetrical posture
- Loadbearing through anteriorly tilted pelvis, protracted shoulder girdle and upper trunk
- Ability to change loadbearing to head and trunk only
- Able to retract chin and turn head freely
- Definite lordotic curve
- Shoulders able to flex and adduct allowing midline hand play above chest
- Free pelvic movement beginning allowing child to touch knees with flexed hips or extend hips and knees
- Feet to midline
- Beginning of lateral load shift
- Unilateral leg raise

LEVEL 5
- Loadbearing on shoulder girdle and pelvis or only on centre of trunk
- Free movement of shoulder girdle and pelvis on trunk
- Able to retract chin
- Pelvis has full range of movement, infants able to play with toes with hips flexed and knees extended and roll into sidelying
- Can return to supine
- Hand and foot play crossing midline

LEVEL 6
- As for level 5
- Pelvis and shoulder girdle moving freely
- Consistent ability to roll into prone by achieving sidelying as in level 5 and then anteriorly tilting pelvis on trunk and extending hips

Supine Lying assessment notes	
COMPONENT GROUP	NOTES AND OBSERVATIONS
Symmetry	
Loadbearing	
Shoulder Girdle Position	
Pelvic Girdle Position	
Lateral Spinal Profile	
Head Movement	
Chin Position	
Arm and Hand Position	
Leg Position	
Activities	

Name	Date

Supine Lying Assessment Chart

Record only the components you observe the child achieving consistently by placing a tick in the box. To assess the child's level of ability, place him in supine on a firm but compliant surface.

COMPONENT GROUP	COMPONENT		CHAILEY LEVEL OF ABILITY 1	2	3	4	5	6	GROUP SCORE
Symmetry	Unable to maintain symmetrical position	☐	1	2					
	Able to maintain symmetrical position	☐			3	4	5	6	
	Able to move in and out of symmetry actively	☐				4	5	6	
Loadbearing	In sidelying (obligatory)	☐	1						
	Head	☐		2	3	4	5	6	
	Shoulder girdle	☐		2	3	4	5	6	
	Trunk	☐		2	(3)	4	5	6	
	Pelvis	☐		2	3	4	5	6	
	Feet	☐		(2)	(3)	4	(5)	(6)	
Shoulder Girdle Position	Retracted	☐	1	2	(3)	(4)	(5)	(6)	
	Neutral	☐			3	4	5	6	
	Protracted	☐				4	5	6	
Pelvic Girdle Position	Posteriorly tilted	☐	1	2	(3)	4	5	6	
	Neutral	☐			3	4	5	6	
	Anteriorly tilted	☐				4	5	6	
Lateral Spinal Profile	Flat back	☐	1	2	(3)	(4)	(5)	(6)	
	Long curve	☐			3	(4)	(5)	(6)	
	Lordotic	☐				4	5	6	
Head Movement	Trunk follows head movement	☐	1	(2)	(3)	(4)	(5)	(6)	
	Head movement followed by pelvic movement in opposite direction	☐		2	(3)	(4)	(5)	(6)	
	Turns head freely	☐			3	4	5	6	
Chin Position	Poked	☐	1	2	(3)	(4)	(5)	(6)	
	Tucked	☐			3	4	5	6	
	Retracted	☐				4	5	6	
Arm and Hand Position	Random	☐	1						
	Out to side, away from body	☐		2	(3)	(4)	(5)	(6)	
	Unilateral grasp to side	☐			3	(4)	(5)	(6)	
	Takes hand to mouth	☐			3	(4)	(5)	(6)	
	To midline	☐				4	5	6	
	Playing with both hands above chest	☐				4	5	6	
	Cross midline	☐					5	6	
Leg Position	Asymmetrical position and movement	☐	1	2					
	Hips abducted and externally rotated	☐			3	4	5	6	
	Hips extended, knees straight	☐				4	5	6	
	Hips and knees both flexed at 90°	☐				4	5	6	
	Feet touching midline	☐				4	(5)	(6)	
	Hips flexed, knees straight	☐					(5)	(6)	
Activities	Turns head to look	☐		2	(3)	(4)	(5)	(6)	
	Unilateral hand play	☐			3	(4)	(5)	(6)	
	Able to touch knees with hands	☐				4	(5)	(6)	
	Able to touch feet with hands	☐					5	6	
	Able to roll into sidelying	☐					5	6	
	Able to roll into prone	☐						6	

OVERALL LEVEL OF ABILITY:

☐ IN EQUIPMENT:
☐ OUT OF EQUIPMENT: TYPE OF SURFACE:_____

Chailey Levels of Prone Lying Ability

LEVEL 1
- Asymmetrical top-heavy posture
- Loadbearing through face, chest, shoulders, forearms and knees and feet
- Pelvis posteriorly tilted
- Hips and knees flexed
- Head to one side
- Chin poked
- Shoulder girdle retracted, shoulders flexed and adducted
- Flat back profile
- Mouthing hand is possible in this position

LEVEL 2
- Asymmetrical posture
- Settles when placed
- More generalised loadbearing through face, chest, upper abdomen, forearms knees and feet
- Pelvis posteriorly tilted
- Shoulder girdle retracted
- Shoulders flexed and adducted with elbows resting behind shoulders
- Hand and arms to side, hips and knees slightly flexed
- Head to one side
- Chin poked
- Beginning to lift head from floor with flat back profile and associated lateral pelvic movement

LEVEL 3
- Symmetrical posture
- Load bearing through lower chest, abdomen, thigh, knees and forearms
- Pelvis and shoulder girdle in neutral
- Props on forearms
- Long curve back profile
- Head in line with spine
- Chin tucked
- Uncontrolled lateral load shift so may topple into supine

LEVEL 4
- Loadbearing through abdomen, thighs and feet, with either hand or forearm propping
- Pelvis anteriorly tilted but not anchoring
- Shoulder girdle protracted
- Angular back profile of upper chest and lower back.
- Able to retract chin
- Free head movement
- Head and upper trunk movement can be dissociated from lower trunk allowing pivoting
- Hand and foot play in midline

LEVEL 5
- Loadbearing through iliac crests, thighs and lower abdomen with hand propping on extended elbows
- Pelvis anteriorly, neutral or posteriorly tilted
- Shoulder girdle protracted
- Angular profile between pelvis and lower back and upper trunk and head
- Able to retract chin
- Free head movement
- Pelvic anchoring enabling efficient pivoting and backward movement
- Able to roll into supine

LEVEL 6
- Free movement of pelvis and shoulder girdle
- Beginning to load bear on hands and knees
- Rocking backwards and forwards in this position

Prone Lying assessment notes	
COMPONENT GROUP	NOTES AND OBSERVATIONS
Symmetry	
Loadbearing	
Shoulder Girdle Position	
Pelvic Girdle Position	
Lateral Spinal Profile	
Head Movement	
Chin Position	
Arm and Hand Position	
Leg Position	
Activities	

Name		Date

Prone Lying Assessment Chart

Record only the components you observe the child achieving consistently by placing a tick in the box.
To assess the child's level of ability, place him in supine on a firm but compliant surface.

COMPONENT GROUP	COMPONENT		CHAILEY LEVEL OF ABILITY 1	2	3	4	5	6	GROUP SCORE
Symmetry	Unable to maintain symmetrical position	☐	1	2					
	Able to maintain symmetrical position	☐			3	4	5	6	
	Able to move in and out of symmetry actively	☐				4	5	6	
Loadbearing	Face	☐	1	2	(3)	(4)	(5)	(6)	
	Shoulders	☐	1	2	(3)	(4)	(5)	(6)	
	Chest	☐	1	2	3	(4)	(5)	(6)	
	Abdomen	☐		2	3	4	5	(6)	
	Forearm and hand	☐	1	2	3	4	(5)	(6)	
	Hands, elbows extended	☐					5	6	
	Pelvis	☐					5	(6)	
	Thighs	☐		2	3	4	5	(6)	
	Knees	☐	1	2	3	4	5	6	
Shoulder Girdle Position	Retracted	☐	1	2	(3)	(4)	(5)	(6)	
	Neutral	☐			3	(4)	(5)	(6)	
	Protracted	☐				4	5	6	
Pelvic Girdle Position	Posteriorly tilted	☐	1	2	(3)	(4)	(5)	6	
	Neutral	☐			3	(4)	(5)	6	
	Anteriorly tilted	☐				4	5	6	
	Anteriorly tilted and anchoring	☐					5	(6)	
Lateral Spinal Profile	Flat back	☐	1	2	(3)	(4)	(5)	(6)	
	Long curve	☐			3	(4)	(5)	(6)	
	Lordotic	☐				4	5	6	
Head Movement	Unable to move	☐	1						
	Difficulty turning head side to side	☐		2					
	Able to turn side to side	☐			3	(4)	(5)	(6)	
	Moves head freely	☐				4	5	6	
Chin Position	Poked	☐	1	2	(3)	(4)	(5)	(6)	
	Tucked	☐			3	4	5	6	
	Retracted	☐				4	5	6	
Arm and Hand Position	Tucked under chest	☐	1						
	To side	☐		2	(3)	(4)	(5)	(6)	
	Elbows behind shoulders	☐		2	(3)	(4)	(5)	(6)	
	Propping on forearms	☐			3	(4)	(5)	(6)	
	Propping on hands, elbows flexed	☐				4	(5)	(6)	
	Propping on hands, elbows extended	☐					5	6	
	Able to release for one hand play	☐					5	6	
Leg Position	Asymmetrical position and movement	☐	1	2					
	Symmetrical midline leg position	☐			3	4	5	6	
	Four point kneeling	☐						6	
Activities	Lifts head with flat back	☐		2					
	Lifts head with curved back	☐			3	4	(5)	(6)	
	Able to pivot to left and right	☐					5	(6)	
	Able to move backwards	☐					5	6	
	Able to roll into supine	☐					5	6	
	Able to attain all fours	☐						6	

OVERALL LEVEL OF ABILITY:

☐ IN EQUIPMENT
☐ OUT OF EQUIPMENT   TYPE OF SURFACE:_____

Chailey Levels of Floor Sitting Ability

LEVEL 1
- Originally described during work with children who had cerebral palsy
- Not observed in our study of normal infants
- Cannot be placed in a sitting position
- Trunk weight cannot be brought forwards over his sitting base
- This may be for a variety of reasons, including a strong tendency to extend, extreme floppiness or fixed deformities

LEVEL 2
- Can be placed in a sitting position
- Needs holding to stay in position
- Trunk weight can be brought forward over his sitting base.
- Pelvis is posteriorly tilted
- Hips are abducted and externally rotated
- Loadbearing through the buttocks and lateral aspect of the feet
- Shoulder girdle is retracted or in neutral
- The back profile is rounded

LEVEL 3
- Can be placed in a symmetrical sitting position
- Can maintain this as long as he does not move
- Pelvis is in neutral tilt
- Hips abducted and externally rotated
- Loadbearing through the buttocks and lateral aspect of the legs and feet
- Chin is tucked
- Shoulder girdle is protracted
- Hands propping or otherwise aiding balance
- Weight is forward over the sitting base

LEVEL 4
- Can be placed in a symmetrical sitting position
- Able to move his trunk forward within his base
- Able to return to upright
- Able to move laterally within base
- Able to rotate trunk within base
- Pelvis is anteriorly tilted
- Hips mainly abducted and externally rotated but can move to a more neutral position
- Can retract chin
- Shoulder girdle is protracted
- Arms can move to shoulder height
- The back profile is upright
- Hands can be brought to midline

LEVEL 5
- As Level 4
- Able to tilt the pelvis anteriorly and posteriorly enabling balance with the trunk behind the base
- This allows unilateral leg movement
- Can reach forwards out of his base
- Can recover balance after leaning to either side

- Hips are predominantly neutral
- Loadbearing through the buttocks and back of thighs
- Arms can move above shoulder height

LEVEL 6
- As Level 5
- Can move from the sitting position forward into prone
- This is by 'off loading' a buttock and leaning forward and sideways in a controlled way

LEVEL 7
- As Level 6
- Child can regain sitting position from prone

Floor Sitting assessment notes	
COMPONENT GROUP	NOTES AND OBSERVATIONS
Ability to be positioned	
Loadbearing	
Shoulder Girdle Position	
Pelvic Girdle Position	
Spinal Profile	
Chin Position	
Trunk Position and Movement	
Hip Position	
Activities	

Floor Sitting Assessment Chart

Record only the components you observe the child achieving consistently by placing a tick in the box.
To assess the child's level of ability, place him on the floor in either long or cross-legged sitting.

COMPONENT GROUP	COMPONENT		CHAILEY LEVEL OF ABILITY							GROUP SCORE
			1	2	3	4	5	6	7	
Ability to be positioned	Cannot be placed	☐	1							
	Placeable but not able to maintain position	☐		2						
	Able to maintain position but not move	☐			3					
	Able to maintain position and move within base	☐				4				
	Able to maintain position and move outside base	☐					5			
	Able to move out of position	☐						6		
	Able to attain position	☐							7	
Loadbearing	Buttocks	☐		2	3	4	5	6	7	
	Feet	☐		2	3	4	5	6	7	
	Lateral aspect of legs	☐		2	3	4	5	6	7	
Shoulder Girdle Position	Retracted	☐	1	2	(3)	(4)	(5)	(6)	(7)	
	Neutral	☐			3	(4)	(5)	(6)	(7)	
	Protracted	☐			3	4	5	6	7	
Pelvic Girdle Position	Posteriorly tilted (uncontrolled)	☐	1	2	(3)					
	Neutral	☐			3	(4)	5	6	7	
	Anteriorly tilted	☐				4	5	6	7	
	Posteriorly tilted (controlled)	☐				(4)	5	6	7	
Spinal Profile	Rounded	☐		2	3	(4)	(5)	(6)	(7)	
	Upright	☐				4	5	6	7	
Chin Position	Poked	☐	1	2	(3)	(4)	(5)	(6)	(7)	
	Tucked	☐			3	4	5	6	7	
	Retracted	☐				4	5	6	7	
Trunk Position and Movement	Behind base	☐	1							
	Forward over base	☐		2	3	4	(5)	(6)	(7)	
	Rotate trunk within base	☐				4	(5)	(6)	(7)	
	Forwards and laterally within base	☐				4	(5)	(6)	(7)	
	Forwards and laterally outside base	☐					5	6	7	
	Recovers balance from behind base	☐					5	6	7	
Hip Position	Abduction and external rotation	☐		2	3	4	5	6	7	
Activities	Variable, uncontrolled, none	☐	1	2						
	Propping to balance	☐			3	(4)	(5)	(6)	(7)	
	Able to raise to shoulder height	☐				4	(5)	(6)	(7)	
	Able to bring hands into midline	☐				4	5	6	7	
	Able to raise above shoulder height	☐					5	6	7	
	OVERALL LEVEL OF ABILITY:									

☐ IN EQUIPMENT
☐ OUT OF EQUIPMENT   TYPE OF SURFACE:_____

Chailey Levels of Box Sitting Ability

LEVEL 1
- Originally described during work with children who had cerebral palsy
- Not observed in the study of normal infants
- Child cannot be placed in the sitting position
- Trunk weight cannot be brought forwards over sitting base
- This may be for a variety of reasons including a strong tendency to extend, extreme floppiness or fixed deformities

LEVEL 2
- Can be placed in a sitting position
- Needs holding to stay in position
- Trunk weight can be brought forward over his sitting base
- Pelvis is posteriorly tilted
- Shoulder girdle is retracted or in neutral
- The back profile is rounded

LEVEL 3
- Can be placed in a symmetrical sitting position
- Can maintain it as long as he does not move
- Pelvis is in neutral tilt
- Chin is tucked
- Shoulder girdle is protracted
- Hands propping or otherwise aiding balance
- Weight is forward over the sitting base

LEVEL 4
- Can be placed in a symmetrical sitting position
- Able to move trunk forward within base
- Able to return to upright
- Able to move laterally within base both ways
- Able to rotate trunk within base
- Pelvis is anteriorly tilted
- Can retract chin
- Shoulder girdle is protracted
- Arms can move to shoulder height
- The back profile is upright.
- Hands can be brought to midline

LEVEL 5
- As Level 4
- Able to tilt the pelvis anteriorly and posteriorly enabling the trunk weight to fall behind the base
- This allows unilateral leg movement
- Arms can move above shoulder height
- Can use hands freely
- Can recover balance after leaning to either side

LEVEL 6
- As for Level 5
- Can sit independently
- Can transfer weight outside of sitting base to leave the position

LEVEL 7
- As for Level 6
- Can move into the sitting position

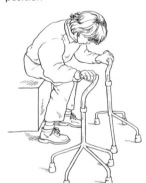

Box Sitting assessment notes	
COMPONENT GROUP	NOTES AND OBSERVATIONS
Ability to be Positioned	
Loadbearing	
Shoulder Girdle Position	
Pelvic Girdle Position	
Spinal Profile	
Head Movement	
Chin Position	
Trunk Position and Movement	
Hip Position	
Activities	

Box Sitting Assessment Chart

Name | Date

Record only the components you observe the child achieving consistently by placing a tick in the box. To assess the child's level of ability, place him in sitting on a flat box, ideally with the femora supported, hips in a neutral position, knees flexed at 90°, and feet flat on the floor spaced apart at the width of the pelvis.

COMPONENT GROUP	COMPONENT		1	2	3	4	5	6	7	GROUP SCORE
Ability to be positioned	Cannot be placed	☐	1							
	Placeable but not able to maintain position	☐		2						
	Able to maintain position but not move	☐			3					
	Able to maintain position and move within base	☐				4				
	Able to maintain position and move outside base	☐					5			
	Able to move out of position	☐						6		
	Able to attain position	☐							7	
Loadbearing	Buttocks	☐		2	3	4	5	6	7	
	Feet	☐		2	3	4	5	6	7	
	Posterior aspect of legs	☐			3	4	5	6	7	
Shoulder Girdle Position	Retracted	☐	1	2	(3)	(4)	(5)	(6)	(7)	
	Neutral	☐		2	3	(4)	(5)	(6)	(7)	
	Protracted	☐				4	5	6	7	
Pelvic Girdle Position	Posteriorly tilted (uncontrolled)	☐	1	2	(3)					
	Neutral	☐			3	(4)	5	6	7	
	Anteriorly tilted	☐				4	5	6	7	
	Posteriorly tilted (controlled)	☐				(4)	5	6	7	
Spinal Profile	Rounded	☐		2	3	(4)	(5)	(6)	(7)	
	Upright	☐				4	5	6	7	
Chin Position	Poked	☐	1	2	(3)	(4)	(5)	(6)	(7)	
	Tucked	☐			3	4	5	6	7	
	Retracted	☐				4	5	6	7	
Trunk Position and Movement	Behind base	☐	1							
	Forward over base	☐		2	3	4	(5)	(6)	(7)	
	Rotate trunk within base	☐				4	(5)	(6)	(7)	
	Forwards and laterally within base	☐				4	(5)	(6)	(7)	
	Forwards and laterally outside base	☐					5	6	7	
	Recovers balance from behind base	☐					5	6	7	
Hip Position	Neutral ab/adduction	☐				4	5	6	7	
	Neutral int/external rotation	☐				4	5	6	7	
Activities	Variable, uncontrolled, none	☐	1	2						
	Propping to balance	☐			3	(4)	(5)	(6)	(7)	
	Able to raise to shoulder height	☐				4	(5)	(6)	(7)	
	Able to bring hands into midline	☐				4	5	6	7	
	Able to raise above shoulder height	☐					5	6	7	

CHAILEY LEVEL OF ABILITY

OVERALL LEVEL OF ABILITY:

☐ IN EQUIPMENT
☐ OUT OF EQUIPMENT   TYPE OF SURFACE:_____

Chailey Levels of Standing Ability

LEVEL 1
- Unable to achieve or maintain position independently
- Needs to be fully supported under axillae
- Minimal loadbearing through side or forefoot
- Stepping reflex may be elicited
- Unable to maintain head upright
- Shoulder retracted
- Pelvis posteriorly tilted

LEVEL 2
- Unable to achieve or maintain position independently
- Needs to be held under axillae or held onto support
- Using support, loadbearing through trunk, forearms, hands and toes or plantargrade feet
- Standing base smaller than or as wide as pelvis
- Able to maintain head upright
- Pelvis posteriorly tilted
- Shoulder girdle protracted
- May bend and straighten knees

LEVEL 3
- When placed at support is able to maintain standing
- Not able to move
- Loadbearing through trunk, forearms or hands and plantargrade feet
- Standing base width of pelvis
- Pelvis in neutral tilt
- Shoulder girdle protracted
- Uncontrolled load shift and leg movement
- Flat back profile

LEVEL 4
- When placed at support able to maintain position
- Able to move within base
- Loadbearing through hands and plantargrade feet
- Trunk upright and able to move away from support
- Standing base as wide or wider than pelvis
- Pelvis anteriorly tilted
- Shoulder girdle protracted
- Can free one hand for play
- Single leg movements may occur

LEVEL 5
- Able to achieve standing using support usually through half kneeling
- Able to move outside of base
- Loadbearing through hands and plantargrade feet
- Trunk upright
- Able to lean backwards and rotate whole trunk
- Free pelvic movement and lumbar lordosis
- Can reach above shoulder height
- Stepping within position
- Leaves position in controlled way using support

LEVEL 6
- Moving freely into and out of position using support
- Cruising initially using three points of support with broad standing base
- Progressing to two points with narrow base
- Free pelvic movement and lumbar lordosis
- Loadbearing through plantargrade feet, occasionally tiptoes
- Decreasing amount of hand support, which is mainly used for balance

LEVEL 7
- Able to stand independently by releasing hands from support for a few seconds
- Able to leave position without support
- Standing base as wide or slightly wider than pelvis
- Arms in medium to high guard position
- Toe grasping

LEVEL 8
- Assumes standing independently from quadruped or squatting position using hands

Standing Ability assessment notes	
COMPONENT GROUP	NOTES AND OBSERVATIONS
Ability to be positioned	
Loadbearing	
Loadshifts	
Shoulder Girdle Position	
Pelvic Girdle Position	
Head position	
Arm and hand position	
Width of standing base	

Standing Assessment Chart

Record only the components you observe the child achieving consistently by placing a tick in the box. To assess the child's level of standing ability, place the child in a standing position against a support at elbow height unless they require full support under axillae or can achieve standing independently.

COMPONENT GROUP	COMPONENT		1	2	3	4	5	6	7	8	GROUP SCORE
Ability to be Positioned	Fully held under axillae, unable to maintain head upright	☐	1								
	Fully held under axillae, able to maintain head upright	☐		2							
	Needs to be held onto support	☐		2							
	Holds on to support if placed	☐			3						
	Holds support with one hand	☐				4	5				
	Able to achieve standing position using a support	☐						6			
	Stands alone	☐							7		
	Assumes standing independently	☐								8	
Loadbearing	Minimal or through side or forefoot	☐	1								
	Trunk on to support	☐		2	3						
	Forearms on to support	☐		2	3						
	Hands on to support	☐		(2)	3	4	5	6			
	Tip toes	☐		(2)	(3)	(4)	(5)	(6)			
	Plantargrade feet	☐		2	3	4	5	6	7	8	
Loadshifts	No load shift	☐	1	2							
	Uncontrolled	☐			3						
	Able to move within base	☐				4	(5)	(6)	(7)	(8)	
	Steps within base	☐					5	(6)	(7)	(8)	
	Able to move outside base	☐					5	(6)	(7)	(8)	
	Able to leave position in controlled way	☐					5	6	7	8	
	Able to attain position	☐					5	6	7	8	
	Able to cruise	☐						6	7	8	
Shoulder Girdle Position	Retracted	☐	1								
	Neutral	☐		(2)	(3)	(4)	(5)	(6)	(7)	(8)	
	Protracted	☐		2	3	4	5	6	7	8	
Pelvic Girdle Position	Posteriorly tilted	☐	1	2	(3)	(4)	(5)	(6)	(7)	(8)	
	Neutral	☐			3	(4)	(5)	(6)	(7)	(8)	
	Anteriorly tilted	☐				4	(5)	(6)	(7)	(8)	
	Free pelvic movement	☐					5	6	7	8	
Head Position	Unable to maintain upright	☐	1								
	Able to maintain upright	☐		2	3	4	5	6	7	8	
Arm and Hand Position	Unable to release hands for play	☐	1	2	3						
	One hand free for play	☐				4	5	6	7	8	
	Reaches above shoulder height	☐					5	6	(7)	8	
Width of Standing Base	Narrower than pelvis	☐	1	2	(3)	(4)	(5)	(6)	(7)	(8)	
	Same as pelvis	☐		2	3	4	5	6	7	8	
	Wider than pelvis	☐				4	5	6	7	8	

OVERALL LEVEL OF ABILITY:

☐ IN EQUIPMENT
☐ OUT OF EQUIPMENT   TYPE OF SURFACE:_____

Using the assessment charts **5.5** 129

6.3 Lying position

A child spends most of his time in lying during the first year of his life. Progression in lying ability forms the foundation for the progression of a child's motor ability. For the first few months of life infant postures are characterised by asymmetrical postures, and movements appear to be random and variable. At about three months of age there is a significant change in postural ability with the development of symmetrical postures and purposeful movements (Prechtl 1984). A close link exists between lying and sitting ability and until a child achieves Level 4 lying in prone and supine he will not be able to sit independently (Level 3). It is therefore important to offer a child with motor impairment the opportunity to experience higher levels of ability in early life to help him improve his motor skills.

As a child grows he is less likely to spend time in the lying position during the day but will still spend many hours in this position at night. Night-time therefore provides the opportunity for postural support to be used to provide gentle stretch and maintain joint positions. Children and young people with existing deformity can gain improvements in muscle length and joint range by sleeping in a corrected position at night.

Supine

For children to bring their hands to midline for play and discover their bodies they will need to be positioned in such a way as to achieve at least a Level 4 lying ability. This includes the following components:

- Symmetrical posture

- Anteriorly tilted pelvis

- Protracted shoulder girdle

- Ability to change to loadbearing areas

- Ability to retract chin

- Definite lordotic curve

- Midline hand play above chest

- Free pelvic movement beginning

- Ability to touch knees with hips flexed or extend hips and knees

- Feet to midline

For a child with a very low level of ability, therapy sessions in supine in the Chailey Lying Support can be very effective. The head and shoulder girdle support is used to protract the shoulder girdle and a small lumbar support encourages a lordosis. Once in this position a child can be encouraged to flex and extend his hips and play with both hands above his chest in midline. These abilities are learnt before rolling. A child will be in a good position to take an active part in his treatment, such as playing with a soft ball or cradle gym.

Prone

For children with motor impairment to take an active part in an activity in prone they will need to be positioned in a way that achieves at least a Level 4 ability. This includes the following components:

- Loadbearing through abdomen, thighs and feet

- Hand or forearm propping

- Pelvis anteriorly tilted but not anchoring

- Shoulder girdle protracted

- Ability to retract chin with free head movement

- Head and upper trunk movement dissociated from lower trunk allowing pivoting

- Hand and foot play in midline

A child with a low level of ability may dislike prone when unsupported because his weight is mainly on his upper trunk and head, making it difficult for him to lift his head up. A simple method of overcoming this is a small contoured wedge, which changes the position so that the load is taken down to the pelvis. This allows the shoulder girdle to protract and load to be taken on the forearms (see figures 114–116 in Chapter 4.10). Initially, a child may need help to maintain this position but gradually his stability will increase as he learns to loadbear through his pelvis. When he can lift his head with a curved back and release one hand he will be able to begin play. He will now be in a good position to take part in activities such as playing with cars, looking in mirrors, listening to a story, playing hide and seek games with his hands, blowing at balloons and watching bubbles.

keypoint

> The Chailey Lying Support can be used in prone or supine as a daytime position for play, sleeping or other activities.

To maximise a child's ability to play, toys need to be positioned where he is able to reach them. The Chailey Levels of Ability can guide you in this. For instance, if his chin is tucked and his shoulder girdle protracted, then toys placed above his chest in midline will encourage him bring his hands together to play. If he can do this he will be able to play with both hands and look at what he is playing with.

For a child who has low levels of lying ability it is particularly important that he feels safe, comfortable and secure enough to permit personal care activities to take place. Be aware that different positions, types of surfaces and textures that a child is lying on often have an effect on his level of ability. During personal care it can be difficult to support a child who has a Level 1 supine lying ability comfortably for bathing, nappy changing and dressing. A child may present with lying ability Level 2 on some surfaces with his clothes on, but have difficulty adapting to that surface when undressed and may revert to Level 1. Surface materials, density of foams and shapes of bath seats can promote a Level 2 or 3 ability where the child is more able to conform to the surface, relax and achieve greater contact. This provides an even distribution of loadbearing.

Chailey Lying Supports

A Chailey Lying Support enables a child to achieve and experience at least Level 4 lying ability, and allows his joints to rest in a neutral position. Used at night for sleeping, it provides long periods of stretch needed to maintain muscle length, preventing the asymmetrical lengthening and shortening that is the major cause of deformity.

A Chailey Lying Support promotes chin tuck, shoulder girdle protraction, neutral pelvic tilt and loadbearing areas of at least Level 4 lying ability. This position gives the biomechanical feedback of a symmetrical position and provides a stable base for movement.

Evenly distributed loadbearing over the whole body's supporting surface minimises the risk of tissue trauma.

The Chailey Lying Support is designed to provide a symmetrical position in either supine or prone. The firm base and cushioned Evazote supports provide a stable, consistent support for the body in symmetrical positions. This will prevent any development of asymmetrical shapes caused by accommodation to soft compliant surfaces.

The diagrams overleaf illustrate the action of forces in prone and supine.

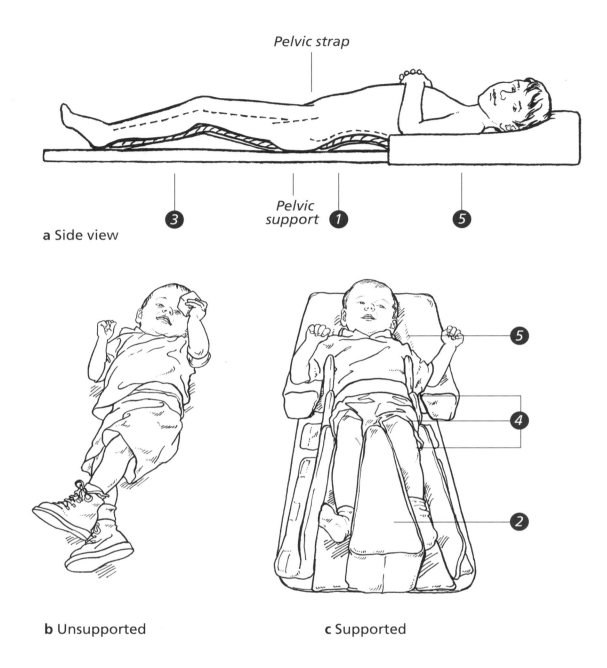

a Side view

b Unsupported   c Supported

1 Anterior pelvic tilt provided by lumbar support extending from the PSIS to the top of the lumbar spine

2 Slightly abducted hip position and symmetrical pelvis provided by abduction block, lateral supports and pelvic strap

3 Knees in slight flexion provided by knee supports

4 Trunk symmetry provided by lateral pelvic and thoracic supports

5 Chin tuck and protracted shoulder girdle provided by head and shoulder girdle support

Figure 121 *Components of the Chailey Lying Support in supine*

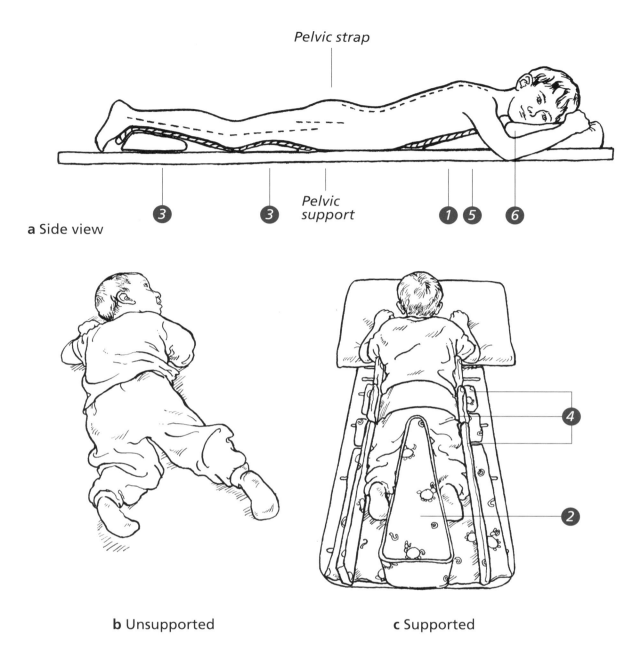

Pelvic strap

Pelvic support

3 **3** **1** **5** **6**

a Side view

b Unsupported   **c** Supported

4

2

1 *Anterior pelvic tilt promoted by contoured chest support which helps shift trunk loadbearing towards the pelvis, maintained by pelvic strap and lateral supports*

2 *Slightly abducted hip position and symmetrical pelvis provided by abduction block, lateral supports and pelvic straps*

3 *Knees supported in slight flexion by thigh and shin supports*

4 *Trunk symmetry provided by lateral pelvic and thoracic supports*

5 *Protracted shoulder girdle provided by a contoured chest support (chest support extended from axillae tapering to the bottom of the sternum*

6 *Chin tuck promoted by protracted shoulder girdle position*

Figure 122 *Components of the Chailey Lying Support in prone*

USE OF CHAILEY LYING SUPPORT FOR SLEEPING

Medical implications must be considered before a lying support is used as a night-time sleeping position. We recommend that a sleep history is taken before supplying a lying support.

The use of postural equipment at night must promote the good quality sleep that is needed for adequate daytime functioning. There is a high frequency of sleep disturbance in children with cerebral palsy due to sleep hypoxaemia caused by upper airway obstruction – probably due to brainstem dysfunction and bulbar problems as well as causes such as hypertrophy of tonsils and adenoids.

The positioning of the child must take into account additional risk factors such as nocturnal seizures, reflux oesophagitis and chest infections causing nocturnal hypoxaemia. Some of these may be aggravated by lying in the supine position, and for children with these difficulties prone positioning may be more suitable (Cartright 1984; Martin et al. 1995). If these factors coexist, appropriate investigations and treatment prior to positioning should be carried out. If there is a risk of nocturnal hypoxaemia, overnight oxygen saturation should be monitored and, in cases of doubt, repeated while a child is in the supine lying support.

Why would we use a lying support for sleeping? We spend a lot of our time sleeping and it is an ideal time to stretch relaxed muscles and gain symmetry.

In the prone sleeping position a child's level of ability must be raised sufficiently by the support for him to be able to turn his head freely whilst maintaining pelvic symmetry.

Supine, rather than prone, is the recommended position for sleeping, for a number of reasons:

• The head and shoulder girdle are more easily aligned

• It allows more freedom of movement for the head, upper and lower limbs

• It is a cooler position

• It is easier to position the child symmetrically

DAYTIME USE OF A CHAILEY LYING SUPPORT

The Chailey Lying Support may be used as a good daytime position, particularly for younger children, for play. It is an opportunity for children to be active in lying and will reduce asymmetry and any tendency to extension, and encourage head, arm and leg movement. It is an opportunity for a child to experience a different lying position from the one in which he sleeps. In prone, a higher chest wedge than the one used for sleeping can be used during play.

USE OF ORTHOSES IN THE CHAILEY LYING SUPPORT

The deforming effect of gravity on the spine is considerably reduced in lying. The Chailey Lying Support provides a contoured surface and lateral supports to maintain the position of the spine. These two factors reduce the need for spinal jackets to be worn in lying. On the rare occasions that one is used in a lying support, the support will need to be shaped so that the contouring is the same, otherwise the child might be very uncomfortable.

Case study

Charlie is 15 months old and has Level 1 lying ability in supine. His loadbearing is through the left side of his body, shoulder girdle retracted, chin poked, pelvis posteriorly tilted and hips and knees extended. Placing him in the Chailey Lying Support gives him experience of what it is like to lie on his back at Level 3. He settles immediately and with his shoulders and pelvis in neutral, chin tucked, hips and knees slightly flexed he starts to experiment with moving his arms and legs. The same thing happens when he is placed in prone in the Lying Support and he quickly starts to practise bringing his head up off the surface. His mother is delighted with the way he is moving and compares it with what his 4-month-old sister is doing when she is on the floor.

6.4 Sitting position

Children should have the opportunity to experience sitting at the appropriate chronological age. In normal development the ability to sit at Level 3 sitting ability starts at about 7 months and progresses rapidly until about 12 months, when the child is able to get in and out of the position (Levels 6 and 7). At this stage of normal development the child will be sitting on the floor, but this is often a very difficult position for children with motor impairment and it might be more appropriate to use a seat, especially for older children. If sitting on the floor is difficult for a child, the reasons for this should be identified. It may be due to muscle length changes, in which case he may need to be positioned in a way that compensates for this.

The aim when providing equipment is to replicate, by introducing support, at least Level 3 sitting ability. At Level 3 the child achieves a symmetrical position and controls the pelvis in an upright position. The shoulder girdle moves into a protracted position and arms are used as support and stability for the trunk. Trunk weight comes forward over the sitting base. Once supported in this position a child will then be able to experiment with trunk movement forwards and back to upright, and then a lateral load shift within his sitting base, giving him the experience of Level 4 ability.

If a child is at Level 1 or 2 sitting ability he will need help to attain Level 3 sitting ability. He may display strategies to prevent falling back or sideways and will need support to stay in this precarious position. If he is put into a reclined or tilted position and has not yet acquired the ability to control having his centre of gravity in this position (this does not happen until Level 5 sitting ability), he will be at a mechanical disadvantage. In this situation he may try to come forward using an abnormal pattern of movement.

If a child is able to achieve Level 4 sitting ability without any help then small items of equipment may improve his ability to Level 5. For instance, a ramped cushion that supports the ischial tuberosities on a flat surface and the femora in a horizontal position will improve loadbearing. This enables him to move within his base more easily by actively tilting his pelvis anteriorly providing, of course, that the chair is the correct height from the floor. It will also help him to free up his arm movements so that he can reach above shoulder height. Once the child is able to achieve Level 5 in sitting, the height of the chair will be the most important feature, allowing him to practise the next level of ability, which is to be able to get in and out of sitting.

Figure 123 *Child on a flat box*

Figure 124 *Child using a ramped cushion*

Opportunities to practise

Look carefully at the components of sitting, and think about how to give the child the practice necessary to achieve his missing skills. Remember the link between lying and sitting, and offer chances to practise these skills in other positions as well. Active movement is necessary for increased strength, stability and control. Normal movement patterns are the most efficient and effective, and these are the ones that we want the child to practise consistently.

The following section will direct you through the process of providing the correct support so that the components of Level 4 sitting ability can be achieved.

Floor Sitting Seat

For younger children floor sitting is the usual sitting posture for play and mobility. This is a posture that children adopt as part of normal development when they are learning to sit. The Floor Sitting Seat is designed for children up to the age of 4 years of age and aims to replicate Level 4 floor sitting ability. It positions a child with an upright pelvis, abduction and external rotation of his hips and with his weight forward over his sitting base. This position offers a basis for developing sitting skills, including trunk control, and maintenance of muscle length around the hip and pelvis. The postural support frees a child's hands from propping so he is able to use them for play. The seat is designed so that a child can be easily placed in it with no need for straps although for safety reasons some children may need a lap strap.

 Question

1 **What does the equipment need to provide to enable someone to achieve a Level 4 sitting posture?**

The seat components include:

- a close fitting pelvic support

- a flat surface for the ischial tuberosities to rest on

- a ramped leg support offering slight knee flexion to allow pelvic movement

- a pommel

- lateral thoracic supports

- a flexible backrest to experience trunk movement behind base

Within the seat a child can flex and extend his knees, move between anterior and neutral pelvic tilt, rotate his trunk within base, move forward over his base and return to upright and potentially move out of the seat by moving forwards and sideways into prone.

Figure 125 *Child using Floor Sitting Seat*

CAPS II seating system

This seating system provides a child with a stable base in sitting. It maintains a symmetrical posture, promoting the control of active movement at a higher level of ability than he can achieve without support. It is designed to emulate an upright sitting posture of at least Level 4 sitting ability.

It can be used on any horizontal base including manual or powered wheelchairs or an indoor mobile base.

> Look back to section 2 and write down the elements that are required for Level 4 sitting ability on a box.

activity

What does the equipment need to provide to enable someone to achieve a Level 4 sitting posture?

• Neutral to anterior pelvic tilt, with no rotation or obliquity

• Horizontal femora with flexed hips, knees and feet at 90°

• Feet supported at height adequate to support femora horizontally

• Neutral hip ab/adduction and rotation

• Trunk symmetry

• Protracted shoulder girdle

• Head in alignment with trunk

• Chin tuck

The explanations with diagrams on the following pages illustrate how this is achieved.

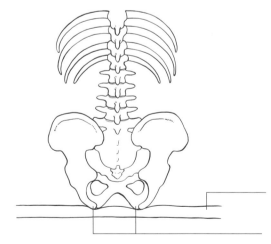

The conforming seat cushion needs to be supported on a flat, firm base.

Ischial tuberosities are supported on the horizontal part of the seat cushion. This enables the pelvis to be supported in a neutral or anterior tilt position and without obliquity, providing a symmetrical and stable position for movement.

Figure 126 *Ischial tuberosities on a horizontal surface*

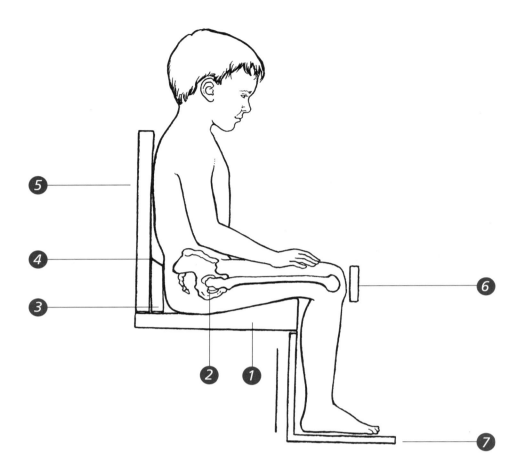

1. *Cushion horizontal beneath the ischial tuberosities, ramped at 15° forwards from the gluteal crease. This accommodates the difference in thigh dimensions and supports the femora in a horizontal position*

2. *Seat length adjustable to maintain hips and knees at 90° enables trunk alignment over stable sitting base*

3. *Sacral pad stepped forward from the backrest accommodates the difference in trunk dimensions whilst maintaining the pelvis in an upright position*

4. *The sacral pad extends from the seat cushion to the approximate height of the lumbosacral junction. It is curved laterally to support the pelvis and sacrum and works in conjunction with the kneeblock*

5. *Backrest at 90° to the seat base to support the trunk in an upright posture and curved laterally to provide lateral stability and encourage shoulder girdle protraction*

6. *Kneeblock maintains the pelvis and hips in neutral alignment*

7. *Footrest height and position maintain femora horizontally and keep the knees at 90° and the feet in alignment with the hips*

Figure 127 *Basic components*

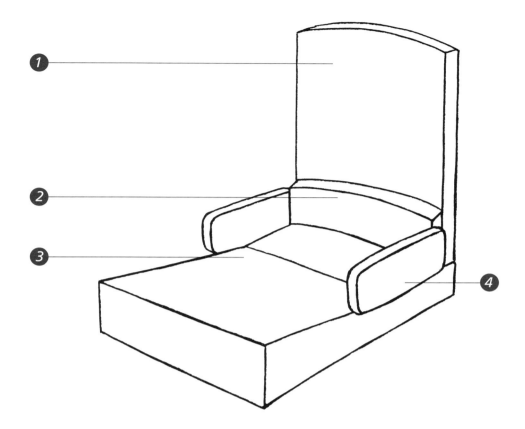

1. *Curved backrest with cushion made from high resilience, low density (very soft) foam to provide support and accommodate bony prominences*

2. *Ramped seat cushion with 15° ramp made from high resilience, high density foam (fairly firm but conforming) which allows stable support on a firm, flat base.*

3. *Sacral support with lateral curve, made from very dense (quite hard) Evazote foam designed to support the pelvis in a symmetrical position*

4. *Adjustable pelvic lateral supports align laterally with the femora and act upon the greater trochanters to help maintain the pelvis in a symmetrical position*

Figure 128 *Basic seat components*

The above components will only work when the seat length is exactly the correct length to maintain the pelvis upright. The seat length needs to be adjustable to accommodate growth of the femur and changes in ability. The pelvic strap is designed to pull down and back to prevent a child standing or extending up and out of the seat, and for safety purposes.

The movements of the hip and pelvis are the most difficult to control and are crucial for a stable sitting base. To achieve and maintain a symmetrical posture all the twelve movements that are possible around the hip joint need to be controlled.

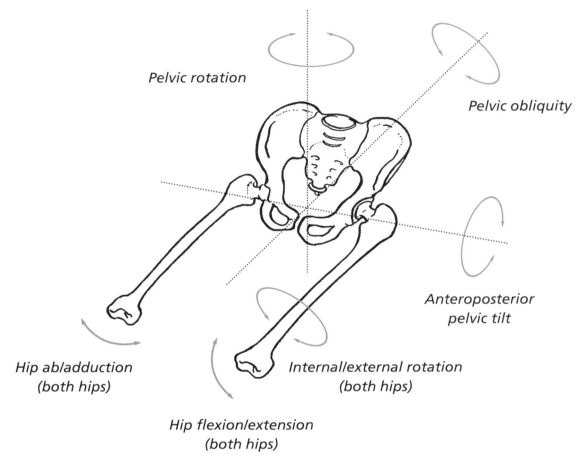

Pelvic rotation

Pelvic obliquity

Anteroposterior pelvic tilt

Hip ab/adduction (both hips)

Internal/external rotation (both hips)

Hip flexion/extension (both hips)

Figure 129 *Twelve possible movements around the hip joint*

Once a seat base with the correct shape and dimensions, posterior support from the sacral pad and lateral supports has been set up, the final component of pelvic stability is provided anteriorly by the kneeblock. Together these components control pelvic tilt, rotation and obliquity, and hip position.

In order to maintain the pelvis in an anterior/neutral tilt and the hips in a neutral position, a force is applied by the kneeblock via the femora to the hip joints. The hip joints lie below the level of the L5/S1 joint and consequently below the level of the top of the sacral pad. The force of the sacral pad and the force of the kneeblock applied equally and in opposite directions serve to maintain the pelvis in an upright position.

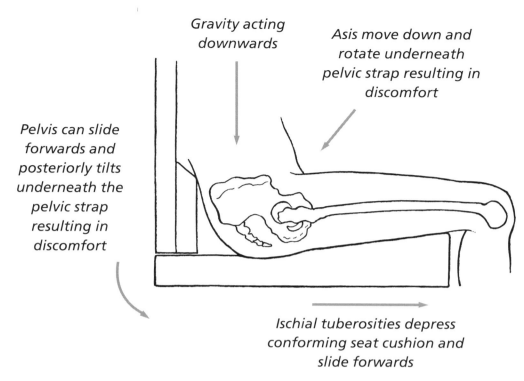

*Gravity acting
downwards*

*Asis move down and
rotate underneath
pelvic strap resulting in
discomfort*

*Pelvis can slide
forwards and
posteriorly tilts
underneath the
pelvic strap
resulting in
discomfort*

*Ischial tuberosities depress
conforming seat cushion and
slide forwards*

Figure 130 *Pelvic strap unable to maintain pelvic tilt*

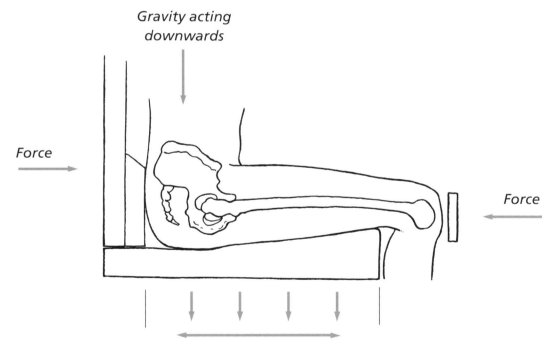

*Gravity acting
downwards*

Force

Force

*Seat length correctly adjusted. Maintains neutral pelvis and
reduces the tendency of the pelvis to posteriorly tilt or to slide
forwards. This minimises the horizontal component of the
trunk weight acting through the knee and sacrum.*

*This maximises the vertical component of the trunk weight
supported by the seat cushion*

Figure 131 *Pelvic position corrected using kneeblock and sacral pad*

The forces applied by the sacral pad and the kneeblock are at a minimum when the pelvis is in a neutral plane, and increase to a maximum, possibly intolerable level, if the adjustment is incorrect and a slumped posture is allowed.

The kneeblock provides control of abduction and adduction of the hip via the medial and lateral pads and each side can be adjusted independently. The kneeblock housing is mounted at a five-degree angle to deflect pressure away from the tibial tuberosity, thus leaving the knee joint itself unloaded.

The footrest position is critical to the correct use of the kneeblock. It will affect the flexion/extension and the internal/external rotation of the hip joints and how the forces are applied through the knee.

Using kneeblocks

THE USE OF KNEEBLOCKS WITH WINDSWEPT HIPS

A child at Level 2 sitting ability needs to achieve symmetry. The potential to have asymmetry of the hips and pelvis is very often a feature at this level of ability. The kneeblock plays an important part in correcting this asymmetry. This is only possible if the kneeblock can be adjusted independently on to each knee.

The kneeblock can be used to correct, control or prevent asymmetry of the pelvis and hips. Look at the diagram below.

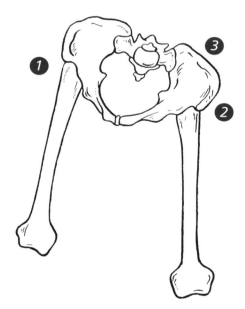

1 *The right hip is adducted and at risk of dislocation*

2 *The left hip is abducted*

3 *The pelvis is rotated forward on the abducted side*

Figure 132 *Rotated pelvis and windswept hips*

In the next illustration the kneeblock has been used to correct this position.

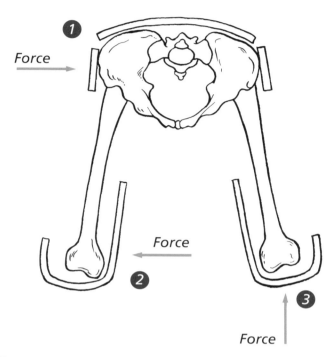

1. The pelvis is positioned on the flat section of the seat cushion and centrally located between the pelvic lateral supports and with posterior support provided by the curved sacral support

2. The adducted hip is brought into a neutral position by an abduction force on to the medial aspect of the femoral condyles. There is no contact to the front of the knee and therefore no force is transmitted to the hip joint on this side

3. Simultaneously a posterior force is applied to the distal end of the femur on the previously abducted leg, holding a de-rotated position at the pelvis and bringing this hip into neutral

Figure133 *Corrected pelvic and hip position*

The forces applied by the kneeblock are counteracted by the sacral pad and lateral pelvic pads.

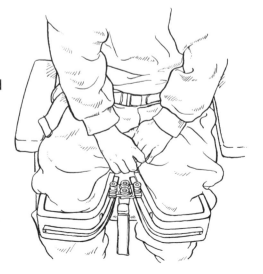

Figure 134 *Kneeblock in use*

THE USE OF KNEEBLOCKS WITH HIP SUBLUXATION

It may be evident when assessing a child's posture that there is a difference in leg length. This is usually apparent shortening and can be due to rotation or obliquity of the pelvis or posterior migration of the hip. Either will cause one leg to appear shorter than the other. A combined clinical assessment and X-ray will help identify the cause of the shortening.

If postural asymmetry is present, it is important to be able to adjust each knee cup individually, allowing the femora to be placed and maintained in the best position achievable. This will encourage proper hip alignment and development to continue.

If a child with subluxation or dislocation of his hips is showing any sign of discomfort or pain then this should be investigated and monitored without delay. It may be necessary to discontinue the use of kneeblocks temporarily, adjust them to reduce the level of corrective forces or consider the use of a unilateral kneeblock or pommel. The situation should be monitored very carefully until you are sure that you have achieved relief of the discomfort or pain.

THE USE OF KNEEBLOCKS WITH HIP DISLOCATION

If a child is known to have a dislocated hip but it is not causing pain or discomfort, there may still be benefits in using a kneeblock to maintain a neutral rotation of the pelvis and help to prevent secondary spinal curvature. You will need to ensure that there is no longitudinal force being transmitted to the hip joint by allowing a little space in front of the knee. Occasionally you may find that it is preferable to have a simple medial pad instead of a complete knee cup on that knee. Where both hips are dislocated, a better option might be a pommel with an adjustable abduction bracket so that good alignment can be still be achieved but no longitudinal force is transmitted to the hip joint.

THE USE OF KNEEBLOCKS FOLLOWING SURGERY

The aim of surgery is to rebalance the length and tension of the adductor muscles and prevent the asymmetrical forces from causing further subluxation of the hip joint.

If there has been bony reconstruction of the femur or acetabulum to relocate a dislocated hip then, once the hip is comfortable, kneeblocks are used post-operatively to maintain the optimal position gained.

Kneeblocks are not contraindicated following surgery provided there is no pain. They may be essential in maintaining the correction gained from the surgery. However they will need to be set up very carefully and monitored frequently during the post-operative period.

Trunk symmetry and support

Thoracic supports help maintain lateral trunk alignment and, if positioned correctly, allow active movement of the trunk forward over the sitting base.

Trunk symmetry can be more easily attained on the stable sitting base that we have just described. Shoulder protraction needs to be present to stabilise the trunk. This is aided by the curved backrest and support from a tray at elbow height. Additional anterior support can be provided close to the trunk by an upright anterior support mounted on the tray. This further enables protraction of the shoulder girdle.

Figure 135 *Child using tray with anterior support*

The stable sitting base, trunk support and shoulder girdle protraction provide the foundation for improving the alignment of head posture with the trunk. This facilitates active movement of the head, arms and hands. A headrest aligned with the backrest contributes to head stability.

Figure 136 *Child sitting with minimal postural support*

Figure 137 *Same child showing improved postural control in CAPS II seat*

Spinal jackets

It is not unusual for a child to use a jacket in a seating system if his spine is at risk of increasing curvature and/or his posture cannot be supported by seating components. If it is to be used all the time the jacket needs to be fitted well over the anterior superior iliac spines, but cut away anteriorly at the base to allow the child to sit in the upright position comfortably, without the jacket causing pressure over the thighs.

For a spinal jacket to work effectively the lower border must cover the iliac crests. Check that the lower back border of the jacket is not too long, causing it to catch behind the seat and affect loadbearing. The backrest cushions on a seating system may need to be altered to accommodate the jacket, as a sacral pad will often not be needed. When a child is wearing a spinal jacket in a seating system the jacket acts as the sacral pad but will not provide lateral and anteroposterior control of the pelvis.

The lower back edge of the spinal jacket should be carefully shaped without undue flaring. This will enable the child to be positioned well into the back of the seat, so that the seat and jacket work together to support the back in an upright position. The lateral pelvic supports need to be positioned so the jacket does not sit on top of them, and the kneeblock must be adjusted to correctly maintain the pelvic and hip position. Spinal jackets are not sufficient on their own to control pelvic and hip position.

CAPS II with Lynx™ Backrest

For children and adults who have some degree of spinal deformity but are still able to sit with a level pelvis the CAPS II seat is now available with a Lynx™ backrest. It provides the benefits of a modular seating system with a contoured backrest. Lynx™ is a sheet made from interlocking X-shaped components. These lock to provide a continuous 3 dimensional surface that can be formed to suit the shape of the occupant. The Lynx sheet is mounted to the CAPS II backrest tubes. The finished backrest is upholstered. These seats are supplied through specialist seating services.

Case study

Becky is 2 years old and has a Minicaps on a Snug Seat frame. She uses this for travelling to and from nursery and also during the day in nursery for all activities. She has Level 2 sitting ability, which means that she needs complete support and control to be provided. Nursery staff have some concerns about her headrest, which they feel needs to be adjusted because her head is always falling forwards. However the real problem is that the seat depth had been set too long, which allows her pelvis to fall back into posterior tilt. Her seat is also tilted backwards, creating a further disadvantage as she struggles to sit more upright. At Level 2 she does not have the ability to change the position of her pelvis for herself. Her trunk is rounded above her pelvis, which makes head control and trunk movement difficult. Shortening the seat depth, supporting her pelvis into a neutral position and bringing the seat base up to horizontal mean that she is able to sit straight and can control her head well. This brings her level of ability in her seat up to Level 3 and she is now able to start to practise small trunk movements forwards and back to upright.

6.5 Standing position

Standing is the least stable posture and requires the highest level of coordination and balance to maintain. As with lying and sitting it is important for children to experience standing at an appropriate chronological age (10–12 months) to promote the normal skeletal development of weight-bearing structures. For children who cannot achieve or maintain standing independently a standing support offers an opportunity to promote motor ability, maintaining muscle length and joint integrity, reduce risk of decreased bone density and improve hand function.

In the early stages of development, standing positions that promote normal movement patterns have the potential to impact on other developmental skills. Children benefit from experiencing a stable position with their trunk forward over their base, which enables them to use their hands efficiently. Normal biomechanical forces will also influence the structure of bones, direction of growth and the congruency of joints.

Active movement within a standing support is essential for a child to be comfortable, for learning movement control and for developing improved muscle strength.

Level of Ability for activity

For children to take part in hand activities they will need to be positioned and supported in such a way as to achieve Level 4 standing ability. This includes the following components:

- Loadbearing through hands and feet

- Ability to move within base

- Trunk and head upright

- Shoulder girdle protracted

- Ability to free one hand for play

- Anterior pelvic tilt

- Standing base as wide or wider than pelvis

- Single leg movements

Children at standing Levels 1, 2 and 3 often need more than one pair of hands or an additional surface to lean on to control their standing posture. The aim of therapy at this stage is to achieve neutral to anterior tilt of the pelvis, which brings the trunk weight over the standing base and increases the ability to loadbear through the legs and feet. With the trunk weight forward over the base shoulder protraction is also easier to achieve.

From this position a child begins to move his trunk within his standing base from forward lean to an upright position that is appropriate for hand activities.

Children at Levels 4 and 5 need postural control to enable them to develop movement within and then outside of their base, in a sequence of forward and backwards within base, then with trunk rotation and finally lateral movement.

Opportunities for practice

If a standing support emulates Level 4 standing ability it will position the child so that he is ready for participation in many activities whilst actively developing motor skills.

Chailey Standing Support

The Chailey Standing Support offers children the support at Level 4 standing ability by providing the components described above. This is achieved by the design of the following elements with the support:

• A horizontal and solid standing base, with the height from the floor such that the child can step on to it

• Adjustable foot supports to provide the correct standing base

• Contoured support for the trunk and thighs, angled slightly forwards at 10° from the vertical at the level of the hips. This supports the trunk forward over the base and the shape encourages some hip flexion. The contoured surface needs to be fairly soft to allow active hip extension and an anterior tilt to the pelvis

• Firm lateral supports over the greater trochanters to stabilise the pelvis and maintain symmetry

• An abduction block keeping the hips in a slightly abducted position and the knees apart

• A pelvic strap to stabilise the pelvis in a neutral/anterior tilt

• Firm thoracic lateral supports to control lateral symmetry of the trunk but set wide enough apart to allow active movement

• A soft narrow anterior thoracic support to allow trunk movement, protraction of the shoulder girdle and free movement of the arms

• A loose chest strap allowing movement is used for safety

• A tray positioned at elbow height for forearm propping if appropriate

Active movement needs to be promoted within the support so that efficient patterns of movement are selected and practised, and the child can learn new motor patterns and gain muscle strength.

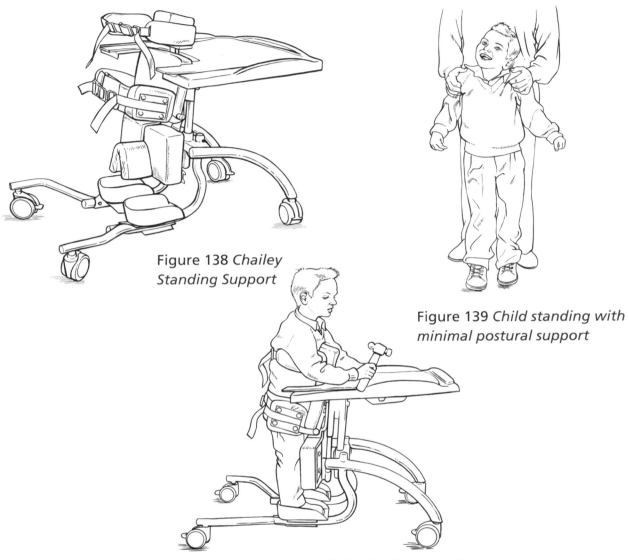

Figure 138 *Chailey Standing Support*

Figure 139 *Child standing with minimal postural support*

Figure 140 *Child in Chailey Standing Support*

Once his ability to stand has been assessed, a child can be placed in a position that meets his postural needs.

The level of support in the Chailey Standing Support can be adjusted for varying abilities.

Children at Levels of Ability 1–4 need a standing support that offers an upright position with support for their thighs, pelvis and trunk to encourage the pelvis into a position of anterior tilt and improve stability. A child will then be able to maintain his position with his trunk forward over his base, shoulder protraction and improved head and shoulder alignment. Once positioned, movement within the support can be encouraged, and the child will begin to control forward lean to upright movements of the trunk as his strength develops.

A child at Level 5 needs to practise pulling up to stand at a support and controlling his trunk outside of his base. He then begins stepping movements in standing, and moving sideways along the support.

At this stage some children may require the extra stability a standing support offers to enable them to practise standing activities and also to use their hands. The chest and lateral thoracic support can be removed to allow greater trunk movement and strength to develop.

A child with the appropriate support has the opportunity to select and practise more advanced patterns of movement. Remember he should always be more able in his equipment than out of it. You can check this by assessing his Chailey Levels of Ability within his support.

The standing support may be used with or without the tray, e.g. for PE activities, sand pit or at a table for group work.

For some children the additional anterior trunk support enables them to gain improved head control and hand use. In these cases the support can be used to improve visual tracking skills and eye pointing. Play and use of switches in the support can begin once a child can free a hand for play.

For many children maintaining their ability to stand and transfer to different positions helps with moving between positions and dressing activities. The use of a standing support that encourages active movement within the support can help.

Case study

Jack has cerebral palsy with his arms more affected than his legs. He needs help to get into standing but can maintain his position once he is there and is beginning to move his legs. He is at Level 4 standing ability and when placed against a support he can maintain his position His shoulder girdle is protracted and he is just beginning to let go with one hand, but he is not confident in letting go for long. This level of ability in standing limits Jack's ability to play with toys in the standing position or use his hands to operate switches, and he has to concentrate on keeping his balance. Jack enjoys standing and uses a Chailey Standing Support without the chest support. In this he is able to use both his hands freely, can lift his arms above shoulder height and is able to move his trunk outside of his base in all directions and recover it. He uses the support in the classroom for painting, sand play and reading. In therapy sessions he has been working on building his upper trunk strength and skills and practising switch use.

The use of standing support for children with existing deformities

SCOLIOSIS OR KYPHOSIS

Some children need to wear a spinal jacket when standing in order to achieve the best achievable position. The height of the lateral pelvic pads and the position of the pelvic strap may need to be adjusted so that they do not cause discomfort. The soft foam allows some conformity with the surface.

KNEES AND HIPS

When the degree of deformity at the pelvis, hips and knees prevents a child from being correctly positioned in the standing support, consideration should be given as to whether it is beneficial. A review of the child's level of standing ability and treatment goals may identify the need for strategies to reduce contractures in other positions such as lying.

Use of orthoses

The Chailey Standing Support is designed to promote normal patterns of movement and this should be considered when using orthoses within the support. Think back to Chapter 4.4 on motor learning. Postural adjustments occur throughout the lower limbs to maintain balance. The use of fixed ankle foot orthoses which limit ankle and knee movements may reduce this. Where control of excessive pronation is needed, orthoses that allow ankle movement are preferred.

Wearing a spinal jacket in a standing support can be uncomfortable. The Chailey Standing Support, however, offers more anterior support than a seating system and many children who wear jackets can maintain a good spinal posture in the standing support without a jacket for short periods.

In some cases jackets will need to be worn in the standing support and the reasons for this will depend on why the jacket was prescribed. If it is necessary to wear a jacket, the shape of the foam may need to be modified to accommodate the jacket.

Frequency and length of time in standing

As with other aspects of postural management, standing practice needs to be part of a regular routine of changes of position. Frequency and length of time will vary according to the reasons for using a standing support. To improve bone density, 60 minutes 4–5 times a week is recommended; other studies suggest that 1-hour sessions three times a week reduce the risk of hip dislocation and control hip flexion contractures (Phelps 1959).

Other considerations for standing

Things to consider when a child is using a standing support include:

- Changes in blood pressure which may cause him to faint. This may be related to a lack of movement in the standing support. Some children who display extreme weakness may also have temporary discomfort due to venous pooling in the lower limbs

- Localised areas of pressure

- Reduced bone density or osteoporosis may present a risk of fracture

- Discomfort and pain

- Functional activities in standing

6.6 Mobility

Children with motor impairment gain independent mobility in a number of ways. All forms of active mobility offer the chance to build muscle strength, and improve fitness levels, and give the child a sense of freedom and independence.

Rolling, commando crawling, scooting in supine and crawling are all methods used by children with motor impairment to move around in their environment, and they provide an essential opportunity for development in all areas. It is important, however, to recognise that some methods of locomotion involve the use of abnormal patterns of movement, such as excessive adduction of the hips in commando crawling and asymmetry of hip position in side sitting. In these cases it is essential to provide a counter action to reduce the long-term effects of the position and perhaps offer alternative movement options.

Walkers

Children who are not walking independently may be offered walking aids for a number of reasons, including an opportunity to explore the environment through play, as a means of learning to walk and to improve muscle, bone and joint structures. The purpose of using mobility equipment needs to be clear to children and families to avoid raising unrealistic expectations. If walkers are used for relatively short periods for play and exploration, what is important is that the child is able to reach toys, cupboards, plants etc., which he might be interested in, and the quality of the movement and position are less important. However, if the purpose of the equipment is to facilitate and improve walking skills, then the position and movement achieved are more crucial and more time will need to be spent practising these skills.

Trikes

Trikes give children, even those with severe physical disability, an opportunity to experience mobility using their own body strength. Muscle strengthening, spatial awareness, manoeuvring and an opportunity to explore a wider environment can all be experienced using a trike. It provides an activity that is comparable to things that their peer group and siblings can do.

The trike with adaptations designed at Chailey Heritage Clinical Services has a saddle seat with anterior thoracic and lateral support, footplates to maintain the foot position and, if necessary, wrist straps to keep the hands in place. A steering guide is available for security and to aid movement.

Figure 140 *Child using adapted trike*

6.7 Using the Chailey Levels of Ability

Prescription/Function

The position that a child achieves with his postural management equipment is crucial to the impact that it has on his function and his potential to improve motor ability, and on the control of deformity. Assessment using the Chailey Levels of Ability both in and out of his equipment identifies whether the equipment has been effective in changing components of the levels of ability to achieve the desired impact. It will also enable you to have realistic expectations of how a child can move in the equipment and use his head and hands for activities, such as play and switch access.

The Chailey Levels of Ability, as well as being helpful for equipment provision and treatment planning, are also useful in thinking about how a child might be able to use his skills to take part in activities.

Using the components from the chart you will be able to identify if a child can:

• tuck or retract his chin

• move within his base

• move outside of his base and recover

• use his hands out to the side

• use his hands in midline

These and other components will help you determine how a child might be able to use his head and hands for activities. This information will indicate whether additional support is needed for some activities, and the best position for toys and/or switches for easy access.

Ensure that the things a child wants to see are within his visual field. You can determine this by thinking about his head and chin position.

The effect of movement on posture can alter a child's ability to maintain stability and posture. Assessment when a child is not participating in activities may be very different from when he is. He may lose his balance or adopt compensatory postures to prevent himself falling.

Time spent getting to know the child and finding out, through play, what motivates him and what activities he would choose will give you valuable information. Careful observation of the child playing in various settings allows the opportunity to record his levels of ability in different situations.

> **It is important that assessment is undertaken when the child is in his resting position, when he is active and, if appropriate, when he is moving.**

keypoint

Communication

Expressive communication is often difficult for children at all levels of ability. Even small utterances may require extreme effort. Where possible, children must be given the chance to communicate with their friends, family and teachers. This is one thing that children feel very strongly about, and for them it is the most important aspect of their lives.

For a child to be able to listen, attend and look efficiently, he needs to be able to maintain shoulder girdle stability with his head in midline. There are many times during the day when a child can, and needs to, practise these skills and we have to make sure the stimulus he is responding to encourages his best stable posture. When a child is actively responding to, or initiating, communication he needs more stability in order to move and point, type or access switches, than when communicating without targeting. Liaison with a speech and language therapist and teacher about a consistent approach and realistic expectations is essential.

Communication aids can be low or high-tech. Low-tech aids might consist of charts, communication books, or simple yes/no signs that the child eye-points to. At Levels 1, 2 and 3 sitting ability the child needs to be stable and fully supported in order to free up his hands (or one hand) to point, or to be able to maintain head control in order to eye-point.

The same applies to the use of high-tech aids where the child might need to use switches. Being stable and properly supported so that he is able to achieve at least Level 3 sitting ability in his equipment is vital. Encourage the practice of small movements of the eyes, hands or fingers, or head in preference to gross movements. Use the movement that the child is able to make most consistently to decide where to place a switch.

Also make sure that objects requiring close visual attention are within the child's visual field, preferably in midline and low enough to be seen when his chin is tucked.

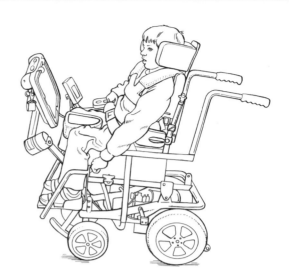

Figure 141 *Child using communication aid*

Eating and drinking

For the child with multiple and complex disabilities one of the first activities introduced may be eating and drinking. Care, time and partnership working are all extremely important. Parents will have a lot to offer on communication and engagement with the child during meal times.

It cannot be assumed that there is one 'ideal' head position for all children to achieve a safe swallow. Video fluoroscopy may well be needed to inform you about the most appropriate position at meal times in order to avoid aspiration (*Eating and Drinking Skills for Children with Motor Disorders,* Chailey Heritage Clinical Services). Seating systems do not mimic the constant sensitive adjustments provided by a mother feeding her child on her lap. As a child grows and it is no longer viable to use a lap, careful compromises need to be considered for a child and the person who is feeding him.

Care needs to be taken when positioning children to enable them to eat and drink efficiently. Children with Level 1 or 2 sitting ability need seating that brings them up to a minimum of Level 3 sitting ability (shoulder girdle protracted and chin tucked). In this position, a child's weight is forward over his sitting base, which helps with swallowing. Swallowing is easier if the chin is tucked. If his head falls back into extension his airway is vulnerable, and swallowing food will be more dangerous, and may result in aspiration.

Being well supported enables children to learn eating skills and enjoy this important part of family and social life.

Transfers

A child who is unable to assist actively with transfers can try practising staying still while his postural support is withdrawn. Staying still and maintaining his balance might be active exercise for a child with a low level of ability.

Most children with a low level of ability are hoisted. Slings and hoisting equipment are chosen to suit the specific needs of the individual. The correct choice of sling is fundamental to safety, comfort and the success of the manoeuvre. Placing the sling is often difficult but the choice of sling material can be helpful. Having swing-away lateral thoracic supports is also very helpful. The sling should not be left in place once the lift is complete unless there are exceptional circumstances.

Some children may be able to control the movement of the hoist for themselves by using the switch controls on an electric hoist. This offers at least some degree of independence and autonomy.

Children who are functioning at Level 4 sitting ability may be able to use a transfer board. This requires good sitting balance (Level 4) and upper body strength, and the child also needs to be well motivated and cognitively aware.

Transfer belts and turntables may be used for those children able to take their weight fully and reliably through their feet (Level 6 sitting ability, or Level 4 standing ability). Children with this level of ability may also benefit from appropriately placed handrails.

Dressing

A child's Chailey Level of Ability will determine how much he is able to participate. Children at lying Levels 1, 2 and 3 need support to feel comfortable and safe while attending to dressing activities. At Levels 1 and 2, arm movements may be random and variable, so assistance with dressing may be limited. At Level 3 a child can use his arms to the side, and with this level of control can take an active part in dressing.

If a sitting position is the one chosen as the best for dressing and undressing, place a child in the sitting position adopted at Level 3 sitting ability, where his trunk is forward over a wide base. For an older child with a very low level of ability, lying in supine may be a better option. Age appropriate positions should be used. For instance a very young child might be dressed on his mother's lap, either in sitting or lying, or both. For an older child it may be possible to organise pants and trousers in a lying position, but to be seated to use postural stability to take part in getting in or out of T-shirts and jumpers. Socks and shoes are often easier to position when a child is seated and able to take an active part.

Consider the surface a child is supported on and how it may affect his stability. Encourage him to assist in movement between positions of stability. If there is an appropriate time to practise these skills, explain what you are going to do and how you would like him to help. In all positions, for example, he will need to take his weight through his left side to allow clothes on or off his right leg, and in upright postures he will need to maintain his trunk weight forward from his pelvis. In all positions, encourage him to keep his head at the midline of his body, with his chin tucked when possible. Gradually build up the speed of the activity.

A child can practise maintaining his posture during dressing and undressing.

Some children might be able to help with socks and shoes once they are sitting in a stable position, or might be able to manage vests, T-shirts and jumpers for themselves. To pull up pants and trousers in standing a child must be able to take weight through both feet reliably (Level 4 standing ability). A handrail might be helpful.

Stability from improved loadbearing and symmetry, and protraction of the shoulder girdle will promote head alignment. Encourage him to keep his head in midline and chin tucked, especially when putting garments over his head.

Toileting

Once a child gets to the stage of being toilet trained there are a variety of special supports available for children with Levels 1, 2 and 3 sitting ability.

At Levels 1 and 2 sitting ability, a child needs complete support and control to maintain a stable position. Depending on his ability the toilet seat might give back, front, side and foot support. If a child's ability allows, the support should offer a position that is less than 90° at the hips. This helps with both positioning and bowel evacuation.

This type of position will also help at Level 3 sitting ability, but at this level the child may only need a grab rail in front of him to help him prop forwards over his base.

At Level 4 standing ability, or Level 6 sitting ability, boys may be able to stand to urinate, perhaps with the help of a handrail.

For children with physical disabilities who do not reach the stage of being ready to toilet train, it will be important to ensure that the surface on which they are placed for cleansing and nappy changing is one that offers them good support where they need it so that they don't feel too vulnerable.

Bathing and showering

Most children love to have a bath, but for a child with severe motor impairment it can be difficult to make this a pleasurable experience. A variety of bath seats and shower chairs are available for children with a low level of ability.

At Levels 1 and 2 sitting ability a child needs full support in order to be safe and comfortable. Bath seats with soft slings are helpful because they conform readily to a child's shape, and lateral supports and straps can be added as required.

Switch access

Assessment of a child's Chailey Level of Ability in the equipment in which he is going to use the switches will provide information about the best position to place them. The use of video and observing the child's movement patterns in equipment without the introduction of an 'active' activity, for example reading a story to the child, often helps as a good starting point for both the child and therapist.

Children will need to use switches for a number of activities including:

• toys

• computers

• communication aids

• mobility

• environmental controls

A child with impaired motor ability will need more stability when operating and reacting to the effects of using a switch than he does when he is not actively engaged in doing something. Remember that we talked in Chapter 3.3 about how we adopt a more stable base of support (i.e. a lower level of ability which we've already mastered) when learning a new skill? If switch use is a new skill, we need to be aware of a child's predominant level of ability and provide and position switches initially within the range of movement achievable at that level of ability. Small controlled fine movements should be encouraged rather than gross uncontrolled movement.

Postural stability is essential for consistent, reliable targeting and use of switches. A child should not lose his postural stability when he is using his switches.

Postural stability and the means of operating switches must complement each other in order to enhance and improve a child's ability in the short and long term. For example, if postural support has enabled a child who could not maintain sitting independently (Level 2) to move within his sitting base (Level 4), switches will initially need to be positioned and useable *within* his sitting base, not behind it or to one side. At this level of ability he needs to be able to maintain Level 4 sitting ability whilst using the switches, and it may be that additional postural support will be needed to achieve this while he is learning to use switches.

> *keypoint*
>
> At Level 1, 2 or 3 sitting ability, switches should be positioned so that they are used *within* the child's base, not behind it or out to one side.

7

References
and index

7.1 References

Alsop, A. and S. Ryan. 1996. *Making the most of fieldwork education*. London: Chapman and Hall.

Arkin, A.M. and J.F. Katz. 1956. The effects of pressure on epiphyseal growth. *Journal of Bone & Joint Surgery* 38-A:1056–1076.

Barnard, S. and G. Hartigan. 1998. Clinical Audit in Physiotherapy: From theory into practice. In *Clinical Audit in Physiotherapy: From theory into practice*. Oxford: Butterworth Heinemann.

Bernstein, S.M. and L. Bernstein. 1990. Spinal Deformity in The Patient with Cerebral Palsy. *Spine: State of the Art Reviews* 4 (1):147–160.

Bleck, E.E. 1987. *Orthopaedic management in Cerebral Palsy*, *Clinics in Developmental Medicine*. Oxford: Blackwell Scientific Publications Ltd.

Bly, L. 1994. *Motor skills acquisition in the first year of life*: Therapy Skill Builders.

Bobath, B. 1972. *Abnormal postural reflex activity caused by brain lesions.* 2nd ed. London: Heinemann Medical.

Bottos, M., Puato, M.L., Vianello, A. and Facchin, P. 1995. Locomotion Patterns in Cerebral Palsy Syndromes. *Developmental Medicine & Child Neurology* 37:883–899.

Carpenter, J. 1998. An Investigation into the Levels of Early Standing Ability, School of Healthcare Professions, University of Brighton, Eastbourne, East Sussex.

Carr, J., R. Shepherd and L. Ada. 1995. Spasticity: Research Findings & Implications for Intervention. *Physiotherapy* 81 (8):421–429.

Cartright, R.D. 1984. Effect of sleep position on sleep apnea severity. *Sleep* 7 (2):110–114.

Chailey Heritage Clinical Services. *Eating and Drinking Skills for Children with Motor disorders*: Chailey Heritage Clinical Services.

Chandler, L.S., M.S. Andrews and M.W. Swanson. 1980. *Movement Assessment of Infants – A Manual*. Rolling Bay WA.

Chapman, C.E. and M. Wiesendanger. 1982. The physiological & anatomical basis of spasticity: a review. *Physiotherapy Canada* 34 (3):125–136.

Charman, R.A. 1998. Motor learning. In *Human Movement*, edited by M. Trew and T. Everett. London: Churchill Livingstone.

Damiano, D.L. , K. Dodd and N.F. Taylor. 2002. Should we be testing and training muscle strength in cerebral palsy? *Development Medicine & Child Neurology* 44:68–72.

De Matteo, C., M. Law, D. Russell and et al. 1993. The reliability and validity of the quality of upper extremity skills test. *Physical & Occupational Therapy in Pediatrics* 13:1–18.

Dietz, V. and Berger, W. 1983. Normal & Impaired Regulation of Muscle Stiffness in Gait: A New Hypothesis about Muscle Hypertonia. *Experimental Neurology* 79:680–687.

Dunn, P.M. 1976. Perinatal observations on the etiology of congenital dislocation of the hip. *Clinical Orthopaedics and Related Research* 119:11–21.

Fetters, L., B. Fernandez and S. Cermak. 1989. The relationship of proximal and distal components in the development of reaching. *Journal of Human Movement Studies* 17:283–297.

Goldspink, G. and P. Williams. 1990. Muscle fibre and connective tissue changes associated with use and disuse. In *Key Issues in Neurological Physiotherapy*, edited by L. Ada and C. Canning. London: Butterworth Heinemann.

Goldspink, G. and P. Williams. 1990. Muscle fibre and connective tissue changes associated with use and disuse. In *Neurological Physiotherapy*, edited by L. Ada and C. Canning. London: Butterworth Heinemann.

Gordon, A. M. and H. Forssberg. 1997. Development of neural mechanisms underlying grasping in children. In *Neurophysiology and neuropsychology of motor development*, edited by K.J. Connolly and H. Forssberg. London: Mac Keith Press.

Green, E.M. 1987. The effect of seating on cognitive function in children with cerebral palsy. Paper read at Annual Meeting of the British Paediatric Association.

Green, E.M., C. M. Mulcahy and T.E. Pountney. 1995. An Investigation into the Development of Early Postural Control. *Developmental Medicine & Child Neurology* 37 (437–448).

Guymer. 1986. Handling the Patient with Speech and Swallowing Problems. *Physiotherapy* 72 (6):276–280.

Hadders-Algra. 2001. Early Brain Damage and the Development of Motor Behaviour in Children : Clues for Therapeutic Intervention? *Neural Plasticity* 8 (1–2):31–48.

Hadders-Algra, M. 2000. The Neuronal Group Selection Theory: a framework to explain variation in normal motor development. *Developmental and Behavioural Pediatrics* 42:566–572.

Hagberg, B., G. Hagberg, I. Olow and L. Wendt. 1996. The Changing panorama of Cerebral Palsy in Sweden. VII. Prevalence and origin in the birth year period 1987–90. *Acta Paediatrica* (85):954–960.

Haley, S.M., S.R. Harris, W.L. Tada and M.W. Swanson. 1986. Item Reliability of the Movement Assessment of Infants. *Physical & Occupational Therapy in Pediatrics* 6 (1):21–39.

Haley, S.M., W.J. Coster, L.H. Ludlow, J. Haltiwanger and P.J. Andrellos. 1992. *Pediatric Evaluation of Disability Inventory*. Boston: New England Medical Center Hospital.

Henderson, S.E. and D.A. Sugden. 1992. *Movement Assessment Battery for Children*. Sidcup: Therapy Skill Builders.

Horowitz, L. and N. Sharby. 1988. Development of prone extension postures in healthy infants. *Physical Therapy* 68 (1):32–39.

Hunt, A., K. Mastroyannopoulou, A. Goldman and K. Seers, et al. 2003. Not knowing-the problem of pain in children with severe neurological impairment. *International Journal of Nursing Studies* 40:171–183.

Keim, H.A. 1978. Clinical Symposia. *CIBA* 30:2–30.

Ketelaar, M., A. Vermeer and P. Helders, J,M. 1998. Functional motor abilities of children with cerebral palsy: a systematic review of assessment measures. *Clinical Rehabilitation* 12:369–380.

Kidd, G., N. Lawes and I. Musus. 1992. *Understanding neuromuscular plasticity: A basis for clinical rehabilitation*: London: Edward Arnold.

Kottke, F.J. 1980. From relex to skill: the training of coordination. *Archives of Physical Medicine and Rehabilitation* 61:551–561.

Lance, J.W. 1980. Symposium Synopsis. In *Spasticity: Disordered motor control*, edited by R.G. Feldman, R.R. Young and W.P. Koella. Chicago: Year Book Medical Publishers.

Lieber, R.L. (2002) In Skeletal muscle, structure, function and plasticity (Ed, Lieber, R. L.) Lippincott Williams and Wilkins, Baltimore.

Leonard, C.T. 1998. *The Neuroscience of Human Movement*. Missouri: Mosby.

Lespargot, A, E. Renaudin, M. Khouri and N. Robert. 1994. Extensibility of hip adductors in children with cerebral palsy. *Developmental Medicine & Child Neurology* 36:980–988.

LeVeau, B. and D. B. Bernhardt. 1984. Developmental Biomechanics. *Physical Therapy* 62 (12):1874–1882.

Lin, J.P., J.K. Brown and E.G. Walsh. 1994. Physiological maturation of muscles in childhood. *The Lancet* 343:1386–1389.

Lonstein, J. E. 1995. The spine in cerebral palsy. *Current Orthopaedics* 9:164–177.

European Computer Driving Licence, ECDL, International Computer Driving Licence, ICDL, and related logos are all registered Trade Marks of The European Computer Driving Licence Foundation Limited ("ECDL Foundation").

CiA Training Ltd is an entity independent of The British Computer Society using the name BCS, The Chartered Institute for IT ("BCS") and is not associated with ECDL Foundation or BCS in any manner.

BCS, The Chartered Institute for IT
APPROVED COURSEWARE

This courseware may be used to assist learners to prepare for the ECDL Certification Programme as titled on the courseware. Neither BCS nor **CiA Training Ltd** warrants that the use of this courseware publication will ensure passing of the tests for that ECDL Certification Programme.

This courseware publication has been independently reviewed and approved by BCS as covering the learning objectives for the ECDL Certification Programme.

Confirmation of this approval can be obtained by reviewing www.bcs.org/ecdl.

The material contained in this courseware publication has not been reviewed for technical accuracy and does not guarantee that candidates will pass the test for the ECDL Certification Programme.

Any and all assessment items and/or performance-based exercises contained in this courseware relate solely to this publication and do not constitute or imply certification by BCS or ECDL Foundation in respect of the ECDL Certification Programme or any other ECDL test.

Irrespective of how the material contained in this courseware is deployed, for example in a learning management system (LMS) or a customised interface, nothing should suggest to the candidate that this material constitutes certification or can lead to certification through any other process than official ECDL certification testing.

For details on sitting a test for an ECDL certification programme in the UK, please visit the BCS website at www.bcs.org/ecdl.

Learners using this courseware must be registered with BCS before undertaking a test for ECDL. Without a valid registration, the test(s) cannot be undertaken and no certificate, nor any other form of recognition, can be given to a learner. Registration should be undertaken with BCS at an Approved Centre.

Downloading the Data Files

There are no data files for this guide.

Aims

The aim of this guide is to provide you with the practical skills required to use a web browser application and to understand and accomplish basic operations associated with searching for information online.

Objectives

After completing this guide you will be able to:

- Understand and use the Internet and *World Wide Web*
- Be aware of security considerations when using Internet technologies
- Stay safe online and recognise appropriate laws and regulations
- Use a modern web-browsing application
- Change browser settings
- Manage bookmarks/favourites
- Search for and critically evaluate information
- Recognise other Internet-based communication tools
- Participate in online communities

Assessment of Knowledge

At the end of this guide is a **Record of Achievement Matrix**. Before the guide is started, it is recommended that you complete the matrix to measure your current level of knowledge. After working through a section, return to and update the **Record of Achievement**. Only when you feel you are competent in all areas should you move on to the next section.

Websites

Websites are constantly changing. At the time of writing all addresses and links are correct, but this may change. If a named website is unavailable you will need to search for an alternative. To help, a list of *Useful Links* to other websites is provided online at **www.bigplanetsupport.co.uk**.

Contents

Section 1
Getting Started

By the end of this section you should be able to:

Understand and Connect to the Internet

Identify Popular Browsers

Start and Close Internet Explorer

Recognise Types of Web Address (URL)

Use Internet Explorer Features

View Web Pages "Full Screen"

Turn Optional Toolbars On and Off

Use Help

Work through the **Driving Lessons** in this section to gain an understanding of the above features.

For each **Driving Lesson**, read all of the **Park and Read** instructions and then, if applicable, perform the numbered steps of the **Manoeuvres**. Complete the **Revision** exercise(s) at the end of the section to test your knowledge.

Driving Lesson 1 - The Internet

▣ Park and Read

The **Internet**, or net for short, is a global network of linked ICT devices that allow people from all over the world to communicate and share information. Many different types of devices are able to connect to the Internet, from desktop and laptop computers to mobile phones. By connecting to the Internet, both you and your equipment are able to interact with and benefit from the many features and services that it offers.

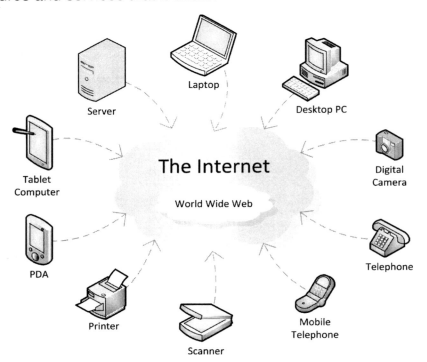

Most people use the Internet to access the **World Wide Web**, or "web" for short. This is the name given to a vast collection of interconnected files called **web pages**. At their most basic, each web page contains information in the form of text and images. However, most web pages today also contain a variety of other multimedia features including video, music and interactive programs.

ℹ *The* World Wide Web *is not the same thing as the Internet – in fact, the web is just one of the many services that runs on the Internet.*

When combined, two or more related web pages form a **website**. This is a fairly loose term which refers to any collection of web pages that belong together (in the same way that the individual pages of a printed magazine belong together). The first page of a website is called the **Homepage** and usually consists of an introduction to the site with "links" to other pages.

ℹ *The language of the web is **HTML** (Hypertext Mark-up Language). This is the programming code that website developers use to create web pages.*

Driving Lesson 2 - Connecting to the Internet

▣ Park and Read

There are many ways of connecting compatible ICT devices to the Internet. The easiest technique is to use cables to link computing hardware and peripherals directly to a router/modem (which in turn connects to the Internet). However, it is becoming more and more practical for modern mobile devices to use wireless technologies instead.

*The connection between a local network device and the Internet is provided by an **Internet Service Provider (ISP)**. This is a third-party communications company that handles the flow of data between your device and the wider Internet. They also supply or rent hardware for connecting to their service such as modems/routers.*

ISPs provide a range of different types of Internet connection. The table below describes some of the most popular types.

Connection	Description
Dial-up	This is an older form of Internet connection which uses a modem connected to a standard telephone line. Although very slow, it is often the only cost effective connection type for people who live in remote rural areas.
Satellite	One of the most expensive types of Internet connection, satellites are useful for people living in remote areas. Although still fairly slow by modern standards, satellite connections are usually much faster than dial-up.
3G and 4G	A popular form of wireless Internet access, 3G and 4G connections provide a direct link between an ICT device and a mobile phone operator's network. Connection speeds are highly variable and depend greatly on mobile phone signal strength. 4G is a newer, faster replacement for 3G (and the lesser-known and rarely used **WiMax**).
DSL/Cable	Popular at home and in small business, DSL (Digital Subscriber Line) and cable connections are wired links to the Internet (using either special telephone lines or fibre optic cables). Because of the high bandwidth, they are usually known as **broadband** connections. Most wireless Wi-Fi routers/modems use DSL or cable connections to access the Internet.
Leased Lines	Popular in big business, these are dedicated wired connections to the Internet with extremely high bandwidth. They are often very expensive!

Driving Lesson 3 - Choosing an ISP

▣ Park and Read

When choosing an ISP to provide an Internet connection, cost and affordability are obvious concerns. However, there are also a number of other important issues to consider before subscribing. For example, is the contract length appropriate (many contracts "lock you in" to a service for 12 to 18 months and they can be difficult to get out of early). It is also important to consider the service's terms and conditions – is that "great deal" really all that great once you factor in hidden charges or bandwidth limitations?

ℹ️ *Many service providers "cap" their Internet allowances (even if advertised as "unlimited") and you could quickly reach and exceed their "fair usage" limits. At this point your connection may be suspended or extra charges incurred.*

One of the biggest requirements of an Internet connection is **bandwidth** (or **Transfer Rate**). This is basically the speed of your Internet access and describes the amount of data that can be transferred over the connection at any one time. As an example, an average MP3 song that is 5Mb in size would take approximately 15 to 20 minutes to download using a dial-up connection. Using a fast home broadband connection, however, this is reduced to only a few seconds.

ℹ️ ***Downloading*** *is the term given to the act of copying a file from an ICT device on a network (such as a computer or server) to your own device. For example, when you use the World Wide Web, each web page you visit is downloaded to your computer so that you can view it.*

ℹ️ ***Uploading*** *refers to the sending of a file from your device to another. For example, you do this whenever you e-mail files to other people or add photographs to a social networking site.*

Bandwidth is measured in **bits per second** (**bps**). As you might guess, this is the number of single bits that can be transferred across a network connection in one second (a bit is the smallest unit of computer data). Although similar to file size measurements, they are calculated slightly differently, as shown below.

Bandwidth	Description
Kilobits (kbps)	1 kbps equals 1,000 bits per second.
Megabits (mbps)	1 mbps equals 1,000,000 bits per second.
Gigabits (gbps)	1 gbps equals 1,000,000,000 bits per second.

ℹ️ *Your Internet connection is like a pipe through which data flows like water. The larger the pipe – or bandwidth – the more information that can pass through it.*

Driving Lesson 3 - Continued

Low bandwidth can result in slow downloads and may restrict how you use the Internet. For example, you may not be able to watch videos online or download large files.

Confusingly, ISPs often advertise bandwidth speeds in Megabits (Mb) instead of than Megabytes (MB). A megabit is only 1024 *bits* rather than 1024 *bytes*.

For example, a "10Mb connection" is a very popular home broadband speed. However, consider the following:

10 Megabits (Mb) = 1.25 Megabytes (MB)

At this speed, it would take *at best* approximately 1 minute, 20 seconds to download a 100MB file (not the 10 seconds you might think). In reality, however, it can take a lot longer as users are rarely able to reach their connection's maximum download speed.

Be aware that home users and organisations will have different bandwidth requirements (which may change over time). Consider your individual or business requirements carefully before entering into a contract with an ISP.

Given the ever-increasing bandwidth requirements of the modern Internet, a fast and reliable broadband service is often the best choice for home and small business users who want to download lots of files and watch videos online.

To help you choose an ISP, it can often be helpful to read online reviews by current customers. Watch out for bad experiences or problems such as poor **uptime** *(no Internet availability) or high* **contention** *(a lot of people sharing the same connection with slow speeds as a result).*

Driving Lesson 4 - Wi-Fi Networks

▣ Park and Read

Short-range **Wi-Fi** connections are ideal for people working "on the move" who need to access Internet resources on their laptops, tablet computers or mobile phones. Connecting is usually a simple case of finding a public network and logging on – it really is that easy! In fact, it is so convenient that you can now commonly find Wi-Fi access points (also known as **hotspots**) in many public places, from trains and planes to coffee shops, airports and hotels.

ⓘ *Wi-Fi simply replaces cables in network. It is not a type of Internet connection in its own right.*

To make sure only authorised people can access a network, Wi-Fi access points are often protected by a **security key**. This is simply a password used by the owner of the wireless router/modem to control who logs on to their network and, in turn, the Internet. Whenever you try to connect to a password-protected Wi-Fi network, your device will prompt you to enter a valid security key.

ⓘ *For security reasons, only connect to secure Wi-Fi networks that require a password. This helps to stop other people remotely accessing your computer.*

⟳ Manoeuvres

1. *Windows* allows you to connect your computer to a wireless Wi-Fi service quickly and easily. To display the **Connect to a network** pop-up, click on the network icons 🖳 or 📶 in the **Notification Area** on the **Taskbar**.

ⓘ *Alternatively, select **Network and Internet | Connect to a network** on the Control Panel.*

Driving Lesson 4 - Continued

i *Wi-Fi access is provided by wireless routers/modems that broadcast their name (known as an* **SSID***, or Service Set Identifier) for users within range to find. The closer the device, the better the signal strength and faster the connection.*

i *If you are using a computer that does not have Wi-Fi, the feature is disabled or there are no networks in range, you will not see any* **Wireless Network Connection** *items in the* **SSID List***.*

2.   Examine the **Connect to a network** pop-up box that appears. If Wi-Fi is enabled and there are networks in range, a list of wireless connections similar to that shown on the previous page will appear.

i *If a network appears with a small shield icon,*  *then this network is "open" and you can connect* <u>without</u> *a password. However, these forms of network are unsafe and best avoided to ensure the security of your computer and its data.*

i *To connect to one of the networks shown, simply select it and click* **Connect***. If the network is protected by a security key, you will be prompted to enter it.*

i *When you connect an ICT device to a new network for the* <u>first</u> *time, Windows will prompt you to choose a* <u>suitable</u> *network location for it (i.e. domain, home/work, public). Depending on your choice, Windows will automatically set up, save and apply the best security settings for that type of connection.*

i *Once connected to a wireless network, the text* **Connected** *appears next to the network's name. In the future, your computer will automatically detect and log on to this network automatically it is available.*

3.   Click once on the network icons 🖥 or 📶 in the **Notification Area** on the **Taskbar** to close the **Connect to a network** pop-up.

i *You may need to pay a small charge to connect to and use a public Wi-Fi access point.*

Driving Lesson 5 - Web Addresses

▣ Park and Read

Websites are stored on computers called **servers**. These are very similar to ordinary home, school or work computers, but they are always connected to the Internet and are accessible to everyone. To locate and access these servers – and the files and web pages they contain – a **web address** is used:

www.ciatraining.co.uk

www.open.ac.uk

www.microsoft.com

www.gov.ie

www.nasa.org

uk.reuters.com

🛈 *Just as every telephone has a unique number on the telephone network, every file and web page on the Internet has its own unique **web address**. This is also known as a **Uniform Resource Locator** (**URL**).*

🛈 *You can tell a lot about a website from its web address. Working from right to left, you can often tell in which country the site is located, the name of the site, and finally the name of the server the site is stored on.*

Notice that most web addresses start with **www**. This usually refers to the default network location for that website on a server. However, for large or more complex websites, the names of other network locations or dedicated servers can be used instead (e.g. uk, news, sport, members, support).

🛈 *Some websites omit the www part of a web address.*

Following the usual www is the **domain name** of the website. This is made up of two or more segments which generally describe the name of the website, the kind of organisation that owns it, and the country where it is located (e.g. uk (United Kingdom), fr (France), es (Spain), de (Germany), etc).

Domain Examples	Type of Website
.co, .com	Company (and general use)
.ac, .edu	Academic/education
.org	Non-profit organisation
.gov	Government
.net	Internet company

🛈 *The addresses of specific subfolders and/or files on a website appear after the domain name (separated by forward slashes, /).*

Driving Lesson 6 - Web Browsers

Park and Read

The *World Wide Web* contains an enormous amount of searchable information covering almost every subject you can think of. In addition, multimedia websites feature games, music, videos, photo sharing, discussion and communication technologies for your entertainment. Perhaps more importantly, public services such as banking, shopping, health care, government and even education can now also be accessed online.

In fact, as the Internet has no international boundaries, you can interact with websites and other people anywhere in the world, from local councils and businesses to multinational companies and organisations. To access this vast worldwide "web" of services and information, you must use a special type of software known as a **web browser**.

A web browser is a program that is able to download and display web pages found on the Internet. It allows you to navigate the *World Wide Web* and interact with the many services available online. It also keeps a record of sites visited for easy future access.

i *There are many different types of web browser available. Popular examples include* Google's Chrome, *Mozilla's Firefox and* Apple's Safari. *However, this guide only covers* Microsoft's Internet Explorer.

Manoeuvres

1. Click once on the **Start** button, ![Start icon] (found at the bottom left of the screen on the **Taskbar**), to show the list of start options available. Nearly all *Windows* applications can be started from here.

2. Move the mouse pointer over **All Programs**. After a moment, a full list of programs will be displayed.

3. To start the *Internet Explorer* program, click 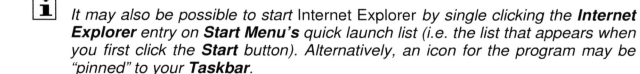.

i *It may also be possible to start* Internet Explorer *by single clicking the **Internet Explorer** entry on **Start Menu's** quick launch list (i.e. the list that appears when you first click the **Start** button). Alternatively, an icon for the program may be "pinned" to your **Taskbar**.*

4. The *Internet Explorer* window will be displayed. Maximise it (so it fills the screen) and leave it open for the next lesson.

i *This guide assumes you already have an Internet connection set up. If the connection to the Internet is not active for any reason, or if you have a dial-up connection, you will be prompted to connect. Please do so now.*

Driving Lesson 7 - The Browser Window

▣ Park and Read

When *Internet Explorer* starts, a web page will usually appear automatically in your browser window known as your **Home Page** (this is not to be confused with the first "welcoming" homepage of every website). Any web page on the Internet can be set as your **Home Page** but this guide uses the *Google UK* search website. If your **Home Page** is different, don't worry, the steps are the same (but the screenshots will appear slightly differently).

☞ Manoeuvres

1. Examine the *Internet Explorer* screen and locate the features shown below.

ℹ️ *Even if* Google *is set as your* **Home Page**, *the site is constantly being developed and may not look the same as the picture above.*

2. Find the **Navigation Buttons**. These can be used to move backwards and forwards through your history of recently visited web pages.

3. Find the **Address Bar**. This contains the web address (or URL) of the web page shown in the **View Window**. The name of the site appears on a **Tab** to the right of the **Address Bar**.

4. Find the **Browser Controls**. These buttons can be used to access useful browser features and settings.

ℹ️ *You will learn more about the features described in this lesson as you progress through the guide.*

5. Leave *Internet Explorer* open and continue to the next lesson.

Driving Lesson 8 - Toolbars

P Park and Read

It is possible to change the layout of the *Internet Explorer* screen by showing and hiding a variety of toolbars, menus and status bars. Hiding features of the browser can give you more space to view websites; however, it also reduces the ease with which you can access certain features and tools.

Manoeuvres

1. There are many ways to customise *Internet Explorer*. Right-click the **Browser Controls** to display a shortcut menu.

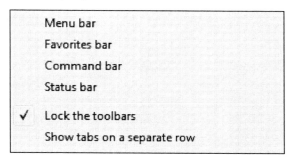

2. Click **Menu bar**. The **Menu bar** is added to the screen, containing drop-down menus with commands to control the operation of the browser. Explore these menus and examine the settings available.

3. Next, right-click the **Browser Controls** again and select **Favorites bar**. As you will see in a later lesson, the bar that appears can contain buttons which, when clicked, will take you directly to your "favourite" web sites.

4. Right-click the **Browser Controls** and select **Command bar**. This bar contains buttons with more commands for controlling the web browser. Examine the features and settings available.

5. Right-click the **Browser Controls** again and select **Status bar**. This adds the **Status bar** to the bottom of the window which features zoom controls and a small panel for displaying useful website information.

6. Click **Tools** from the **Command bar** and select **Full Screen** from the menu to remove all bars from the display (except the **Status Bar**). This view gives you more space in which to read and interact with websites.

Driving Lesson 8 - Continued

i   *In **Full Screen** mode, the toolbars will automatically hide when the mouse pointer is moved over the **View Window**. They will reappear temporarily when the mouse pointer is moved to the very top of the application window.*

7.   To return to normal view, move the mouse to the top of the screen until the toolbars reappear. Notice the three **Window Control Buttons** at the top right of the window.

Window
Control Buttons

8.   Click the **Restore** button, 🔲, to restore the browser's toolbars.

i   *Alternatively, you can enter and exit full-screen view by pressing <**F11**>.*

9.   By right-clicking the **Browser Controls**, turn off the **Menu bar**, **Favorites Bar**, **Command bar** and **Status bar**.

10.   Leave *Internet Explorer* open for the next lesson.

Driving Lesson 9 - Browser Help

▣ Park and Read

Internet Explorer contains an online **Help** facility that may assist if you experience problems using the program.

⤷ Manoeuvres

1. To open *Internet Explorer's* **Help** facility, press the **<F1>** key on your keyboard.

ℹ️ *Help can also be accessed from the **Menu bar** (if displayed).*

2. The **Windows Help and Support** window is displayed. A **Getting Started** article may be shown on opening, containing links to various topics.

3. Click any link to display more information about that topic.

4. Click the **Home** button, 🏠, to return the **Help and Support** home page.

5. Click the **Browse Help** button, 📖. The page that appears groups the **Help** topics into sections (like chapters in a book).

6. Click on any of the **Contents** shown to open that section and display a list of topics and further categories. Click on any topic to display help text for that topic, or click another category for a further list of relevant topics (and maybe even more subcategories).

7. Help on specific topics can be quickly located. Type **virus** in the search box at the top of the window and then click the **Search Help** button, 🔍.

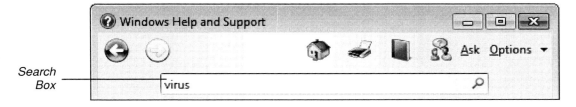

Search Box

8. A list of topics which contain the word **virus** is displayed. Select an entry from the list to display the relevant help text.

9. Next, click the **Ask** button, 👥 Ask. Read the list of additional support options that are displayed.

10. Click the **Close** button, ❌, at the top right corner of the **Windows Help and Support** window to close it. Leave *Internet Explorer* open.

Driving Lesson 10 - Closing the Browser

▣ Park and Read

To end the current browsing session, the web browser must be closed. With a dial-up connection, you should also disconnect from the Internet (if you are not prompted to disconnect automatically).

↱ Manoeuvres

1.   Click the **Close** button, 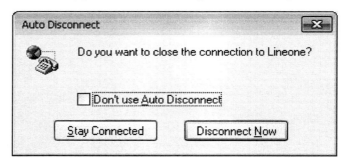, at the top right corner of the *Internet Explorer* window.

ℹ️ *Alternatively, select **File** and then **Exit** from the **Menu Bar**, if displayed.*

2.   If you have control over your Internet connection, via a router for instance, you may wish to switch it off at this stage. However many applications are designed to operate with an active Internet connection (*Microsoft Office's* online help system, for example) and so it may be advisable to leave the connection in operation.

3.   If you have a dial-up connection it is more likely that you will want to close the connection after use. An **Auto Disconnect** dialog box, similar to that shown below, should appear after closing *Internet Explorer*.

4.   Select **Disconnect Now** to end the current session.

ℹ️ *If the **Auto Disconnect** dialog box does not appear when using a dial-up connection, you can disconnect manually by clicking the network icon, 🖳, on the **Taskbar** and selecting the **Disconnect** option.*

Driving Lesson 11 - Revision

▣ Park and Read

At the end of every section you get the chance to complete one or more revision exercises to develop your skills and prepare you for your ECDL certification test. You should aim to complete the following steps without referring back to the previous lessons.

⌐ Manoeuvres

1. What is the difference between the Internet and the *World Wide Web*?

2. What is HTML?

3. What is a URL and what is it used for?

4. What is a domain name?

5. Name three different types of popular web browser.

6. Start *Internet Explorer*.

7. What is the **Address Bar** used for?

8. What are the **Navigation Buttons** used for?

9. What additional bars can be included at the top of the *Internet Explorer* window?

10. Close *Internet Explorer*.

[i] *Sample answers can be found at the back of the guide.*

[i] *Now complete the **Record of Achievement Matrix** at the back of the guide. You should only move on when confident with the topics and features described in this section.*

Section 2
Navigation

By the end of this section you should be able to:

Use the Address Bar

Recognise and Follow Hyperlinks

Move Back and Forward Through a Website

Open New Browser Tabs and Windows

Store and Organise Bookmarks

Use the Favorites Bar

Find and Delete Browser History

Stop and Refresh Web Page Downloads

Work through the **Driving Lessons** in this section to gain an understanding of the above features.

For each **Driving Lesson**, read all of the **Park and Read** instructions and then, if applicable, perform the numbered steps of the **Manoeuvres**. Complete the **Revision** exercise(s) at the end of the section to test your knowledge.

Driving Lesson 12 - The Address Bar

🅿 Park and Read

The quickest and easiest way of visiting a web site is by manually typing its address, or URL (Uniform Resource Locator), into the **Address Bar**.

Always make sure you enter a web address precisely. One character out of place and you may be taken to another website.

↱ Manoeuvres

1.   Start *Internet Explorer* and make sure you are connected to the Internet. Your default **Home Page** will be displayed.

2.   Click once in the **Address Bar** of the browser window to highlight the text already there. Enter **www.bigplanetsupport.co.uk**.

3.   Press <**Enter**> or click the **Go to** button, ↱, to instruct *Internet Explorer* to locate and download the homepage of the *Big Planet Support* website.

*Notice that Internet Explorer automatically adds **http://** to the start of the address. This represents the **protocol** used by the World Wide Web (i.e. the set of rules that determine how computers transfer data) and is a required part of every URL. Most websites use the protocol **http** (**Hypertext Transfer Protocol**) and so start with **http://**.*

4.   After a moment, the homepage of the *Big Planet Support* website will be displayed in the browser's **View Window**. Notice that it replaces the previous web page.

Driving Lesson 12 - Continued

i *Big Planet Support is a dedicated website created specifically to accompany this guide.*

5.   Read the text on the *Big Planet Support* homepage.

i *The first web page that you see when you visit a website is called the homepage. It is the front door to a site and usually contains links to all other accessible areas.*

6.   You will enter more addresses into the **Address Bar** as you progress through this guide. For now, leave *Internet Explorer* open for the next lesson.

Driving Lesson 13 - Hyperlinks

Park and Read

One of the most important and powerful features of the Internet is the **hyperlink** (also known simply as a **link**). A hyperlink is a picture, a button, or a piece of text which, when clicked, immediately takes you to a different location on the web. Often a hyperlink will simply take you to another page within one website, but they can also link to a page on an entirely different website anywhere in the world.

As any one web page can be linked to many more pages, which in turn can be linked to many more, it is possible to browse the *World Wide Web* using only hyperlinks. Indeed, you may find links to new topics that you did not consider and find yourself on a path far removed from your original location. This process of following links is referred to as "surfing the web".

Manoeuvres

1. The *Big Planet Support* website should currently be open in the **View Window**.

2. Locate the navigation hyperlinks on the left of the homepage. These "links" will appear on every web page on the *Big Planet Support* website.

 To help you find your way around, it is standard practice for websites to include navigation hyperlinks at the top or left side of all pages.

3. Move your mouse pointer over **Hyperlinks**. The pointer changes to a hand, 🖑, indicating this is a link to another web page.

4. Click <u>once</u> to download and display the **Hyperlinks** page (you should not double-click links). Read the information about the types of hyperlinks that exist.

 If necessary, use vertical scroll bar on the right to view all of the content.

5. Click the underlined word **here** in the the text. This is a hyperlink that opens another web page.

Links are commonly found within lines of text, as the example <u>here</u> shows.

Driving Lesson 13 - Continued

6.   Read the information that is displayed. Then, click the link **Return to the previous page** link to return to the **Hyperlinks** page.

7.   Pictures can also be hyperlinks. Click the image labelled **An Image Hyperlink**. Another page is downloaded and displayed.

8.   Click the link **Return to the previous page** to return to the **Hyperlinks** page.

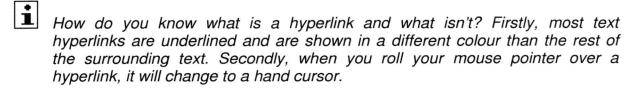

How do you know what is a hyperlink and what isn't? Firstly, most text hyperlinks are underlined and are shown in a different colour than the rest of the surrounding text. Secondly, when you roll your mouse pointer over a hyperlink, it will change to a hand cursor.

9.   Click the **Image Gallery** link on the left navigation panel. A page containing links to three further sub-pages is displayed (i.e. **Cartoons**, **Computers** and **Places**).

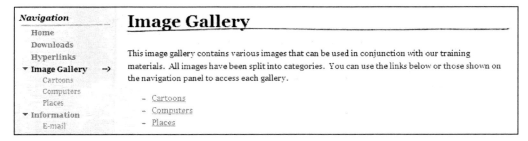

10. Click the **Places** link to display another page containing pictures of various locations around the world.

*You can also click the **Places** submenu link, shown under **Image Gallery** on the navigation panel, to display the **Places** page.*

11. Click on any image that interests you to view a larger version of it.

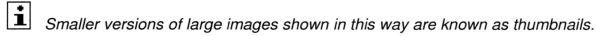

Smaller versions of large images shown in this way are known as thumbnails.

12. Click the **Cartoons** submenu link, under **Image Gallery**, to display another collection of images. Click on any of these to view a larger version.

13. Click the **Computers** submenu link to display yet another collection of images. Again, click on one to view a larger version.

14. Leave *Internet Explorer* and the website open for the next lesson.

Driving Lesson 14 - Navigation Buttons

▣ Park and Read

Internet Explorer records all of the web pages that you view and the order in which you view them. In each browsing session, it is easy to move between them by using the **Back** and **Forward** buttons.

The **Back** button moves backwards through your list of recently viewed pages – one at a time – until the first one is reached. The **Forward** button does the opposite, moving you forward until the most recently viewed page is reached.

Back
Button

Forward
Button

Also, to return directly to your starting **Home Page** (without needing to use the **Back** button), you can use the **Home** button.

⌐ Manoeuvres

1. The *Big Planet Support* site should still be open from the previous lesson. As you clicked a number of links to reach the page currently on display, the **Back** button will be active.

2. Click the **Back** button <u>once</u> to return to the previously visited page.

3. Repeat this action, stepping back through each page visited, until the button becomes ghosted (pale grey). This means that the first page viewed in this session has been reached (which should be your **Home Page**).

🛈 *Holding down the **Back** or **Forward** button displays a drop down list of all pages visited before or after the current one. Any page can be selected from the list to jump directly to it.*

4. Now click the **Forward** button once. *Internet Explorer* will go to the next page in the sequence of viewed pages.

5. Repeat this action and move forward through the list of all recently viewed pages until the **Forward** button becomes ghosted. This indicates that the most recently viewed page has been reached again.

🛈 *You can also use <Alt →> to move forward and <Alt ←> to move backwards.*

6. Click the **Home** button, 🏠, to the right of the **Address Bar**. You will return directly to your personal **Home Page** without needing to click the **Back** button multiple times.

7. Leave *Internet Explorer* open for the next lesson.

Driving Lesson 15 - New Tabs

🅿 Park and Read

Normally, when you click a hyperlink, the web page it connects to is downloaded and displayed (replacing the web page that was previously open). However, it is possible to have more than one page open at the same time, each contained within its own **Tab**.

↱ Manoeuvres

1.   Enter **www.bigplanetsupport.co.uk** into the **Address Bar** again.

ℹ *As you type the* Big Planet Support *site's address into the **Address Bar**, you may notice that the full address appears automatically to save you time. This is known as **autocomplete**. Simply press <**Enter**> to accept the suggestion.*

2.   Press <**Enter**> or click the **Go to** button, ➔, to display the *Big Planet Support* website's homepage.

3.   Notice that the name of the site appears on a tab at the top of the screen.

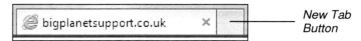

New Tab Button

ℹ *The **New Tab** button can be used to open a new, blank tab.*

4.   Click the **New Tab** button. A new **Tab** is opened showing the default tab page. Some recent sites that you have visited may be listed

ℹ *Alternatively, <**Ctrl T**> will also open a new, blank tab.*

5.   Enter **www.ecdl.org** into the **Address Bar** and press <**Enter**>. A new website is downloaded and displayed.

6.   Click the first tab, labelled **bigplanetsupport.co.uk**, to activate it.

ℹ *The background of the currently active tab is lighter than the others.*

7.   Notice that this page still shows the *Big Planet Support* site's homepage.

8.   Click the second tab to activate it again.

9.   Open a new, blank tab. This time, enter the address **www.bbc.co.uk** to visit that website. There are now three tabs open.

Driving Lesson 15 - Continued

10. By clicking each tab in turn, experiment with moving between tabs.

*You can also move between tabs by holding <**Ctrl**> and pressing <**Tab**>.*

11. Make the third tab (*BBC*) active.

Notice that the currently active tab (or the tab under the mouse pointer), has a ***Close Tab*** *button, ×.*

12. Click the **Close Tab** button once to close it.

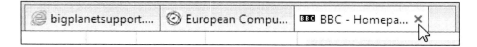

13. Similarly, close the second tab, leaving only the first tab open (containing the *Big Planet Support* website's homepage).

14. Leave this page open for the next lesson.

Driving Lesson 16 - Tabbed Browsing

▣ Park and Read

Tabs can really help improve your productivity when browsing. For example, you can open a new tab to explore links or perform different tasks, returning to the first tab when you are finished.

⤷ Manoeuvres

1. The *Big Planet Support* site's homepage should currently be the only tab open. *Right-click* once on the **Image Gallery** hyperlink. A pop-up shortcut menu appears.

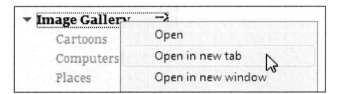

2. Select **Open in new tab**.

ℹ️ *You can also hold <**Ctrl**> and click a link to open it in a new tab.*

3. The **Image Gallery** web page is opened in a new tab which appears at the top of the browser window. If the new tab is not automatically selected, click it once now to activate it.

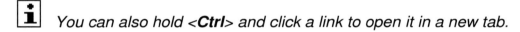

4. Click the **Computers** hyperlink shown on the **Image Gallery** page. Then, click any of the image previews (known as "thumbnails") to open a larger version of that picture.

ℹ️ *Each tab maintains its own list of recently viewed web pages that can be accessed using the **Forward** and **Back** buttons.*

5. Close the current tab. The *Big Planet Support* site's homepage should now be the only tab open. Notice that it is still on the same page that you left it.

6. Next, follow the **Useful Links** hyperlink. A page containing a number of hyperlinks to other websites is displayed in the current tab.

ℹ️ *The creator of a web page can design a link to always open in a new tab/window.*

Driving Lesson 18 - Favorites

▣ Park and Read

When browsing the web, you will often come across interesting websites that you would like to revisit on a regular basis. To make it quick and easy to do this, *Internet Explorer's* **Favorites** feature can be used. In a few easy steps a web page can be "bookmarked" so that you can jump directly back to it at any time.

↰ Manoeuvres

1.   The *Big Planet Support* site's homepage should currently be open. To "bookmark" this page, locate the **Browser Controls** and click the **Favorites** button, ☆.

2.   The **Favorites Center** appears. This contains a list of all bookmarked sites arranged into folders (a number of default folders may appear).

3.   To add the *current* web page to your list of **Favorites**, click the **Add to favorites** button, Add to favorites ▼.

ℹ️ *Alternatively, click **Favorites** from the **Menu bar** and select **Add to favorites**.*

4.   In the **Add a Favorite** dialog box that appears, change the text in the **Name** field to **Big Planet Support**.

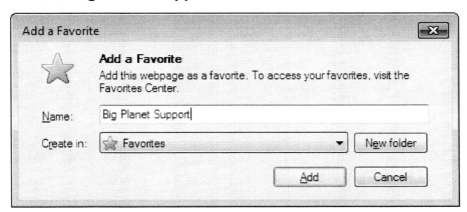

Driving Lesson 18 - Continued

5.   Click **Add** to add the site to your list of bookmarks.

6.   Next, enter **www.bbc.co.uk** into the **Address Bar** and press **<Enter>**.

7.   The BBC's homepage appears. Click, ⭐, and then click **Add to Favorites** to bookmark this site. Change the name to **BBC** and click **Add**.

8.   Enter **www.nasa.gov** into the **Address Bar** and press **<Enter>**.

9.   When the **NASA** homepage appears, add it to your list of **Favorites**. Change the name to **NASA**.

10.   Enter **www.gov.uk** in the **Address Bar** and press **<Enter>**.

11.   The site which appears gives access to many UK public services. Browse the homepage and then add it to your list of **Favorites** with the name **Government**.

12.   Return to your default **Home Page** by clicking the **Home** button, 🏠.

13.   Several sites have now been added to your list of bookmarks. Click ⭐ to display the **Favorites Center** again, and make sure the **Favorites** tab is selected at the top of the panel.

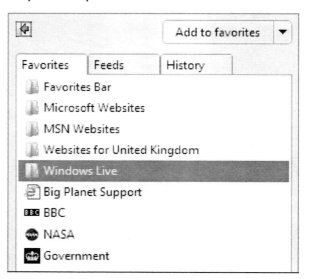

14.   Move your mouse pointer over the **Big Planet Support** bookmark. It will change to a hand cursor to inform you that this is a hyperlink.

Driving Lesson 18 - Continued

[i] *Notice the **Tooltip** that appears containing the name and web address of the bookmarked website.*

[i] *To display any bookmarked site in the list of **Favorites**, simply click its entry.*

15. Click the **Big Planet Support** bookmark. You will be taken directly to the *Big Planet Support* website. By default, the new site will replace the existing site in the **View Window**.

[i] *You can click the **Pin the Favorites Center** button, ▣, to prevent the panel from disappearing when you select a link or click the main **View Window**. It will then remain on screen until you manually close it.*

16. Open the **Favorite Center** again. Then, click **BBC** to go directly to that site.

17. Experiment with the **Favorites Center** and visit all of the new bookmarks created in this lesson.

18. When you are finished, use the **Favorites Center** to return to the **Big Planet Support** site's homepage.

19. Leave *Internet Explorer* open for the next lesson.

Driving Lesson 19 - Organising Favorites

🅿 Park and Read

Your bookmarks are simply a list of *Windows* shortcuts. As such, they can be easily organised into folders or moved and renamed.

↱ Manoeuvres

1. Click ⭐ to display the **Favorites Center** again. Then, click the drop-down arrow on the **Add to favorites** button.

2. From the list of options that appears, select **Organize favorites**. The **Organize Favorites** dialog box is displayed.

Driving Lesson 19 - Continued

3.   Click the **New Folder** button. A new folder is created. Name it **ECDL Bookmarks** and press <**Enter**>.

 It is also possible to create folders within folders to add additional levels of bookmark organisation.

4.   Next, click once to select the **BBC** bookmark and then click the **Move** button.

5.   On the **Browse For Folder** dialog box that appears, select the newly created folder, **ECDL Bookmarks**, and click **OK**. The **BBC** bookmark is moved.

6.   Select the **NASA** bookmark and click **Rename**.

7.   Change the name of the entry to **Space Exploration**, then press <**Enter**>.

 You can also drag and drop bookmarks to move them.

8.   Drag the **Space Exploration** bookmark onto the **ECDL Bookmarks** folder and drop it. The bookmark is moved.

9.   Using the same technique, move the **Government** bookmark to the **ECDL Bookmarks** folder.

10.   Click **Close** to close the **Organize Favorites** dialog box.

11.   Enter **www.ecdl.org** into the **Address Bar** and press <**Enter**>.

12.   When the web page has finished downloading, click ⭐ to display the **Favorites Center** again.

13.   To add this page directly to your new **Favorites** folder, click the **Add to favorites** button, | Add to favorites ▼ |.

14.   When the **Add a Favorite** dialog box appears, change the **Name** to **ECDL Homepage**.

15.   Notice the **Create in** drop-down box. This can be used to save the bookmark to a pre-existing folder in your **Favourites**.

 *You can also create a new folder from this dialog box by clicking the **New folder** button.*

Driving Lesson 19 - Continued

16. Drop down the **Create in** box and select the **ECDL Bookmarks** folder created earlier.

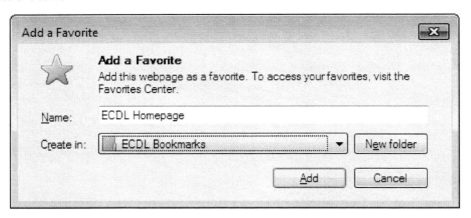

17. Then, click **Add** to add the new bookmark.

18. Click 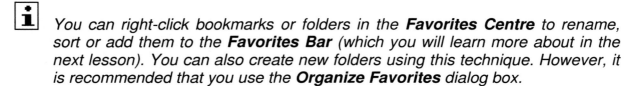 to display the **Favorites Center** again. There will now be an **ECDL Bookmarks** folder in the **Favorites Center**. Click on it to display the contents.

ⓘ *You can right-click bookmarks or folders in the **Favorites Centre** to rename, sort or add them to the **Favorites Bar** (which you will learn more about in the next lesson). You can also create new folders using this technique. However, it is recommended that you use the **Organize Favorites** dialog box.*

19. Experiment with the **Favorites Center** and visit some of the bookmarks in the new **ECDL Bookmarks** folder.

20. Leave *Internet Explorer* open for the next lesson.

Driving Lesson 20 - The Favorites Bar

📭 Park and Read

Bookmarked sites can be added to the **Favorites Bar**. This bar can be permanently displayed above the main **View Window** so that web pages can be accessed instantly without needing to display the **Favorites Center**.

🔼 Manoeuvres

1.   Right-click the **Browser Controls** and select **Favorites Bar**. The bar that appears can contain individual buttons for bookmarked sites.

2.   Enter **www.ciatraining.co.uk** into the **Address Bar** and press <**Enter**>. The homepage that appears can be easily added to the **Favorites bar**.

3.   Click the **Add to Favorites bar** button, ⭐, on the **Favorites Bar**. A new bookmark is created and added to the bar.

ℹ️ *Alternatively, you can drag the web page icon, 🌐, from the* ***Address Bar*** *to the* ***Favorites Bar****. This icon changes depending on the site being viewed.*

4.   Enter **www.wikipedia.org** into the **Address Bar** and press <**Enter**>. Using whichever technique you prefer, add this site to the **Favorites Bar**.

5.   Experiment by clicking each of the new bookmarks and observe the result. The **Favorites Bar** is a really handy way of keeping your most used bookmarks at your finger tips.

6.   Display the **Favorites Center** and click on the **Favorites Bar** folder to expand it. Notice the new bookmarks appear here.

ℹ️ *Bookmarks placed in the* ***Favorites Bar*** *folder appear on the* ***Favorites Bar****.*

7.   It is easy to remove entries from the **Favorites Bar**. Right-click on the **Wikipedia** button on the **Favorites Bar** and select **Delete** from the shortcut menu. The bookmark is removed.

8.   Remove the **CiA Training** bookmark on the **Favorites Bar** also.

9.   Right-click the **Browser Controls** and select **Favorites Bar**. The **Favorites Bar** is hidden once again.

Driving Lesson 21 - Deleting Favorites

◨ Park and Read

To allow you to navigate to your favourite web pages more quickly, it is good practice to remove unwanted bookmarks that you no longer want or need. To do this, bookmarks and folders can be easily deleted from the **Favorites Center**.

⟰ Manoeuvres

1. Click ☆ to display the **Favorites Center** again. Then, click the drop-down arrow on the **Add to favorites** button.

2. From the list of options that appears, select **Organize favorites**. The **Organize Favorites** dialog box is displayed.

3. Expand the **ECDL Bookmarks** folder. There are four bookmarks contained within.

4. Select **Government** by clicking it once. Then, click the **Delete** button. The bookmark is permanently removed.

5. Use the same technique to delete the **Space Exploration** and **ECDL Homepage** bookmarks.

6. Next, select the **ECDL Bookmarks** folder. To delete this folder and all of its contents, click the **Delete** button. A **Delete Folder** prompt will appear.

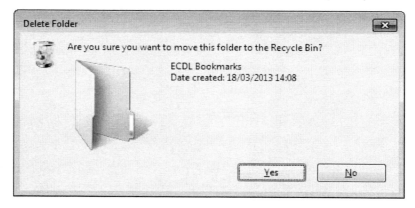

7. Read the dialog box and then click **Yes**. The folder and all of its contents are permanently removed.

8. Click **Close** to close the **Organise Favorites** dialog box.

ℹ️ *As you saw in the previous lesson, you can also right-click bookmarks or folders in the* ***Favorites Centre*** *to delete them.*

9. Leave the **Big Planet Support** bookmark in your **Favorites Centre**. You can use this to help navigate to the *Big Planet Support* website later.

Driving Lesson 22 - Browsing History

▣ Park and Read

As you browse the *World Wide Web*, *Internet Explorer* keeps a record of all the web pages visited. This is known as your **browsing history** and can be viewed in the **Favorites Center**. If you ever need to return to a recently viewed web page, but can't remember its location, you will find this feature very useful.

⌐ Manoeuvres

1.   Click the drop-down arrow to the right of the **Address Bar**, ▾. Notice the list of recently visited websites (which may appear as web addresses or by name).

ℹ️ *Your recently visited website list may appear differently to that shown above.*

2.   There is a list of recently typed web addresses, a list of recently visited pages (**History**) and a list of recently visited **Favorites** pages.

ℹ️ *The **History** and **Favorites** lists can be expanded by clicking the ▾ buttons.*

3.   Select any of the items shown to jump back to that page.

4.   A more complete and structured history list is available in the **Favorites Center**. Click the **Favorites** button and then select the **History** tab. The **History** view will appear.

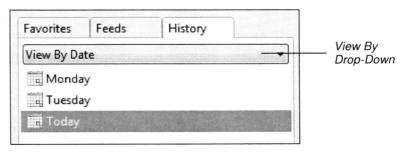

View By Drop-Down

Driving Lesson 22 - Continued

5. The default ordering of your history is **View By Date**. All sites visited (up to the default history time limit) are grouped into time periods.

6. Click **Today** to view a list of sites you have visited today.

7. Click the entry for the *Big Planet Support* website (**bigplanetsupport**, **www.bigplanetsupport.co.uk**) to see a further list of pages visited within that site today (if applicable).

8. Click on any entry to close the **Favorite Center** and return to that page.

9. Click the **Favorites** button again. This time, click the **View By** drop-down button on the **History** tab. Notice you can sort your **History** by **Most Visited** (web pages in order of visit frequency) or **By Site** (web pages in alphabetical order).

10. Click **By Site** and observe the effect.

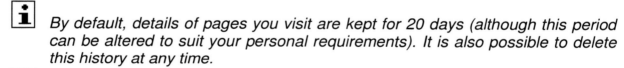 *By default, details of pages you visit are kept for 20 days (although this period can be altered to suit your personal requirements). It is also possible to delete this history at any time.*

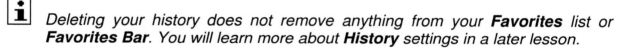 *Deleting your history does not remove anything from your **Favorites** list or **Favorites Bar**. You will learn more about **History** settings in a later lesson.*

11. Locate the **Browser Controls** and click the **Tools** button, ⚙.

12. To delete your browsing history, select **Safety** and then **Delete browsing history**.

13. A dialog box appears with options for deleting various aspects of your history. Read the descriptions below each checkbox to see the type of history information you can delete.

14. Check **Temporary Internet files**, **History** and **Form data** only. In practise, you may wish to delete other types of history also.

15. Click **Delete**. After a short delay a **Notification Bar** will appear to show that the history has been deleted (which you can dismiss by clicking ×).

16. Open the **Favorites Center** again and view your **History** – none of the websites visited earlier should appear.

17. Check the **Address Bar** drop-down list. This has also been cleared.

Driving Lesson 23 - Revision

▣ Park and Read

At the end of every section you get the chance to complete one or more revision exercises to develop your skills and prepare you for your ECDL certification test. You should aim to complete the following steps without referring back to the previous lessons.

⌐ Manoeuvres

1.   Visit the *Yahoo* website **www.yahoo.com**.

ⓘ *You may be redirected to a local version of this site (e.g. uk.yahoo.com).*

2.   When the *Yahoo* homepage appears, use any of the available hyperlinks to view topics of interest to you.

3.   Use the **Back** button to return to the *Yahoo* website's starting homepage.

4.   Add the current *Yahoo* homepage to your **Favorite Center's** list of bookmarks (name it **Yahoo Homepage**).

5.   Use the **Forward** button to return to the most recently viewed page.

6.   Now visit the *CNN* website **www.cnn.com**.

7.   Bookmark this site's homepage with the name **CNN Homepage**.

8.   Browse the *CNN* website by selecting any hyperlinks of interest to you. Practise using the **Back** and **Forward** buttons to navigate the site.

9.   Create a new top-level folder in your **Favorites** and name it **Revision**.

10. Move the **Yahoo Homepage** and **CNN Homepage** bookmarks into the new **Revision** folder.

11. Visit the *Yahoo* homepage again by using a bookmark.

12. Display your **History** and use it to revisit the *CNN* homepage.

13. Delete your browsing **History**.

14. Delete the **Revision** bookmarks folder and all of its contents.

15. Close *Internet Explorer* and any open tabs.

ⓘ *Now complete the **Record of Achievement Matrix** at the back of the guide. You should only move on when confident with the topics and features described in this section.*

Section 3
Searching the Web

By the end of this section you should be able to:

Find Information using Search Engines

Search for Keywords and Phrases

Perform Website Searches

Find Text on a Web Page

Refine Searches with Advanced Options

Critically Evaluate Information Found Online

Work through the **Driving Lessons** in this section to gain an understanding of the above features.

For each **Driving Lesson**, read all of the **Park and Read** instructions and then, if applicable, perform the numbered steps of the **Manoeuvres**. Complete the **Revision** exercise(s) at the end of the section to test your knowledge.

Driving Lesson 24 - Search Engines

▣ Park and Read

The Internet can be used to find information on almost any subject you can think of. However, finding the exact information you want from the billions and billions of websites on the *World Wide Web* is not always easy. To help, you can use a **search engine**.

As you probably already know, a search engine is a website that you can use to search for **keywords** on other web pages. Although a search engine may look simple, behind the scenes it is connected to a very large and complex database. When you perform a search, the search engine very quickly selects every web page in the database that contains your keywords. These pages are then presented to you as a list of hyperlinks.

There are many useful search engines available on the web, some of which are more specialised than others. Today, the best and most popular general search engines include:

Google: www.google.co.uk
Yahoo: www.yahoo.co.uk
Ask: www.ask.com
Bing: www.bing.com

In this lesson you will use the *Google* search engine. This is probably the best search engine available and is highly recommended for general everyday use. Of course, the search techniques that you learn in this lesson will apply equally well to any other search engine that you may choose to use in the future.

⌐ Manoeuvres

1.   Open *Internet Explorer* and enter **www.google.co.uk** into the **Address Bar**. Press **<Enter>** and the *Google* search engine appears.

Search Box ————

Search
Button ——————

i *Websites are constantly being developed and improved. As such, the* Google *search pages and results may not look exactly as shown in this section. However, the basic functionality should remain the same.*

Driving Lesson 24 - Continued

2. Let's assume that you are planning a holiday in the UK and would to find a list of popular theme parks. Click once in the **Search Box**, enter the keyword **parks** and then press <**Enter**>.

🛈 *Alternatively, enter the keyword **parks** and click the **Search Button** (if present). This is labelled **Google Search** on the previous screenshot but may change.*

🛈 Google *may automatically start searching as you enter keywords. It may also provide a number of search suggestions as you type. If the search text you are entering appears you can select it to save time.*

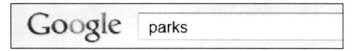

3. *Google* finds every site in its database which contains the required keyword **parks**. Make a note of the number of results found (which is usually shown towards the top of the page).

About 3,560,000,000 results (0.15 seconds)

🛈 *Due to the ever-changing nature of the* World Wide Web, *you will probably find a different number of results than that shown above.*

4. All of the web pages found are placed in order of relevance (the first ten or so are the most relevant and are shown first). Scan the results and notice that a number of pages have been found which have nothing to do with theme parks.

5. Let's make the search more specific (known as "**refining**"). At the top of the page change the keyword text to **theme parks** and press <**Enter**>.

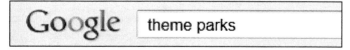

🛈 *The web pages that a search engine finds are often referred to as **hits**. As well as providing hyperlinks to web pages where your keywords are found,* Google *also shows a small extract of the text on those pages.*

6. Fewer results are found. Scan the small extracts for each "hit" and notice that the web pages are now much more relevant.

7. To narrow the search even further, change the keyword search text to **UK theme parks**. Press <**Enter**>. Fewer, more relevant results are found.

Driving Lesson 24 - Continued

 Surround keywords with quotation marks to obtain results matching an exact phrase, e.g. **"Tom and Jerry"** *or* **"The Battle of Hastings"**.

8.   Have you noticed that the search keywords can appear in any order in the results? To search for the specific phrase **UK theme parks** only (with all of the words in that exact order) place quotation marks around the keywords in the search box at the top of the page and press <**Enter**>.

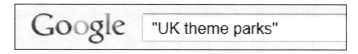

9.   The number of results will be further reduced and only web pages that feature the exact phrase "**UK theme park**" somewhere in their text will appear.

 Commercially sponsored websites may be displayed at the very top of the results list or on the right side of the screen. Although usually relevant, these sites are also designed to sell you products or services.

10.   Recall that you were searching for the names of theme parks in the UK. Examine the results found and then visit the web page that seems most relevant.

11.   If the selected web page does not contain relevant information, click the **Back** button and try another. If the first set of *Google* search results is not relevant, you can view more by clicking the **Next** hyperlink (or similar) at the bottom of the page.

12.   When you are finished, use the **Back** button to return to *Google's* starting homepage.

 As well as searching for keywords in web pages, many search engines also allow you to search for keywords in news articles, discussions, maps, books, and image and video descriptions. These features are usually available towards the top or left side of a search engine's homepage.

13.   Explore the many search features available on *Google's* homepage. For example, try searching for the keywords **theme park** in *Images*, *Videos*, *News* or *Discussions*.

14.   When you are finished, return to *Google's* starting homepage.

Driving Lesson 25 - Advanced Search

P Park and Read

The previous lesson demonstrated a common problem encountered by Internet users: a search can often produce millions of hits. Fortunately, it is possible to narrow a search considerably using the following tips:

Exclude words	Use a minus symbol before an unwanted word or phrase to exclude it, e.g. **french wine -champagne**.
Specify location	Many search engines allow you to restrict searches to sites within a specific country or region (e.g. UK only). This often helps you find more relevant results when searching for local information or services.
Specify Language	Restrict the results of a search to pages written in a specific language.
Specify Date	Restrict the results of a search to pages or files that were uploaded or changed within a specific time frame.
Specify Media	Restrict your search to files of a specific type (e.g. images, videos, documents, etc.)

↱ Manoeuvres

1. *Internet Explorer* should currently be open with the *Google* search engine's homepage (**www.google.co.uk**) on display.

2. You would like to find information about bass, a type of fish. In the **Search Box**, enter the keyword **bass** and press **<Enter>**. Examine the results found.

3. Notice a lot of hits are related to music. You are not interested in this, so exclude that word from the search results. At the top of the page change the search text to **bass -music** and press **<Enter>**.

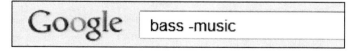

Google   bass -music

ℹ *Be careful not to insert a space between the minus symbol and the excluded keyword.*

4. Examine the websites found which are much more relevant. The keyword **music** does not appear in any of the results.

ℹ *Although excluding words is sometimes useful, it is usually best to refine your keywords instead. For example, rather than exclude the keyword **music** in the above example, try searching for **bass fish** instead.*

Driving Lesson 25 - Continued

5.   Next, you would like to find information about trips to France. However, you are not interested in going to Paris or Nice. In the **Search Box**, replace the previous search with the keywords **France trips -Paris -Nice** and press <**Enter**>.

6.   Examine the results found. The websites listed will not feature the keywords **Paris** or **Nice**.

 *Some search engines also have an **Advanced Search** option which can be used to find web pages or files published from a specific location, in a specific language or within a certain date range.*

7.   Locate the **Advanced Search** link. This can often be found near to the **Search Box**, at the bottom of the results page, or as an option in the site's "search tools".

8.   Examine the advanced search options that appear. Notice that you can restrict results by language, region, date updated and file type.

9.   From the options available, restrict results to web pages updated within the last month.

10. Perform the advanced search and observe the result. Then, return to the advanced search options.

11. From the options available, restrict results to files of type **PDF**.

12. Finally, restrict results to web pages published in France and in the French language. Perform the search and observe the result.

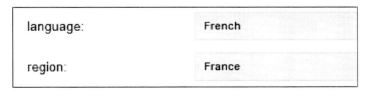

13. Feel free to explore more of *Google's* advanced search features. When you are finished, return to your **Home page** by clicking the **Home** button.

14. Leave *Internet Explorer* open and continue on to the next lesson.

Driving Lesson 26 - Search Tips

▣ Park and Read

When you use a search engine such as *Google* to find information, remember these following useful tips:

- Enter only important, descriptive keywords. Use more than one keyword for more accuracy (search engines will generally ignore common words like **and**, **an**, **of**, **where**, **when**, **is**, etc).

- The more precise your keywords, the more likely you are to find useful results. For example, **theme park** will produce more specific results than just **park**.

- Be descriptive and enter keywords as you think they will appear on a web page. For example, **park admission prices** will produce better results than **park costs**.

- If initial results are too broad, you can refine your search by adding more keywords.

- Remember that you can use quotation marks to find specific phrases.

- Use the minus operator to exclude results that contain keywords you do not want.

- To help refine your searches further, consider performing an advanced search and restrict results by language, region, date or file type.

- It doesn't matter if you use upper or lower case text.

- Don't bother to include general punctuation marks as these are usually ignored.

- Be prepared to follow more than one search result to find the information you need. It really does pay to be patient and explore a selection of results.

🛈 *These search techniques will work with all general search engines, not just* Google*.*

Driving Lesson 27 - Website Searches

▣ Park and Read

Many websites have their own search features which only reference information contained within their pages. For large websites that contain a lot of information, this can be a useful feature.

However, there are also many online reference books, encyclopaedias and dictionaries available to use for free. For sites such as these, the internal search features are even more important.

⟰ Manoeuvres

1. Enter **en.wikipedia.org** into the **Address Bar** and press <**Enter**>. The *Wikipedia* website loads. This vast online encyclopaedia contains information contributed by volunteers worldwide.

2. Locate the site's **Search Box**. This can usually be found towards the top-right corner of every page on the site.

3. Click once in the **Search Box** and enter the keyword **blackbird**.

4. Ignore any listed suggestions and press <**Enter**>. A large list of possible topics is listed. Remember, only the *Wikipedia* site is being searched.

5. Browse the results to see the various topics available.

6. Locate and click the hyperlink entry for the **Common Blackbird**. A comprehensive page of information is displayed.

ℹ *Most websites have a search feature like this for finding information within a single site.*

7. Using the same technique, search *Wikipedia* for information on *Captain Cook*. When was he born?

8. Next, search *Wikipedia* for information on the *Red Admiral* butterfly (*Vanessa Atalanta*). What is its average wing span?

9. Finally, search *Wikipedia* for information on the city of *Dublin*. At which river mouth is the city located?

10. Leave *Internet Explorer* open for the next lesson.

ℹ *Sample answers can be found at the back of the guide.*

Driving Lesson 28 - Finding Text on a Page

▣ Park and Read

Internet Explorer has a useful **Find** facility which can be used to search for text on a web page.

ℹ️ *The **Find** feature only searches the currently selected tab.*

⬈ Manoeuvres

1. Return to the *Big Planet Support* website by entering its address into the **Address Bar** (or by using the bookmark in your **Favorites Center**).

2. Click the **E-mail** hyperlink on the left navigation panel (you may have to expand the **Information** heading first).

3. Press **<Ctrl F>** (i.e. hold down the **<Ctrl>** key and press **<F>**). The **Find Bar** appears.

ℹ️ *Alternatively, if the **Menu Bar** is visible, you can click **Edit | Find on this page**.*

4. In the **Find** box, enter they keyword **message**. All **6 matches** on the page are highlighted.

5. Notice that the first match is automatically selected.

6. Click **Next**. *Internet Explorer* will select the next occurrence of the keyword **message** on the page and ensure that it is in view.

7. Click **Next**. Repeat this action until the first occurrence of the keyword is highlighted again.

ℹ️ *The **Next** and **Previous** buttons will continually cycle through all of the matches found.*

8. Try searching for the keyword **e-mail**. Experiment with the **Next** and **Previous** buttons to cycle through the 9 matches discovered.

9. Close the **Find** bar by clicking the **Close the Find bar** button, ⌧, at the left end of the bar.

10. Leave the *Big Planet Support* site open and continue to the next lesson.

Driving Lesson 29 - Critical Evaluation

⚑ Park and Read

Don't always believe everything that you read or hear online, in magazines or on TV. Although the information may have been approved by experts and checked for accuracy, this is not always the case. You need to stop and consider how trustworthy the information is before you believe it or use it in your own work, especially if it is found on public websites where very little quality control exists. This is not always easy to do, but the following tips will help:

- Consider the source of the material that you are reading. Who has written it and why, and do they have any evidence to support their claims?

- Consider the publisher's authority in their area. Are they well known for producing reliable and accurate information? Do they reference and build upon other credible work (and is their work in turn referenced or held in high regard by others)?

- What is the intention of a website or a publisher? Is the information provided aimed at entertaining you, informing you of facts, presenting a viewpoint, persuading you of a belief, or trying to sell you something?

- Forums or "blog" posts will most likely be based on biased (one-sided) opinion. You should take care when using information of this type.

- The articles stored on editable web pages or "wiki" sites (e.g. *Wikipedia*) are created by the general public (who are usually not experts) and should not be fully trusted.

- Well known and legitimate business websites are fairly trustworthy, but they are also likely to be biased towards promoting their own products and company goals.

- Materials obtained from well-known government or scientific sources (e.g. the *National Geographic* website) are usually a good source of reliable and accurate information.

- Consider the age of the information you find. It could be out-of-date or no longer relevant.

- Finally, if you decide to use a piece of information, try to confirm specific details by reading around the subject. Do other authors agree?

Remember, if you are making decisions or basing your work on information found online, you need to be confident that the facts and figures used are totally reliable, accurate and fit for purpose. The quality and relevance of your work depends on it, and you may be asked to justify and defend your choices later.

Driving Lesson 30 - Revision

P Park and Read

At the end of every section you get the chance to complete one or more revision exercises to develop your skills and prepare you for your ECDL certification test. You should aim to complete the following steps without referring back to the previous lessons.

Manoeuvres

1.   Visit the *Google* search engine (**www.google.co.uk**).

2.   Use *Google* to find out about the history of the **Ferris Wheel**. In particular, find out when the first one was created and who built it.

3.   Consider the following famous quote: "**Here age relives fond memories of the past, and here youth may savor the challenge and promise of the future**". Use *Google* to find out who said it.

4.   Use *Google* to find information about **grizzly bears**. Notice how many hits you receive.

5.   Refine your search to find information about grizzly bears in **Canada**. The number of hits should decrease.

6.   Exclude the keyword **Ontario** from your search. The number of hits should decrease even further.

7.   Now only show web pages published in the last year.

8.   What is the average high temperature of the **British Columbia** town of **Victoria** in **July**?

9.   Visit the *Wikipedia* website (**en.wikipedia.org**).

10.   Use the search feature on *Wikipedia* to find out more the planet **Neptune**. Read the information provided. How relevant, accurate and reliable is it?

11.   Use *Internet Explorer's* **Find Bar** feature to find each occurrence of the word **Neptune**. Step through each match found.

12.   With regards to Neptune, find information about **Triton** – what is it?

13.   Return to your default **Home Page**.

i *Sample answers can be found at the back of the guide.*

i *Now complete the **Record of Achievement Matrix** at the back of the guide. You should only move on when confident with the topics and features described in this section.*

Section 4
Web Page Interaction

By the end of this section you should be able to:

Download Files

Save Pictures

Copy and Paste Text and Pictures

Use Print Preview and Page Setup

Print a Web Page

Print a Text Selection

Complete an Online Form

Translate Text

Work through the **Driving Lessons** in this section to gain an understanding of the above features.

For each **Driving Lesson**, read all of the **Park and Read** instructions and then, if applicable, perform the numbered steps of the **Manoeuvres**. Complete the **Revision** exercise(s) at the end of the section to test your knowledge.

Driving Lesson 31 - Downloading Files

▣ Park and Read

Many types of files, including documents, music and video files, can be downloaded from the Internet and saved, viewed or played on your computer.

ⓘ *Be aware of copyright law before downloading or accessing creative works online. You will learn more about copyright in a later section.*

⟲ Manoeuvres

1. Return to the *Big Planet Support* website by entering its address into the **Address Bar** or by using the bookmark in your **Favorites Center**.

2. Click **Downloads** on the navigation panel on the left. The page that appears contains links to various files for you to download and try.

3. Click on the hyperlink **Apollo.wav**. A **Notification Bar** will appear at the bottom of the screen prompting you to **Open** or **Save** the file.

4. Click **Open**. After a short delay while the file is downloaded and security checked, your media player application (*Windows Media Player* by default) will open and the file will start to play.

ⓘ *If a different program has been set up to be the default media player, the file will start to play in that application instead. The controls may vary between different media players but will be functionally similar.*

Driving Lesson 31 - Continued

 *The **Apollo** file has not been permanently downloaded. It is stored in your browser's **Temporary Internet Files** folder and will be deleted automatically at a later date. The following actions will show how to save objects permanently.*

5.   When the audio clip finishes playing, close the media player.

6.   Next, click on the hyperlink **Berlioz.wav**. When the **Notification Bar** appears prompting you to **Open** or **Save** the file, select **Save**. The music file is saved into your **Downloads** folder.

7.   When the file is finished downloading, select **Open** on the **Notification Bar** to play the audio clip. Close the media player when it finishes playing.

8.   To have more control over the location of the saved file, right-click on the **Berlioz.wav** link and select **Save target as** from the shortcut menu.

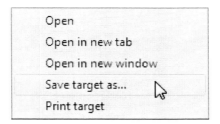

9.   The **Save As** dialog box appears. Navigate to your **Documents** library.

10.   Leave the **File name** and **Save as type** settings as they are and click **Save**. A **Notification Bar** may appear briefly to inform you of download progress.

11.   Click the **Start** button and select **Documents** to open your **Documents** library. A copy of the **berlioz.wav** file has been downloaded into this folder and will remain there until deleted.

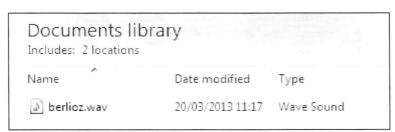

12.   Close the **Documents** library window and return to *Internet Explorer*.

13.   Any file can be downloaded from the Internet using this technique. Right-click the **Testimonial.doc** link on the **Downloads** page and select **Save target as** from the shortcut menu.

14.   In the **Save As** dialog box make sure the save location is set to your **Documents** library. Then click **Save**.

15.   Similarly, save **Ocean.avi** to your **Documents** library.

Driving Lesson 31 - Continued

16. Click the **Start** button and open your **Documents** library. The files **berlioz.wav**, **ocean.avi** and **Testimonial.doc** will be listed.

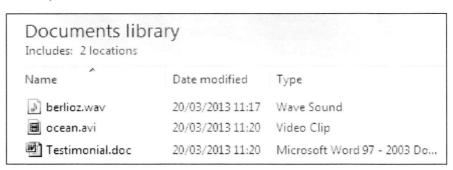

17. Double click the **ocean.avi** file to start the demonstration movie. Close the media player when it is finished.

i *Always be careful when downloading files of any sort from the Internet. Unless you completely trust the source of the file, it may contain viruses and other malware that can harm ICT devices or allow criminals to steal information. If you do download a file, scan it first using your computer's antivirus software.*

i *Antivirus software can also be used to scan files "on-demand", which is useful for checking downloaded files <u>before</u> you open them. To do this, simply right-click the file and select the option to scan it with your antivirus program.*

18. Delete the files **berlioz.wav**, **ocean.avi** and **Testimonial.doc** from your **Documents** library.

19. Use the **Navigation Pane** on the left to change the location to the **Downloads** folder and delete the **berlioz.wav** file that was saved there.

20. Close the window showing the **Downloads** folder and return to *Internet Explorer*.

Driving Lesson 32 - Saving Pictures

▣ Park and Read

Individual images on a web page can be saved to your computer. As you will learn later, you must be very careful how you use the saved image as it is likely to be copright protected.

☞ Manoeuvres

1. The *Big Planet Support* website should still be open. Navigate to the **Image Gallery** and then to the **Places** page (or simply click the **Places** link under **Image Gallery**).

2. A list of pictures of places from around the world is shown. Click one that interests you to view a larger version of that image – you are going to save this picture to your computer.

3. Using your mouse, right-click on the image. From the pop-up menu that appears, select **Save picture as**.

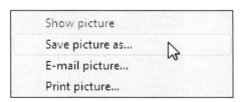

4. The **Save Picture** dialog box appears. Make sure the **Pictures** library is selected as the location to save the image.

5. You can specify an image's file name when saving. Rename the file **picture**.

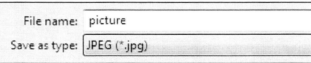

 *Notice the **Save as type** drop-down box. Images come in a variety of different formats – this one is a JPEG which is the format most often used for pictures. Others include Bitmap, PNG and GIF.*

6. Click **Save** to save the image to your **Pictures** folder.

7. Minimise *Internet Explorer*, open the **Start Menu** and select **Pictures**. The downloaded **picture** file should appear in the list.

8. Double-click the **picture** file to open it in your computer's default image viewer.

9. Close the image viewer and then delete the **picture** file.

10. Close the **Pictures** library and return to *Internet Explorer.*

Driving Lesson 33 - Printing a Web Page

▣ Park and Read

You can print documents, or parts of documents, directly from the Internet.

☞ Manoeuvres

1. The *Big Planet Support* website should still be open. Click the **Internet** link on the navigation panel (you may need to expand **Information** first).

ℹ *Web pages rarely appear in print exactly as they do on-screen. For this reason, it is always advisable to use **Print Preview** before printing.*

2. Locate the **Browser Controls** and click the **Tools** button, ⚙. From the menu that appears, select **Print** and then **Print preview**.

3. Examine the window that appears. In particular, notice the useful buttons on the **Toolbar**.

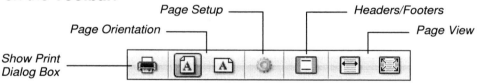

4. From the **Page View** settings, click **View Full Width** to zoom in. Notice that the text is cut off on the right side of the page.

5. From the **Page Orientation** settings, click **Landscape**. All of the text can now be seen.

6. From the **Page View** settings, click **View Full Page** to zoom out.

7. Click **Turn headers and footers on or off** to switch off the headers and footers. Observe the result.

8. Click **Turn headers and footers on or off** again to restore the headers and footers. The information displayed is useful.

9. Click the **Page Setup** button to display the Page Setup dialog box. Examine the settings shown.

ℹ *The **Page Setup** dialog box can be used to change the size of paper used, the margins, and the contents of the headers and footers.*

10. The default settings are fine for most general print outs. Click **OK** to close the dialog box.

11. Finally, click the **Print Document** button to display the **Print** dialog box.

Driving Lesson 33 - Continued

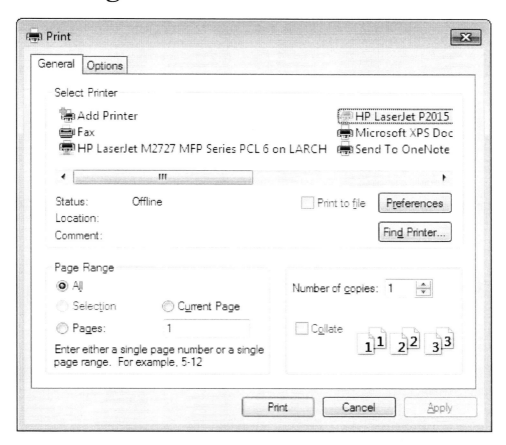

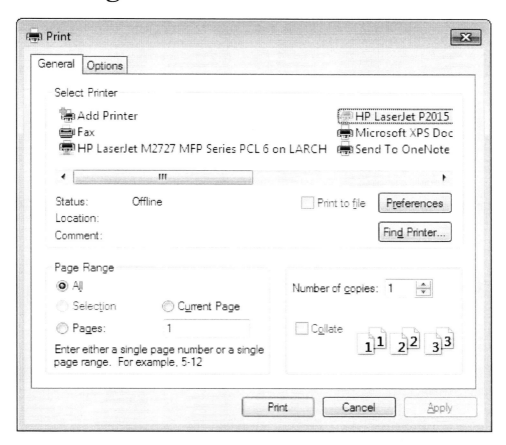 *When browsing, you can also press <**Ctrl P**> to display the **Print** dialog box.*

12. Select a printer to use from the **Select Printer** list (assuming that one is available; your default printer should already be selected).

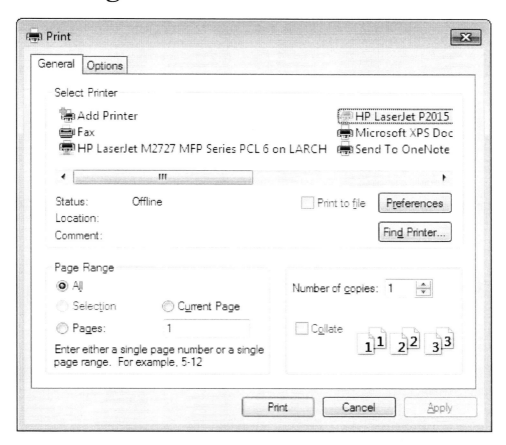 *The **Page Range** settings can be used to specify which pages (from the print preview) should be printed.*

13. Make sure that **All** is selected in **Page Range** and **Number of copies** is set to **1**.

14. Click **Print** to print the page. The **Print** dialog box automatically closes and a copy of the web page is sent to your printer.

 *To save printer ink, Internet Explorer does not always print background colours. You can change this setting from **Page Setup**.*

15. Leave *Internet Explorer* open for the next lesson.

Driving Lesson 34 - Printing a Selection

▣ Park and Read

As well as printing whole web pages, it is also possible to print only a selection of a page's text (including any selected images).

↱ Manoeuvres

1. The *Big Planet Support* website should still be open. Make sure the **Internet** page of information is currently on display.

2. Click and drag to select the *second* paragraph of text starting "**The Internet, or net for short...**".

    > This page contains information about the Internet that can be used in conjunction with CiA Training and Big Planet Publishing materials.
    >
    > The Internet, or net for short, is a global network of interconnected computer systems that allows people from all over the world to communicate and share information. Most people use the Internet to access the World Wide Web; a vast collection of linked documents called web pages (stored on other computers connected to the Internet).
    >
    > More and more, as an alternative to conventional shopping, the Internet is being used to purchase goods. Many different types of item and services can be bought online. There are sites selling almost

3. Click the **Tools** button, select **Print**, and then select **Print preview**.

4. To print only the selected text, click the drop-down box labelled **As laid out on screen**. Examine the options shown, and then select **As selected on screen**.

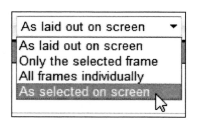

5. Observe the effect. Then, click the **Print Document** button to display the **Print** dialog box.

6. Notice that **Selection** is currently checked under **Page Range**. This only prints the selected text (and can be selected directly from the **Print** dialog box without needing to adjust settings in the **Print preview**).

7. Click **Print**. The selected text is sent to your printer.

8. Leave *Internet Explorer* open for the next lesson.

Driving Lesson 35 - Copy and Paste

 Park and Read

It is possible to copy text and images from a web page and then to paste them into a document. Again, you must be very careful how you use material obtained from the Internet as it is likely to be copright protected.

Manoeuvres

1. The *Big Planet Support* website should still be open with a paragraph of text on the **Internet** page selected.

2. Right-click the selected text and select **Copy** from the shortcut menu that appears. The copied text is placed in memory.

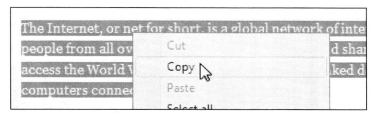

3. Using the **Start Menu**, find and open *Microsoft Word*.

4. With the cursor flashing in the top left corner of a blank document, click the **Paste** button on the **Ribbon**.

 Click the ***Paste*** *button's icon, not the drop-down arrow below it. Alternatively, press <**Ctrl V**>. If you do not have Microsoft Word, WordPad can be used instead.*

5. The copied text is pasted into the document. Press <**Enter**> to start a new line and use the **Taskbar** to return to the *Big Planet Support* website.

6. Click the **Places** link on the navigation panel (you may need to expand **Image Gallery** first).

7. Right-click any image that you like from those shown. Select **Copy** from the shortcut menu that appears. The copied image is placed in memory.

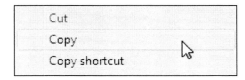

8. Return to *Microsoft Word* and click the **Paste** button again. The copied image is pasted into the document.

9. Press <**Enter**> to start a new line and use the **Taskbar** to return to the *Big Planet Support* website.

Driving Lesson 35 - Continued

i *As you browse the Internet and find websites of interest, you may find that you would like to include a link to it in your document..*

10. Click the **Home** link on the navigation panel to return to the *Big Planet Support* site's homepage.

11. Click once in the **Address Bar** to auto-select the web address.

12. Right-click the selected address and choose **Copy** from the shortcut menu that appears. The copied address is placed in memory.

i *Alternatively, press <**Ctrl C**>.*

13. Return to *Microsoft Word* and click the **Paste** button again. The copied web address is pasted into the document.

i *Notice that the web address appears as a hyperlink. It can be clicked from within* Word *to open the page in your web browser.*

14. Close the document without saving.

i *You can also paste web addresses into any Internet communication program of your choosing (e.g. your favourite e-mail program) in order to share it with others.*

15. Close *Word* but leave *Internet Explorer* open for the next lesson.

Driving Lesson 36 - Online Forms

🅿 Park and Read

Similar to paper-based forms that you complete with a pen or pencil, an **online form** can be completed by typing information into labelled boxes on a web page. That data can then be "submitted" and sent to the form's owner.

Online forms available on the *World Wide Web* are used for many different purposes, from requesting information or sending feedback to adding comments to blogs and shopping online. Despite these many different uses, you'll be happy to know that the vast majority of online forms look and work in exactly the same way.

↱ Manoeuvres

1. The *Big Planet Support* site should currently be open. Click **Online Forms** on the navigation panel on the left. The page that appears contains links to various online forms for you to try.

ℹ️ *The online forms provided are for demonstration purposes only and are typical of the many web-based forms used by websites on the* World Wide Web. *Even though the details you enter are not sent to anybody or recorded anywhere, you should not enter any real personal details.*

2. Click once on **Feedback Form** to open the linked web page in a new tab. An online feedback form for the fictitious business *Quality Theatre Company* appears.

Quality Theatre Company

We are constantly trying to improve the performances you see at the theatre. Please take a few moments to let us know your thoughts on the productions we show. Please note: this is an example form. Any text you enter will not be sent to anyone or any organisation.

*Required

About You

Please provide your contact details:

Your Name: *

Your Email Address: *

3. Read the information on the page and scroll down to view the entire online form. Notice the **Submit** button at the bottom of the page.

Driving Lesson 36 - Continued

4. Consider the following statement:

    Last **Monday** you attended the *Quality Theatre Company's* production of **The Tempest** at their **Studio** venue. It was great and you thought both the theatre and the performers were **very good**. It was better than **Hamlet** and **Othello** which you saw last year.

5. Complete the online form by entering the relevant information (based on the statement above) into each box.

i *Notice that some boxes are marked with a red asterisk (✷), indicating that this information is required. If you do not enter valid information into these boxes you will receive an error message.*

6. When you are finished, click the **Submit** button, Submit , to send your feedback information to the theatre. You will receive a confirmation that your comments have been received.

i *Some forms feature a **Reset** button, Reset , that can be used to quickly clear all of the information entered into a form. If present, this can usually be found next to the **Submit** button.*

7. Close the new tab for the completed form, 🔵 Thanks! ✕ , to return to the *Big Planet Support* tab.

8. Now click once on **Booking Form**. An online form for a fictitious *Online Library Services* website appears.

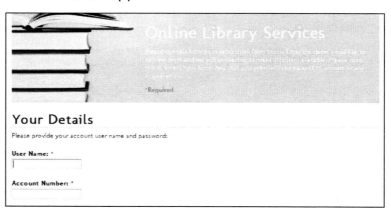

9. You would like to reserve **The Tempest** by **William Shakespeare** from your local library for next **Friday** (your account number is **OLS1234**). Complete and submit the form.

10. When your receive confirmation of your reservation, close the new tab to return to *Big Planet Support* site and leave it open for the next lesson.

i *Always make sure you enter (and double-check) your personal details correctly when completing an online form. To provide a record of the data you submit, websites will often send you an automatic confirmation e-mail.*

Driving Lesson 37 - Translate a Web Page

▣ Park and Read

There are many powerful online tools that can translate text into different languages in seconds. This is useful for reading web pages that were created in another language.

⌐ Manoeuvres

1. The *Big Planet Support* website should still be open. Click the **Translation** link on the navigation panel. A page containing a single paragraph of French text appears.

2. Click and drag to select the paragraph of text.

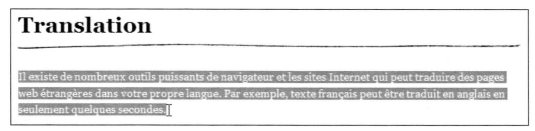

3. To translate the selected text into your own language, right-click it to display a shortcut menu. Without clicking, place your mouse pointer over **Translate with Bing**.

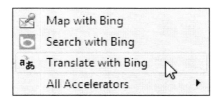

ⓘ Bing *is a popular search engine created by* Microsoft. *Most search engines have text translation capabilities.*

4. *Internet Explorer* uses the *Microsoft Translator* service on the *Bing* website to translate the selected text. A preview appears in a window.

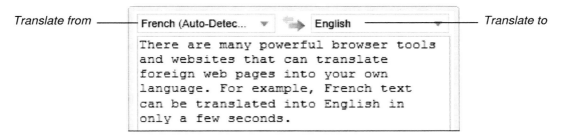

ⓘ *Notice that "Translate from" and "Translate to" are automatically selected. Alternative selections can be made by clicking the drop-down boxes.*

Driving Lesson 37 - Continued

5.   Now click the **Translate with Bing** item on the shortcut menu. This opens the *Microsoft Translator* site in a new tab.

6.   Examine the website. You can type or paste text in a variety of languages into a box on this page. The *Microsoft Translator* service will then translate it into any of the other languages supported.

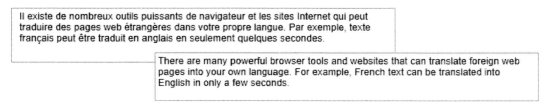

Il existe de nombreux outils puissants de navigateur et les sites Internet qui peut traduire des pages web étrangères dans votre propre langue. Par exemple, texte français peut être traduit en anglais en seulement quelques secondes.

There are many powerful browser tools and websites that can translate foreign web pages into your own language. For example, French text can be translated into English in only a few seconds.

7.   Experiment with the various translation tools and features available. Try entering your own text and translating it to a different language.

ℹ️ *The* Microsoft Translator *service also has the ability to translate entire websites.*

8.   Enter the web address of your favourite website (e.g. **www.bbc.co.uk**) into the translation box.

Translate from: English

Translate to: Italian

Translate

www.bbc.co.uk

ℹ️ *The Bing website is constantly being developed and may not appear exactly as shown here. However, the basic functionality should remain the same.*

9.   Translate this web address. The *Microsoft Translator* service opens the site and translates all of the on-screen text *in place*. This may take a few moments to complete.

ℹ️ *You can follow links on a translated website and* Microsoft Translator *will translate those pages too.*

10. Explore and experiment with the many useful features of the *Microsoft Translator* service.

ℹ️ *Try performing an advanced search in* Google *to find web pages in another language. Then, use the* Microsoft Translator *service to translate them into English.*

11. When you are finished, return to your **Home page** and leave *Internet Explorer* open for the next lesson.

Driving Lesson 38 - Revision

▣ Park and Read

At the end of every section you get the chance to complete one or more revision exercises to develop your skills and prepare you for your ECDL certification test. You should aim to complete the following steps without referring back to the previous lessons.

⌐ Manoeuvres

1. Visit the *Big Planet Support* website and follow the **Downloads** link on the navigation panel.

2. Download the audio file **Berlioz.wav** to your **Documents** library. Once downloaded, find this file on your computer and play it.

3. Download the spreadsheet file **Turnover.xls** to your **Documents** library. Once downloaded, find this file on your computer and open it.

4. Find a picture from the *Big Planet Support* **Image Gallery** and save it to your **Documents** library with the name **image**.

5. Copy another picture from the *Big Planet Support* **Image Gallery** and paste it into a blank *Word* or *WordPad* document.

6. Return to the *Big Planet Support* website and follow the **E-mail** link (you may need to expand **Information** first).

7. Copy the second paragraph of text on this page (starting "**E-mail is an extremely important and efficient communication tool...**").

8. Paste the copied text into your *Word* or *WordPad* document.

9. Close the *Word* or *WordPad* document <u>without</u> saving changes.

10. With the second paragraph of text still selected in *Internet Explorer*, open a **Print preview** of the page.

11. Change the orientation to landscape and select to print only the selected text. Print 1 copy.

12. Close *Internet Explorer* and any other programs opened in this section.

13. Use **Windows Explorer** to delete the files **berlioz.wav**, **turnover.xls** and **image.jpg** from your **Documents** library.

14. Close any open windows and return to your **Desktop**.

 *Now complete the **Record of Achievement Matrix** at the back of the guide. You should only move on when confident with the topics and features described in this section.*

Section 5
Settings & Security

By the end of this section you should be able to:

Change Your Home Page

Understand and Block "Pop-ups" and Cookies

Recognise and Use Secure Websites

Control Internet Use

Browse the Web Safely

Understand Data Protection

Appreciate Copyright Law

Respect Intellectual Property

Work through the **Driving Lessons** in this section to gain an understanding of the above features.

For each **Driving Lesson**, read all of the **Park and Read** instructions and then, if applicable, perform the numbered steps of the **Manoeuvres**. Complete the **Revision** exercise(s) at the end of the section to test your knowledge.

Driving Lesson 39 - Home Page Settings

▣ Park and Read

The **Internet Options** dialog box allows you to customise *Internet Explorer* to suit your individual preferences. For example, the default **Home Page** or the number of days that pages are kept in your history can be changed (along with more advanced Internet and security settings, as you will learn later).

⤵ Manoeuvres

1. Open *Internet Explorer* and wait for your default **Home Page** to appear.

2. Locate the **Browser Controls** and click the **Tools** button, [⚙]. From the menu that appears, select **Internet options**.

3. The **Internet Options** dialog box appears. Make sure the **General** tab is selected.

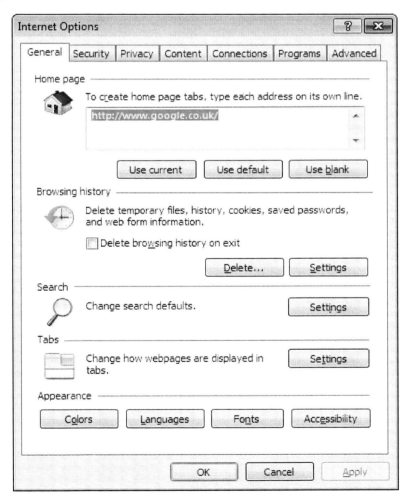

4. In the **Home page** section, replace the default address shown with the web address **www.bigplanetsupport.co.uk**.

Driving Lesson 39 - Continued

Notice the **Use current** button. This can be used to set your **Home Page** to the location of the site currently open in the **View Window**.

5. Click **OK** to confirm the change – the dialog box closes. Your **Home Page** is now the *Big Planet Support* website.

6. Click your **Home** button, [⌂]. The *Big Planet Support* website appears.

Feel free to set your **Home Page** to whichever web page you prefer.

7. Click the **Tools** button, [⚙], and select **Internet options** again. In the **Browsing history** section, click the **Settings** button. Examine the **Temporary Internet Files and History Settings** dialog box that appears.

Notice that Internet Explorer *stores copies of web pages for faster viewing next time you visit. These are called* **Temporary Internet Files**. *In addition,* Internet Explorer *will keep track of pages visited in your* **History** *for 20 days.*

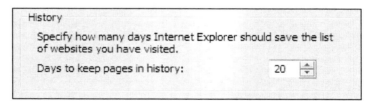

8. The default settings are generally ideal for normal use. Click **Cancel** to return to **Internet Options**.

9. In the **Browsing history** section again, click the **Delete** button. The **Delete Browsing History** dialog box (that you saw in an earlier lesson) appears.

10. Make sure only **Temporary Internet files** is selected this time, and click **Delete**. Wait for a few moments as the temporary files are cleared.

11. Click **OK** to close **Internet Options** (and close the **Notification Bar** informing you that *Internet Explorer* has finished deleting your browsing history, if it appears).

InPrivate Browsing *allows you to browse the Internet without history records or temporary Internet files being created. You can enter* **InPrivate** *mode by clicking* **Tools | Safety | InPrivate Browsing**.

12. Leave *Internet Explorer* open for the next lesson.

Driving Lesson 40 - Blocking Pop-ups

▶ Park and Read

When browsing the *World Wide Web*, you may find that some hyperlinks open new tabs or windows when clicked. This is perfectly normal behaviour. However, some websites try to randomly "**pop-up**" new windows in order to show you advertisements. These can be a real nuisance!

Fortunately, *Internet Explorer's* built-in **Pop-up Blocker** automatically prevents websites from opening new windows without you first clicking a link. When this happens, a yellow **Notification Bar** appears at the bottom of the screen.

 *If you would like a blocked pop-up window to continue opening, click the **Allow once** button on the **Notification Bar**.*

↱ Manoeuvres

1. Locate the **Browser Controls** and click the **Tools** button, ⚙. From the menu that appears select **Internet options**.

2. The **Internet Options** dialog box appears. Display the **Privacy** tab.

3. Locate the **Pop-up Blocker** checkbox. By default, this should be turned on.

 *If the **Pop-up Blocker** is turned on, any window that a website attempts to open automatically will be blocked. The **Notification Bar** shown in* Park and Read *above will be displayed.*

4. Click the **Settings** button to the right of the **Pop-up Blocker** checkbox.

5. The **Pop-up Blocker Settings** dialog box appears. Familiarise yourself with the various options that are available to control how pop-ups are handled (a **Medium** blocking level is recommended).

 *If you find you often need to allow pop-ups to open on websites that you trust and use regularly, you can add them to your **Allowed sites** list.*

6. Click the **Close** button and close the **Internet Options** dialog box.

 *The Big Planet Support website contains a link to a handy resource for testing your popup blocker. To find this, visit **Useful Links | Course Support**.*

Driving Lesson 41 - Cookies

▣ Park and Read

Cookies are small, simple text files that websites use to store information on your computer. They usually record useful data such as user-account details, page views, settings and shopping cart contents. However, they can also be used to track your surfing habits and build marketing profiles.

ℹ *In general, cookies are beneficial and enhance your browsing experience. They are not malicious and cannot damage your computer.*

↱ Manoeuvres

1. Click the **Tools** button, ⚙, and select **Internet options**. Make sure the **Privacy** tab is selected.

2. Notice the privacy slider under the **Settings** header. This can be used to increase or decrease your Internet browser's privacy settings (and control how websites are able to store cookies on your computer).

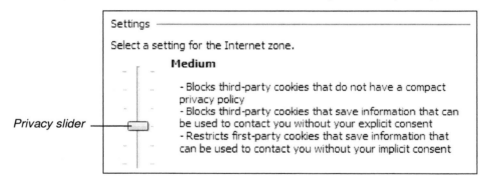

3. **Medium** is recommended and should be selected by default. Read the settings that apply at this privacy level.

4. Next, try dragging the privacy slider up and down. The higher the slider, the higher the privacy restrictions (and the less websites are able to store cookies on your computer).

ℹ *Generally speaking, the more secure and private you make your computer, the less useful it becomes – you will need to find a reasonable balance between the two that most suits you.*

5. Return the privacy slider to **Medium** level. This provides a sensible balance between privacy and the usability of websites.

6. Click **OK** to close the **Internet Options** dialog box.

ℹ *It is now the law for websites to ask for your permission to store cookies on your computer. For reputable websites it is perfectly safe to allow this.*

Driving Lesson 42 - Secure Websites

🄿 Park and Read

When shopping or subscribing to services on the Internet, it will usually be necessary to supply financial information (usually credit or debit card details) to the seller. This process will always involve some risk, although probably no more than supplying the same details over the telephone. Fortunately, there are protection systems in place on websites to make the process much safer.

First and foremost, <u>only</u> enter personal, financial and sensitive information into **secure websites**. These sites can be identified by **https** at the start of the URL and a small padlock symbol, 🔒, on the right of the **Address Bar**.

ℹ️ *Notice the additional **s** that has appeared at the end of the **http** protocol in the URL. This indicates that the connection with the server hosting the web page is **secure**. All information you send and receive over this connection will be **encrypted** (scrambled). Encryption prevents people from being able to intercept and read internet communications.*

ℹ️ *To allow a secure connection, a "certificate" must be obtained by a website's owner to verify their identity and their site's official URL. This is called a **digital certificate**.*

↱ Manoeuvres

1. The *Big Planet Support* site should currently be open. Click **Online Forms** on the navigation panel on the left. The page that appears contains links to various online forms which are provided for demonstration purposes.

2. Click once on **Query Form** to open the linked web page in a new tab. An online question and answer form for a fictitious business appears.

ℹ️ *This web page is **secure**. All information you enter and submit will be encrypted (scrambled) so that only the intended recipient can read it.*

3. Notice that a padlock icon, 🔒, appears on the right of the **Address Bar**. The URL also starts with **https**.

Padlock icon

4. Click the padlock icon to view this website's **digital certificate**. In practice, you should check that the certificate's URL matches the expected, genuine web address of the site you are using.

5. Close the tab containing the **Q&A Forum** web form, returning to the *Big Planet Support* site.

Driving Lesson 43 - Controlling Internet Use

▣ Park and Read

There is an extraordinary amount of information, imagery, video, opinion and debate available on the *World Wide Web*. As a result, there also exists content that can be considered objectionable or offensive. Indeed, there is some content placed on the web for the sole purpose of being offensive! Whilst the average person may consider this to be an acceptable price to pay for unrestricted access, there are situations where all possible steps should be taken to prevent exposure to offensive or explicit material (particularly where children are concerned).

 Parents and guardians can help protect their children by physically supervising and restricting the time they spend online.

If physical supervision is not always possible, Internet browsers (and some firewalls) include **content filters** which restrict access to web pages based on a rating system. Commercial software also often includes the ability to monitor and restrict chat room and social networking site access, currently an area of increasing concern.

 *Internet Explorer's built-in **Content Advisor** tool can be used to restrict access to websites and file downloads based on their content. Settings are available in the **Content** tab of the **Internet Options** dialog box. However, you will need Administrator privileges on your computer to be able to turn this feature on.*

Unfortunately, no matter how hard you try, you will eventually read distasteful comments online. The inappropriate behaviour of others on the *World Wide Web* is a constant problem, and you will do well to simply ignore it. However, if another person's behaviour is particularly offensive or gives you cause for concern (for example, if you feel a child is at risk from strangers or from online bullying), you can report it to the website's owners and/or the police.

⬈ Manoeuvres

Are the following statements true or false?

1.	The content of websites is guaranteed to be tasteful and free from objectionable comments.

2.	People who communicate with others via the Internet tend to act in a very professional manner.

3.	If you are concerned about a person's behaviour, you can report them to the website's owners. In extreme cases you can report them to the police.

4.	Adults should monitor a child's online activities, educate them about the nature of the Internet, and warn them of potential threats.

Driving Lesson 44 - Staying Safe

P Park and Read

The risks involved in using Internet technologies are the same as those found in many other aspects of everyday life (although they are sometimes easier to stumble across online). This lesson touches on some of the more important safety issues that you must be aware of when using the Internet...

- Firstly, always be careful when downloading files of any sort from the Internet. Unless you completely trust the source of the file, it may contain malicious software ("**malware**") that can harm your computer or allow criminals to steal information from it.

 If you do download a file, scan it first using antivirus software <u>before</u> you open or run it.

- Avoid illegally downloading copyright music, videos and pirated programs. As well as getting you into a lot of trouble, these files can often contain malware.

- Try to only visit reputable websites. Adult pages or sites that promote or enable illegal activities (i.e. file sharing) often aim to mislead you or infect your computer with malware.

- If you ever submit sensitive, personal information online (for example, when purchasing items on shopping websites), only do so on the sites of well-known, legitimate businesses. Also make sure the URL begins with **https** and the padlock symbol, 🔒, appears in the **Address Bar**.

- It is recommended that you "log out" of online accounts once you have finished using them. This prevents anyone who uses the computer after you from gaining access.

- <u>Always</u> ignore advertisements and invitations to win prizes and download free software – these are rarely genuine.

- Do not trust that people are who they say they are. This may seem obvious, but people can very easily exaggerate or lie about their identities to mislead you. Never give personal or financial details to – or arrange to meet offline – people you don't know.

- Always keep your computer up-to-date by regularly downloading the latest antivirus and software security updates.

- When at work or in education, remember that personal use of the Internet is usually not allowed.

It is your responsibility to protect your own safety and that of others who you work or study with. If you allow a virus or other type of malware to gain access to and damage your own computer, it can also spread and cause harm to other systems that you share a network with – be careful!

Driving Lesson 45 - Data Protection

Park and Read

Businesses are now more connected and reliant upon technology than ever before. As a result, they create and store a lot of important information about their customers, from personal and contact information to usernames, passwords and financial details. This information is very sensitive and valuable, and customers trust businesses to keep it safe from loss, theft or damage.

Data Protection laws protect all personal data that a business or organisation stores about people. In particular, it requires that only information that is needed for a "specific purpose" can be recorded (and only when the owner has given their permission). The laws also require that information is kept up-to-date and secure at all times and isn't given away to other people.

Protection rights and obligations can differ between countries. If you reside or work outside of the UK and Ireland, it is important that you familiarise yourself with the relevant data protection laws in your territory.

In summary, data protection laws require that all information about any identifiable individual shall be:

- Kept accurate and up to date.
- Obtained and processed fairly and lawfully.
- Processed only for specified and legitimate purposes.
- Adequate, relevant and not excessive for those purposes.
- Used for the original purpose only and for no longer than is necessary.
- Processed in line with the rights of the individual.
- Secure and protected against loss, damage and inappropriate use.
- Not transferred to countries unless they also have adequate data protection laws.

 The Information Commissioner is an independent authority set up in the UK to provide guidance on data protection and to uphold information privacy laws. In Ireland, this entity is called the Data Protection Commissioner.

With so many businesses dependent on the creation and management of customer information, imagine what would happen if that data was lost or stolen? At the very least, customers would lose confidence and stop supporting the business. However, if the information fell into the wrong hands and was used to commit a crime (e.g. identity theft or credit card fraud), this could be very costly and embarrassing.

If data is seen to have been lost through negligence, consequences can range from an inspection through to criminal prosecution with severe damages payable to those affected. This will not only cost the business a lot of money but also the jobs of anyone responsible for the loss!

Driving Lesson 46 - Copyright

▣ Park and Read

Copyright laws automatically protect any original work (e.g. text, images, music, videos, software, games, etc.) from being copied, used, altered, distributed or sold without the express permission of their owner. In practice, this prevents you from distributing the work of others or stealing material from the Internet and passing it off as your own work.

⚹ *The creative works of a person are their **intellectual property**. That is, a person automatically owns and has exclusive copyright to anything they create.*

To use the creative work of another person, you must first get their permission (and perhaps pay a small fee). In return, you will be granted a "licence" to use that work. This is a legal contract between you and the owner of the work and specifies exactly what you can and cannot do with it.

⚹ *How do you know if a document, web page, image, video or music file is copyright protected? It's easy – copyright <u>automatically</u> applies as soon as the material is created. However, many people make copyright explicit to discourage infringement. To do this, they include a **copyright notice** alongside their work (e.g. Copyright © CiA Training 2013).*

However, there are "fair use" exceptions which allow you to use small parts of somebody else's work for research, commentary or review. If you do this, you must **reference** it correctly by describing where you got the information from (known as its **source**). This gives credit to the original creator and protects you from being accused of stealing copyright-protected work and passing it off as your own (known as **plagiarism**).

So, if you reference somebody's material in your own work, you must mention all of the following:

- The full name of the person or company that created and owns the material.
- The name of the publication that contains the material (if relevant).
- Where you found the material, such as a book's page number or an Internet address.
- The year that the material was created, updated or published.

⚹ *If you copy another person's text word-for-word, you must place "speech marks" around it to show it is a direct quote.*

It is common practice to simply include the author's surname (or company name) and publication date in brackets after you reference their material in your text. You should then include full details in a list of sources at the end of your work (known as a **bibliography**).

Driving Lesson 47 - Revision

▣ Park and Read

At the end of every section you get the chance to complete one or more revision exercises to develop your skills and prepare you for your ECDL certification test. You should aim to complete the following steps without referring back to the previous lessons.

↱ Manoeuvres

1. Display the **Internet Options** dialog box.

2. Set your **Home Page** to the search engine **www.bing.com**.

3. Use your **Home** button to visit your new **Home Page**.

4. By default, how many days will *Internet Explorer* save a list of your visited websites (known as your **History**)?

5. What is a pop-up and how can they be prevented from appearing?

6. What is a cookie?

7. Cookies are harmful to a computer and must be blocked! True or false?

8. How can you tell if a website is secure?

9. What do you understand by the term encryption?

10. What type of tool can be used to control or restrict Internet use?

11. Which law protects all personal data that a business or organisation stores about people?

12. For your answer to 11, describe the main obligations of this law.

13. Which law protects any original, creative work from being copied, used, altered, distributed or sold without the express permission of their owner?

14. If you use a small extract of text created by somebody else in a review of their work, what should you always do?

15. Set your **Home Page** to your preferred web site.

16. Close *Internet Explorer*.

ℹ️ *Sample answers can be found at the back of the guide.*

ℹ️ *Now complete the **Record of Achievement Matrix** at the back of the guide. You should only move on when confident with the topics and features described in this section.*

Section 6
Communication

By the end of this section you should be able to:

Recognise Popular Online Communication Tools

Identify Popular Online Communities

Get Involved and Share Content

Understand the Rules of Netiquette

Safely Interact with Other People using ICT

Be Aware of Important Privacy and Security Issues

Work through the **Driving Lessons** in this section to gain an understanding of the above features.

For each **Driving Lesson**, read all of the **Park and Read** instructions and then, if applicable, perform the numbered steps of the **Manoeuvres**. Complete the **Revision** exercise(s) at the end of the section to test your knowledge.

Driving Lesson 48 - Communicating Online

▣ Park and Read

There are many ways to interact with other people online. As the Internet has no international boundaries, you can talk freely to friends, family, colleagues and organisations throughout the world – instantly and with little or no cost. In fact, modern ICT has completely changed the way we communicate with each other, giving us access to a worldwide network of advice, debate, feedback, opinion, conversation, support and knowledge.

Aside from the *World Wide Web*, the following table briefly describes the most popular Internet communication technologies available today.

Technology	Description
Chat Rooms	Chat rooms are online spaces that allow people with similar interests to come together and talk about topics which interest them. Text is typed into a shared window that all connected users see.
Instant Messages	With instant messaging (**IM**) tools you always know when your contacts are online and you can easily start a text or video based conversation with them. These tools are very useful for communicating with friends, family and colleagues instantly.
E-mail	Short for electronic mail, this basic ICT system for sending messages and files to other people is still the most dominant form of online communication today – especially in business.
VoIP	*Voice over Internet Protocol* (VoIP) software such as *Skype* can turn an ICT device (and optional webcam) into a phone, allowing you to talk to friends, family, colleagues and customers anywhere in the world.
Conferencing	Using the same kind of technology as VoIP, video conferencing tools allow two or more people to attend an online meeting together.
SMS/MMS	The **Short Messaging Service** (SMS) is a standard feature of most mobile networks, providing a way to send small text-based messages to and from mobile phones. The more advanced **Multimedia Messaging Service** (MMS) supports the exchange of richer media such as pictures, videos and files.

Along with simple telephone voice calls, the technologies mentioned above help people interact and work together "on the move". They also make it much easier for people to work from home (known as **teleworking**), which reduces office and travel costs and gives employees more flexibility in their job.

Driving Lesson 49 - Online Communities

▣ Park and Read

There are many ways to use modern technology to communicate electronically with people from all over the world, and new and innovative uses for the Internet appear daily. As a result, whole new **virtual communities** have appeared online in which members get together to exchange views, share interests, exchange files, and communicate with friends, family and colleagues.

The following table briefly describes some of the most popular platforms which support the creation of online communities.

Technology	Description
Forums & Bulletin Boards	Businesses and people with similar interests and expertise use forums and bulletin boards to spread news, exchange views, request support, and post shared messages. Other members can then read and comment on those contributions, creating "**threads**" of conversation.
Social Networking	Social networking sites such as *Facebook* and *Twitter* allow people to communicate with friends and family online by sharing photos, videos, links and comments. You can also chat with friends in real time anywhere in the world.
Games	Many games now feature large and elaborate online worlds in which players can meet and interact virtually. As the technology matures, people are also finding more practical and serious uses for it (e.g. collaboration and education).
Virtual Learning Environments	Web-based learning environments allow students to access resources, learn new skills, interact with teachers and tutors, and sit tests virtually.
The Cloud	The "cloud" is the name given to a range of online storage areas and Internet-based tools and services. Popular collaboration technologies such as *Office 365* and *GoogleDocs* operate in the cloud, allowing people to access, co-create, share and edit files from anywhere in the world using only their web-browser.

Today, online communication allows geographically distant individuals to come together and work on projects in teams. As a result, the various technologies and community platforms are becoming more and more popular in business where employees work in separate locations or from home.

Driving Lesson 50 - Sharing Content

🄿 Park and Read

There are many ways that you can express yourself creatively online and share text, music, video and pictures with others.

Although it is possible to control who sees your content, it is more common for people to publish material publicly for everyone in the world to see.

The following table briefly describes some of the most popular types of technology that can support the creation and publication of online content.

Technology	Description
Blogs	A blog (which is short for web-log) is simply an online journal in which you can "post" anything that is on your mind. They are very easy to set up and readers are often encouraged to comment on individual posts.
Microblogs	Microblogs are similar to normal blogs but are based on the creation of very short text messages (usually no longer than 140 characters). Due to their immediacy and speed of use, microblogging services such as *Twitter* can be a useful source of topical opinion, debate and breaking news.
Wikis	A wiki is simply a website that you can edit using your web browser. They are useful for creating online repositories of information that a community can contribute to themselves. The encyclopaedia *Wikipedia* is the most popular example of a wiki.
Podcasts	Podcasts are audio or video programmes that can be played back on a computer, mobile phone or portable media playing device. They are often released as episodes, similar to a TV series, and cover a variety of topics from education to entertainment. With the right hardware, you can easily create your own podcasts.
Media Sharing	There are many popular websites that allow you to upload and "self-publish" your <u>own</u> pictures, videos and music files. Anyone in the world can then access your content and offer useful comments and constructive feedback. Content can range from small, home-made photo albums to major international music releases.

Always remember that your views and opinions are as valid as everyone else's. You are encouraged to explore your creativity, share content and contribute to online communities that are of interest.

Driving Lesson 51 - Netiquette

▣ Park and Read

When you are working online it is very easy to forget your basic manners and say things that you would never say in a face-to-face conversation. So, before you interact with others online or via e-mail, try to familiarise yourself with the rules of **netiquette** – "network etiquette":

- Behave online as you would in real life and respect other people and their opinions.

- Be clear and keep your contributions brief, accurate and relevant.

- Where subject or topic headings are available, always be sure to use clear, sensible and meaningful titles.

- Be tolerant of others and never send angry messages (known as **flames**).

- Use appropriate language (especially when representing a business).

- Don't use UPPERCASE words – this is the same as shouting.

- Make sure your contributions are spelled correctly and make sense.

- Avoid forwarding irrelevant junk e-mail, jokes and chain messages.

- Always respect copyright and data protection laws.

- Keep personal, financial and contact details safe and do not give this information out to others unnecessarily.

- Don't post anything that could get you into trouble or embarrass you in the future!

 Whether at work or in education, you have a responsibility to act professionally and make a good impression when communicating with others.

Unfortunately, no matter how well-mannered you are online, you will eventually read comments or interact with others who are not so considerate. Inappropriate behaviour and offensive material is a constant problem on the Internet and you will do well to simply ignore it. However, if any behaviour or content is particularly offensive or worrying (for example, if you feel you are being bullied or that another person is at risk) you must report it to a person in authority.

Driving Lesson 52 - Privacy and Security

◨ Park and Read

The Internet is an amazing resource and people find new uses for it every day. However, all of this potential and freedom does have a price – your privacy and safety. Fortunately, you can avoid many of the potential risks of using Internet communication technologies with a little common sense...

- First and foremost, never publish personal information such as your name, address, date of birth or telephone number. Carefully consider who could read that information and what it could be used for.

 *Publishing your personal information online makes it easier for you to become a victim of **identity theft**, where someone uses your details to purchase items, open accounts, apply for credit, etc.*

- Never post or e-mail sensitive information to anyone. E-mail is not a secure communication channel (unless messages are encrypted).

- Explore and customise your privacy settings. Most online publishing and social media websites have a range of privacy settings that you can – and should – adjust to suit your own preferences.

 Do not assume a website's default privacy settings are sufficient. Many sites are designed to encourage sharing with little regard for protecting one's identity.

- If talking personally or confidentially with another individual online, use a direct, private, one-to-one communication channel. E-mail is perhaps best, but most social media websites also offer **Direct Messaging** features for this very purpose.

- Many online social media websites and mobile applications feature services that can track and publish your physical location (known as **geotagging**). There are obvious security issues associated with this and, if concerned, you should block or disable these features.

- Know your friends. Unless you are intentionally trying to reach a wider audience, only accept invitations or requests to join groups and social networks from people that you know and trust.

- Think about the consequences of what you are saying online and never share inappropriate, embarrassing or intentionally hurtful content.

- Always consider your audience. Remember that employers, family and friends might be able to see any content that you publish.

- Try to ignore inappropriate behaviour online. To help, most social media websites provide features to "block" people or, if their behaviour is particularly offensive or worrying, report them to the service's owners.

Driving Lesson 53 - Revision

🄿 Park and Read

At the end of every section you get the chance to complete one or more revision exercises to develop your skills and prepare you for your ECDL certification test. You should aim to complete the following steps without referring back to the previous lessons.

↱ Manoeuvres

1. Name some popular ways of communicating with other people on the Internet.

2. Name some popular Internet platforms which support the creation of online communities.

3. Name some popular types of technology that can support the creation and publication of online content.

4. In online communications, what is a flame?

5. In online communications, what is wrong with creating posts using only UPPERCASE letters.

6. The default privacy and security settings on social networking websites are fine. True or false?

7. Offensive behaviour is a part of social media - there is nothing you can do about it. True or false?

8. Creating a vast network of "friends" is what social media is all about – it doesn't matter that I don't know who most of them are. True or false.

ℹ️ *Sample answers can be found at the back of the guide.*

ℹ️ *Now complete the **Record of Achievement Matrix** at the back of the guide. You should only move on when confident with the topics and features described in this section.*

Answers

Driving Lesson 11

1.   The Internet is a global network of linked ICT devices that allow people from all over the world to communicate and share information. The World Wide Web (a vast collection of interconnected web pages) is the name given to just one of the many services that runs on the Internet.

2.   HTML (Hypertext Mark-up Language) is the programming code that website developers use to create web pages.

3.   A URL (Uniform Resource Locator) is another name for a web address. They are used to uniquely identify and find web pages or files on the Internet.

4.   A domain name is made up of two or more segments which generally describe the name of the website, the kind of organisation that owns it, and the country where it is located.

5.   Examples include Internet Explorer, Chrome, Safari, Opera, and Firefox.

7.   The Address Bar contains the web address (or URL) of the web page shown in the View Window.

8.   The Navigation Buttons can be used to move backwards and forwards through your history of recently visited web pages.

9.   Menu bar, Favorites bar, Command bar and Status bar.

Driving Lesson 27

7.   November 7, 1728.

8.   Approximately 45-50mm (1.8-2.0in).

9.   River Liffey.

Driving Lesson 30

2.   George W. Ferris created the first Ferris wheel in 1893.

3.   You could have used the search "Here age relives fond memories of the past" to find out that that it was Walt Disney who said this.

8.   Approximately 21 degrees Celsius.

12.   Triton is a moon of the planet Neptune.

Driving Lesson 43

1.   False.

2.   False.

3.   True.

4.   True.

Driving Lesson 47

4.   20.

5.   A pop-up is a tab or window opened automatically by a website, often to show an advertisement. A pop-up blocker can be used to stop them from appearing.

6. Cookies are small, simple text files that websites use to store information on your computer. They usually record useful data such as user-account details, page views, settings and shopping cart contents.

7. False. Cookies are generally beneficial and enhance your browsing experience. They are not malicious and cannot damage your computer. However, they can be used to track your surfing habits and build marketing profiles.

8. Secure websites can be identified by https at the start of the URL and a small padlock symbol on the Address Bar.

9. Encryption is the process of scrambling information to prevent other people from being able to read it. All information you send and receive over a secure Internet connection will be encrypted.

10. Along with personal supervision, content filters are useful tools for monitoring and restricting web access (preventing adult or objectionable web pages from downloading).

11. Data protection.

12. In brief, data protection laws require that only relevant information that is needed for a specific purpose can be recorded (and only when the owner has given their permission). The laws also require that information is kept up-to-date and secure at all times and isn't given away to other people. Gathering or using information illegally, or transferring it to a country without similar protection laws, is obviously prohibited.

13. Copyright.

14. You must reference material correctly by detailing the owner of the original work and where you got it from (known as its source).

Driving Lesson 53

1. Examples include chat rooms, instant messages (IM), e-mail, VoIP, video conferencing and SMS/MMS.

2. Examples include forums and bulletin boards, social networking, games, virtual learning environments and cloud-based technologies.

3. Examples include blogs, microblogs, wikis, podcasts and social media websites (e.g. photo, video and music sharing platforms).

4. A flame is an angry message.

5. Uppercase letters are used to indicate SHOUTING.

6. False. Many social websites are designed to encourage sharing with little regard for protecting your identity.

7. False. Although it is true that inappropriate behaviour is a constant problem online, social websites often have tools to block or report offensive individuals.

8. False. Unless you are intentionally trying to reach a wider audience, only accept invitations or requests to join groups and social networks from people that you know and trust.

Record of Achievement Matrix

The **Record of Achievement** matrix can be used to measure progress through this guide. This is a learning reinforcement process – you judge when you are competent.

Three tick boxes are provided for each exercise. Column 1 should be ticked for **no knowledge** of the subject or topic covered, 2 for **some knowledge**, and 3 for **competent**. A section is only complete when you have ticked column 3 for all exercises.

Tick the Relevant Boxes   **1**: No Knowledge   **2**: Some Knowledge   **3**: Competent

Section	No.	Driving Lesson	1	2	3
1 Getting Started	1	The Internet			
	2	Connecting to the Internet			
	3	Choosing an ISP			
	4	Wi-Fi Networks			
	5	Web Addresses			
	6	Web Browsers			
	7	The Browser Window			
	8	Toolbars			
	9	Browser Help			
	10	Closing the Browser			
2 Navigation	12	The Address Bar			
	13	Hyperlinks			
	14	Navigation Buttons			
	15	New Tabs			
	16	Tabbed Browsing			
	17	Stop and Refresh			
	18	Favorites			
	19	Organising Favorites			
	20	The Favorites Bar			
	21	Deleting Favorites			
	22	Browsing History			
3 Searching the Web	24	Search Engines			
	25	Advanced Search			
	26	Search Tips			
	27	Website Searches			
	28	Finding Text on a Page			
	29	Critical Evaluation			
4 Web Page Interaction	31	Downloading Files			
	32	Saving Pictures			
	33	Printing a Web Page			
	34	Printing a Selection			
	35	Copy and Paste			
	36	Online Forms			
	37	Translate a Web Page			

Tick the Relevant Boxes   **1**: No Knowledge   **2**: Some Knowledge   **3**: Competent

Section	**No.**	**Driving Lesson**	**1**	**2**	**3**
5 Settings and Security	39	Home Page Settings			
	40	Blocking Pop-ups			
	41	Cookies			
	42	Secure Websites			
	43	Controlling Internet Use			
	44	Staying Safe			
	45	Data Protection			
	46	Copyright			
6 Communication	48	Communicating Online			
	49	Online Communities			
	50	Sharing Content			
	51	Netiquette			
	52	Privacy and Security			

Notes

Index